Foretelling Widowhood

FORETELLING WIDOWHOOD

MRIDULA TRIVEDI
T.P. TRIVEDI

MOTILAL BANARSIDASS PUBLISHERS
PRIVATE LIMITED • DELHI

*First Edition: Delhi, **2008***

ISBN: 978-81-208-3222-0 (Cloth)
ISBN: 978-81-208-3223-7 (Paper)

MOTILAL BANARSIDASS
41 U.A. Bungalow Road, Jawahar Nagar, Delhi 110 007
8 Mahalaxmi Chamber, 22 Bhulabhai Desai Road, Mumbai 400 026
203 Royapettah High Road, Mylapore, Chennai 600 004
236, 9th Main III Block, Jayanagar, Bangalore 560 011
Sanas Plaza, 1302 Baji Rao Road, Pune 411 002
8 Camac Street, Kolkata 700 017
Ashok Rajpath, Patna 800 004
Chowk, Varanasi 221 001

Printed in India
**BY JAINENDRA PRAKASH JAIN AT SHRI JAINENDRA PRESS,
A-45 NARAINA, PHASE-I, NEW DELHI 110 028
AND PUBLISHED BY NARENDRA PRAKASH JAIN FOR
MOTILAL BANARSIDASS PUBLISHERS PRIVATE LIMITED,
BUNGALOW ROAD, DELHI 110 007**

Dedicated to my most affectionate, loving and caring mother Late Smt. Brij Raj Kumari Sharma

May, 1901 – Dec. 12th, 1985

धर्मपत्नीं मिलित्वैव ह्येकं जीवनमावयोः ।
अद्यारभ्य यतो मे त्वम् अर्द्धांगिनीति घोषिता।।

From today itself, I (declare) my wife as my equal half and emerge ahead to create a new life blending my (essence) with her.

CONTENTS

सुवर्णवृद्धिं कुरु मे गृहे श्रीः
विभूतिवृद्धिं कुरु मे गृहे श्रीः।
विज्ञानवृद्धिं कुरु मे गृहे श्रीः
सौभाग्यवृद्धिं कुरु मे गृहे श्रीः।।

O Goddess *Mahālakṣmī*! bless our home with gold, splendour, knowledge and fortune.

PREFACE

Foretelling Widowhood is the fruit of research work carried out by us during the last two decades. A work of predictive astrology, it amalgamates a plethora of principles enshrined in various classical texts and practical study of birth charts of those who have been unfortunate enough to suffer the immeasurable grief and plight of untimely widowhood. Untimely widowhood is the biggest tragedy that can befall a woman and is irreversible. In olden days, widowhood in general and untimely widowhood in particular was considered an unpardonable sin and a woman had to commit *Satī*, that is to mount the pyre of her late husband. Was not this inhuman? Women would be ever grateful to Raja Ram Mohan Rai whose untiring efforts led to rooting out of this obnoxious practice.

A common belief among masses, as also amongst self-styled astrologers, is that *maṅgalī* females or those females having *kuja doṣa* in their birth charts are predisposed to suffer widowhood. We would like to humbly opine that this belief is only partially correct. It is not certain that females having *kuja doṣa* will essentially undergo the miseries of marital disaster such as widowhood. Many females, who suffered untimely widowhood, were not *maṅgalī* either from ascendant, or from Moon or from Venus. This is definitely a wrong concept that widowhood will curse only a *maṅgalī* female. In fact, much is not known about the *kuja doṣa* and its actual effect.

This thought provoking voluminous work contains 9 chapters. First two chapters, *Planetary Dimensions and Zodiac* and *Essentials of Astrology*, cover a few important but basic information and principles regarding confusions and doubts about a number of astrological concepts such as *nāḍī doṣa, nīca bhaṅga rājayoga*, Combustions & *bādhakas, retrograde planets, Mars–Saturn* conjunction, Jupiter–Venus etc.,

We have also exercised a lot in formulating timing of widowhood and dealt with 32 cases of widowhood in Chapter 3 entitled *Early Widowhood : An Astrological Exploration* with detailed analyses and findings.

Timing an event is the tougher task to perform than predicting. We have used certain classical aphorisms in Chapter 4 entitled as *Timing Widowhood.* We have also discussed the timing of widowhood cases in detail. We hope that this would act like bridgestones in timing an event for students of astrology.

It has been observed that there are many misconceptions about Jupiter, e.g., it can prevent widowhood if it has an influence over 7th or 8th house, but our observations in this regard is that, nearly fifty percent cases of widowhood occur during the major or sub period of Jupiter, which has been explained in Chapter 5 named *Widowhood and Misconceptions about Jupiter.*

Few females are fortunate enough to be blessed with *akhaṇḍa saubhāgya yoga.* Sages have mentioned a lot about the combinations on widowhood but they have discussed less on *akhaṇḍa saubhāgya yoga.* We have detailed this properly in Chapter 6 on *Akhaṇḍa saubhāgya Yoga.*

Chapter 7, *Birth in Jyeṣṭha nakṣatra* is an important as many misconceptions and wrong impressions prevail among us regarding the birth in *jyeṣṭha nakṣatra.* Adversities can certainly be reduced and eliminated if advice of sages like *Kālidāsa* are strictly followed and other remedial measures undertaken.

The work wouldn't have been complete in all respects, had the chapter on the untimely loss of wife had not been included. While it can not be gainsaid that women who suffer early widowhood. have to normally undergo more pain and sufferings than men. It can only be claimed on the risk of sounding insensitive that the men do not suffer pain at the loss of their spouses. In a happy conjugal life, loss of either spouse is traumatic. Therefore we have included *Determinants for Death of Wife* as chapter 8.

The book would have been incomplete without the remedial measures – some common and some rare. It will not be out of place to mention that prevention is always better than cure. We have mentioned as many as 38 remedial measures in chapter 9 entitled *Remedies For Marital Maladies and Widowhood.* Most of these measures have been tested by us over hundreds of women in whose birth charts potent combinations of loss of husband were present. We advise all such women who want to be blessed with *akhaṇḍa saubhāgya* to select a remedial measure suitable to their planetary combination and follow it with firm faith and dedication.

We express our immense gratitude and sincere thanks to venerable Mr. Narendra Prakash Jain of M/s Motilal Banarsidass for the decision to publish this work and having already earlier published our six books in Hindi:-

1. *Vaivāhik Vilamba Ke Vividha Āyāma Evam Mantra*

2. *Vaivāhika Sukha : Jyotiṣīya Sandarbha*
3. *Santāna Sukha : Sarvāṅga Cintana*
4. *Śani Śamana*
5. *Śatru Śamana*
6. *Kālsarpa Yoga*

We offer heartfelt appreciation to our daughter Deeksha who always inspires us for writing on astrological subjects, son Vishal who spared some of his valuable time in processing and compiling the book – their respective spouses Rahul and Shilpi, and our grandchildren Yug and Ansh. We also offer our sincere thanks to Dr. Rakesh Asthana, the Chief Medical Officer in Central Health Service for editing.

We are quite confident that *Foretelling Widowhood* will be warmly welcomed by the readers of astrology. However we would be indebted to them for their reactions and opinions.

We trust and pray that this work will preclude widowhood at practical and theoretical levels and would empower and enable those afflicted by the ire of most malefic Mars and misfortune of marital maladies to everlasting conjugal life of highest order. Hence, truest reward for this humble effort would be the happiness and joy of those, thus bestowed.

Mridula Trivedi & T. P. Trivedi
24, Mahanagar Extension,
MRIDUL VATIKA
(Opp. E-40 Corporation Quarters)
Pili Colony, LUCKNOW-226 006 (UP)
Tel: 0522 – 2326625, 2327869

समः शत्रौ च मित्रे च तथा मानापमानयोः।
शीतोष्णसुखदुःखेषु समः संगविवर्जितः ।।
तुल्यनिन्दास्तुतिर्मौनी सन्तुष्टो येनकेनचित।
अनिकेत स्थिरमतिभक्तिमान्मे प्रियो नरः।।

That person is dear to me who like seers
becoming free from all attachment is
of stable disposition and entreats
equally friends or foes, honour or
dishonour, cold or hot season,
critique or praise.

Chapter-1

PLANETARY DIMENSIONS AND ZODIAC

Zodiac is an imaginary belt in the heaven about 9 degrees either side of the Sun's path within which the planets and the constellations move from east to west. This zodiac is known as *bhava cakra or rāśicakra.*

This zodiac is an imaginary circle of 360° which is divided into twelve equal parts and each part is of 30°. Generally, we name the divisions as *rāśi* and entire *cakra* the *rāśicakra.*

The east-west movement of the heavenly bodies is just an apparent movement. Actually the planets in the solar system travel from west to east while the stars on the background are almost fixed, that is, their distance is so big from us that their movements appear as if non-existent.

Of the several movements of our earth, two are important for our day to day life. The earth rotates round its axis completing one rotation in about twenty-four hours of our time and revolves round the Sun completing one revolution in 365 days 6 hours 9 minutes 9 seconds.

The twenty-seven zodiacal constellations have been considered important for calendric astronomy same as the twelve signs of the zodiac.

Importance of the *rāśicakra* and the *nakṣatra cakra* are described in length in the following lines.

SIGNS AND THEIR CHARACTERISTICS

The importance of zodiacal signs is immense. There

is not a thing on earth which does not come under the sway of one or the other sign. Each sign is important in its own sphere and, therefore, it necessitates that each of these twelve signs be studied for the respective matters they represent.

1. Signs (*rāśis*) and their *tattvas*
    a) Fiery signs (*agni tattva*) – Aries, Leo, Sagittarius.
    b) Earthly signs (*bhū tattva*) – Taurus, Virgo, Capricorn.
    c) Airy signs (*vāyu tattva*) – Gemini, Libra, Aquarius.
    d) Watery signs (*jala tattva*) – Cancer, Scorpio, Pisces.
2. Movable (*cara*) and fixed (*sthira*) signs
    a) Movable (*cara*) - Aries, Cancer, Libra, Capricorn.
    b) Fixed (*sthira*) - Taurus, Leo, Scorpio, Aquarius.
    c) Common (*dviṣvabhāva*) - Gemini, Virgo, Sagittarius, Pisces.
3. Odd and even signs
    a) Odd signs – Aries, Gemini, Leo, Libra, Sagittarius, Aquarius.
    b) Even signs – Taurus, Cancer, Virgo, Scorpio, Capricorn and Pisces.
4. Masculine and Feminine
    a) Masculine – Aries, Gemini, Leo, Libra, Sagittarius and Aquarius.
    b) Feminine – Taurus, Cancer, Virgo, Scorpio, Capricorn and Pisces.
5. Cruel and Mild Signs
    a) Cruel – Aries, Gemini, Leo, Libra, Sagittarius and Aquarius.
    b) Mild – Taurus, Cancer, Virgo, Scorpio, Capricorn and Pisces.

6. Fruitful and Barren Signs
   a) Fruitful – Cancer, Scorpio, Pisces.
   b) Barren – Gemini, Leo, Virgo.
7. *Śīrṣodaya* and *Pṛṣṭhodaya* Signs
   a) *Śīrṣodaya* signs (rising by their heads) Leo, Virgo, Libra, Scorpio and Aquarius
   b) *Pṛṣṭhodaya* signs – (rising by hinder parts)- Aries, Taurus, Cancer, Sagittarius and Capricorn
   c) *Ubhayodaya* signs – (rising by head and hair) – Gemini, Pisces. All *sīrṣodaya* signs are powerful during day time. All *pṛṣṭhotodaya* signs are powerful during night time. *Ubhayodaya* sign Gemini is powerful during night while Pisces is powerful during twilight.
8. Signs ruling different parts of the body
   Aries - head; Taurus-face, throat; Gemini-breast; Cancer-heart; Leo-heart; Virgo-stomach; Libra-waist, hips and sexual organs; Sagittarius-thighs; capricorn-legs; Aquarius-ankles; Pisces-feet. These divisions help a lot while analysing the horoscope for diseases.
9. Metals and Tastes
   a) Aries, Leo, Scorpio – Copper; taste-bitter and hot.
   b) Taurus, Libra – Silver; taste-sour.
   c) Gemini – Brass; taste-mixed.
   d) Cancer – Bronze; taste-salty.
   e) Virgo – Bronze; taste-mixed.
   f) Sagittarius and Pisces – Gold; taste-sweet.
   g) Capricorn and Aquarius – Iron; taste-astringent.

10. Directions
    a) East : Aries, Leo, and Sagittarius.
    b) South : Taurus, Virgo and Capricorn.
    c) West : Gemini, Libra, and Aquarius.
    d) North : Cancer, Scorpio and Pisces.

11. Nocturnal and Diurnal Signs
    a) Nocturnal (*rātribalī* signs) – Aries, Taurus, Gemini, Sagittarius, Capricorn.
    b) Diurnal (*dvibalī*) signs – Cancer, Leo, Virgo, Libra, Scorpio, Aquarius. Pisces is powerful during twilight.

12. Seasons
    a) Summer – Pisces, Aries, Taurus, Gemini.
    b) Rainy – Cancer, Leo, Virgo, Libra.
    c) Winter – Scorpio, Sagittarius, Capricorn, Aquarius.

13. Caste
    a) *Kṣatriya* – Aries, Leo and Sagittarius.
    b) *Śūdra* – Taurus, Virgo and Capricorn.
    c) *Vaiśya* – Gemini, Libra and Aquarius.
    d) *Brāhmaṇa* – Cancer, Scorpio and Pisces. According to Tajik school of thought Taurus, Virgo and Capricorn are classed as *Vaiśya varṇa* while Gemini, Libra and Aquarius are *Śūdra varṇa.*

14. Colours
    a) Red – Aries, Leo and Sagittarius.
    b) White – Taurus, Cancer and Libra.
    c) Ash – Gemini, Scorpio and Aquarius.
    d) Black – Virgo, Capricorn and Pisces.

15. Short and Long
    a) Short – Aries, Taurus, Aquarius, Capricorn.
    b) Long – Leo, Virgo, Libra, Scorpio.
    c) Normal – Gemini, Cancer, Sagittarius, Pisces.

16. Mental qualities
    a) Arrogant – Aries, Taurus, Gemini.
    b) Vacillating – Cancer.
    c) Judicious – Leo, Sagittarius, Pisces.
    d) Intellectual – Virgo.
    e) Brutal – Libra.
    f) Aggressive – Scorpio.
    g) Indolent – Capricorn and Aquarius.
17. *Vāta/Pitta* etc.
    a) *Vāta* (wind) – Taurus, Virgo and Capricorn.
    b) *Pitta* (bile) – Aries, Leo, Sagittarius.
    c) *Śleṣmā* (phlegm) – Cancer, Scorpio and Pisces.
18. Lean (*śuṣka* signs)
    Aries, Gemini, Leo, Libra, Sagittarius and Aquarius.
19. *Kīṭa* (*insect*) signs –
    Scorpio, Pisces, Cancer and second half of Capricorn.
    Catuṣpada (*quadruped*) Signs – Aries, Taurus, Leo, second half of Capricorn.
    Nara (human) signs – Gemini, Libra, Aquarius, Virgo and first half of Sagittarius.
20. *Ūrdhvamukha* (face-up) signs –
    3rd, 6th, 9th and 12th signs from the Sun.
    Adhomukha (facing down) signs –
    4th, 7th, 10th signs from the Sun and the signs in which the Sun is posited.
    Tiryakmukha signs –
    2nd, 5th, 8th, 11th signs from the Sun.
21. *Rāśi Gandantan*
    Last one *ghaṭī* (24 mts) each of Cancer, Scorpio, Pisces and the first ghati of Leo, Sagittarius and Aries.
    Rāśi Sandhi
    Last *navāṁśa* of Cancer, Scorpio, Pisces. Both *rāśi sandhi* and *gandanta* are bad symbols.

22. Angles : The ascendant, 4th, 7th and 10th are called angles or *kendras*.

a) The 5th and 9th from the ascendant are trines or *koṇas*.

b) The 6th, 8th and 12th from the ascendant are called evil houses or *trikasthānas*.

c) The 3rd, 6th, 10th and 11th from the ascendant are known as *uccaiḥsthānas*.

d) The 2nd and the 7th are called *mārakasthānas* or houses of death.

e) The 4th and 8th from the ascendant are known as *caturasras*.

f) The houses adjoining the angles (i.e. the 2nd, 5th, 8th and 11th) are designated as cadent houses or *apoklimas*.

g) The houses adjoining *apoklimas* (viz. the 3rd, 6th, 9th and the 12th) are known as *panapharas* or succedent houses.

Apart from the nine planets from the Sun to Ketu, Hindu astrology also recognizes sub-planets or *upagrahas*. These positions should also be inserted in the horoscope for they are capable of giving certain effects independent of the nine *grahas* or planets.

The five *upagrahas* are *dhūma, vyatīpāta, pariveśa, indracāpa* and *upaketu*. These are non-luminous or *aprakāśaka grahas*. The actual positions of these are to be calculated as given in the *Bṛhat Parāśara Horā Śāstra* (Ch. 3 *Ślokas* 61-64).

To get *Dhūma* 4 signs 13 degrees and 20 minutes of arc to the Sun's longitude. *Dhūma* from 12 signs to ascertain the position of *Vyatīpāta Dhūma* is reduced. The position of *Pariveśa* is obtained by adding 6 signs to *Vyatīpāta*. To get the position of *indracāpa* the longitude of *Pariveśa* deducted from 12 signs. *Upaketu* will be ahead of *indracāpa* by

16 degrees 40 minutes and one sign or 30 degrees behind the Sun.

From the above we can deduce the following simple standard formulae to know the positions of the five *aprakāśaka grahas* when the sun's longitude is given.

a) Sun + 133^0 20′=*Dhūma*
b) *Dhūma* + 53^0 20′ = *Vyatīpāta*
c) *Vyatīpāta* + 180^0 = *Pariveśa*
d) *Pariveśa less* 53^0 20′= *Indracāpa*
e) *Indradhanuṣa* + 16^0 40′= *Upaketu*
f) *Upaketu* + 30^0 = The Sun.

There are four kinds of *Varga* evaluations, viz.

a) *Ṣaḍvarga* (6 divisions only considered) – *rāśi, horā*, decanate, *navāṁśa, dvādaśāṁśa* and *triṁśāṁśa.*
b) *Saptavarga* (7 divisions): *saptāṁśa* calculations to *ṣaḍvarga* to get *saptavarga divisions.*
c) *Daśa Varga* (10 divisions): *khalāṁśa, daśāṁśa* and *ṣaṣtiaṃsa* calculations is added to the *saptavarga* scheme.
d) *Ṣoḍaśa Varga* : These are 16 divisions or *vargas.*

Now, the special technical names given in this context are:-

a) *Ṣaḍvarga* scheme, if a planet is in two good *vargas*, it is called *kiṁśuka varga.* Similarly if it has 3 good *vargas* then *vyañjana;* 4 good *vargas, cāmara;* 5 good *vargas, chatra;* and 6 good *vargas, kuṇḍala.*
b) When *saptavarga* scheme is considered, the above names for the 6 good *vargas* remain the same as for *ṣaḍvargas* while 7 good *vargas* get the name *mukuṭa.*
c) When *daśavarga* scheme is considered, the number of good *vargas go* with the following names—

2. *Pārijāta* 3. *Uttama* 4. *Gopura*
5. *Siṁhāsana* 6. *Pārāvata* 7. *Devaloka*
8. *Brahmaloka* 9. *Śakravāhana*
10. *Śrīdhāma*

d) Lastly, when *ṣoḍaśavarga* scheme is considered the good *vargas* go with the undermentioned special names.
2. *Bhedaka* 3. *Kusuma* 4. *Nāgapuṣpa*
5. *Kanduka* 6. *Kerala* 7. *Kalpavṛikṣa*
8. *Candanavana* 9. *Pūrṇacandra*
10. *Uccaiḥśravā* 11. *Dhanvantari*
12. *Sūryakānta* 13. *Vidruma*
14. *Śakrasiṁhāsana*
15. *Goloka* 16. *Śrīvallabha*

In these divisional considerations, good *vargas* mean the planet's exaltation sign, *mūlatrikoṇa* sign, own sign and the signs of the lord of an angle from the *āruḍha lagna*. The divisions of a combust planet, defeated planet, weak planet and a planet in bad *avasthās* like *śayana* are inauspicious and be not considered good.

For convenience sake, the sages used these terms in their *ślokas*. When the term *Sūryakāntāṁśa* appears, it denotes that the planet is in 12 such good *vargas* out of the 16 divisions, or when the term *pārāvatāṁśa* is used it means the planet is in 6 such good divisions in the *daśavarga* scheme. So to say, these are brief terms.

Vargottama is however a different term. It means that the planet occupies one and the same *rāśi* and *navāṁśa*.

Nāḍiaṁśas: Each *rāśi* is divided into 150 *nāḍiaṁśas*, measuring 12' of arc. A *nāḍiaṁśa* is again divided into two parts which are respectively known as *pūrvabhāga* (former part) and *parabhāga* (latter part). Some *Nāḍī* texts make each *rāśi* into

600 *nāḍīaṁśas* thus making the entire zodiac into 7200 parts.

Description of *Nakṣatra*

The zodiac is an imaginary elliptical band 18^0 wide described round the star sphere at the centre of which runs the Ecliptic; to this narrow band are confined the Sun, Moon and the planets and can never be seen on any other part of the sky except the zodiac.

The zodiac is divided into twelve equal lengths in each of which the Sun transits for a period of one month of the year. They are the signs of the zodiac.

The *nakṣatras* or the *kālamaṇḍala* or circle of time. They are twenty-seven in number. Each of which has peculiar functions as per its quality.

A question may arise as why Oriental Astro-Science takes selected few planets and a selected few constellations in preference to the innumerable ones studded in the sky. The simple answer to this is that, such of them who influence our lives on this planet earth have been accepted by the givers of this science in preference to the rest.

The 360 degree of zodiac is divided into twelve equal parts. Each part is a sign of 30 degrees longitude. In the same way, these 360 degree have been divided into 27 equal parts called constellations, that is, stars or star groups. Hence, stars forming a group are called constellations. In 1982, the International Astronomical Union recognized 88 constellations; but for the Astrological purposes 27 constellations have been recognized and each of these has been assigned to a planet. The 28th *nakṣatra* group is called *abhijit* which is in the sign of Capricorn extending from 6^0 40$'$ to 13^0 20$'$ and is ruled by the Moon. This *abhijit* has not been given the status of a constellation like the other 27 *nakṣatras*. The names of the 27 asterisms are as follows. 1-*aśvinī*, 2-*bharaṇī* (*dvija*), 3-*kṛttikā*, 4-*rohiṇī*, 5-*mṛgaśirā*, 6-*ardrā*, 7-*punarvasu*, 8-*puṣya*, 9-*aśleṣā*, 10-*maghā*, 11-*pūrvāphālgunī*, 12-*uttarāphālgunī*, 13-*hasta*, 14-*citrā*, 15-*svāti*, 16-*viśākhā*, 17-*anurādhā*, 18-*jyeṣṭha*, 19-*mūla*, 20-*pūrvāṣaḍhā*, 21-*uttaraṣāḍha*, 22-*śrāvaṇa*, 23-*dhaniṣṭhā*, 24-*satabhiṣā*, 25-*pūrvābhādrapadā*, 26-*uttarabhādrapadā*, 27-*revatī*. The longitude of a constellation is 13^0 $20'$. Each *rāśi* includes 9 quarters (*padas*) of the constellations. In the table No. 2 *Meṣa rāśi* (Aries) is formulated by the four *padas* of *aśvinī*, four *padas* of *bharaṇī* and one *pada* of *kṛttikā*. The rest three *padas* of *kṛttikā* go to the next *rāśi vṛṣabha* and herein all the 4 *padas* of *Rohiṇī* plus 2 *padas* of *Mṛgaśirā* are to be found– thus completing the 9 *padas* in a *rāśi* and so on it goes with the rest.

The placement of Moon in a constellation marks the broad period (*daśā*) of the planet which governs the constellation. For instance, *Moon is in Leo* 20^0 *in a horoscope*. This point falls in the constellation of *pūrvāphālgunī* of which Venus is the governing planet and therefore, the person born under this constellation will experience the broad period (*daśā*) of Venus, the constellational lord. This is as per the *viṁśottarī daśā* system, propounded by the great sage *Parāśara*.

Man is a twelve fold being – three fold spirit, three fold body, three fold mind and three fold soul. These divisions are very clearly seen in the twelfth signs of the zodiac.

1. Three Fiery signs indicating three aspects of Spirit
   (a) Aries - Divine spirit
   (b) Leo - Life spirit
   (c) Sagittarius - Human spirit
2. Three Earthly signs representing three aspects of body
   (a) Taurus - Mineral or Physical body
   (b) Virgo - The Etheric or Vital body
   (c) Capricorn - The Astral or Desire body.
3. Three Airy signs showing Mind
   (a) Gemini - Conscience or reasoning mind
   (b) Libra - Sub-conscious mind that is, memory
   (c) Aquarius - Super-conscious or creative-intuitive mind.
4. Three watery signs representing three aspects of soul.
   (a) Cancer - Conscience soul (b) Scorpio - Intellectual soul (c) Pisces - Emotional soul.

CONSTELLATIONS AND THEIR CHARACTERISTICS

No. 1 - Sex of the constellations:

a) Male - *aśvinī, punarvasu, puṣya, hasta, anurādhā, srāvaṇa, purvabhādrapadā* and *uttarabhādrapadā.*

b) Female - *bharaṇī, kṛttikā, rohiṇī, ardrā, aśleṣā, maghā, pūrvāphālgunī, uttarāphālgunī, citrā, svāti, viśākhā, jyeṣṭhā, pūrvāṣāḍhā, uttarāṣāḍhā, dhaniṣṭhā* and *revatī.*

c) Eunuch - *mṛgaśirā, mūlā* and *satabhiṣā.*

No. 2 – *Guṇas:*

a) *Sāttvika–punarāvasu, aśleṣā, viśākhā, jyeṣṭhā, pūrvābhādrapadā* and *revatī.*

b) *Rājasika–bharaṇī, kṛttikā, rohiṇī, pūrvāphālgunī, uttarāphālgunī, Hasta, pūrvāṣāḍha, uttarāṣaḍha* and *Śrāvaṇa.*

c) *Tāmasika–aśvinī, mṛgaśirā, ardrā, puṣya, maghā, citrā, svāti, anurādhā, mūlā, dhaniṣṭhā, satabhiṣā* and *uttarābhādrapadā.*

No. 3 – Movable/Immovable:

a) Movable – (Mobile) *punarvasu, svāti, śrāvaṇa, dhaniṣṭhā* and *śatabhiṣā* – Auspicious for journey or movement.

b) Immovable – *rohiṇī, uttarāphālgunī, uttarāṣāḍhā* and *uttarābhādrapadā* – Auspicious for the work of fixed nature, such as entering into a new house etc.

No. 4 – Nature:

a) *Ugra* (Aggressive) – *bharaṇī, uttarāphālgunī, mūlā, purvābhādrapadā* – Auspicious for starting any work of aggressive nature like war, quarrelling etc.

b) *Miśra* (Mixed) – *kṛttikā* and *viśākhā* – Auspicious for mixed type of works.

c) *Laghu* (Light) – *aśvinī, puṣya, hasta* – Auspicious for sale-purchase, art and education etc.

d) *Maitra* (Friendly) – *mṛgaśirā, citrā, anurādhā* and *Revatī* – Good for starting friendship and wearing new clothes.

e) *Dāruṇa* (Hard) – *ārdrā, aśleṣā, jyeṣṭhā* and *mūlā* – Good for etc.

f) *Adhomukhī* (Down faced) – *bharaṇī, kṛttikā, aśleṣā, maghā, pūrvāphālgunī, viśākhā, pūrvāṣāḍhā* and *purvābhādrapadā* – Good for digging well, tank etc.

g) *Ūrdhvamukhī* (Up-faced) – *rohiṇī, ārdrā, puṣya, uttarāphālgunī, uttarāṣāḍhā, śrāvaṇa, dhaniṣṭhā, śatabhiṣā* and *uttarābhādrapadā* – Good to draw government favour.

h) *Triaṅgamukhā* (Tripple-faced) – *aśvinī, mṛgaśirā, punarvasu, hastā, citrā, svāti, anurādhā, jyeṣṭhā* and *revatī* – Good for journey, purchase etc.

i) *Dagdha* (Burnt) – *bharaṇī* on Sunday, *citrā* on Monday, Tuesday with *uttarāṣāḍhā, dhaniṣṭhā* on Wednesday, Thursday with *uttarāphālgunī*, Friday with *jyeṣṭhā* and Saturday with *revatī* becomes *dagdhā*. These days are inauspicious to start with any work.

No. 5 – Blind stars :-

a) *Andha* (Blind) – *rohiṇī, puṣya, uttarāphālgunī, viśākhā, purvāṣāḍhā, dhaniṣṭhā* and *revatī*.

b) *Mandākṣa* (Limited vision) – *aśvinī, mṛgaśirā, aśleṣā, hastā, anurādhā, uttarāṣāḍhā* and *satabhiṣā*.

c) *Madhyākṣa* (Average vision) – *bharaṇī, ardrā, maghā, citrā, jyeṣṭhā, pūrvābhādrapadā* and *abhijit*.

d) *Sulocanā* (Pretty eye) – *kṛttikā, punarvasu, purvāphālgunī, svāti, mūla, śrāvaṇa* and *uttarābhādrapadā*.

The visionary classifications of the constellations is suggestive that the person having his Moon in blind or *andha* constellations is of a superfluous intuitional judgement whereas *mandākṣa* is little better in the matter. The *madhyākṣa* sees through things with a mediumistic view while *sulocana* sees things through and through. This interpretation may be classed as a philosophical one of the constellations.

Mandi : *Mandi*, the poisonous one is the son of Saturn as described in Indian Astrology. Determination of its position in a birth chart is the most important task.

For day born, the duration of a day (sunrise to sunset) is called a *divāmāna*. Divide this by 8. Each part is governed by a planet. The day lord is the lord of the 1st part and remaining parts are ruled by the planetary order of the weekdays.

Similarly, to determine the position of *Mandi* for night birth, divide the *rātrimāna*, duration of the night (sunset to sunrise) by 8. The first part is ruled by the planet 5th from the day lord and the remaining parts in the same order as mentioned in case of day born. Here also, the part ruled by Saturn goes to *Mandi* or *gulikā*.

Here is a table for easy reference.

1. To find out *Mandi* during day time: -

	Day	1st	2nd	3rd	4th	5th	6th	7th	8th
1	Sun	Sun	Moon	Mars	Mer	Jup	Ven	Sat	X
2	Mon	Moon	Mars	Mer	Jup	Ven	Sat	X	X
3	Tue	Mars	Mer	Jup	Ven	Sat	X	X	X
4	Wed	Mer	Jup	Ven	Sat	X	X	X	X
5	Thu	Jup	Ven	Sat	X	X	X	X	X
6	Fri	Ven	Sat	X	X	X	X	X	X
7	Sat	Sat	X	X	X	X	X	X	X

2. To find out Mandi during night time:-

	Day	1st	2nd	3rd	4th	5th	6th	7th	8th
1	Sun	Jup	Ven	Sat	X	X	X	X	X
2	Moon	Ven	Sat	X	X	X	X	X	X
3	Tue	Sat	X	X	X	X	X	X	X
4	Wed	Sun	Mon	Mars	Mer	Jup	Ven	Sat	X
5	Thu	Mon	Mars	Mer	Jup	Ven	Sat	X	X
6	Fri	Mars	Mer	Jup	Ven	Sat	X	X	X
7	Sat	Mer	Jup	Ven	Sat	X	X	X	X

Example – For instance, a boy is born on 9th July 1985, Tuesday at 1.30 pm IST in Bhubaneshwar. In any local almanac the duration of the day can be found. The author's calculations are based on the *Rāṣṭriya Pancāṁga* prepared by the Director General of Meteorological Centre for the year 1985. According to this, the sunrise of 9th July is at 5.13 am and sunset at 6.31 pm for Bhubaneshwar. So the *Divāmāna* is 13th 18m=798 minutes. Dividing this by 8, we get 97m 30 seconds per part, that is, 1h 37m 30 sec. Since the day is Tuesday, 5th division of the day will be ruled by Saturn. 4th division ends after 6 hrs. 30 mts of sunrise, that is, 5h 13m+6h 30 = 11.43 am. From 11.43 am beings the fifth division governed by saturn, which is time when *Mandi* rises. At 11-43 am, of 9th July 1985, the sign Virgo rises in the East. So *Mandi* is to be fixed in the sign Virgo in the birth chart or Virgo is to be called as the *Gulikā Lagna* for this chart. The *lagnasphut* (longitude of *gulikā lagna*) at 11.43 am is Virgo 21°30′ so the *gulikā* or *mandi* is in Virgo 21°30′ of the chart.

Importance – One can rectify the asundance of a horoscope considering its position. That may be in trine from mandi itself, or the 7th, 5th or 9th from the rasi or the *navāṁśa* occupied by Mandi, its dispositor or the Moon.

Fortuna: What is Pars Fortuna? Fortuna, also called Pars Fortuna, is a magnetic point in the horoscope represented by the earth symbol.

It is to be determined by adding the longitudes of the ascendant with that of the Moon subtracting the longitude of the Sun from the total, that is, *lagnasphuta (+) candrasphuta (-) ravisphuta* = Fortuna.

Example – For instance, the Sun is in Virgo 15°20′ the Moon is in Capricorn 13° 30′ and the ascendant falls in Libra 28°, so the position of Fortuna is to be as follows.

Lagnasphuta is 6° 28′ + *candrasphuta* 9°13′ 30″= 16°11′ 30″- *ravisphuta* 5° 15′ 20″= 10° 26′ 10″. So Fortuna is to be placed in the 26° 10′ of Aquarius.

A critical example now. Suppose ascendant is in Aries 15° 2′, Moon is also in 15° of Aries. So 0° 15′ + 0° 15′= 1° 0′ 00″. The Sun is in 5° 15′ or Leo 15°. therefore, the ascendant and Moon total fall short of the longitude of the Sun. Here add one circle that is, 12 signs and deduct the longitude of the Sun which will be 1° 0′ 00″+ 12°=13°0′ 00″ – 5° 15′= 7° 15 00″ or Scorpio 15°. Fortuna's position will be at Scorpio 15°.

Effects – Fortuna is both a sensitive and a fortunate point in the zodiac, which improves the matters signified by the house it occupies.

Prāṇapadā : What is *Prāṇapadā* ? A *prāṇa* is equal to 15 lltas and one *daṇḍa* is equal to 4 *prāṇas*. A human being takes birth only when the ascendant falls either in the *Prāṇapadā* itself or in the 5th, 7th or 9th *bhāvas* therefrom or in the 5th or 9th counted from the 7th house from *Prāṇapadā*.

How to calculate? Convert the given time into *vighaṭīs* and divide the same by 15. If the Sun is in a movable sign add the resultant *rāśi*, degrees with it, if in fixed sign add 240 degrees with above and in case dual sign 120 degrees to be added. Example – For instance, the child is born at 20 *ghaṭīs* 20 *vighaṭīs* after sunrise. Converting the same into *vighaṭīs*, we get 1220. Dividing it by 15 the result comes 81-5 means 81 *rāśis* 5^0, Dividing this by 12, we get 9 signs 5^0 or 275^0. If the Sun is in a movable sign (suppose in *Libra* 10^0) then 275^0 + 190^0 = 465^0. Since one sign is of 30^0 it will be 15^0 15′. Deducting 12 signs it comes to 3^0 15′of Cancer 15^0, wherein *Prāṇapadā* will be placed.

Importance – The importance of *Prāṇapadā* lies in its use for rectification of birth time as mentioned above.

CALCULATIONS OF *upagrahas*

Like *grahas*-Planets, there are five *upagrahas* or subplanets. They are 1-*Dhūma*, 2-*Vyatīpāta*, 3-*Pariveśa*, 4-*Indracāpa*, 5-*Upaketu*. They are *highly malefics* in their behaviour and effects.

How to calculate them? Note the longitude of the Sun of a nativity and calculate these *non luminous-aprakāśa Grahas* as per the formula given below:-

1. Sun's longitude + 133^0 20′= *Dhūma*
2. *Dhūma* + 53^0 20′= *Vyatīpāta*
3. *Vyatīpāta* + 180^0 = *Pariveśa*
4. *Pariveśa* – 53^0 20′= *Indracāpa*
5. *Indracāpa* + 16^0 40′= *Upaketu*

Upaketu, if increased by 30 degrees will be equal to the Sun's longitude of the given horoscope.

S.No.	Upagrahas	Exaltation	Debilitation	Own Sign
1	Dhūma	Leo	Aquarious	Capricorn
2	Vyatīpāta	Scorpio	Taurus	Gemini
3	Pariveśa	Gemini	Sagittarius	Sagittarius
4	Indracāpa	Sagittarius	Gemini	Cancer
5	Upaketu	Aquarius	Leo	Cancer

Though the calculations of these subplanets are not necessary for the horoscope, still their roles are very much felt at the time of minute study of a chart. Hence the necessity of this chapter.

How they behave? – They behave as per the moods or whims of their dispositors, the lord of the houses they occupy. Since they are highly malefics and afflict the *bhāva*, mostly negative results can be expected from them.

Planets and Their Characteristics

S. No.	Elements	The Sun	The Moon	The Mars	The Mercury
1	Sex	Male	Female	Male	Eunuch
2	Temperament	Hot	Cold	Hot	Convertible
3	Caste	Kṣatriya	Kṣatriya	Kṣatriya	Vaiśya
4	The age	50 yrs	70 yrs	17 yrs	10 yrs
5	Status	King	Queen	Commander	Child (Kumār)
6	Qualities	Sāttvika	Sāttvika	Tamas	Rajas
7	Elements	Fire	Water	Fire	Earthly
8	Taste	Pungent	Saltish	Bitter	Mixed

9	Direction	East	N.W Corner	South	North
10	Nature	Malefic	Benefic & malefic	Malefic	Convertible
11	Controlling senses	Eye	Tongue	Eye	Nose
12	Controlling limbs	Head	Face	Chest	Hips
13	Shape of the planet	Quadra-ngular	Circular	Triangular	Triangular
14	Stature	Tall	Short	Tall	Dwarf
15	Control over body	Male life	Female life	Blood	Skin
16	Bodies	Legs	No legs	Four legs	Two legs
17	Esoterically	Soul	Mind	Power	Speech
18	Own house	Leo	Cancer	Aries, Scorpio	Virgo, Gemini
19	Exaltation	Aries 10^0	Taurus 3^0	Capricorn 28^0	Virgo 15^0
20	Mūla *trikoṇa*	Leo 20^0	Taurus	Aries 12^0	Virgo 16^0 $20'$
21	Debilitation	Libra 10^0	Scorpio 3^0	Cancer 28^0	Pisces 15^0
22	Karakatwa	Father	Mother	Brother	Uncle
23	Colour	Red	White	Deep red	Green
24	Season	Summer	Rainy	Summer	Autumn
25	Metal	Copper	Silver	Copper	Lead
26	Gemstone	Ruby	Pearl	Coral	Lead
27	Humours	Bile	Phlegm	Bile	Nervous system
28	Presiding deity	Śiva	Pārvatī	Kārttikeya	Viṣṇu

29	Presiding goddess	Mātaṅgī	Kamalātmikā	Bagalā	Bhuvaneśvarī
30	Daśā period (viṁśottarī)	6 yrs	10 yrs	7 yrs	17 yrs
31	Daśā period (aṣṭottarī)	6 yrs	15 yrs	8 yrs	17 yrs
32	Birth place	Kaliṅga	Yavana countries	Avantī	Magadha
33	Dhātus	Bones	Blood	Marrow	Skin
34	Grains	Wheat	Rice	Aḍhaka	Green gram
35	Periods	Six months	A moment	A day	Two months
36	Trees	Tall & strong	Creepers	Thorny	Fruitless
37	Places in a house	Worship room	Bath room	Kitchen	Dancing hall
38		Quadrupeds	Like a reptile	Quadrupeds	Like birds
39	Combustion		12^0	17^0	11^0

S. No.	Jupiter	Venus	Saturn	Rāhu	Ketu
1	Male	Female	Eunuch	Female	Eunuch
2	Warm	Cold	Cold	Neutral	Neutral
3	Brāhmaṇa	Brāhmaṇa	Śūdra	Outcaste	Cāṇḍāla
4	30 yrs	16 yrs	80 yrs	100 yrs	—
5	Prime Minister	Prime Minister	Servant	Servant	Beggar
6	Sāttvika	Rajas	Tamas	Tamas	Tamas
7	Ether	Water	Wind	Wind	Fire
8	Sweet	Sour	Astringent	Bitter	Bitter

9	N.E.Corner	S.E.	West	S.W.	—
10	Benefic	Benefic	Malefic	Malefic	Malefic
11	Ear	Taste	Skin	Skin	—
12	Stomach	Sex organ	Bone	Hands	Legs
13	Ecliptical	Octagonal	Tall	A line	A line
14	Tall	Normal height	Short	Tall	Tall
15	Liver	Throat/ kidney	Bowels	Teeth	Stool
16	Two legs	Two legs	Four legs	No legs	No legs
17	Wisdom	Sensual pleasure	Sorrow	Enjoyment	Experience
18	Sagittarius, Pisces	Libra, Taurus	Capricorn, Aquarius	Virgo	Pisces
19	Cancer 5^0	Pisces 27^0	Libra 20^0	Gemini 21^0	Sagittarius 21^0
20	Sagittarius 5^0	Libra 20^0	Aquarius 20^0	Gemini 20^0	Sagittarius 20^0
21	Capricorn 5^0	Virgo 27^0	Aries 28^0	Sagittarius 21^0	Gemini 21^0
22	Children	Husband/ wife	Servant	Paternal grand parents	Maternal grand parents
23	Yellow	White	Blue	Grey	Brown
24	Dewy	Spring	Winter	—	—
25	Gold	Silver	Steel	Lead	Lead
26	Yellow saphire	Diamond	Blue saphire	Gomed	Cat's eye
27	Phlegm	Wind/ phlegm	Wind	Wind	Bile

28	Viṣṇu	Lakṣmī	Yama	Kārttikeya	Brahmā
29	Tārā	Lakṣmī	Dakhinakālī	Chinnamastā	Dhūmavatī
30	16 yrs	20 yrs	19 yrs	18 yrs	7 yrs
31	19 yrs	21 yrs	10 yrs	12 yrs	Nil
32	Sindhu	Nikata	Saurāṣtra	Simhal	Parvat
33	Fat	Semen	Muscles	Anus	Worms
34	Bengal gram	Cowgram	Sesamum	Black gram	Horse gram
35	A month	A fortnight	A year	Some hours	—
36	Fruit bearing	Creepers	Thorny	Bushes	Bushes
37	Strong room	Bed room	Garage	Latrine	Dirty place
38	Human beings	Human beings	Like birds	Shaven head	Like a snake
39	15^0	9^0	17^0	-	-

न ह्यतो धर्माचरणं किञ्चिदस्ति महत्तरम् ।
यथा पितरि शुश्रूषा तस्य वा वचनक्रिया ।।

Being obedient to father and devotedly
serving to him is such a religion (duty)
that no other religion is greater
than this (Lord *Rāma*).

Chapter-2

ESSENTIALS OF ASTROLOGY

Following principles have been traced from various works of astrology. These are most important observations of various astrologers and a few of these have been taken from classical works. These principles of astrology will help the beginners for the advanced study of astrology. These principles of the science of astrology have been experienced on over thousand of birth charts and the results have always been astonishingly, precisely accurate and correct. We have included the general principles of astrology also for the ready reference to students, such as the rules of *nīca bhaṅga rājayoga*, combustion, *bādhakas*, cancellation of *nāḍī doṣa* and the like.

Principle 1- *Navāṁśa*

One important use of *navāṁśa* is to assume that a planet is in association with the planet in whose *navāṁśa* that is situated. *navāṁśa* chart may be studied independently, provided the time of birth is absolutely correct.

Principle 2 - *Dispositors*

(a) The dispositor gives the results of the planets, which are occupying their signs. For advance study of the theory of the dispositors, a book name *Dispositors* by J.N.Bhasin may be referred.

b) The dispositor usually carries the effects of the planets posited in their sign, e.g., *Mars* in Pisces, then its dispositor Jupiter opposite to its life saving nature, because of carrying the effects of *Mars*, will kill the native (or concerned individual).
1, 5, 9 are fiery signs
2, 6, 10 are earthly signs
3, 7, 11 are airy signs
4, 8, 12 are watery signs
lords of these houses are also fiery, earthly, airy or watery in nature. They incorporate these nature (fiery, earthly, airy and watering). but if any house is occupied by a planet, its lord will act in accordance with the nature of the planet posited in its sign, even though its own nature may be different.

Principle 3 - Planets And Separation

The Sun, Saturn and *Rāhu* possess separative tendencies. The 12th house and the lord thereof also has separative tendency. Dispositors of these planets also have separative tendency. These planets give rise to separation during their *daśā bhukti*. If any house receives malefic impact of at least three of these, the auspicious results of that house will be spoiled.

Principle 4 - Jupiter And Sun

For Virgo *lagna*, Jupiter in 11th in Cancer gives daughters as it owns two *kendras*. Retrograde Jupiter in 11th gives male child. Generally, it may be clearly understood that it is not at all essential that male planets like Jupiter or Sun, tend to bless one with male children only.

Principle 5 - Effect Of Sun

The Sun creates problems, tensions and trouble from the person where the Sun is placed. In 7th, the Sun causes disputes with wife, in 5th with children, in 4th with mother and so on. Sun promotes 3rd, 10th and 11th houses if placed therein. In the 5th house, Sun gives daughter and not son. In 7th, Sun gives unhappy married life and separation because the native ignores his/her spouse. In 4th Sun may give rise to heart trouble, especially if *Ketu* is associated in 4th.

Principle 6 - Moon

Moon should be regarded as malefic if it is placed within 72^0 from the Sun. Moon is a benefic from 8th lunar day of bright fortnight to the 7th lunar day of dark fortnight.

Principle 7 – *Sudarśana* System

Sudarśana is the system introduced by *maharṣi Parāśara.* According to this, position is analyzed in relation to Sun *lagna* and Moon *lagna* also in addition to general *lagna. Sudarśana Cakra* contains these three charts in one, e.g., if any house is afflicted as well as disposed, in relation to all the three *lagnas*, the matters of that house will largely be hampered or promoted accordingly.

Principle 8 - Cancellation Of *Naḍī Doṣa*

1. There is no *nāḍī doṣa* if birth takes place in *Rohiṇī, ardrā, mṛgaśirā, kṛttikā, puṣya, srāvaṇa, revatī,* and *uttarābhādrapadā.*

   (Jyotiṣa Cintāmaṇi)

2. If the Moon sign of either of the couple is owned by Jupiter, Venus or Mercury, *Nāḍī Doṣa* will be cancelled or it will be ineffective.

   (Vivāha Kautūhala)

3. *Nāḍī doṣa* will be cancelled if *janma nakṣatra* of the boy and girl is same but the *pada* is different, i.e., if both are born in different quarters of the same constellation.

4. If both, boy and girl are born in the same *nakṣatra* but the Moon sign is different.
5. If the Moon sign of the boy and girl are same but constellation are different.
6. If Moon sign of boy and girl are ruled by the same planet, i.e., if there is *ekādhipatya* the *nāḍī doṣa* is automatically gets cancelled.

Principle 9 - Marriage Time

a) So many rules have been laid down for timing of marriage but we are not able to time all marriages correctly. I have experienced that 4th house does play a vital role in the timing of a marriage. Fourth house creates a feeling of own home, belonging to some one and being responsible to him or her fully. Marriage is not merely a union of two physical bodies but it is a sacred bond of love, care and responsibility for whole life. Marriage causes lot of variations, additions and emotions in the mind of every person. Therefore, the 4th house must be considered for timing of marriage in addition to the 7th and 2nd house.

b) Transit of Jupiter is very important in timing marriage. After fixing up appropriate *daśā* and *bhukti* for marriage, see the influence of transiting Jupiter. It should influence by way of aspect or it should transit over the 7th house, *lagna*, its lords or *kārakas* like Moon or Venus.

c) The rules of *Phaladīpikā* about the importance of Jupiter's transit over the sum of longitude of *lagna* lord and 7th lord or to the trine position does not work accurately.

Principle 10 - Late Marriage

a) If the Sun, Moon, 7th lord and *kārakas* are under the influence of Saturn, the marriage will be delayed. If the *luminaries* and *kārakas* fall in

Saturn's *navāṁśa*, the marriage will be delayed. Influence of retrograde planets either by placement or aspect over the 2nd or 7th house or their lords will also cause delay in marriage. Combination of Moon and Venus is also a negative combination for early marriage. If Venus falls in the sign of luminaries, i.e., Cancer or Leo and is also hemmed between them, the marriage will be delayed.

b) Mutual aspect or conjunction of Saturn and Mars in respect to 7th house will also create obstacles in marriage. Placement of concerning planets in fixed signs and *navāṁśa* will also cause some delay in marriage. The intensity of adverse planets causing delay in marriage should be properly judged, so that probable *daśā* and *bhukti* for marriage may be judged correctly.

Principle 11 - Widowhood

The Sun or Mars in the sign of their exaltation or own sign identical to the 1st or 7th house will cause widowhood. If Sun is placed in the 1st or 7th house for Leo, Aries or Libra *lagna*, the widowhood will be there. Placement of *Mars* in the 1st or 7th house for Aries, Libra, Scorpio, Taurus, Capricorn or Cancer ascendant, will cause widowhood. These clues should be studied with other favourable or unfavourable combinations. These should not be applied verbatim. Specific combination of widowhood are explained in this book.

Principle 12 - Two Wives

If Venus or 7th lord is hemmed between two malefics or *pāpas*, two wives will be there. It is not essential that both wives are legally married to the native. One may be a secret and responsible for relationship with any female just like that of wife. This is an important rule and has been verified in dozens of horoscopes.

If Venus is placed in movable sign and *navāṁśa* (not *vargottama*), the native will have two wives.

Venus in Cancer and Moon in Capricorn, the native will have two marriages.

Placement of Moon and Venus in the 7th house in association gives rise to *bahukalatra yoga*, i.e., number of wives will be there.

If the lord of the 7th house and Venus falls in the dual sign in male nativity, two marriages will take place. If these fall in the *navāṁśa* of Mercury or Jupiter, more than one marriage will surely be there.

If Moon joins the 7th or 3rd house from *lagna* and Mercury is placed in the 10th house as reckoned from *lagna* lord, the native wiil be surrounded by women.

If the 7th lord is strong, exalted or it is retrograde in the lagna, more than one marriage will take place.

If the 7th lord is strong, and well placed, marriage will take place in a decent and rich family and *vice-versa*.

Principle 13 - Short Life Of One Partner

If Moon is placed in the 6th or 8th house with a malefic in the *lagna* and the same position is present in the horoscope of partner, the husband or wife will die soon after marriage.

Principle 14 - Death Within 8 Years

a) If Moon is placed in the *lagna* and Mars is posited in the 7th house, the death of boy or girl will come within 8 years of marriage.

b) If Sun and Saturn are conjoined in the 7th house in association with *Rāhu* or *Ketu*, the native will be killed by the spouse.

c) If Mars and Jupiter are conjoined in Cancer or Capricorn, spouse will be destroyed. If retrograde

Jupiter, joins *Mars*, the same results will come in evidence.

d) If one is born in Taurus ascendant, and *lagna* lord Venus falls in Scorpio, the early loss of spouse will take place.

e) Saturn in the 3rd house, will give marriage with a girl who has already lost her father. The danger to the life of mother-in-law within one year of marriage will be there.

f) Mars in the 8th house will cause diseases of uterus to the wife of the native. In a female horoscope, it will also cause widowhood.

g) The native will lose all his wealth, illicit relations, if *Rāhu* falls in the 7th house with a malefic in the sign of a malefic planet.

h) Saturn and Moon placed in the 7th house deny marriage. *Mars* conjoined with Mercury in the 7th house is very adverse and causes marital mishaps. *Mars* with Venus in the 7th house makes one rich through the spouse though the combination is very adverse for marital happiness. Jupiter, Mercury and Saturn in the 7th house gives a dumb spouse instead of riches. Jupiter *Mars* in the 7th house denotes a very prosperous husband.

Principle 15 - Children

Taurus, Leo, Virgo and Scorpio are honoured at *alpasuta rāśi*. The girl who is born in these signs, will be blessed only with a few children. However, if the sign comes under the influence of many benefics, many children will be born.

Principle 16 - Family Of Spouse

The wife will come out from a decent and rich family if the 7th lord is stronger than *lagna* lord and is well placed under the aspect of benefics or it is exalted. The family of wife will be a reputed one.

Principle 17 - Beauty And Physique Of Spouse

The planets placed in the 7th house or the planets who lend their aspect over the 7th house, decide the beauty of spouse. The 7th lord should not be taken much into consideration in the judgement of beauty, structure, age and complexion of the wife as this is generally done so by mistake.

Principle 18 - Direction Of Marriage

The direction indicated by the planet who becomes the lord of the 7th house as reckoned from Venus, will be the direction of the house of wife from where she will come out.

Principle 19 - Result Of Planets

Generally, the planets give the results, good or bad more strongly for the houses they are placed in or aspect as compared to the houses they own.

Principle 20 - *Daśā*

a) The planet ruling a person as the sub-period lord invariably influences the main *daśā* lord irrespective of their position in the horoscope, e.g., in Mercury, Mars period, Mars will harm the aspects of Mercury, relatives, brain etc.

b) *Daśā bhukti* lord if placed in a same house, gives bad results.

c) *Śani*-Venus is always bad.

d) *Śani Rāhu* is always bad.

e) *Rāhu* is conjoined with *Kendra* or *trikoṇa* lord gives very good results regarding the house it controls.

f) *Daśā* lord should be taken as *lagna* under separate chart keeping the *daśā* lord in *lagna* should be prepared for the examination of *daśā bhukti* results correctly. Similarly, while studying the details of sub-period keeping the sub period lord in the *lagna* another chart should be prepared for accuracy, correctness, preciseness of *daśā bhukti* results.

g) Mars *Rāhu* in 7th creates havoc including Mars Saturn and *Rāhu* Saturn in the married life. That may cause separation, widowhood, deaths and miseries.

h) If a child dies within 5 years, it is due to mother's ill luck, if 5 to 12 years, father's ill luck and after 12 years due to own sins.

i) Jupiter Sun Yoga – very good and will promote the house.

Principle 21 - Libra Ascendant And Jupiter

For Libra ascendant, Jupiter owns 3rd and 6th house but he gives benefic results as an exception to general rule. Though usually astrologers consider Jupiter as malefic for Libra ascendant.

Principle 22 - Distinction Between Life And Wealth Prospects

When the lord of any house aspects its own house, prospects of that house are promoted, e.g., for Capricorn natives, Saturn's aspect on *lagna* gives honour and wealth but shortens the life.

Mars for Aries natives, if placed in 10th aspects *lagna*, will give honour and wealth but the body would be subjected to injurious and short life.

Principle 23 - 11th Lord

If the lord of the 11th house is a malefic planet and he is placed in 5th house, it is not good for life prospects of elder brother. If such lord is afflicted by aspects of malefics, birth of elder brother denied.

Principle 24 - Sun And Venus

If Sun is located in any sign of Venus and is aspected by Moon, the man is fond of call girls.

Principle 25 - Debilitation Of *Lagnādhipati*

S. No.	Ascendant	Ascendant lord	Debilitated in	Trouble
1	Leo	Sun	3rd	ears
2	Cancer	Moon	6th	stomach
3	Aries	Mars	4th	chest
4	Scorpio	Mars	9th	back-hips
5	Gemini	Mercury	10th	knee
6	Virgo	Mercury	7th	urinary
7	Sagittarius	Jupiter	2nd	face
8	Pisces	Jupiter	11th	leg
9	Taurus	Venus	5th	stomach
10	Libra	Venus	12th	feet
11	Capricorn	Saturn	4th	chest
12	Aquarius	Saturn	3rd	breathing canal

Principle 26 - Disease

a) Lord of 6th in 6th, 8th, 10th and 1st, one suffers from boils.

b) Lord of 6th in 7th and 8th lord in 8th, causes Piles.

c) 6th lord with different planets

6th lord + Sun in 1st — high fever

6th lord + Moon in 1st — watery diseases

6th lord + Mars in 1st	billions trouble
6th lord + Mercury in 1st	consumption
6th lord + Jupiter in 1st	sexual
6th lord + Venus in 1st	nervous
6th lord + Saturn in 1st	spleen or carbuncle

watery diseases are gallbladder swelling, ulcer, bilious complaints, sexual troubles.

d) Mars in 6th, one suffers from high fever in 12th year and 6th year. 6th lord in 8th house, - same result.

Jaundice, Saturn Mars in 6th aspected by *Rāhu* or Sun – Chronic disease, heart or lung troubles.

e) Diseases and *lagna* lord

Sun as *lagna* lord represents	bone, Eye
Moon as *lagna* lord represents	blood
Mars as *lagna* lord represents	muscles
Jupiter as *lagna* lord represents	liver, fat, gall bladder
Mercury as *lagna* lord represents	veins, skin
Venus as *lagna* lord represents	Urinary tract, semen
Saturn as *lagna* lord represents	veins, nerves

f) Any planet that occupies the *lagna* becomes strongest representative of the tissue that it represents.

Such as Mars's affliction in *lagna* shows affliction or troubles in muscles and blood pressure. The placement of the afflicted Sun in ascendant, shows eye trouble and trouble connected with bones.

g) Any planet which occupies the 6th house, causes the disease represented by the planet such as Saturn in 6th under affliction may give neurological problems, kidney complaint, pain in legs, arthritis, asthmatic complaints etc.

h) Moon represents mind, Mercury represents brain. Affliction of both by conjunction of Saturn, *Rāhu, Ketu* causes mental disease such as depression or even insanity if the 5th house is also heavily afflicted.
Here aspect of *Rāhu-Ketu* or Saturn to radical Moon in *gochara* is enough to render a person suffer mentally.

i) *Triśamsa* chart must be referred for illness and diseases.

j) Mars in Virgo or in 6th house rules blood and wounds. Moon controls blood.

k) Blood Pressure – Mars governs the blood cells while Moon governs the watery portion of blood. Constellation belonging to Sun, Mars and *Ketu* have a stable blood pressure.

l) *Kṛttikā, mṛgaśirā, uttarāphālgunī, hasta, citrā, jyeṣṭhā, uttarāṣāḍhā, dhaniṣṭhā,* generally produce high blood pressure, i.e., hypertension.

m) *Aśvinī, rohiṇī, svātī, mūla, ardrā, satabhiṣā,* and *revatī* produces low blood pressure.

n) Mars in the constellation of *Ketu* generally produces high blood pressure.

o) Mars in the constellation of Sun or *vice-versa* produces high blood pressure.

p) 5th and 9th houses are important for blood pressure and heart, i.e., 5th house governs right ventricle, 9th governs left ventricles.

q) For Myocardial infraction (Heart attack) 4th, 5th, 8th houses should be afflicted.

r) Transit Sun passes through radical Mars, there is slight increase in blood pressure.

s) Transit Moon over Sun and Mars causes low blood pressure.

t) Transit Moon over *Ketu* causes depression.

u) Sun's debilitation generally causes heart trouble if it is identical to 4th or 6th house.

v) Severe heart trouble, when Sun and Moon are away by 120 degree or more, provided other combination of heart trouble are present. Protection against heart diseases particularly violent attack and consequent deaths will result if following combinations are there:-

I. Strong Jupiter in *lagna*

II. *Gajakesarī yoga*

III. Sun in Gemini

Principle 27 - *Rāhu* And *Saturn*

Evil planets in 6th or lord of 6th with Saturn or *Rāhu* will cause the native to suffer always. Planets placed in the 6th house will give trouble for which they are *kārakas* such as Saturn in 6th causes neurological problems, wind disorder, asthma, arthritis, hernia, spondylitis etc.

Principle 28 - Relatives

6th lord with benefics in *kendra* gives good friend. Lord of *lagna* in 6th aspected by 6th lord – gives constant trouble with relatives.

Lord of 9th in 6th aspected by 6th lord, one suffers from fire or thieves.

Principle 29 – Certain Transit Rules

a) Saturn's transit in 1st house, health will certainly suffer, mind is harassed. Strong and benefic Saturn – one gains a lot but loses all. One should not make important changes during Saturn's transit from *lagna*.

b) Mars transit in 1st house is more evil than Saturn but for short time.

c) Jupiter's transit in *lagna* indicates bright and joyous period, good health and spirits, active, young time to make changes. Saturn's transit in 2nd house, financial loss dragging annoyances. Mars in 2nd – quick and violent misfortune. Jupiter in 2nd – self money is obtained easily.

d) Saturn in 10th transit – Bankruptcy, ruin, Jupiter in 10th transit – most fortunate provided there are no evil transit or direction at that time. Promotion, increase in salary, business prosper, popularity, all of these are evident during the transit. Mars in 10th transit – misfortune.

e) Saturn's transit in 5th house in a favourable or exalted sign, may give rise to birth of a child.

f) Sun, Mars transit in 2nd house from Moon may give wealth.

Principle 30 – *Deśakana*

Varāhmihira's Classification of various parts of the body

Houses	1st *Deśakana* 0° – 10°	2nd *Deśakana* 10° – 20°	3rd *Deśakana* 20°- 30°
1	nead	neck	nerves
2, 12	eyes	shoulders	rectum
3, 11	ears	hands	testicles
4, 10	nostrils	sides	thighs
5, 9	cheek	heart	knees
6, 8	chin	stomach	shanks
7	mouth	novel	feet

2nd to 6th left side
8th to 12th right side

Principle 31 - Mars-Saturn Conjunction

a) Saturn-Mars conjunction in Cancer (*karka*) is definitely a hazardous combination with serious distructive results.

b) Saturn-Mars conjunction in Aries, Gemini, Libra, Capricorn and Pisces, it gives destructive results. Not so bad in other cases. If Jupiter Venus conjunction is there and results get modified.

c) Saturn-Mars conjunction in 7th, 8th, 11th are more prone to destructive results. Next bad house is ascendant. This helps if in *lagna* gives prosperity. Jupiter-Venus conjunction or opposition is present or when the conjunction is in the sign other than Cancer.

d) Saturn-Mars mutual aspect involving Aries, Libra, Scorpio and Pisces, i.e., Saturn occupying one of these signs and Mars in other sign but in mutual aspect with Saturn creates more destructive results.

e) Saturn in Sagittarius in mutual aspect with Mars, helps the native by creating good results.

f) Saturn in Cancer with mutual aspect of Mars is usually present in the horoscopes of prominent persons.

g) Mars in Aries, Saturn in Cancer, the end of life is unnatural but with Mars in Capricorn mixed results are noted.

h) Saturn in 2, 3, 4 and 7th in mutual aspect with Mars is more destructive than other houses.

Principle 32 - Jupiter-Venus

Jupiter-Venus conjunction is a great asset in general for the native. Jupiter-Venus conjunction in Taurus, Aries, Cancer, Leo, Scorpio and Pisces give very auspicious results.

9th is the best house for the combination.

1st, 5th, 7th, 11th is also good.

4th, 10th works well.

6th, 8th, 12th ineffective.

Opposition of Jupiter-Venus being Jupiter in 1st, 2nd, 5th, 7th house gives quite auspicious results. Jupiter in 4th or 10th house, Venus in opposition mixed results.

Daśā Bhukti of these two planets will be quite auspicious but it will be quite inauspicious, if any of them is afflicted or adversely placed.

Principle 33 - Means of Livelihood

Sun-Saturn influence makes one doctor. However, Mars and Sun makes one a Surgeon. Influence of Moon can make one Pediatrician. Role of Jupiter, Mars and Sun in respect to 10th house is likely to make one successful. If 6th, 8th and 12th houses are involved with these planets, one is sure to become a Doctor.

For determination of profession, following should be judged.

Ascendant	Shows the aptitude of the native.
10th house	Actual type of work done (*Karma*).
8th house	Career which will be taken up by the native.

Besides these, 2nd, 11th should also be judged for income.

Sun – Creator, owner, promoter, manager, physician; employment in Govt. brokerage or communication, wood or timber, forest department.

Moon – Salt, mind, mental work, liquids, unsteadiness, movements, changes, sea etc. Dairy farms, water works, irrigation, textiles, midwife.

Mars – Fire, engineering, lands, operations, calling involving instruments, armaments and tools like police, military, medical departments, geological institutions, furnace, railway engine, barber, royalty.

Mercury – Clerks, accountants, auditors, copyists, driver, travellers, traders, authors, postman, messengers, arbitrators, printing, newspaper work, computer, publisher.

Jupiter – Banks, treasuries, income tax and revenue, charitable and educational institutions, lawyers, auditors, editors, judges, counsellors, postal department, advisors, temples, church, advertisement, agricultural goods, seeds, fertilizers.

Venus – Artist, musician, dress maker, perfumes, poets, building, engineer, weavers, car decorators, jewellers, income tax and all leather work, cement, carpenter, eminence, authority and power, tea leaf.

Rāhu – If occupies house of Mercury, he promotes good researches, scholars, lawyers, speculators, medicines, especially antibiotics, telephones, electricity, aviation etc.

Ketu – Secret service, cunning or tricky job depends on the lord of the house occupied by him.

Principle 34 - Govt. Job

Lord of *lagna* if placed in 10th, 8th or trines or *vice-versa* – Govt. job. If the *lagna* or the 10th lord is related with the 6th house or its lord of those lords placed therein, one is likely to be engaged in service only (not in business).

10th house governs government job. Aspect of Saturn on the *kāraka* of profession, denotes service, i.e., aspect of Saturn on 10th or 10th lord.

On 2nd earning through tongue
On 3rd by commission or writing
On 4th house, education, water
On 5th ministerial service, publication
On 6th wood timber, stones, instruments, hospital prison, punishment, execution of cruel orders
On 8th trade, disputes, partnership, court.
On 8th astrologer, legacy, insurance, mystic secret affairs
On 9th legal charitable and religious profession, preceptors, medicines also.
On 10th Govt. job or job in which public is involved.
On 11th receipts of fees, gains, trade
On 12th jail, hospitals, travel to foreign lands, expensive profession.

Kāraka of 10th house – Jupiter, Sun, Mercury and Saturn. Lord of 2nd and Mercury combined shows bankers (Dr. K.N. Rao).

Mars, Mercury and Saturn makes one engineer, especially with Mars Mechanical Engineer and Mercury, Civil Engineer.

Engineer —

- Mercury in 10th owning 10th, skilled engineers are born in *lagna* 3, 6, 9, 11
- Gemini ascendant with Mercury in 1, 10
- Virgo ascendant with Mercury in 1, 10, 9
- Sagittarius ascendant with Mercury in 1, 7, 9, 10
- Aquarius ascendant with Mercury in 1, 5, 9, 10 or combination with Saturn makes successful engineer.

Lawyers – Jupiter, Mercury, lord of 6th house, Venus, provided these are related with the 5th, 6th and 10th house.

Teachers – Jupiter, Mercury in ascendant, 3, 6, 9 are most suitable for teachers.

Jupiter – Saturn in 10th makes one Teacher engaged in research-work.

Mercury-Venus; Jupiter-Venus; Mercury-Jupiter; Moon-Mercury; Saturn-Sun; Mercury-Jupiter; Sun, Moon, Mercury – makes one interested in writing work, learning and journalism.

Principle 35 - Numbers

Sun	1
Moon	2
Jupiter	3
Uranus	4 (negative Sun)
Mercury	5
Venus	6
Neptune	7 (negative Sun)

Saturn 8
Mars 9

A-1, B-2, C-3, D-4, E-5, F-8, G-3, H-3, I-1, J-1, K-2, L-3, M-4, N-5, 0-7, P-8, Q-1, R-2, S-3, T-4, U-6, V-6, W-6, X-5, Y-1, Z-7

No. 1 and 4 are interchangeable.

No. 2 and 7 are interchangeable.

Persons of No. 2 are mixed up with No. 8

By adopting a suitable name in harmony with one's birth chart, one can change one's luck.

V.N.Rao —

6 5 1 2 1 6 1 5 2 1 7 = 37 = 10 = 1

Date of birth 15-10 –1930

1. Birth of primary numbers 15 = 1+5 = 6
2. Fadic number 15-10-1930 = 6 + 1 + 13 = 20 = 2
3. Compound number = 20
4. Name number = 37 = 3+7 = 10 = 1
5. Root No. 1

Principle 36 – Planetary Aspects

(a) Aspects are found at 30°, 60°, 90°, 120°, 180°, 210°, 240°, and 270°. 300°, 330° within a range of + and – 8°. in case of Sun, the range is upto 17° aspects are mutual, Saturn aspects Sun at 60°. it also means that Sun aspects Saturn at 300°

The range of aspects to and from the Sun varies from planet to planet.

For Mars it is	17°
For Mercury it is	14°
For Saturn it is	15°
For Moon it is	12°
For Jupiter it is	11°
For Venus it is	10°

For Retro Mercury it is 12^0
For Retro Venus it is 8^0

Beyond these degrees (forward and backward) no aspect is formed.

b) Conjunction of Saturn and Sun is less harmful than aspect.

Pinciple 37 - Distance Between Sun and Mercury

Sun and Mercury are never beyond 28^0 conjunction with 5^0.

Pinciple 38 - Distance Between Venus and Sun

Sun and Venus are never beyond 48 degrees.

Principle 39 - Heart Troubles

Person of Cancer rising will have low vitality. When the Sun is in the ascendant, the native has more vitality. Cancer rules heart and gastric pain.

Cancer people are fond of foods and are healthy eaters. Their health is afflicted often due to wrong diet.

Sun in Cancer or Capricorn, if afflicted indicates heart troubles. There are many forms of heart trouble. Instead of going deep into it, the astrologer should foretell about the problem connected with heart only. If any doctor is a student of astrology as well, and knows the anatomy, he can be more precise in correctly pinpointing the particular problem of heart, on the basis of aspect, conjunction and signs involved. We have discussed this in quite detail in our article. *Planets and Cardiac Troubles*.

An affliction of *Ketu* indicates weakening of heart by poison from some malfunctioning organ or from another disease or affliction. If *Ketu* and Sun occupies 4th house, heart trouble is indicated. If conjunction takes place in Cancer in 4th house, it is worst.

Prominent indicator of Hypertension
Prominent angular Sun + an afflicted Saturn or Mars.

After study of innumerable horoscopes, it was found that:-

a) *Rāhu*, Mars and Sun in 4th house cause heart trouble either by aspect or conjunction.
b) Afflicted Sun is connected with lords of 6th or 8th.
c) The 4th or 5th house or their lords if afflicted (house is more important than lord) and connection is established with 6th or 8th lord. Heart attack comes in the period of 6th and 8th lords or planets owing or occupying 2nd or 12th from Sun or 4th lord.
d) In many cases, Venus is found considerably afflicted – Venus rules Veins.

Principle 40 - Combustion of Planets

Within 17 degree from Sun's longitude	Jupiter is combust
Within 15 degree from Sun's longitude	Saturn is combust
8 degree at West from Sun's longitude	Venus is combust
10 degree at East from Sun's longitude	Venus is combust
12 degree retrograde from Sun's longitude	Mercury is combust
14 degree Direct from Sun's longitude	Mercury is combust
72 degree from Sun's longitude	Moon is combust

Principle 41 - *Bādhakas* for Movable and Immovable Signs

Common sign	7
Stationary sign	9
Movable sign	11

Elements allotted to the signs–

Aries, Leo, Sagittarius	Fire
Gemini, Libra, Aquarius	Air
Cancer, Scorpio, Pisces	Water

क्रमाच्च रागद्विशरीरभानामुपान्त्यधर्मस्मरगास्तदीशाः ।
खरेशमान्दिस्थितराशिनाथा ह्यतीव बाधाकरखेचराः स्युः ॥

Jātaka Pārijāta, Śloka 48, *chapter* 2

In the case of movable, immovable and dual signs, planets occupying respectively the 11th, 9th or 7th from them or their lords will prove exceedingly troublesome if they happen to own at the same time the houses occupied by the lord of *Khara* or *Mandi*.

Principle 42 - *Vedha*

When transiting planets comes under *Vedha*, its good or bad effects are checked. Position of *Vedha* for each and every planet is different. In the following table, position of Vedha is given above the line whereas which position of planet will be checked, will come under the line, e.g., when Sun will be transiting in the 11th house and any other planet will be transiting in the 5th house, auspicious effects of the Sun of the 11th house will be checked and so with other positions as well. Rules of *Vedha* must be applied while examining transiting results of all planets.

Sun	<u>11, 3, 10, 6</u>	Except Saturn
	5, 9, 4, 12	
V.V.Sun	<u>4, 5, 9, 12</u>	
Converse Vedha	3, 6, 10, 11	
Mars	<u>3, 6, 11</u>	
	12, 9, 5	
V.V.Mars	<u>5, 9, 12</u>	
	3, 6, 9	

Mercury	2, 4, 6, 8, 10 / 5, 3, 9, 1, 8
V.V.Mercury	3, 6, 7, 9, 12 / 2, 5, 8, 10, 11
Jupiter	2, 5, 7, 9, 11 / 12, 4, 3, 10, 8
V.V.Jupiter	3, 4, 10, 12 / 2, 5, 9, 11
Venus	1, 2, 3, 4, 5, 8, 9, 11, 12 / 8, 7, 1, 10, 9, 5, 11, 6, 3
V.V.Venus	6, 7, 10 / 2, 5, 9
Saturn	3, 6, 11 / 12, 9, 5
V.V.Saturn	5, 9, 12 / 3, 6, 11

Principle 43 – Malefic Nature of Planets

Sun in Aquarius
Moon in Capricorn
Mars in Libra
Venus in Aries
Jupiter in Gemini
Mercury in Pisces
Saturn in Cancer or in Leo
Rāhu in Sagittarius
Ketu in Gemini

Chronic physical ailments, improper growth, paralysis, financial difficulties, loss of parents, loss of shelter, loss of appetite, loss of reliable and friends, loss of good company.

Ketu in Gemini – Financially ruined, physically handicapped, asthma, lungs diseases.

Mars in Libra – Mental ailments, retardation, paralysis and invalid.

Ketu in Leo – Chronic heart trouble, *Rāhu-Ketu* eclipse Sun, Moon, Leo and Cancer are inimical – heart trouble.

Sun in Aquarius – Suffer from heart and brain disorder, too many obstacles in life. Very bad for finance, low acts, no happiness from Sun, no prosperity, strong likes and dislikes and honest.

Moon in Capricorn or (Scorpio) – Misfortune through woman, undetermined, lack of control of appetites, secret enemies, difference in occupation, harsh speech, dropsy, kidney, tumor, in stomach, nervous disorder, danger through voyages.

Mars in Libra – Mental ailments, mental retardation, paralysis, permanent physical disability. Hot tempered, impulsive, aggressive, hostile, cruel hatred, passion, delayed marriage, disappointment in love. Illegal sexual attachments, wine concubines.

Mercury in Pisces – Wicked, not very learned, cruel hearted, not happy with children, speaking, singing or writing power or spiritualism.

Jupiter in Gemini – Weak body, stomach and lung trouble, less vitality, timid, weak, tact and common sense, sexually weak, good judgement, quick decision, prompt action, truthful and trustworthy.

Venus in Aries (or Virgo) – Too much heated, body susceptible to allergic ailments, over sexy, brain disorder, fond of woman, wine and prostitutes badly.

Saturn in Cancer or Leo – Cruel hearted, jealous, difficulties after marriage, heart and stomach disorders, change of residences. Danger through accident and over work. Sorrows through love affair and children.

Rāhu in Sagittarius – Suffers from acute sciatica pains, lungs and heart troubles, financial troubles, poor, hospitalization, very bad for high position. asthma, pleurisy and tuberculosis.

Ketu in Gemini – Gives acute asthma, lungs and heart trouble, imprisonment, hospitalization. Very bad for all respects strictly invalid.

Principle 44 - Pitfalls in Prediction

1. *Yoga bhaṅga* must be seen.
2. Opposition of Moon-Venus-Mars the strength of horoscopes.
3. A *Yoga* formed around the Sun or Moon is powerful.
4. Second comes the *Yoga* formed with the *lagna* and cone.
5. In *Adhi Yoga*, if Venus joins 7th from Sun – Yoga gets spoiled.
6. Venus placed in the 7th from Moon, cancels the *kārakatva* results of Venus which happens to be marital partner and marital happiness.
7. Aspect of Saturn on Jupiter spoils the effects of *Malawaya Yoga*.

Principle 45 - Ailment

1. *Lagna* should be Leo, Virgo, Scorpio or Sagittarius.
2. Moon in Cancer aspected by Mars.
3. Lord of *puṇya Saham* in Cancer, Leo, Scorpio or Capricorn unaspected by benefics.

Principle 46 - Findings by Sri P.S. Shastri

Rāhu

Own house	Aquarius or Pisces
Exaltation	12 degree Gemini
Mooltrikoṇa	Virgo
Friends	Sun, Mercury, Venus
Enemies	Moon
Neutral	Others

Kāla Sarpa Yoga – *Rāhu* to *Ketu* and not *Ketu* to *Rāhu*, no planet should be within 12 degree of either of *Rāhu* or *Ketu*.

- Only Mercury can control the evils of *Rāhu*.
- In Budha's major period, *Rāhu* gives very good results but reverse is not always true.
- *Sarpa doṣa* arises when *Rāhu* owns 5th or occupies 5th.
- *Rāhu* is very helpful for *kuṇḍalinī* or in worship of *Śakti*.
- *Rāhu*–Mars conjunction indicates danger from reptile.
- *Rāhu-Śanī* – skin trouble, pon venomous bites.
- Conjunction of *Rāhu* with *Śanī* or *kuja* is bad for health
- With Moon – effect on mind and body
  with Sun – highly critical
  with Jupiter – might result in heterodoxy
  Rāhu owns Aquarius and for all purpose, this should be taken to act like *Śanī*.

Ketu

Own house	Taurus
Mūlatrikoṇa	Pisces
Exaltation	6 degree of Sagittarius
Friends	Moon, Mars, Jupiter
Enemy	Sun

Principle 47 - Miscellaneous

1. Mars in 5th kills 1st son after birth especially for Libra ascendant.
2. *Ketu* in 2nd gives daily income unexpectedly.
3. *Mars* in 3rd does not give younger brother or kills him.
4. Saturn in 10th takes one to dizzy hights from zero.
5. Jupiter in 5th obstructs the birth of son.

Principle 48 - Matching of Horoscope

Fiery sign has affinity to airy sign. Earthy sign got affinity to watery sign. Friendship of *Rāśi* lords, must be there. This is most important for happy married life.

Principle 49 - Retrograde Planets in Exaltation by Dr. Shastri

a) If debilitated planet is retrograde, it will give exaltation results and *vice-versa.*
Debilitation is cancelled if any planet is exalted in the sign of the debilitated planet, square to the Moon but Moon is unfortunate in this respect because no planet is exalted in Scorpio. Moon's exaltation is not Taurus. This is pure speculation.

b) All retrograde planets should be considered as strong The benefit of such a strength, of course, goes to the house which the retrograde planet owns. The results may therefore, depend on the fact whether it owns a good house and is strong. In which case, the house and benefits. When the retrograde planet is lord of an evil house, it of course, increases the evil nature thereof. Keeping in view the fact that Jupiter owns a good house, the following *śloka* No. 40 of *Chapter* 15 seems to have been penned by author of *Sarvārthacintāmani.*

वक्रं गतस्यापि गुरोर्दशायां महार्थतां याति सुतार्थदारान्
युद्धे जयं भूपतिमित्रतां च सुगन्धजाताम्बरवाग्विलासम्।

i.e., during the ruling period of a retrograde Jupiter, a person gets much wealth, sons, wife. He is victorious in battle, gets favour from government, scented articles, clothes and excellence of speech.

There is no doubt that Jupiter lord of a good house in retrogression will give good results but this is subject to the overriding condition that Jupiter in such a condition should not be under heavy affliction. If he is, say under as many as four malefic influences, then, inspite of his retrogression, Jupiter will give bad results.

c) For retrograde planets, in general *Phaladīpikā* (Chapter IV, Sloka No. 4) says:-

वक्रं गतो रुचिररश्मिसमूहपूर्णो नीचारिभांशसहितोऽपि भवेत्स खेटः ।
वीर्यान्वितस्तुहिनरश्मिरिवोच्चमित्र स्वक्षेत्रगोऽपि विबलीहतदीधितिश्चेत् ।।

A planet possesses strength when he is retrograde, as his rays are brilliant and full, even though he may be posited in a debilitation or inimical sign or *aṁśa*. Like the Moon, a planet even if occupying an exaltation, friendly or his own sign or aṁśa becomes weak, should he be eclipsed due to vicinity to Sun.

When Jupiter is retrograde, it denotes also the existence and prosperity of the things etc. of which it is the significator. For example, if in a birth chart, when the other factors for main issues viz. the 5th house, its lord, the 9th house and its lord are all weak, but Jupiter is retrograde and unaspected by malefics, the native will have a number of male issues.

Principle 50 - My Experience About *Viṁśottari Daśā* System

a) Jupiter and Venus are inimical in nature. One is *deva guru* and other is *dānava guru*. Sub period of Venus in the major period of Jupiter or sub period of Jupiter in the major period of Venus are adverse for family happiness, prosperity and general health provided one of them is adversely placed in a malefic sign or malefic house.

However, if both are favourably placed in benefic houses and signs and they are in quadrant or in trine from each other. Their *daśā bhukti* will be excellent.

b) When Venus and Saturn are equally powerful in a horoscope, occupying exaltation or vargottama positions, they in their mutual *daśā bhukti* will cause the down fall of the native, even though he is an emperor. If one of the planets is strong and the other weak, the stronger one will cause the *Yoga*. If both the planets are weak and placed in 6th, 8th or 12th from each other or own those houses or conjunctions, they will bestow on the native's prosperity. If one of them owns an auspicious house and other a malefic one, even then both of them will produce good effects. Such is the opinion of some sages.

Principle 51 - Special Significance of Jupiter

For Women, Jupiter has a special significance, in as much as Jupiter is the significator of Husband *in their horoscope.* When in the birth chart of a women Jupiter becomes the lord of the house representing the husband, viz., the 7th, it naturally represents the husband par excellence. Affliction of such Jupiter obviously tells heavily on the longevity of the husband. The view that Jupiter is the significator of husband (and not Venus as held by some) is supported by the author of the famous work *Phaladīpikā*, while enumerating the traits of Jupiter, *Mantreśwara* says:-

वैदुष्यं विजितेन्द्रियं धवसुखम्।

i.e., learning, control over senses and the longevity of husband, should be considered from Jupiter.

In this context, it may be added that exalted Jupiter, whatever its merits, is generally bad for the longevity of the relation represented by the house in which its sign Sagittarius falls, particularly in cases in which Jupiter in such a position is afflicted too. For example, in regard to exalted Jupiter in the 8th house of a birth chart with *Ketu*, the author of *Devakeralam* remarks at page 130:-

स्वपितुर्भगिनी चाद्या विधवा चिरजीवनी ।

i.e., the eldest sister of father will become a widow but will live long. The author of this book opines that Jupiter should be regarded for *Saubhāgya* of the female. In addition to merits, education, nature and personality, popularity etc. whereas Mars signifies *Vaidhavya*. The affliction of Jupiter by Mars in the concerning houses may not save widowhood even if Jupiter aspects the 8th house or placed therein.

Principle 52 - Saturn Represents Animals

In *chapter* 56 of BPHS, we read in *Ślokas* 12 to 14

लग्नात् षष्टाष्टमे मन्दे व्यये नीचेऽस्तगेऽप्यरौ ।
गोमहिष्यादिहानिश्च बन्धुद्वेषी भविष्यति ।।

i.e., if Saturn is in debilitation or eclipsed in 6th, 8th and 12th house, the native sustains loss of animals like cows and buffalows and becomes an enemy to his relatives. From the above *śloka*, it is evident that Saturn can be a representative of animals. In fact being lowest in scale no other planet is more qualified to be a representative of the animal class than Saturn. In fact Saturn also acts for "Species" such as of animals. For example, if Saturn occupies the sign Sagittarius in the 6th house, then Jupiter lord of the 6th house would represent a horse. This fact further indicates earning from horses (on races) if Jupiter has an intimate relation with the *lagna* and its lord.

Principle 53 - Mars and Moon both represent blood

That Moon represents blood is a fact very well known (see however *Jātaka Pārijāta* 2-28). Mars also represents blood and if afflicted brings about trouble in blood, in this connection *Jātaka Pārijāta* 6-95 reproduced below is relevant.

जातः शोणितपित्तमेति वसुधापुत्रे तथास्ते क्षति ।

i.e., if Mars is in the 7th house of the birth chart, the native suffers from blood and bile troubles. ~~Mars in 8th~~ house gives piles, fistula and accidents.

In cases where a planet represents both, it naturally becomes strongest representative of blood. and if it is afflicted, brings about blood trouble in more severe manner. Mars in the sign of Moon, i.e., Cancer, makes Moon a pucca representative of blood, similarly, Moon in the sign of Mars, say Scorpio, *lagna* makes Mars a pucca representative of blood, which of course is polluted, diseased etc. if the Moon or Mars as the case may be, is afflicted by *Rāhu* and Saturn factors of disease. When there is such an affliction of Moon or Mars and Mercury too is in any of the lagnas or is lord of any of the lagnas and afflicted by *Rāhu* or Saturn, the trouble spreads to skin as well and this becomes a case of leprosy, leucoderma, eczema, allergy to skin.

Principle 54 - Moon *Lagna*

Candrakalānāḍī has the following to say in *śloka* 30 at page 300 in regard to the importance and the necessity treating Moon as a *lagna*.

चन्द्रलग्नं शरीरं स्यात् लग्नं स्यात् प्राणसंज्ञकम् ।
ते उभे संपरीक्ष्यैव सर्वनाडीफलं स्मृतम् ।।

The house occupied by Moon is body, while the *lagna* house like breath, it is by a thorough examination of the house with reference to both *lagna* and *candralagna* then prediction can correctly be made.

This is an important rule and one which is of immense in practice. For example, the sign of a planet happens to be from both the *lagna* and the *candralagna* and the lord of that sign is heavily afflicted, the yoga will be disastrous for career of the man. If on the other hand, it is strong and we aspected the man will get rapid promotion etc. in life, the idea is that the lord of a particular house from lagna assures an added importance and a sense of certainty in its act when it is also lord of the same. No. of house from the *candralagna* as well. This is of course an actual working of *Sudarśana* (See Rule 42). *Mānasāgarī paddhati* also expresses a similar view and says:-

चन्द्रः सर्वत्र बीजाभो लग्नं च कुसुमप्रभम् ।
फलेन सदृशोऽंशश्च भावः स्वादुरसः स्मृतः ।।

i.e., in giving effects Moon acts as a seed, *lagna* as a flower, *navāṁśa* etc. as fruits and house as the taste of those fruits.

Principle 55 - Plurality

Mercury is the planet of plurality par excellence. The *Yoga* for twin births is not complete without the cooperation of Mercury. This can be inferred from the fact that every other planet represents only one of the humours but mercury represents all the three of them. From a reading of *śloka* 49 of *Chapter* 6 of *Jātaka Pārijāta* given below it is clear that Mercury has a special role of plurality to play.

त्रिकोणगेज्ञे विबलैस्तथाऽपरैर्मुखाङ्घ्रिहस्तैर्द्विगुणस्तदा भवेत् ।

i.e., if Mercury is stronger than the rest of the planets and is placed in a *koṇa* house, the native will have double face, feet, arms etc. By location in the *koṇa* Mercury will influence the *lagna* with ease and since it will have an effective and somewhat exclusive influence on the *lagna*, its quality of plurality will have ample opportunity to play its part and make the limb involved more than one in number. The *Uttar* Calamity says that Mercury represents मिश्रपदार्थान्, i.e., mixed objects which implies plurality.

When there is intimate link between the *lagna* and the 3rd house, and its significator Mars and Mercury too is involved in the *yoga*, the birth of twins takes place. For a practical illustration, please see the birth chart with Gemini *lagna* given at page.

Principle 56 - Medical line

Sun is intimately related to medical line भैषज्योर्ण तृणाम्बु धान्य कनक व्यापार मुक्तादिकै is part of *Śloka* 44 of *chapter* 15 of *Jātaka Pārijāta* and says that medical practice, wool etc. are related to Sun.

Principle 57 - Music and musical instruments

That Venus represents music is well known. For example, the author of *Jātaka Pārijāta* says in *Śloka* 101 of *Chapter* 8 as under:-

शुक्रे स्वोच्चगते विलासवनितासंगीतनृत्यप्रियो ।

i.e., Venus in exhaltation makes a person indulge in luxury, women, music and dancing.

For exaltation of Mercury, the author of *Sarvārthacintāmaṇi* says in *Śloka* 2 of *Chapter* 14

उच्चस्थितस्यापि शशांकसूनोर्दशामहत्वम् कुरुतेऽर्थसौख्यम् ।
देहस्य पुष्टिं धनधान्यपुत्रा गोवाजिमृदंगनादम् ।।

i.e., the ruling period of an exalted Mercury gives eminence, affluence good health, good items of wealth in kind, elephants and the hearing of the sound of the musical instrument called *Mṛdaṅga*. Thus Venus relates to music proper and Mercury to instruments of music.

Film line is intimately connected with both of them and hence these two planets have much influence on the *lagna* of film factors.

The house of the horoscope concerned in the matter of music is the 3rd as it is 2nd from second and also part of the respiratory canal.

2nd house represents speech, sweetness, softness or harshness of wife as the case may be. Venus and Mercury in 2nd house gives rise to musical throat. The 5th house must also be well disposed. If Mercury or Venus are placed in 5th house and 2nd house is well disposed with benefics like Jupiter and Moon will be blessed with art of singing.

Principle 58 - Quickness of results

Amongst the planets, Mercury is one that is known for giving quick results. In regard to this planet, *śloka* 69 of chapter 1 of *Sarvārthacintāmaṇi* records:-

हास्यप्रियः पित्तकफानिलात्मा सद्यःप्रतापी ननु पुंश्चलश्च

i.e., Mercury is Jocular, has all the three humours phlegm, bile and wind, is eunuch and gives its results very quickly. If Mercury is lord of a good house, such as 5th or 9th and is quite strong, it will give good luck soon after the start of its *daśā*. Similarly if it is badly afflicted say as lord of the 8th house, it can cause immediate death.

Another factor that works for quickness in results is the intensity of the influence. If the intensity of the influence. If the intensity of the influences is comprised of malefic planets, the bad results follow quickly. If, however, the intensity is one of benefic influence, the desirable event takes place at an early date. For example, much influence of benefics on the factors for marriage, i.e., 7th house, its lord and its significator would bring about marriage at an early date.

Principle 59 - Cause of divorce, abdication, *sannyāsa* etc.

Sun, Saturn and *Rāhu* are the three main causes for separation, forsaking, leaving etc. this separation may take place in the shape of divorce, or abdication or *sannyāsa* but it is essentially the result of the separative influence of the above noted three planets. In regard to Sun, *Jātāka Parijata Śloka* 23 *Chapter* 16 opines in regard to its location in the 7th house as under:-

उत्सृष्टा मदनस्थिते दिनकरे ।

i.e., if Sun occupies the 7th house of the birth chart of women, she will be given up by her husband i.e., divorce etc. *Rāhu* and Saturn also play the part of severance. *Śloka* 93 of *Chapter* 5 of *Jātaka Pārijāta* states that:

धर्मे शनौ चाथ गुरौ तृतीये करच्छिदः स्यान्निधने व्यये वा ।
कर्मस्थिताश्चेद्यति राहुमन्दसौम्याः करच्छेदयुतोऽत्र जातः ।।

Jātaka Pārijāta, Śloka 93, *Chapter* 5

If Saturn is situated in the 9th house and jupiter joins the 3rd house, then both the hands of the native are severed same results are observed if jupiter is placed in the 12th house and *Rāhu* in the 8th house, i.e., if *Rāhu,* Saturn and Mercury are situated together in the 10th house, the hands are severed. Severance, it may be added, is here the result of the separative influence of Saturn and *Rāhu* on Mercury which stands for the arm. It is significant to note that this evil *yoga* has occurred in the 8th from 3rd, i.e., the death house of arms. *Jaimini Sutra* 12 of is more explicit. It says:

शनिराहुभ्यां अपवादात् त्यागो नाशो वा ।

i.e. Saturn and *Rāhu* cause bad name and are instruments of separation and destruction (of wife etc.) Thus the Sun, Saturn and *Rāhu* are instruments of separation as distinct from "killing" outright, which is the function of Mars and *Ketu.* This statement of *Jaimini Sūtra* is relevant to old days when removal of hands was an important punishment for the culprits even at this time, this is relevant in various Muslim countries like Saudi Arabia, removal of hands is big punishment to thieves and dacoits.

Principle 60 - Strong and weak planets

Under the following conditions, planets become strong and give good results if they are benefics for the *lagna* concerned. The good results will of course, be mainly in respect of the house in which their *mulatrikoṇa* sign falls.

A. When they are in good houses such as *kendras*.
B. When they are in their exaltation, own or friendly sign.
C. When they are near about the middle of the sign.
D. When they occupy friendly *vargas* (*Sapta varga, Ṣoḍaśa varga.*
E. When they are farthest away from Sun.
F. When they are in houses where they get Directional Strength (*digbala* like Sun and Mars in 10th house, get full *digbala*).
G. When they are aspected by benefics.
H. When they are located with benefic planets.
I. When they are surrounded by natural benefic planets.
J. When they are retrograde.
K. When they are well placed from *lagna* (2nd, 4th, 5th, 7th, 9th, 10th, or 11th from it).
L. When they are well placed from the main *daśā* lord.
M. When they are friends of main *daśā* lord.
N. When they are in friendly *nakṣatras*.

When planets have the traits opposite to those listed above, they give bad results i.e.:-

a) When they are located in bad houses such as 6th, 8th and 12th.
b) They are in inimical signs.
c) When they occupy the very start (0^{0} - 3^{0} $20'$) or the fag end of the sign (26^{0} $40'$ - 30^{0} $00'$).
d) When they occupy inimical vargas.
e) When they are in the same sign as the Sun and particularly they are within their respective degree of combustion (12, 17, 13, 11, 9 and 15 from Moon to Saturn respectively).
f) When they occupy a house opposite to the one which they get directional strength.
g) When they are aspected by malefics.

h) When they are located with a malefic planet.
i) When they are surrounded by malefics.
j) When they occupy bad houses from *lagna*, i.e., 3rd, 6th, 8th or 12th.
k) When they are enemies to the main *daśā* lord.
l) When they are badly placed from the main *daśā* lord.
m) When they occupy inimical *nakṣatras*.

Some of the more important points noted above, have been incorporated in the following *Ślokas* 2 and 3 of *Sarvārthacintāmaṇi Chapter* 16.

गोचरस्थे फलं सौख्यं सर्वस्मिन् पाकपादगृहे गोचरत्वं
नाम स्वर्क्षतुंग त्रिकोणस्थ
षडष्टान्त्यविवर्जितिः अनस्तगो मित्रगस्तु गोचरस्थो भवेद्ग्रहः।

i.e. planet technically called in Gocara or transit always gives good results in its ruling periods when the transiting planet is one which is not located in 5th, 6th, 8th or 12th house as Moon or its own position. It is not eclipsed by Sun but is located in his own, exhalted, *mūlatrikoṇa* or friendly sign.

Principle 61 - Factors Enhancing Value

The lord of the 2nd and 11th house are not only in themselves factors that denote by their strength the abundance of wealth, these are also factors that enhance the value of the person, or thing that they influence by their association or aspect. This point has been brought out by *Śloka* 89, *chapter* 4 of *Sarvārthacintāmaṇi* as under:-

धनेशलाभेशसमन्विते वा क्षेत्रे तदीशेऽप्यथ कारके वा
वैशेषिकांशे शुभदृष्टियुक्ते बह्वर्थरूपं गृहमाहुरार्याः

i.e., if the lord of the 2nd and the 11th houses are associated with the 4th house, the lord of the 4th house or with the significator of the 4th house (Mars=property), is in *vaiśeṣika aṁśa* and is under the aspect of good planets, the man possesses very valuable house. The value is aptly awarded by the lord of the 2nd and 11th houses. These houses being of finance and gains respectively, denotes value. People with Aquarius as their ascendant can benefit immensely by this fact as Jupiter the significator of finance himself becomes lord of two houses of finance (2nd and 11th) and thus triply represents value. If Jupitor in such cases is strong and aspects the house and the significator of any object, that object will be enhanced much in value. In Leo nativities Mercury becomes the lord of the 2nd and 11th houses and as such, is a factor for value like Jupiter. When in a Leo nativity Mercury and Jupiter both have combined influence, their enhancing quality is obviously increased especially for Leo or Cancer ascendant. This is very important factor which should be understood properly for accurate application and correct predictions.

Principle 62 - Basis of Determining Benefic or Malefic Nature of Planets

Benefics and malefics criterion for Indian Astrology has two types of planets:-

(a) Natural (b) Conditional

natural type and the conditional type each have their own separate benefic and malefic planets. The two types are explained below:-

Natural benefics and malefics

Jupiter and Venus are natural benefics. Sun, Mars, Saturn, *Rāhu* and *Ketu* are natural malefics. In natural condition, i.e., without reference to any particular *lagna*, Moon is treated as benefic provided it is not within 72 degrees from Sun in distance. If it is, whether in the dark or bright fortnight, it considered and acted as malefic. Mercury when acting alone is a benefic. If with malefics, it becomes a malefic, with benefics, it is of course a benefic. *Rāhu* acts like Saturn while *Ketu* acts like Mars.

Conditional benefics and malefics

Planets lord of the 1st, 4th, 7th and 10th houses of the horoscope cease to be natural benefics or malefics as the case may be. The lords of the trines, i.e., 5th and 9th houses whether they are natural benefics or natural malefics always give good results. Lords of 3rd, 6th and 11th houses give bad results. Lords of 2nd and 12th houses gives the results of the house in which their sign other than the one in these houses falls. In the cases of Sun and Moon owning one sign only, becoming lords of the 2nd or 12th house they give the results dependent on their strength and the influence they are under the house etc. in which placed. The lord of the 8th house is considered as bad.

Note: In the above analysis, the lord of the 11th house has been declared as a malefic. In our personal view, the badness is intended to refer to health. As far as finances are concerned, the lord of the 11th house gives good results, unless of course it is weak.

In regard to the conditional planets, the rule for finance is that if a particular planet is benefic for a particular *lagna*, the stronger it is the better and useful the results. If such a planet is weak and afflicted, it gives bad results and the more it is afflicted the worse the results. If, however, a planet is malefic for a particular *lagna* and is strong the stronger it is the more harmful it becomes. If such a malefic planet is weak and afflicted, it gives good results and the more it is afflicted the better are the results.

Principle 63 - Aspects

In Indian Astrology, every planet aspects the house, sign or planet placed 7th from it. In counting the 7th place, the house in which the aspecting planet is located is also taken into account. The following planets, in addition to having the above noted 7th aspect have the following special aspects. Mars aspects the house etc. placed 4th and 8th from it. Jupiter aspect the house etc. 5th and 9th from it. Saturn aspects the house etc. placed 3rd and 10th from it

a) *Rāhu* and *Ketu* have also aspects like Jupiter i.e. these shadowy planets aspect the house etc. placed 5th and from them.

b) In the case of aspect by Rāhu and *Ketu*, it should be kept in mind that they also throw along with their own influence or the influence of the malefic planet or planet with whom they may be associated or under whose influence they may be located. For example, if *Rāhu* and Mars are located in the 6th house, the 9th aspect of *Rāhu* on the house of weak will convey to that house the influence of Mars as well. Similarly if *Rāhu* is located in the 6th house and Mars is in the 3rd house or the 12th or 11th, the influence of *Rāhu* on the 2nd house will be also include the influence of Mars by whom *Rāhu* is aspected.

c) A planet located 10th from any house etc. throws ¾ its normal aspect on the house. This aspect may be called *kendra* aspect (square aspect).

In this connection, please see the following *śloka* No. 3 of *chapter* 26 of BPHS (*Brihat Parāśara Hora Śāstra*)

त्रिदशे च त्रिकोणे च चतुरस्रे च सप्तमे,
पादवृद्ध्या प्रपश्यन्ति प्रयच्छन्ति फलं तथा ।

i.e., planets have one fourth aspect or influence on 3rd and 10th house from them, half on those 5th and 9th from them, $3/4^{th}$ on 4th and 8th from them and full on the 7th from them.

Principle 64 - Dispositors etc.

Planet situated in good or bad conditions in a house or sign gives good or bad effects to the house over which the planet concerned has lordship. But these effects will further be modified by the position of the planet who in turn is the lord of the sign occupied by them. For example, if Sun is lord of 5th house in any horoscope and is in the 7th house, it would be considered weak by virtue of its occupying the debilitation sign. But if Venus lord of the debilitation sign of Sun is in turn located in Aries, Sun would be considered as strong because of this placement of Venus in his exhaltation sign. This means then that the lord of the sign occupied by any planet works as the planet. We can thus say that:-

If the sign or signs of a planet are not occupied by any planet, it would give the results good or bad in accordance to its lordship as a conditional planet for the *lagna* involved. If however, one of its signs is occupied by a planets, it would give the results good or bad of the planets occupying its sign. If both of its sign are occupied by planets, it would give the effects of the planets who have more affinity of traits with it.

Principle 65 – Malefic Planets in Trines

It has been our experience that natural malefic planets Sun, Mars and Saturn when located in the 5th or 9th house of the horoscope lose much of their strength, say about 1/3rd of it. For example, it has come in our experience that Saturn in its sign of exaltation, is not conducive to the longevity of the person in whose *lagna* its sign Aquarius falls. This is apparently due to the fact that in such cases, Libra the exaltation sign of Saturn falls in a trine from Aquarius. The above view is borne out by *Mānasāgarī Paddhati* which, for example says in regard to the location of Saturn in the 5th house.

शनैश्चरे पंचमशत्रुगेहे पुत्रार्थहीनो भवतीह दुःखी,
तुङ्गे निजे मित्रगृहे च पङ्गौ पुत्रैकभागी भवतीति कश्चित् ।

i.e., Saturn in inimical sign makes one bereft of son and wealth and one is unhappy. He gets one son only if Saturn is in its own sign or sign of exhaltation or in a friendly sign. The word 'दुखी' lends support to the view that it is not merely the traits of the 5th house that suffer, here but also those of Saturn as significator.

Principle 66 – Mental deficiency

Mental deficiency is caused by the affliction of Moon and Mercury located in *Kendra. Vide Śloka* 18 of *Chapter* 6 of *Jātaka Pārijāta* केन्द्रस्थितौ सौम्यनिशाकरौ वा सौभ्यांशहीनौ भ्रमसंयुतः स्यात्। Why has the condition of their location in *Kendra* been imposed is an interesting question. The answer is that planets by their location in *Kendra* influence the *lagna*. When the said affliction will influence the *lagna* too, directly another factor standing for brain will be involved in affliction, lending, weight to the onset of the disease. We will see in the case of study of the sixth house that a condition of the location in *kendra* was imposed there too. Moon and Mercury represents the emotional and rational powers respectively. The fourth house is one of emotions and the first and 5th of rational thinking. Thus a complete *Yoga* for mental derangement or lunacy would be formed only when all these factors are involved. That is why we have opened thus in *Horā Śataka*—

लग्नं चतुर्थं च तथा हि चन्द्रमा दिशन्ति
सर्वे मनसो हि वेदनां।
भावं च वाणमपि सोमजस्तथा दिशेच्च वृत्तिमथ
तर्कसंभवाम् ।।
वेदनाया यदा क्षोभं तर्कशक्तिश्च क्षीयते ।
जातकस्य तदा नूनमुन्मादो जायते भुवि ।
जातस्य हि यदा लग्नं चतुर्थवाणमेव च ।
सोम सोमात्मजश्चैव नष्टा उन्मत्त एव सः ।।

i.e., the fourth house and Moon denotes the emotional side of man. Mercury and the 5th house denote the rational faculties of man. When both the emotional and the intellectual faculties of man are shocked, disturbed and reduced, lunacy results. That is the reason why when these factors are afflicted by malefic planets (by association or aspect) madness comes to be in evidence.

Principle 67 – Planets in *Lagna* and Disease

In regard to the location of Mercury in *lagna*, *lagna* is considered body as a whole. *Lagna* in its broad sense includes the Sun *lagna* and the Moon *lagna*. Due to this representative character of *lagna* and to the fact that *lagna* stands for "Self", any planet that happens to be located in *lagna* fully represents the tissue of which it is the significator. For example, Mercury which stands for skin, if afflicted in a place other than *lagna*, would no doubt denote some trouble in skin but the assertion to that effect can not be made with any measure of certainty. On the other hand, if Mercury is afflicted while located in *lagna*, it can be said with certainty that it would bring about trouble in skin, the reason being that Mercury in *lagna* assumes a wider role which skin has in body. The disease called leucoderma arises from affliction if Mercury satisfies the above condition, i.e., when it is suffering in any of the three *lagnas*. The principle applicable to Mercury as explained above, may applied to other planets. For example, if Mars is in *lagna* and is weak and afflicted by *Rāhu* and or Saturn, the person is likely to suffer through muscles and blood trouble and so on.

The sign in the *lagnas* too represent their respective limbs more effectively than in any other house. This is evident from the following *śloka* No. 49 of *chapter* 60 of *Jātaka Pārijāta*—

कुब्जः स्वर्क्षे शशिनि तनुगे मन्दमाहेयदृष्टे,
पंगुमीने यमशशिकुजै वीक्षिते लग्नसंस्थे ।

i.e., If Moon occupies her own sign (Cancer) in the ascendant and is aspected by Saturn and Mars, the man becomes "hunch backed". Similarly if there is the sign Pisces in the *lagna* and is aspected by Saturn, Moon and Mars, the man becomes lame. In the first case the sign Cancer in *lagna* represents fully the chest: which it normally stands for, and by affliction gets it bent. In the second case the sign Pisces, comes to *lagna* and gives full representation to feet for which it stands and hence by affliction brings about lameness. In short, the idea is that feet suffer in such a case more severely than would have been the case, had Pisces been afflicted anywhere else than in *lagna*.

Principle 68 – Aristorcratic factors

Sun and Moon are called राजानौ, i.e., Royal planets. In modern times, the term can be interpreted as referring to people high up in social and political spheres – the aristocratic class as a whole. Any factor that would be influenced by them would be infused with their aristocratic or royal character. Thus the status of that factor will be boosted. For example, if the 7th house is influenced by Sun and a strong Moon, the wife or husband as the case may be, will come from a family enjoying high financial status. *Śloka* 43 of *chapter* 28 of *Sārāvalī* given below, runs in the same strain—

कर्मपरामलांगीं नृपतिसुतां रोषणां धनोपेताम् ।
भार्यां ददाति शुक्रश्चन्द्रगृहे भानुसन्दृष्टः ।।

i.e., Venus if located in the sign of Moon (Cancer) and well aspected by Sun, makes the wife as active, with a pure body, a princess, ambitious and rich. Wife coming from a royal family or a family very high in power and pelf is thus due to the influence of royal planets Sun and Moon on the significator of wife. Astronomically, seventh aspect of Sun on Venus is not possible. What is intended is the influence of Sun which must be there on Venus in order to make wife royal or aristocratic.

Principle 69 – Longevity

The longevity of a person has to be determined by the strength of both his first and 8th house *Veda* the following *śloka* No. 4 of *chapter* VII of *Sarvārthacintāmaṇi*—

रन्ध्रेशयारेणापि विलग्ननाथे युते रिपौ वा व्ययराशियुक्ते,
षष्ठान्त्यपे वा यदिलग्नयुक्ते दीर्घायुरस्येति शुभेक्षितश्चेत् ।

When the lord of the *lagna* and that of the 8th house are together in 6th or 12th house and are well aspected, they confer long life etc. authors have dealt with the first and the 8th house separately and held these as houses of longevity. In regard to longevity vis-a-vis the first house, the author of *Sarvārthacintāmaṇi* says in *śloka* 107 of the second *chapter*—

लग्नाधिपोऽतिबलवानशुभैरदृष्टः केन्द्रस्थितः शुभखगैरवलोक्यमानः ।
मृत्युविधूय विदधाति सुदीर्घमायुः सार्द्धगुणैर्बहुभिरूर्जितया च लक्ष्म्या ।

i.e., when the lord of the ascendant is strong and not influenced by malefics and is on the other hand, located in *kendra* and aspected by benefics, it removes danger of death and brings about very long life and bestows on the native many good qualities and great wealth. Thus the house of life and death being the first and the 8th house, the nature of influence exerted on these houses and their lords indicates the mode of death, its cause etc. the following *ślokas* are relevant in this context—

षष्ठाष्टमव्यये चन्द्रे लग्ननाथे वीक्षिते,
मन्दमान्द्यगुसंयुक्ते तस्य दुर्मरणं वदेत् ।

if Moon and the lord of the *lagna* are located in or associated with the sixth, eighth or twelfth house of the horoscope and are afflicted by Saturn, *Mandi* or *Rāhu*, then death in miserable manner should be predicted. The idea is that the manner of the affliction of *lagna* and Moon gives a hint in regard to mode of death.

पापक्षिते तुहिनगावुदये कुजेऽस्ते त्यक्तो विनश्यति ।

i.e., if malefic planets aspect the Moon in *lagna*, i.e., Mars does it, particularly by its location in the seventh house, the child is forsaken by its mother and dies—

मरणात् जीवितमरणां गुह्यस्थानं च मरणहेतुं च,
अन्नसुखं मृतिदंशं परिभवमपि चिन्तयेत् प्राज्ञः ।

From the 8th house of the horoscope, should be decided the question of life and death, the rectum, mode of death food, service, venereal disease and dishonour.

Principle 70 – Traits of first house

The first house of the horoscope is designated by many terms, one of which is *janma*, i.e., birth. This name is very appropriate as the very first event that happens to the soul with its advent into this world is his very birth. Astrology has therefore, associated birth and all things intimately connected with birth with the first house, the lagna or ascendant. The place at which a birth takes place, i.e., whether it is in air, on earth, below earth, in water etc. is considered and decided by a study of the first house. For example, the author of *Devakeralam* writes in *śloka* No. 848 at page No. 78—

मकरॉशकगे मन्दे चन्द्रे राहु समन्विते,
लग्नेशे शनि संयुक्ते वनप्रान्ते प्रसूतिमान् ।

i.e., if Saturn is located in the *lagna* in the *navāṁśa* belonging to itself and *rāhu* is with the Moon, the native will be born in a jungle. From this *śloka*, it is clear that the nature of the place of birth is determined by the nature of the planet influencing the most the *lagna* and the *candra lagna*. For a birth in a boat or ship, the author of *Jātaka Pārijāta* states in *śloka* No. 61 in *chapter* 3—

लग्ने जलजेऽस्तगेऽपि वा चन्द्रे पोतगता प्रसूयते ।

i.e., if there is a watery sign (4, 8 or 12) in the ascendant and Moon aspects the same from seventh house, the *Yoga* indicates birth in a boat. Here also the same principle has been applied.

In fact the principle is very wide in its application and we can say that whatever is governed by conditions at birth or whatever that is had by persons from birth, such as stature of the body, caste in which one is born, etc. is all determined by a study of the influences being thrown on the *lagna* and the *candralagna*.

The first house of the horoscope is the quintessence of the whole horoscope. It has such major roles as longevity, wealth, health, honour and position. When therefore, first house get strengthened, these qualities are boosted. There are different ways in which this house may get strengthened. One is when a benefic planet occupies. It, another is when a benefic planet aspects it, another is when benefic planets surround it, i.e., one occupies the 12th and the other the second house of the horoscope yet another is when natural benefic planets are located in the sixth, seventh and eighth from it. The last case goes by the name of *Lagnadhi yoga*. Moon too is treated as *lagna* hence here is reproduced a *śloka* 42 of *chapter* VI of *Phaladīpikā* extolling the qualities of the *lagna* when boosted—

सौम्यैरिन्दोर्घून षड्न्ध्रसंस्थैस्तद्वल्लग्नात्संस्थितैर्वाधियोगः ।

नेता मन्त्री भूपतिः स्यात्क्रमेण
ख्यातः श्रीमान्दीर्घजीवी मनस्वी ।

i.e., if natural benefics occupy the sixth, seventh and eighth house either from the *lagna* or Moon, *Rājayoga* is created. If the benefics are in ordinary strength, the man becomes a leader of men, if in medium strength, a minister and if in high strength, the *Yogas* makes the man a king, i.e., a person holding real ruling powers.

Principle 71 – *Daśā Bhukti*

A. If Saturn and *Rāhu* are conjoined together, the prosperity and success will be promoted much during the period of the stronger planet out of the two.

B. If *Rāhu* or Saturn are conjoined with a *yogakāraka* planet, the *daśā* will be excellent and the native will attend much progress during the *daśā bhukti* of these malefics. If Saturn is a *yogakāraka* there, the major or sub period of Saturn will be very promising.

C. If *Rāhu* falls in Aries, Taurus, Gemini, Cancer, Scorpio, Sagittarius or Pisces, anywhere in the horoscope, that will certainly bless the native with one or the other good results at least.

D. Any planet placed at 30^0 of the sign. Occupied by it, will certainly create obstacles problems and troubles during its *daśā bhukti*.

E. If Mars is conjoined with a debilitated planet, the good effects of *Rāhu* will be curtailed and the malefic effect of the debilitated planet will be enhanced.

F. Sub period of a planet should be divided in three equal parts. The planet will exhibit the results of the house and its position in the 1st one third part. It will give the effects of the sign occupied by 2nd part and in the last part of its *daśā*, the planet will show the results of aspects.

Principle 72 – *Navāṁśa*

The first house may also be boosted through the *navāṁśa*, i.e., when the *navāṁśa* sign in the *lagna* is the same as the *lagna*. Such a *lagna* is called *vargottama lagna* and has been extolled in *śloka* 6, of *chapter 9* in *Sarvārthacintāmaṇi*—

शुभं वर्गोत्तमे जन्म वेशिस्थाने च सद्ग्रहे,
अशून्येषु च केन्द्रेषु कारकाख्यग्रहेषु च ।

i.e., a birth should be considered lucky or fortunate where the *lagna* is *vargottama*, or where a natural benefic planet occupies the second house from the sun, or where the *kendras* first, fourth, seventh and tenth houses in a horoscope are not vacant, or where there is *kāraka yoga*, i.e., where planets in exaltation or in their own signs and located in mutual *kendras* and also in *kendras* from the ascendant. All the four situations, it would be observed become conducive to the *lagnas* in one way or the other. Hence the importance of the *lagna* can not be ignored.

Principle 73 – Planets Aspecting Own Signs

Any sign that is aspected by its lord or is associated with it and is also influenced by association or aspect by natural benefic planets and has no influence on it of any malefic planets denotes the prosperity of the traits and characteristics of the house in which it is located. This is supported by the following *śloka* No. 1 of *chapter* 11 of *Jātaka Pārijāta*—

ये ये भावा स्थितज्ञामरगुरु पतिभिः संयुक्ता वीक्षिता वा,
नान्यैर्दृष्टा न युक्ता यदि शुभफलदा मूर्तिभावादिकेषु ।

Following *śloka* from *Bṛhad Horā Parāśara* may also be quoted in this reference.

यो यो भावः स्वामिदृटो युतो वा
सौम्यैर्वा स्यात्तस्य तस्यास्ति वृद्धिः
पापैरेवं तस्य भावस्य हानि
निर्दृष्टिव्य जन्मतो प्रश्नतो वा।

The importance of this *śloka* is the same as above with the additional proviso that this principle is true in regard to both the natal and the horary chart.

We present this principle to the reader with the highest recommendation. It will be found applicable to all prominent personalities whatever their walk of life. In case where the said principle is applicable to the ascendant and the *candra lagnas* (the sign occupied by Moon at birth) it confers greatness as would be illustrated in the body of the book. We may, however, add in this connection that when it is a case of a natural malefics such as Mars or Saturn aspecting its own sign any where while it may and does enhance the social and financial status of the person concerned, it is not conducive to the life of the person etc. represented by the house so aspected.

Another point that we would like to add is that when under the above rule a house is aspected etc. by its lord, the benefit of such an aspect or association goes not only to the house so aspected but also to the house where in the other sign of the planet concerned is located. For example, if in the case of a Scorpio nativity, Mars lord of the ascendant is located in the 12th house from it where it aspects its own sign Aries located in the sixth house, the benefit goes not only to the sixth house but also to the first house where the other sign

Scorpio of Mars is located.

Sarvārthacintāmaṇi is more explicit on the point. Here is *śloka* No. 2 of *chapter* 2 thereof—

> भावाः सर्वे शुभपतियुता वीक्षिता वा शुभेशैस्तद्वत्तद्वयाषा
> सकलफलदा पापदृग्योगहीनाः ।
> पापा सर्वे भवनपतयश्चेदिहाहुस्तथैव खेटैः सर्वैः शुभमपि
> फलं निम्नमूढारिहीनैः ।

i.e., Any house that is conjoined to or aspected by a natural benefic planet, that happens to be its lord and is influenced by association or aspect by natural benefic planets, gives best results, provided it is not influenced by association or aspect by a natural malefic planet. When any house is conjoined to or aspected by a natural malefic planet, who is its lord and is similarly conjoined with or aspected by natural benefics also gives best results, provided of course that the planet so aspecting is not its enemy, eclipsed or otherwise very weak.

Principle 74 – *Lagna* and Life

The *lagna* not only denotes infancy and the very early age of man, it also indicates life as a whole, or the entire period of life. Here is *śloka* 2342 of *Devakeralam*—

> भाग्ये लग्नाधिपेऽत्युच्चे गुरुणा च निरीक्षिते,
> जन्मप्रभृति च श्रीमान् न कदाचिद् दरिद्रकः ।

i.e., if the lord of any *lagna* is exalted in its highest degree in the 9th house and is also aspected by Jupiter, the native is rich throughout life and is never in want.

Sarvārthacintāmaṇi in *śloka* 94 of *chapter* II stresses the same rule when it says—

लग्ने शुभेशोभनदृष्टि युक्ते बाल्यात्सुखंतन्नहि पापयोगात्,
दुःखी भवेत्पापबहुत्वयोगे लग्ने तु बाल्यान्मरणान्तकालम् ।

i.e., if there is a benefic planet in the *lagna* and another benefic aspects it, but there is no malefic influence on the *lagna*, the native enjoys comforts throughout life. If on the other hand, there are more than two malefic influences on the *lagna* (without any benefic influence) the entire life of the native is miserable. These principles show how intimately the question is related to the strength of the *lagna*.

Principle 75 – Children

If Cancer sign falls in the 5th house and Jupiter is placed there, one will beget daughters only; if Saturn occupies the 5th in Cancer, male children will be born. Mercury in Cancer in 5th gives few sons and placement of Moon in 5th house in Cancer gives more daughters and less sons. For this, following *śloka* of *Jātakadeśa mārga* may be referred—

मन्दे कंकिणि पुत्रगे बहुसुतः सौम्ये तथाऽल्पात्मजः
शीतांशौ बहुकन्यकाल्पतनयो जीवे तु कन्याप्रजः ।
शुक्रेऽर्केऽसृजि च द्वितीयदयितालब्धात्मजः स्यान्नरो
प्यस्तं चन्द्रगृहे फलं सदसतां मिश्रे बलाढ्याद्वदेत् ।।

Principle 76 – Things made alien by sixth house

The 6th house of the horoscope does not merely stand for ones enemies and the traits of enmity, it also stands for the trait of alienness, i.e., not belonging to us, foreign etc. For example, *śloka* of *Jātaka Pārijāta* reads as under—

स्त्री पुत्रपे बलिनि शोभन खेट दृष्टे षष्ठाधिपेन सहिते सति वीक्षिते वा ।
जारेण पुत्र जनि लाभमुपैति तस्या धवो बहुकलत्रयुतोऽप्यपुत्रः

If the lord of the 4th house is strong and well aspected but is either with or aspected by the lord of the 6th house and the horoscope belongs to a lady, she gets a son from a person other than her husband. If the horoscope belongs to a male, he does not get a son even if he marries many women.

Alluding to birth *Jātaka Pārijāta* says illegitimate in *śloka* 68 of *chapter* 12 –

षण्मातृपौ पितृस्थाने पितुश्च व्यभिचारदौ
मातृ तातारि देहेशैरेकस्थैः परजातकः ।

i.e., if the lord of the 4th, 9th, 1st and the 6th are together any where the birth should be considered as bastard. The cause for such a birth is of course, the association of the foreign element denoted by the lord of the 6th house with factors for self, mother, father (1st, 4th and 9th houses respectively).

Principle 77 – Present, Past and Future

Time is indefinite. Human birth itself is what gives it a start and creates the illusion of time, hence we take the first house, i.e., the house of birth as the "present". In order to have a triangular conception of time, we have the triangle constituted by the 1st, 5th and 9th houses of the horoscope, where 9th stands for the past, for it represents a point in time that has long past the horizon, i.e., the present, the 5th stands for the future for it represents a point, i.e., sign which has still to rise in the eastern horizon (*lagna*). While dealing with the traits of the 5th house *Uttarakālāmṛtā* has said—

नाना काम्य महा प्रयोग पितृवित्ते दूर चिन्ता क्रमात्
Chapter 5 *śloka* 8

i.e., 5th house relates *inter alia* to much coveted affairs, immense work, paternal property and fore-sightedness, which implies that the 5th house is related to future. It is in recognition of this fact that "speculation business" (*saṭṭā*) is associated with 5th house. The ability to read the future of man is also accordingly associated with this house.

For the 5th house from Moon of Jupiter *Mānasāgarī paddhati* says—

चन्द्रात्पंचमजीवे दिव्यदृष्टिर्भवेन्नरः

i.e., a man has supernatural vision if Jupiter is located 5th from Moon. The vision is of course the ability to be quick to sense the future.

Principle 78 – Foreign Travel

The 8th house of horoscope is concerned, *inter alia*, with overseas journeys. While dealing with the nature of events connected with the 8th house location of Moon, the author of *Sarvārthacintāmaṇi* states in *śloka 29* of *chapter* 13.

रन्ध्रस्थितस्यापि दशाप्रपन्ना
देहस्यकाश्यं जलभीतिदुःखम् ।
विदेशयानं सकलैर्विरोधं
कुभोजनं मातृजनेषु कष्टम् ।।

i.e., during the ruling period of Moon when she is situated in the 8th house, there is emaciation of body (Moon being a *lagna* factor stands for body) fear of drowning (both the 8th house and the planet Moon are watery in nature and the 8th is house of destruction), travel to foreign countries (being journey overseas), opposition to all (Moon stands for the masses as a significator and is located in a very bad house), eating third rate dishes (Moon being related to eating and 8th to badness) and trouble to mother and relatives like mother (Moon is significator for mother). Some people associate foreign travel with the 9th house which is really a house of long travel within one's own country, for Saturn located in the 8th house *Mānasāgarī paddhati* has in *śloka* 8 of *chapter* II said देशान्तरे तिष्ठति, i.e., one goes and stays in foreign land in trouble.

Principle 79 – Scantiness and dearth trait of 6th house

The 6th house by its association with others through itself or through its lord, brings about reduction, want, dearth, scantiness, restriction etc. to the traits with which it is associated. *śloka* 76 of *chapter* 6 of *Jātaka Pārijāta* is relevant in this context and reads as under—

कामेश्वरः शुक्रयुतो रिपुस्थः कलत्रषण्ढत्वमुदीरयन्ति,
षष्ठेशलग्नाधिपती समन्दौ केन्द्रत्रिकोणे यदि बन्धनं स्यात् ।

i.e., if Venus and lord of the 7th house (both represent wife) are located in the 6th house, the yoga renders wife stirile. Similarly if the lord of the *lagna*, in company of the lord of 6th and Saturn is located in *kendra* or *koṇa*, the man gets imprisoned. We thus see that the 6th house reduces the functions of the party with which it is associated. When associated with representative factors of wife it has reduced considerably, her power as a woman to procreate and when associated with *lagna* it has, in collaboration with another factor for reduction, reduced and restricted the movements of the body leading to "imprisonment". Thus 6th house and its lord act as restricting influences. *Pārāśara* also expresses the same principle when it says in 24-63 of *Bṛhat Pārāsarahorā Śāstra*—

षष्ठेशो सहजे जातः क्रोधी विक्रमवर्जितः ।

i.e., when lord of the 6th house goes to the 3rd house of valour it makes the man devoid of valour.

Principle 80 – Marriage relates to 2nd house as well

Normally we examine the 7th house of the horoscope in connection with problems relating to marriage. But the 2nd house of the horoscope is also relevant to the question of marriage particularly to the question of the time of its coming about, as the second house is the house of "family" and a family of one's own is created only with marriage. In this connection, *śloka* No. 60 of *chapter* 6 of *Sarvārthacintāmaṇi* states as under—

लग्ने कुटुंम्बे यदि दारभावे शुभान्विते शोभनवर्गयुक्ते,
तदीश्वरे शोभनदृष्टियुक्ते बाल्ये विवाहादिकमाहुरार्याः।

i.e., if in the 2nd and the 7th houses of the horoscope there are vargas of benefic planets (decante, *navāṁśa* and other similar division are called *vargas*) and if these houses and their lords are associated with or are aspected by benefics, the man gets married in a very early age. *Pārāśara* too has made a similar statement in *śloka* 24 of *chapter* 16 BPHS as under—

कुटुम्बस्थानगे शुक्रे दारेशो लाभराशिगे,
दशमे षोडशाब्दे च विवाहः प्रायशो भवेत् ।

i.e., if Venus is in the 2nd and lord of the 7th house is in the 11th, the man generally marries in his 10th or 16th year of life, i.e., early in life. In passing it may also be added that the cause of early marriage in the above case has been due to the participation in the *yoga* of the lord of the 11th house – the house of gains or acquisition.

Principle 81 – Cinema

Representation of *Bṛhat Pārāsarahorā Śāstra chapter* 24 *śloka* 113 links "pleasure" to the 5th house. This work and *śloka* 24 of *chapter* 2 of *Jātaka Pārijāta* hold that the planet Mercury has a special relation to "pleasure resorts". Thus by a combination of Mercury and the 5th house we can have such modern pleasure resorts as the cinema, the clubs the circus and the like. For example, if the sign Gemini of Mercury is located in the 5th house, the 5th house may be considered as a cinema and its relation to other factors in the birth chart interpreted accordingly. The *śloka* of BPHS referred to above is as given below—

कर्मेशे सुतभावस्थे सर्वविद्यासमन्वितः,
सर्वदा हर्षसंयुक्तो धनवान् पुत्रवानपि ।

i.e., when the lord of the 10th house occupies the 5th, the native is very well educated, always in happy mood, wealthy, and blessed with sons. The word *hya* – is noteworthy as signifying itself as one of the chief traits of the 5th house. The other *śloka* runs as under—

देवतोयतटवह्निविहाराः कोशगेहशयनोत्करदेशा
भानुपूर्वनिलया परिकल्प्या कोणनिलयावहि केतुः

It is meant that place of frequent resort of Sun is a temple, of Moon a watery place, of Mars where fire is mostly in evidence, of Mercury a place of intellectual enjoyment or playing etc.

Principle 82 – Loss of wealth by Govt. orders

The 10th house represents the Govt. the 12th house being 3rd from the 10th would therefore, represents the arms of Govt., i.e., means of execution of the intentions of Govt. thus the 12th house of a horoscope represents the orders of Govt., which if adversely effect the 2nd house may mean loss of wealth through Govt. orders, i.e.. as a measure of punishment etc. in this context *śloka* of *Sarvārthacintāmaṇi* is relevant. It reads in part as under—

व्ययेशो धनभावस्थे ... ... राजदण्डाद्‌ धनक्षयः

i.e., when the lord of the 12th house is located in the 2nd house one may lose wealth as a punishment awarded by Govt.

For the same reason, the lord of the 8th can perform the functions of the orders of the Govt. as the 8th house is 11th from the 10th and constitutes the 2nd arm of the Govt. in fact, just as the 1st, 3rd, 10th and 11th houses are the houses representing the deliberate actions of any person, in the same manner the 1st, 3rd, 10th and 11th house of the Govt. would represent deliberate action by Govt. these houses in the case of Govt. would be 10th, 12th, 7th and 8th houses respectively from the main horoscope of the native concerned.

Principle 83 – Prediction through definition & correlation

Prediction in Astrology gets facilitated if we can translate the problem under consideration into astrological factors and then proceed to examine each of those factor. For example, in cases of lunacy or mental derangement, we know that this disease results from the derangement of brain as well as through the shock to the emotional side of our being.

We have, therefore, to examine such factors in the birth chart as stand for the emotions and the brain. Now the brain is represented in astrology by the first house, its lord, the 5th house, its lords and the planet Mercury. Similarly emotions are represented by the 4th house, its lord and the planet Moon. Thus when the factors enumerated above are afflicted, lunacy results.

The author of *Jātaka Pārijāta* puts the same thing in essence when it says in *śloka* 81 of *chapter* 6—

केन्द्रस्थितौ सौम्य निशाकरौ वा
सौम्यांशहीनौ भ्रमसंयुतः स्यात् ।

i.e., the native will suffer from lunacy if Mercury and Moon (brain and emotion respectively) are located in *kendra* but without any benefic influence on them.

Principle 84 – Factors for darkness

The following *śloka* No. 70 of *chapter* 3 of *Jātaka Pārijāta* enumerate the factors that represent darkness—

मन्दर्क्षांशे शशिनि हिबुके मन्ददृष्टेऽब्जगे वा
तद्युक्ते वा तमसि शयनं नीचसंस्थैश्च भूमौ ।
यद्वद्राशिर्व्रजति हरिजं गर्भमोक्षस्तु तद्वत्
पापैश्चन्द्रात्स्मरसुखगतैः क्लेशमाहुर्जनन्याः ।।

If Moon is in the signs (10, 11) or the *navāṁśa* of Saturn or is located in the 4th house from *lagna*, or is aspected by Saturn, or is located in watery signs (4, 8, 12) or is situated with Saturn anywhere in the horoscope, the birth should be declared as having taken place in darkness. If three or more planets occupy their sign of debilitation, the birth takes place on earth (and not on bed). Thus the following are the factors of darkness.

a) The sign of Saturn.
b) The 4th house.
c) Saturn.

We can, of course consider a fourth factor in the form of *Rāhu* who acts always like Saturn. The term darkness here has a symbological significance and may denote *incognito* conditions of man or conditions where he remains in darkness as seen by the general public.

Principle 85 – Masses

The mutual link, in any manner, between the lords of the first house (self) and the 4th house (masses) indicates an interest in masses, i.e., in the country of birth. It is thus a *Yoga* for patriotism and is present in the horoscope of all patriots. For example Sardar Patel, famous architect of free India, a Cancer nativity, had lord of 4th in 4th. He had lord of 4th house from Moon *lagna* linked to the lord of the said lagna. Akbar the great, a great lover of his country and its people, had an exalted Mars in the 4th house and Saturn lord of the 4th located in *lagna* with the lord of the *lagna* (ascendant) who squares the 4th house. Haider Ali, another great patriot had Libra as his ascendant. Saturn lord of his 4th house was aspecting the 4th house while Venus lord of the ascendant was in his fourth house. Bal Gangadhar Tilak, another patriot of first water, had Venus lord of the 4th house located in Cancer in the ascendant. Similarly Dr. Rajendra Prasad, first President of India had Sagittarius as his ascendant with the second sign of Jupiter falling in the 4th house. His Jupiter, the lord of the 4th house was aspecting the ascendant.

Pandit Madan Mohan Malviya, with Cancer as his ascendant had his Venus lord of the 4th house in 7th thereby aspecting the ascendant. He had also an exchange between the lord of Moon *lagna* and that of the 4th house from it. Shri Jawaharlal Nehru, first Prime Minister of India had a Venus in dignity in Libra in the 4th house and Moon as the lord of ascendant placed in Cancer itself 10th from it, thus creating an intimate link with the 4th house.

Principle 86 – Charitable deeds

The 9th house is the house of religion and high thoughts and therefore of charitable deeds. The lords of the 10th house and 11th house of the horoscope are equally the houses of good and charitable deeds. The following authorities are relevant in this context—

1. सिंहासनांशके दाननाथे लग्नेशवीक्षिते
   कर्मेशेनापि संदृष्टे महादानकरो भवेत्
2. चतुर्थे दानभावेशे कर्मेशे केन्द्रमाश्रिते
   व्ययेशे गुरुसंदृष्टे महादानकरो भवेत्
3. लाभेशे केन्द्रभावस्थे महादानकरो भवेत्

i.e.,

(i) If the lord of the 9th house is in the *varga* called *simhāsana* and is aspected by the lord of the *lagna* and is also aspected by the lord of the 10th house, one is a great philanthropist.

(ii) If the lord of the 9th house occupies the 4th, the lord of the 10th house is in a *kendra*, and the lord of the 12th house is aspected by Jupiter one is a great philanthropist.

(iii) If the lord of the 11th house is located in a *kendra* house one is a great philanthropist.

We should, therefore, treat the lords of the 9th, 10th and 11th house as conducive to good and charitable deeds.

Principle 87 – Sub and main period lords

The planet having its sub period in the *vimśhottari daśā* system, should always be considered as influencing for good or for bad, the planet having its main ruling period, irrespective of the fact, whether the sub-period lord actually influences in any way the main period lord. This principle is born out by authoritative texts. For example, the following *śloka* No. 23 of *chapter* XVI of *Sarvārthacintāmaṇi* may be referred to in this connection—

कर्मस्थरविदाये तु शुभभुक्तिर्यदा तदा
करोति विपुलं राज्यं कीर्तिश्च आचन्द्रतारकी

i.e., during the main ruling period of Sun located in the 10th house and the sub ruling period of a benefic planet there is ever lasting fame and also acquisition of ruling powers. In *Sarvārthacintāmaṇi* VXI-6 we again read—

धनस्थवासरेशस्य पापभुक्तो धनक्षयं वाक्यपारुष्यं मनोदुःखं
नेत्ररोगं महद्भयम् ।

i.e., during the sub period of a malefic planet in the main period of the planet, that is the *lord* of the day of birth located in the 2nd house (wealth) one has loss of wealth, harshness of speech, mental worry, eye trouble and much fear. It would be noted that the author has nowhere stated in the *śloka* that the planet havings its *bhukti* should in any way influence the planet having the main ruling period. such influence is, however, implied very strongly as evidenced by the results stated.

Principle 88 – Table showing planetar friendship etc.

Planet	Sun	Moon	Mars	Mercury	Jupiter	Venus	Saturn	Rāhu	Ketu
Whom it considers as a friend	Jupiter Mars Moon	Sun Mercury	Moon Jupiter Sun	Rāhu Venus Sun	Sun Mars Moon	Mercury Saturn Rāhu	Mercury Venus Rāhu	Venus Mercury Saturn	Venus Mercury Saturn
Whom it considers enemy	Saturn Rāhu Venus	Rāhu Ketu	Mercury Rāhu	Moon	Mercury Venus	Sun Moon Moon	Sun Mars Moon	Sun Mars Moonas	Sun Mars
Whom it considers a neutral	Mercury	Saturn Venus Jupiter Mars	Saturn Venus	Jupiter Saturn Mars	Rāhu Saturn	Jupiter Mars	Jupiter	Jupiter	Jupiter

Principle 89 – Houses and their affairs

Houses are the imaginary divisions of the earth created by super imposition of the zodiac on it through the ascendant, i.e., the sign rising in the eastern horizon at the moment of birth at a particular place. The houses are evolutionary in conception and deal with all affairs of life. Some of the more important of which are given below—

First House – Conditions at birth, such as the nature of the place of birth, the body as a whole, the limbs of the body individual, colour of the body, stature of the body, longevity, honour, self, sex of partner, brain, wealth, means of livelihood, wife of the eldest brother of father, husband to the eldest sister of father, mode of death, mental traits.

Second House – Food, eating and drinking habits, accumulated wealth, banks, treasuries, right eye, speech, oratory, education, boyhood, throat, face, elder coborns to mother, family, death, princely people.

Third House – Activity, arms, younger brothers, deliberate self, short journeys, communications, writings, respiratory canal, courage, defence department of Govt. victory or defeat, youth, friends, ears, air travel, longevity, wife of the younger, brother to wife, husband at younger sister to wife, father-in-law.

Fourth House – Nadir, well, water, darkness, mother, emotions of all types, masses, longevity of father, comfort, conveyances, property, mind, lands, farming, progress, chest, lungs, blood, residence, transfers, place of birth.

Fifth House – Creative mind, power of authorship, progeny, abortions, lady love, places of pleasure such as cinemas, belly, heart, advising capacity, ministership, lottery, speculation, father, future, intellect, deity one worships, elder coborns of wife or husband, wife of elder brother, husband of elder sister, foresight.

Sixth House – Hurdles, opposition, enmity, scantiness, debts, disease, younger brother or sister of mother, intestines, injuries, theft, vices, foreign elements, violence, kidneys, longevity, eldest brother or sister.

Seventh House – Private parts of the body, urine, semen, sex, marriage, wife, divorce, road, status of wife or husband, trade, eldest brother or sister to father, impotency, partnership, death, ruling powers.

Eighth House – Longevity, death and destruction, mode of death, foreign travel, seas, sin, mysterious things, research, testicles, dishonour, adventure, husband to the eldest sister of mother, wife to the elder brother of mother, mental torture.

Ninth House – High thinking, religion, spirituality, merit of previous life, past life, father, son, thighs, favour from Govt. windfalls, career, high officials, long inland journeys, younger brother to wife or husband, wife of younger brother, husband of younger sister.

Tenth House – Religious deeds, wealth of father, govt. ruling powers, zenith, height, position, honour, actions by self kins, mother to wife or husband, longevity of younger brother and sisters, results of actions.

Eleventh House – Income and gains, elder brothers and sisters, lower portion of the legs, longevity of mother, wife of son, husband to daughter and her marriage, deliberate self, injury, disease, younger brother to father etc.

Twelfth House – Expenses, waste, left eye, *mokṣa*, feet, sea side, a watery place, overuse, losses, separation, luxury, enjoyments of bed, sleep, orders of the govt. defence department, temple or places of worship, the career of public, wife of the younger brother to mother, husband to younger sister to mother, imprisonment, spy.

Principle 90 – Sandhis or junction points

Just as a turning point on roads is dangerous to life, just as the period of transition from puberty to youth is fought with danger to character, just as the public transit from slavery to freedom involves danger to life, just as the turning away of one season and coming up of a new is full of possibilities of disease, similarly the interval between the termination of one sign and the start of another is dangerous to the realization of the traits of the planets in these junction points. The author of the *Phaladīpikā* has gone even to the length of saying—

स्वोच्चे सुहृत्क्षेत्रा गतो ग्रहेन्द्रः षड्भिर्बलै र्मुख्यबलान्वितोऽपि
सन्धौ स्थितः सन्नफलप्रदस्स्यादेवं विचिन्त्यात्र पदेद्विपाके ।

i.e., if a planet even if it be located in its sign of exaltation, in its own sign, or the sign of a friend and having all the six types of strengths, would be without any results, if it is located at the junction point. For the above reason, a planet located at a point where both sign and a *nakṣatra* terminate simultaneously such as the end of signs Cancer, Scorpio and Pisces, would be still more dangerous for planets particularly Moon to occupy. These 3 points are called *gandas*. The reason is obvious for in such a contingency the planet is not able to act in accordance with the traits of the proceeding sign nor with those of the coming one. It is, as if it is in a no man's land.

Principle 91 – Educational attainments

Even in texts, there is confusion in regard to the house to be considered for academic education. Some are of the opinion that it relates to the 2nd house, others opine that the house of education is 4th, while there are still others who hold that 5th house is the house of education. We are in favour of the 2nd house. Authors who have stated the 4th as the house of education have also mentioned the 2nd house also as one of education. The author of *Phaladīpikā* is most clear and explicit on the point. He says in XVI-5.

अर्थस्वामिनि मुख्यभावजुषि सत्स्वर्थे कुटुम्बश्रिया
सर्वोत्कृष्टगुणी धनी च सुमुखी स्याददूरदर्शी नरः ।
सम्बन्धे शशितुर्द्वितीयपतिना लोकोपकारक्षमां
विद्यामर्थमवाप्नुयादथ शनैः क्षुद्राल्पविद्यारतः ॥

i.e., if Sun is located with the lord of the 2nd house of a horoscope, one is capable of doing good to the public. He also earns wealth and education. If, however, the lord of the 2nd is located with or is under the influence of Saturn, the native gets very little education and of a low type too.

Principle 92 – Fourth house as birth place

The fourth house is generally treated by people as one's residence, which of course, it is. But it is also the place of birth like the *lagna*. On this point, the author of *Phaladīpikā* observes in *śloka* 14 of *chapter* XVI—

दुःस्थे सुखेशो कुजसूर्ययुक्ते
सुखेऽपि वा जन्मगृहं प्रदग्धम्

i.e., if the lord of the 4th house occupies any of the bad houses, 6th, 8th or 12th, alongwith Sun and Mars or if Sun and Mars are located in the 4th house, the house in which one is born is a burnt one. If Sun as the lord of *lagna* is located in the 4th house and if Moon aspects it from the 10th house, the *yoga* indicates that the person is born in the house of his mother, i.e., in her parent's house.

Principle 93 – Moon in 6th house – danger to life

While dealing with the question of *ariṣṭa*, i.e. danger to life in infancy, authors like *Varāhamihira* and others have stated that Moon by occupying certain houses of the horoscope and being weak therein brings about death in infancy. These houses are 1st, 5th, 7th, 8th, 9th and 12th. The list makes no mention of the 6th house which is also dangerous for Moon to occupy. Moon in 6th house if weak and afflicted may not kill one in infancy but certainly it is strong factor for shortening life considerably. In this context, see the following *śloka* from *Jyotiṣatattva*—

दैन्यामान्ये सुन्दरीमन्दिरस्थे
दोषानाथे द्वादशे दारहतान्

i.e., If the planet Venus is located in the 7th house and Moon in the 12th house, the *Yoga* takes away life of wife. The life of wife is obviously endangered here by the 6th position of Moon from the 7th house and its significator.

While dealing with Moon's positions in various houses, the author of *Sārāvalī* says the following for the 6th position of Moon—

रजनिकरे स्वल्पायुः षष्ठगते भवति संक्षीणे

i.e. if Moon is in the vicinity of Sun and is in the 6th house, one is very short-lived.

The author of *Jātaka Pārijāta* has said the same thing in *chapter* 8, *śloka* 75 -

अल्पायुः स्यात् क्षीणचन्द्रेऽरिसंस्थे

Principle 94 - *Sudarśana* - an illustration

Jupiter, Venus and Mercury are throwing their combined good influence on the 5th house. The 5th house is moreover not aspected by any malefic planet and yet there is the true statement of the subject in regard to suffering of a chronic nature. What is the answer of Astrology? *Sudarśana* is the answer. Let us see, lord of 5th from *lagna* is Mercury. Lord of 5th from *Candra lagna* is Jupiter and *lord* of 5th from the *Sūrya lagna* is Venus. All these 3 planets are located under the strong aspect of an exhalted malefic Saturn and that too as the lord of the sign occupied by two malefics, Sun and *Ketu*, it was thus as a result of the affliction by the disease giver Saturn of the *lord* of the 5th house from all the three *lagnas* that this chronic trouble came into existence. If you examine the problem merely from *lagna* alone, you are sure to fail, as then you are likely to think that since both the 5th house and its *lord* is under the influence of Jupiter and Venus there should be no trouble in the belly. Thus *Sudarśana* teaches us to have an integrated view from all *lagnas*.

Principle 95 – Cordiality

There are two main rules for determining cordiality between two relations as seen from the horoscope of any one person. The first rule is that if the *lord* of the house of the relation concerned is strong and so also is the Significator of that relation, there will be cordiality between the subject and his relation involved. For example see the following—

लग्नेशात् पितृभावेशे संपूर्णबलसंयुते
कारके वा शुभदृष्टे जातः पितृवशानुगः

i.e., if the *lord* of the 9th house from *lagna* is full of strength (by house position, sign position, association aspect etc) and so also is the *kāraka*, i.e. Significator of father (Sun) the subject will be obedient to his father.

The 2nd rule for cordiality is that the two planets involved should not be located in 6th, 8th position from each another or the *lagna* etc. the following *śloka* No. 28 from *chapter* 20 of *Phaladīpikā* is relevant.

दशेशशत्रोररिगेहभाजो लग्नेशशत्रोरपि वाथभुक्तौ,
शत्रोर्भयं स्थान-भयं तदास्यस्निग्धोऽपि शत्रुत्वमुपैति नूनम् ।

i.e., a planet that is enemy to the planet having its main ruling period, or is located in the 6th house or its enemy of the lord of *lagna*, will turn even the best of friends into enemies in its sub period and there is great fear of not only enemies but also of losing honour.

Principle 96 – Jupiter and illegitimate birth

From a perusal of the following *śloka* No. 6 of *chapter* 5 of *Bṛhatjātaka*, it would be seen that Jupiter has a substantial role in determining whether a particular birth is real or an illegitimate one.

> न लग्नमिन्दुं च गुरुनिरीक्षते न वा शशांकं रविणासमागतम्
> सपापकोऽर्केण युतोऽथवा शशी परेण जातं प्रवदन्ति निश्चयात्

i.e., when in the horoscope of a person, the *lagna* and the *Candra lagnas* are not aspected by Jupiter or if Sun and Moon are located together but are not aspected by Jupiter or if Sun and Moon are in the same sign with Saturn and Mars, the birth should be declared as from some one other than the known father of the native. It seems the influence of Jupiter on Sun and Moon (factors of birth and representatives respectively of father and mother) is a legalizing and validating influence that makes a birth real. It is, therefore, stated in the above *śloka* that without such an influence birth becomes illegitimate.

But in actual life, we see that a birth is illegitimate in spite of Jupiter's influence on the lagna factors stated. However, Mercury does play a vital role in illegitimate birth of a person, as Mercury is also illegitimate child of Moon.

Principle 97 – *Rahu's* aspect–an illustration

Rāhu and *Ketu* – the shadowy planets throw their influence or aspect as it is called on the house etc. located 5th and 9th from them. Here *Parāśara* opines in this content—

सुत मदन नवान्त्ये पूर्ण दृष्टि तमस्य,
युगल दशाम गेहे चार्घ दृष्टिं वदन्ति ।

i.e., *Rāhu* and *Ketu* have full aspect on 5th, 7th or 9th houses and half on second and tenth. Based on the above principle and on the shadowy nature of these planets, we have stated that the shadowy planets also convey the effects of the planets under whose influence they are situated.

Principle 98 – Separative nature and planets

When a king loses his kingdom or abdicates, when a person leaves his home and hearth and becomes a *sannyāsin*, when a divorce takes place between the wife and the husband, there is always evidence in the birth chart, of influence of a 'separative' nature being exerted on the houses concerned. We have observed in *Horāśataka*—

Chāyā Ātmaja Paṅgu Divakareṣu Khet Dveyo Diśati Yātrā Nij Prabhāvam Nūnam Prathakta Viśayadhi Tasmāt Daśme Yathāḥ Rāja Nyāsam Āhuḥ.

Translation: Out of *Rāhu*, Saturn and Sun, when two or more planets throw their influence on a house etc, the native is separated from the traits of that house. Just as, if *Rāhu* and Saturn are aspecting the 10th house (and it's lord) one has to lose his kingdom or job. The principle of "Separation" illustrated above is of universal applicability. In the field of health and disease, when we find that the 6th part of the *kāla puruṣa*, i.e., the 6th house, it's lord, the 6th sign (Virgo) and its lord (Mercury) are all afflicted through association or aspect, by Saturn and *Rāhu*, one suffers from Hernia, which is obviously a disease wherein the intestines (represented by the 6th part of the *Kālapuruṣa*) are dislocated, i.e., separated from their normal location, in the human system.

Principle 99 – Element of Houses

The *lord* of the first, fifth and the ninth houses are generally fiery in nature because these houses are of that nature.

The lord of the 2nd, 6th and the 10th houses represent the 'earthly' qualities. The lord of the 3rd, 7th and the 11th house represent 'air' and those of the 4th, 8th and the 12th houses represent 'water'. If, however, these houses are occupied by any planet, the lord thereof will represent the element of the planet in occupation, and not the nature of the planet that is the lord of the house. For example, *Ketu* and Mars are situated in the 12th house in Pisces, then the lord of the 12th house, i.e., Jupiter, according to the normal rules stated above stands for 'water', being lord of a watery house, but in this case, it will not act as water but will act as 'fire', since it will carry the effects of the firy planets-*Ketu* and Mars which occupy the sign of Jupiter in the 12th house. It is thus clear that when a fiery planet occupies a fiery house containing a fiery sign, such as Mars and *Ketu* located in Aries in the 5th house, it's lord will represent 'fire' in many capacities and as such will cause much harm to the house etc. it may influence.

Principle 100 – Karmic control theory

One of the most important dimensions of astrology is *karmic* control theory of planets. As per Hindu astrology, *Rāhu* and *Ketu* are shadowy planets which play significant role in predicting one's destiny. According to Hindu system of astrology, a planet can get modified by it's ownership of a certain house or it's placing in the birth chart. Why can't lords of the houses occupied by *Rāhu* and *Ketu* be considered in predicting one's fortune. In Hindu mythology, destiny of a person in the present life is *sum* of his past *karmas* (good or bad) and actions in the present life. As a matter of fact, *Rāhu* and *Ketu* acts as a vacuum tube connecting unknown past karmas and the known present or *Rāhu* and *Ketu* bridge the gap between the previous form of soul to the present soul structure.

In the domain of *karmic* control theory, astrologer must pay proper attention towards modification of astrological predictions. *Karmic* control planets are nothing but dispositors of *Rāhu* and *Ketu* or lords of the houses occupied by *Rāhu–Ketu*. *Ketu* is the inlet point for past karmas, the planet ruling the sign of *Ketu* is called the incoming or past life *karmic* control planet. The planet ruling the sign of *Rāhu*, controls the *Karmic* distribution in present life. that is why, it is known as *karmic* distribution planet. The *karmic* control planets imparts strong effects on the destiny of native depending upon their location in the birth chart and aspects they make with other planets. The aspects made by the *karmic* control planet to other planets are of utmost importance in the *karmic* understanding.

As per oriental text of Hindu astrology, if the *karmic* control planets are together, they will make the native great even if no other planetary combination is present to form any *Yoga*. If this *Yoga* produced by *karmic* control planets is afflicted, the person born will still be great, but this combination will destroy the person also. Another important known observation is that whenever any planetary configuration has given rise to a *Rāja Yoga* and if this *Yoga*, in one way or the other is associated with *karmic* control planet, the power of this *Yoga* will get boost-up many times but if this *yoga* is afflicted, the native will still be great but he will be destroyed also due to his karmic destiny. Besides this, if *Rāhu* and Sun are in conjunction, considerable personal elevation of the native is indicated wherever the combination is located in the birth chart.

Principle 101 – The 12th house

The planet Venus feels very happy in the 12th house. This is contrary to the general rule which says that a planet in the 12th house becomes weak and causes harm to the traits it represents. Why is Venus strong and happy in the 12th house? The answer lies in the fact that the traits of the 12th house and the planet Venus are similar and complementary. Both Venus and the 12th house represent *bhoga* or enjoyment and luxury. Due to this affinity, Venus in the 12th house is strong. Hence people in whose horoscopes Venus is placed in the 12th house in a friendly sign, have generally long living wives. That the planet Venus gives good results by it's location in the 12th house is the opinion of the authors of *Bhāvārtha Ratnākara* and *Uttara Kālāmṛta*. These authors also hold the view that the location of Venus in the 6th house too causes affluence. Here also the reason is the same, viz., the affinity between Venus and the 12th house, which it would aspect by being situated in the 6th house.

Principle 102 – Influence of planets

Any house, sign or planet is considered to be under the influence of a planet placed tenth from it. The nature of influence of course will depend on the fact whether the planet in 10th place is benefic or malefic in nature. This type of *kendra influence* should always be given due consideration, in addition to the usual examination of the planetary aspects. The planetary aspect are explained below.

I. Every planet aspects fully, i.e., throws its influence on the house, sign or planet placed 7th from it.

II. Jupiter, Mars and Saturn throw their influence in the manner indicated in (I) above. In addition they have their special aspects as under.
    a) Jupiter aspects fully the house, sign or planet placed 5th or 9th from it.
    b) Mars aspect fully the house, sign or planet placed 4th or 8th from it.
    c) Saturn aspects fully the house, sign or planet placed 3rd or 10th from it.

Aspects of planets are of utmost importance in astrology as these have enormous modifying influence.

Principle 103 – Debilitated Planets

Debilitated (*nīca*) planets give bad effects in regard to the element for which they stand. For example, Sun and Mars are "fiery" in nature and when debilitated, set limbs on fire. Venus and Moon are "watery" in nature and when debilitated bring in an element of liquidity in the limb which they afflict.

For example, a debilitated Moon in the fifth gives "pleurisy", Jupiter through its debilitation associates swollen condition in the trouble. Similarly Saturn brings in an element of pain, Mercury through its debilitation brings about trouble involving many complications.

Principle 104 – Malefic becomes strong

Benefic planets Jupiter, Venus, Mercury are weak in 3rd and 6th houses where malefics become strong by location.

Principle 105 – The sixth house

This is an evil house and indicates miseries, problems, deaths, enmity, ailments and grief. The 6th house is 9th from 10th and 10th from 9th, therefore, the 6th house governs the future prospects and promotion in the professional career of a native. Whenever the 10th or 6th lord occupies the 6th house, one earns his livelihood through service and not by business. Promotion, extensions, suspension, demotion and termination should also be judged from 6th house in addition to 10th house. The 6th house is also called the house of service, therefore, the prospects of service come under the control of 6th house.

Principle 106 – The 8th House

The 8th house is the most misunderstood house as it is dealt for the matters connected with deaths. The 8th house is the house of mysteries, similar to Scorpio sign. The 8th house governs legacy, i.e., inherited property through will of any person. The relationship of the 4th and 8th house show gain of property through legacy. Hidden treasure kept under the ground should also be judged from the 8th house if 2nd and 5th house also support. The 8th house is 11th from 10th and 10th from 11th, therefore, accomplishment of elevated ambitions comes under the control of 8th house. It has been observed in the horoscopes of various class I officers, IAS, Chairman, Managing Directors, Ministers, GM's secretaries, that is the 8th house plays a prominent role in the judgement of their profession. The 10th house has an influence of the 8th lord or the 8th lord occupies the 10th lord. As per general principles of astrology, 10th house should be spoiled if 10th lord occupies 8th and 8th lord occupies 10th. But it is just opposite owing to reasons mentioned above. The 8th house also controls the crowd and masses. Mr. S.Kannan, the popular research oriented scholar of astrology has emphasized a lot over the 8th house in his various articles published in *The Astrological Magazine* of Bangalore. The 8th house 12th from the 9th house, therefore, it controls foreign travels also. Death of father should be judged from the 8th house and mother's death should be judged from 3rd house. Placement of the *lord* of the *lagna* in the 8th house is not adverse for longevity until unless it is aspected by malefics. If 8th house is strong in *bhāvabala*, the native will live long.

Principle 107 – *Māraka*

It is believed that lord of 2nd and 7th house are *māraka*. The death is the last phase of life and if 1st house denotes childhood then the 12th house should rule the death. In my experience, I have found that 12th house has a prominent role in causing one's death. The 8th house governs the longevity, then the 12th from 8th, i.e., the 7th governs death. Similarly, as per the principle of *Bhavat Bhāvam*, the 8th from 5th, i.e. the 3rd house rules longevity. The 12th from 3rd house is the 2nd house which rules death. So the 2nd house is a *māraka*, the 7th house is stronger *māraka* and the 12th house is strongest *māraka*. 22nd *DeśaKana* signifies the source of death.

Principle 108 – Saturn's *Mahādaśā*

An important rule of *daśā* that the 4th *daśā* from birth will be adverse provided it is Saturn's *mahādaśā*. It means that if the birth has taken place during the major period of Mars, then the major period of Saturn will be bad as it is 4th *daśā* from Mars *daśā*. This rule needs further research in my experience of about 35 years that this principle does not hold good. I have found that the natives born in *Mṛgaśirā*, *Citrā* or *Dhaniṣṭhā*, enjoyed the major period of Saturn if Saturn was well fortified and strong.

Principle 109 – Lords of Triangles

If lords of triangles conjoin in the ascendant or 10th house, one earns great name, fame and fortune provided the conjunction is unafflicted.

Principle 110 – Lords of 6th and 8th house

If lords of 6th and 8th house are malefics especially for Gemini and Cancer ascendant and conjoin in the ascendant, the 6th or 8th unnatural end of life may come in evidence before 36th year of age provided the conjunction is unaspected by benefics.

Principle 111 – Lords of angles/triangles

If lords of angle are placed in triangle or vice-versa, that gives good results even if they are malefic or benefic. If the lords of angles are placed in angles or if the lords of triangles are placed in triangles that does not give good results. Irrespective of the fact of their being malefic or benefic in nature.

Principle 112 – Jupiter in the 7th House

Placement of Jupiter in the 7th house should not always be appreciated. If Jupiter falls in the 7th house in watery sign in Cancer, Scorpio, Pisces, that brings disaster in married life, the wife or husband may not have a real or intimate feeling with spouse. Partner may leave or run away or may even expire, exactly depending upon other planetary combination.

Principle 113 – Profession

The judgement of native's profession is mostly examined from the 10th house only. The lord of *navāṁśa* occupied by 10th lord usually signifies the nature of occupation but this is only a supplementary principle. Planets placed in the 10th house and *navāṁśa* lord occupied by them also has a lot to do one's profession. The 2nd house and its lord do play a significant role in examination of vocation. The 11th house is also important for the confirmation of the job undertaken by the native.

Principle 114 – *Maṅgalī doṣa* and cancellation

It is said by sages that Mars causes *maṇgalī doṣa* if it is posited in the 1st, 2nd, 4th, 7th, 8th and 12th house. However, *maṇgalī doṣa* will not exist if Mars occupied always be appreciated. If Jupiter falls in the 7th house in watery sign in Cancer, Scorpio, Pisces, that brings disaster in married life. the wife or husband may not have a real or intimate feeling with spouse. Partner may leave or run away or may even expire. exactly depending upon other planetary combination.

Principle 115 – Effective *kuja doṣa*

We have observed that Mars harms the married life and to the spouse in the horoscope of males if its influence is there in 7th house. Therefore, placement of Mars in the 12th, 1st, 4th and 7th house in a male nativity brings havoc in conjugal bliss in male nativities. Males should be treated *maṅgalī* if Mars is placed in any of these houses. A female native will be *maṅgalī* if Mars influences the 7th or the 8th house because the 8th house represents happiness and span of married life in addition to the life span of husband. Placement of Mars in 1st, 2nd, 4th, 5th, 7th, 8th and 12th house will make a female *maṅgalī*. Here our observation about the placement of Mars in 5th house in female horoscope is quite negative in respect of her married life. She may suffer loss of husband, divorce or miserable married life. We have penned an article about the role of Mars in 5th house for females in *The Astrological Magazine* and have also written a *chapter* on it in my exhaustive book on marriage named *Predicting Marriage.*

Principle 116 – *Candra maṅgala* and *guru maṅgala*

A common belief among us is that aspect or conjunction of Jupiter or Moon with Mars nullifies *maṅgalī doṣa* but it is not correct under our observation. We have studied innumerable horoscopes and our humble observation in this regard is just opposite to the general view. We have also written various article on the subject that conjunction or aspect of Jupiter or Moon with Mars enhances the intensity of *kuja doṣa*. Mars gets exalted where Jupiter is debilitated and Mars gets debilitated where Jupiter is exalted but they are mutual friends. Similarly, Mars is debilitation in the sign of Moon and Moon is debilitated in the sign of Mars, what kinds of friends they are? Mars gets exalted in Saturn's sign and Saturn gets debilitated in Mars's sign Aries. Mars has a peculiar relationship due to its very complicated nature. After examination of hundreds of horoscopes, we have observed that *kuja doṣa* gets enhanced whenever Mars is posited in the sensitive houses and is under the influence of Jupiter or Moon either by conjunction or by aspect. There had been lots of controversy about the subject in the columns of the letters to the Editor in *The Astrological Magazine* and finally the most famous astrologers like Dr. P.S. Shastri, Mr. H.R. Shanker, Mr. K.N. Rao and Dr. Nimai Banerjee etc. accepted and appreciated this observation of Mars and Jupiter, Mars and Moon whole-heartedly.

Principle 117 – Sun and Saturn

Sun and Saturn are father and son but they are ideal enemies. They are reverse in nature in most of the respects. The Sun is exalted in Aries while Saturn is debilitated there and vice-versa. Sun rules East, Saturn rules West. The Sun is king and the Saturn is servant and so on. Mr. H.N. Katve who should be honoured like *Varāhamihira* of present era, has revealed an astonishing fact about relationship of Sun and Saturn. He has specified in his classical work *śani–vīcāra* about the relationship of the Sun and Saturn by association and opposition. If a native has the combination of Sun and Saturn in his horoscope, the progress of his father will be heavily checked after the birth of the child, if the Sun is weak and Saturn is strong. In case if the Saturn is weak and Sun is strong, the Sun will not be able to progress, prosper, or promote his professional career and financial aspect so long as his father is alive. In fact, if the Sun and Saturn are conjoined or placed opposite to each other about 180^0 apart, the native's who are father and son in birth, were bitter and strong enemies in the previous births. They fought a lot in the earlier birth. In such a case, one will have to face defeat. The nature has arranged that the native who was defeated, will gain from the fortune of the other person by becoming his father and son. This is an automatic adjustment by the nature. The native who born in the previous birth will lose his fortune or his son or father will take his fortune and will progress. In many cases, the father snatches the fortune of son and prospers a lot. In other cases soon after the birth of son, downfall or even the death of father takes place because he had troubled his son (in the previous birth) very much and the son will snatch the fortune of his father. The son will prosper and the father will be ruined.

Principle 118 – Career

For the judgement of profession, the nature of the ascendant and its *lord*, the position of the Moon and the strength of the 6th house of service should also be taken into account. A benefic in the 6th or *lord* of *lagna* or the 10th in 6th usually indicates that the native is destined for service. For smooth service career, *lords* of *lagna* and the 10th should be on friendly terms with *lord* of the 6th, otherwise due recognition of one's ability is not forthcoming from one's boss or employer. Again, a planet in the 10th or the 10th lord receiving the aspect of a benefic denotes uncommon ability for successful administration and management. Mercury rules intelligence and Jupiter intuitive insight. When these planets are well disposed in a horoscope, the native is intelligent and efficient.

Principle 119 – Occupation and planets

The following combinations by aspect or by conjunction related to the 10th house give rise to specific means of livelihood.

Mercury and Sun	Executive post, mercantile activities, export and import business.
Mercury and Saturn	Brokerage, postal service, librarian, book trade, clay manufacturing.
Mercury and Venus	Writing of poetry, screen-play, drama, ambassadors, and representatives.
Mercury and Moon	Cinema, exhibition.
Mercury and Saturn	Buffoonery, cartoon-drawing, automobile driving.
Mercury and Mars	Service in Telephone Exchange, printing, drugs, surgery, auditing and accountancy.
Mercury and Jupiter	Research, religious and philosophical writings, corporation and councils.
Jupiter and Sun	Religious organisations, posts of power and authority.
Jupiter and Saturn	Occultism, hypnotism, clairvoyance, contractors, charitable work, poor homes.
Jupiter and Mercury	Technology, ministership.
Jupiter and Moon	Authorship, journalism.
Venus and Moon	Shipping agency, hotel keeping, sale of wine, scents, cosmetics and fancy goods.

Venus and Mercury	Music teaching.
Venus and Saturn	Sale of betel leaves, soap, musical instruments, cosmetics, inks, lime, shoes of good quality.
Venus and Mars	Robbery, dacoity, automobile driving, menial jobs.
Moon and Rāhu	Air-hostess.
Mars and Rāhu	Space travel and space science.
Mercury and Rāhu	Radio-station, watch-merchants, photography.
Venus and Rāhu	Radio-artist.
Saturn and Rāhu	Circus

These combinations get modified according to the benefic aspects they receive.

Again the position of the lord of the 10th is worth considering, especially in its relation to *lagna* or to another benefic aspecting it. If lord of 10th is placed with 9th lord, the native earns through writing. If lord of 10th is in 9th with *Ketu* and aspected by Jupiter, the native earns through religious and spiritual preachings. If lord of 10th is in 11th with Mars, the native earns through scientific pursuits. If lord of 10th is with Saturn, the native earns through hard toil and even asceticism. If lord of 10th is in 9th house or with Mercury, the native earns through writing. If lord of 10th is with lord of 9th and Mercury, the native earns through writings on astrology.

If lords of 4th and 9th are in the 10th house, and lord of 10th is in 11th house, the native earns through big business and manufacturing of goods. (The nature of the commodity differs in keeping with the characteristics of the planets aspecting 10th house).

The importance of *lagna* and its lord and their relative position to 10th house stabilizes a native's source of income. Lord of 10th in *lagna* or aspecting *lagna* definitely brings luster and distinction to one's career or means of livelihood. Again, if lord of 10th is exalted and aspects *lagna* or is posited in 10th house, it is an important factor in ensuring smooth means of livelihood, involving less struggles.

Principle 120 – Promotion

How to judge the prospects of promotion in a horoscope? The house concerned with promotion is the 10th. Strong planets in the 10th house have their say in matters of professional prospects. While examining the 10th house, the following factors should be kept in view:-

1. Lord of the 10th house.
2. Lord of the sign occupied by the lord of the 10th house.
3. Planets in the 10th house.
4. Planets aspecting the 10th house or its lord.
5. The position of the Sun in the horoscope, especially its association with the 10th house, since the Sun is indicator of professional prospects.
6. A powerful Sun in the 10th house is a clear indication of rise in one's career.
7. Lord of 10th is to be counted from *lagna*, from Moon, from Sun and from 6th house, the house which indicates service.

The position of the 6th house is also to be taken into consideration. 6th house is the 10th house from the house of fortune, the 9th house. Moreover, an excellent *Rāja Yoga* in the horoscope bearing on 10th house or 6th house is in the invisible hemisphere. Its connection with the lord of the 10th, the visible house, brings a native's service prospects into limelight and prominence. For sudden supercession and professional gains, lord of the 10th and the 2nd conjoin in a *kendra* and the 6th house is strong.

1. Lord of 6th exalted, lord of 10th in 11th along with lord of the 9th house.
2. Lord of 6th aspecting 6th, lord of 10th aspecting 10th and a powerful *Rāja Yoga* present in the horoscope. One touches the highest post in one's field.
3. Lord of the 10th or 6th from Moon aspected by a benefic and the presence of 3 planets in *kendras*.
4. Lord of 10th in 10th, *lord* of 6th in 6th and lord 11th or 2nd aspecting 10th house.
5. Lord of 10th aspecting 6th house, lord of 6th house aspecting 10th house and lord of 11th aspecting 10th house.
6. Lord of 10th in 10th, lord of 9th aspecting 10th house and lord of 6th in 2nd or 11th house.
7. Lord of 10th aspecting 10th house, lord of *lagna* aspecting 10th house and lord of 11th in 9th and 9th lord strong.
8. Lord of 10th in 11th with lord of 6th and lord of 9th or 2nd in 6th.
9. Lord of 10th in 10th, lord of 6th exalted in *lagna* and lord of 9th in *lagna* aspecting 9th or 10th house.
10. Lord of the 10th in 9th, lord of the 11th in the 10th and lord of the 6th aspecting the 6th.
11. Lord of the 10th in the 9th, lord of *lagna*, 2nd and the 11th in the 10th and lord of 9th aspecting the 6th house.

12. Lord of the 9th in 9th house; lord of the 10th in 10th house and lord of the 6th aspecting the 6th house.

Sudden promotion by supersession

1. Lord of the 10th house in combination with lord of 2nd, lord of 6th aspecting 10th house, and lord of a *trikoṇa* in 10th house.
2. Lord of 10th in 11th, lord of 9th, 10th and *lagna* placed in 11th or 2nd and lord of 6th in a *kendra*.
3. Lord of 10th house aspecting 9th, 10th or 11th lord of 9th in 10th, lord of 11th and 6th aspecting 10th house.
4. Lord of 10th in 11th or 2nd, lord of 6th and 10th in association either by aspect or conjunction.
5. Lord of 9th aspecting 10th house and lords of 6th, 2nd and 11th combine in a *kendra* or receive the aspect of a powerful benefic.
6. Lords of 9th and 10th in the 10th house, lord of 11th aspecting the 10th house, lord of the 10th from 10th house aspecting 9th house, and lord of the 6th too aspecting 10th house.
7. Lord of the 10th in the 9th, lord of the 9th in the 2nd, aspecting the 9th house or 10th house, lord of the 6th in *lagna* and lords of 2nd and 11th are in the 10th.

Principle 121 – Time and duration of mental ills

Mental tensions and ailments appear:-

1. When malefic planets transit over the natal Sun or Moon or *lagna* lord.
2. When malefic planets in their transit afflict the 6th, the 8th or the 12th lord.
3. When Saturn aspects the radical Moon or Sun or vice-versa in transit.
4. When lord of *lagna* in transit has its connection with the 8th or 12th house or its lord.

5. When Mars or the Sun passes over natal *Rāhu* or vice-versa.
6. When what rules, the Moon, Mercury, Saturn and Nodes occupy houses of their fall or their inimical signs.

Principle 122 – Sudden gains

Sudden gains are possible through speculation, lottery, race, buried treasure and prizes and awards. We give below some of the combinations of sudden gains—

1. If lords of 10th and 2nd combine in a *kendra* (angle) or *trikoṇa* (*trine*).
2. If lords of 2nd and 1st reckoned from the lord of 2nd is in *kendra* (angle).
3. If lords of 2nd and 11th are in a *kendra*.
4. If benefics occupy 3, 6, 10, 11 houses from the Moon.
5. If *yogakāraka* is connected with 5th house, success in speculation is assured, provided the 5th house is strong.
6. If Jupiter is strong and connected with the 5th house as well as the 2nd house, success in speculation or gambling is achieved
7. If lord of *lagna* is in the 11th, combined with lord of 9th, and lord of 11th is in the 2nd, lottery *Yoga* is formed.
8. If benefics are in 3rd, 5th, 7th and 11th houses.
9. If lords of 2nd, 9th, 11th are strong and free from the evil aspects of 6th and 8th lords.
10. If lord of 1st or 2nd is in 10th, wealth from State is indicated.

Principle 123 – Transits

The result of transiting planets should be examined from radical Moon only and not from ascendant. Moon is a planet of timing events. At the time of birth, the rising *nakṣatra* decides the balance *daśā bhukti* in any *daśā* system and that helps in timing events. Thus it is the *nakṣatra* which helps in working out the major or sub period. Thus Moon is the factor whose movement decides the time of occurrence of the events. Therefore, timing through transits of planets should be considered for their actual results from their radical Moon only.

Principle 124 – 10th Lord and transit of Jupiter and Saturn

If Saturn will cross over the radical location of 10th lord, problems in profession will certainly arise. Similarly, if Jupiter will cross over the lord of 10th house, the professional prosperity will be highlighted, merits will be recognized and all round success in career will come in evidence. It may be noted that transits of planets help in working out precise and accurate time of events. Transiting planets do not give rise to any event which is not indicated in the birth chart. Good or bad event will take place when a particular planet will transit in a particular sign or house. Events will be prominent when vital planets like Saturn, Jupiter, *Rāhu, Ketu,* Sun either cross the position of any radical planet or opposite to them or aspect them in one or the other way. *Nakṣatra* are also important in which the particular planet will be transiting or the *navāṁśa* in which a planet is transiting will certainly play a vital role in shaping out time of event. This requires lot of practice and experience.

We have given 124 astrological principles of great importance to help the readers and especially for those students and beginners who face lots of confusion in astrological dictums. One can acquire immense knowledge of science of astrology of various fields if he carefully understands these principles and apply the same in practical nativities. These principles have been taken from various classical works, our observations and from the writings of great, famous and successful astrologers of our country such as *Dr. B.V. Raman, Dr. Nimai Banerjee, Dr. P.S. Shastri, Mr. K.N. Rao, Mr. J.N. Bhasin, Mr. B.S. Gupta* and *Mr. Gopesh Kr. Ojha* etc. I feel deeply obliged to all of them and express my humble regards and innumerable thanks.

ॐ नमो ज्योतिर्लोकाय कालाय
निमिषाय पतये महापुरुषायाभिधीमहि ।।

O God ! you are the residing place for all *jyotirgaṇas*, and establisher of *devas* who are settled in form of *Kālacakra* and *Puruṣa*. Therefore we beseech you.

Chapter-3

EARLY WIDOWHOOD : AN ASTROLOGICAL EXPLORATION

Much has been written and experienced by sages and modern astrologers about the widowhood of females. Mostly position of Mars in the sensitive houses where Mars gives rise to *kuja doṣa* is held responsible for such tragedies particularly in the horoscopes of females. It is true but definitely not absolute.

Widowhood is always a setback but if it comes soon after marriage or due to accidental or suicidal death of husband, this is extremely bad, giving rise to extreme degree of terrible plight and sorrow to the native. Here, I want to discuss certain planetary combinations for such tragic death of husband soon after marriage. Every case has different combination. A serious study of all such cases will make the observations most accurate and precise.

Following planetary combinations cause early widowhood. The cause of death of the husband may either be accident, mishappening, suicide or incurable ailment depending upon the planetary configurations in the horoscope of female. It is not at all essential that the loss of husband will take place with female suffering from *kuja doṣa*. Many females may lead a happy married life inspite of having a strong *kuja doṣa*, while many others may lead unhappy married life or may suffer widowhood without having any kind of *kuja doṣa* in their birth chart. I will first of all illustrate a few cases where the females were not *maṅgalī* and they suffered the tragic death of their husband. After that I will explain the cases of *maṅgalī* females who lost their husbands within a short span of their marriage. Prior to it, it will be relevant to quote related aphorisms as mentioned in various classics.

लग्नाच्चन्द्रात्पापाः सप्तमेऽष्टमे वा विधवा ।
भौमर्क्षे राहो सप्तमेऽष्टमे व्यये वा विधवा ।
द्यूनगे पापे विवाहानन्तरं सप्तमाब्दे रण्डा ।
षष्ठाष्टमेशौ षष्ठे व्यये पापयुतौ नवोढा रण्डा ।।
खलैः कलत्रे च गतालका स्यात् ।
विषकन्यायोगश्च वैधव्यकरः ।।
वैधव्यं स्यात् पापरवयेऽष्टमस्थे ।

1. One becomes widow if malefics join 7th and 8th house from *lagna* and Moon.
2. If *Rāhu* falls in the sign of Mars and occupies 7th, 8th or 12th houses, widowhood occurs.
3. If malefics are placed in the 7th house, one becomes widow within 7 years of her marriage.
4. If the lord of the 7th joins 8th house and the lord of the 8th occupies 7th house under the aspect of malefic planet, one becomes widow soon after marriage.
5. If the lords of the 6th or 8th houses are conjoined in the 6th or 12th house with malefics the female will become widow soon after marriage.
6. Malefics in the 7th house can make one widow.
7. If the female is a *viṣakanyā,* i.e., if Saturn falls in the ascendant, Mars joins 9th house and the Sun occupies the 5th house.
8. Malefics in the 8th house can make one widow.

चन्द्रः पापेन संयुक्तश्चंद्रो वा पापमध्यगः ।
चन्द्रात् सप्ताष्टमे पापा भर्तुर्नाशकरा मतः ।।
क्रूरो व्योमचरः स्त्रीणामष्टमस्थो विलग्नतः ।
नीचारिपापवर्गेषु पत्युर्मृत्युकरः स्मृतः ।।

If Moon conjoins with malefics or is hemmed between malefics, the husband will expire. The same misfortune of loss of her husband will come if the 7th and 8th houses reckoned from Moon, are occupied by malefic planets.

If Moon is posited in the 8th house in the sign of debilitation or in the inimical sign or in the *vargas* of evil planets, death of husband occurs before the native.

लग्नात्सप्ताष्टमे पापाः प्राणेशस्यान्तकारकाः ।
चन्द्रात्सप्तमगाश्चैव भर्तृघ्नी दर्शजापि वा ।
वैधव्ययोगजनितावनिताविवाहो
दारघ्नयोगजकुमारवरेण कार्यः ।।
लग्नव्ययाम्बुनिधनाप्तकुजो मिथोघ्नः ।
विवाहोक्तप्रश्नसमयोक्तवैधव्ययोगा विचार्याः ।।
क्रूरे मृत्यौ मश्त्युपो यन्नवांशे
वैधव्यं स्यात्तद्दशान्तर्दशादौ ।।
क्रूरे मृत्यौ चेच्छुभाः स्वे तदा नारी स्वयं म्रियेत् ।।
लग्नेशसप्तमेशशुक्राः शन्यार युक्ताश्चेद्विधवा ।।

1. If malefics are placed in the 7th and 8th houses from *lagna*, one becomes widow.
2. If a female is born on *amāvasyā* (no-Moon day), i.e., when the Sun and Moon are associated, she suffers widowhood.
3. Girls, who have a combination of widowhood, should be married with a boy having *darha yoga* in his horoscope.
4. Placement of Mars in the 1st, 4th, 8th or 12th houses causes destruction of both.

5. Consideration of widowhood should also be made on the basis of query chart.
6. If the lords of the *lagna*, the 7th house and Venus are conjoined with malefics like Saturn and Mars, one suffers from widowhood.
7. The husband may expire during the *daśā bhukti* of the *navāṁśa* lord occupied by the lord of the 8th house, provided the 8th house is occupied by malefics.

सप्तमेशोऽष्टमे यस्याः सप्तमे निधानाधिपः ।
पापेक्षणयुताद्‌ बाला वैधव्यं लभते ध्रुवम्‌ ।।
सप्तमाष्टपती षष्ठे व्यये वा पापपीड़ितौ ।
तदा वैधव्यमाप्नोति नारी नैवात्र संशयः ।।

The woman decidedly suffers widowhood if the 7th lord of her horoscope falls in the 8th house and the *lord* joins the 7th house and malefics lend their evil aspects over these planets. If the *lords* of the 7th and 8th houses are conjoined in the 6th or 12th houses in association with malefics, the lady certainly suffers widowhood.

सौम्याभ्यां प्रवरा शुभत्रययुते जाया भवेद्‌ भूपतेः
सौम्यैकेन पतिप्रिया मदनभे दृष्टे युते जन्मनि ।
पापैकेन पुनर्विलोलनयना पापद्वयेनाधमा
पापानां त्रितयेन सा परकुलं हत्वा पतिं गच्छति ।।

If there are three benefics in the 7th house of the horoscope of a female, she will live like a queen. If one benefic is there in the 7th house, she will be loved by her husband.

1. If one malefic occupies the 7th house, she will possess captivating eyes.
2. If two malefics are there in the 7th house, she will be involved in indecent acts.

3. If three malefics are present in the 7th house of the birth chart of a lady, she will go to her lover's house after killing her husband.

जनुः काले मदनभवने वासरमणौ पतिं त्यक्त्वा
नूनं कुपितहृदया भूमितनये ।
अवश्यं वैधव्यं सपदि कमलाक्षी रविसुते जरां
पापैर्दृष्टे निजमतिविरोधं व्रजति सा ।।
निशाकरात्सप्तमभावसंस्था महीजमन्दागुदिवाकराश्चेत् ।
तनोरिभे जन्मनि नैधते वा दिशान्ति वैधव्यमलं मदे वा ।

If the Sun is posited in the 7th house of a female, she will leave her husband.

If Mars is there in the 7th house, she will be angry with her husband and will keep such negative feelings in her heart.

If Saturn falls in the 7th house, it will make her widow definitely. If malefics aspect such adversely placed Saturn in the 7th house, she will become widow without marriage, i.e., she will remain unmarried.

If in the 7th house from Moon in 3rd, 1st, 7th houses from *lagna*, Mars, Saturn, *Rāhu* and Sun are placed, she will suffer widowhood.

पापग्रहे सप्तमलग्नगेहे भर्ता दिवं गच्छति सप्तमेऽब्दे ।
निशाकरे चाष्टमवैरिभावे तदाष्टमाब्दे निधनं प्रयाति ।।

Husband dies in the 7th year after marriage if malefics are posited in the *lagna* and the 7th house. If Moon falls in the 6th or 8th house, the husband expires in the 8th year after marriage.

दाराधिपे सोमसुते सपापे नीचारिमूढे यदि नाशभावे ।
पापान्तरे पापदृशा समेते जाता पतिघ्नी कुलनाशकर्त्री ।।

The female will kill her husband and the whole family will be destroyed, if Mercury is the lord of the 7th house and falls in the 8th in the sign of its debilitation or in inimical sign or it is hemmed between malefics and is also aspected by malefics. However, if Mercury owns 7th house, the 8th house will either be Cancer or Libra. As such, 7th lord Mercury can not be debilitated in the 8th house in any conditions. So if Mercury is afflicted, weak or under *pāpakartarī Yoga* or is associated as aspected by malefics in the 8th house, the wife may kill her husband.

लग्नाद्विधोर्वा यदि जन्मकाले शुभग्रहो वा मदनाधिपश्च ।
द्यमनस्थितो हन्यनपत्यदाषडुं च विषांगनाख्यम ।।
केन्द्रकोणे शुभाः सर्वे त्रिषडायेऽप्यसद्ग्रहाः ।
तदा भौमस्य दोषो न मदने मदपस्तथा ।
वैधव्यदोषजनितावनिताविवाहो दाघ्नदोषजवरेण समं प्रकार्यः ।।

The 7th house from *lagna* and Moon, is occupied by benefics, the combination for widowhood and childlessness will automatically be cancelled. If benefics are placed in *kendra* and *trikoṇa*, 3rd, 6th and 11th houses are occupied by malefics, the 7th lord falls in the 7th and the girl is free from *kuja doṣa*, widowhood will be cancelled. The girl having combination of widowhood should be married with a boy in whose birth chart *darha yoga* is present. In that case, there will be no loss of husband.

पातालेऽपि तनौ रन्ध्रे जामित्रे वापि च व्यये ।
स्थितःकुजः पतिं हन्ति न चेच्छुभयुतेक्षितः ।।

If Mars benefit the aspect or association of benefics be in 1st, 4th, 7th, 8th or the 12th, the husband dies.

इन्दोरप्युक्तगेहेषु स्थितौ भौमेऽथवा शनिः ।
पतिहन्ता स्त्रियाश्चैवं वरस्य यदि स्त्रीमृतिः ।।

If Mars or Saturn occupies these houses from the Moon sign, then also the native's husband dies. If such planetary dispositions occur in a man's chart then his wife dies.

अंगारके मदनमदिरमिन्दुभावं मन्दान्विते हरिभगे जननेऽगंनायाः ।
वैधव्यमेव नियतं कपटप्रवंधाद्धारांगना भवति सैव वरांगनापि ।।

If in a horoscope, Mars being in the sign of Cancer is placed in the 7th house or Mars and Saturn being in the sign of Leo are situated in the 7th house, then the native will certainly be widowed.

यस्मिन् योगे समुत्पन्ना पतिं हन्ति कुमारिका ।
तस्मिन् योगे समुत्पन्नो पत्नीं हन्ति नरोपि च ।।
स्त्रीहन्ता परिणीता चेत् पतिहन्त्री कुमारिका ।
तदा वैधव्ययोगस्य भंगो भवति निश्चयात् ।।

If a man takes birth under a *yoga*, similar to the *yoga* in which a woman takes birth and attains widowhood, he will become a widower. If a woman with such a *yoga*, it will cause cancellation of such a *yoga*.

पत्युः कलत्रेषु रन्ध्राद्द वैधव्यस्य द्विजोत्तम ।
असंगतं कलत्रेषु पत्योः तत्फलमीरयेत् ।।

From the 7th house, the husband and from the 8th widowhood are to be examined, which can not be applied to males and must be applied to female horoscopy only.

स्त्रीणां वैधव्यदो योगः पुंसां जन्मनि चेद्द भवेत् ।
तदा पत्नीविनाशः स्याद्रुभयोश्चेच्छुभं स्मृतम् ।।

If the combinations for widowhood in a woman's chart obtain in a man's chart, it leads to destruction of wife. However, if present in the charts of both the man and the woman, it is auspicious for both of them.

Following *śloka* has been given in *Jyotiṣatattva prakāśa* in *Chapter* 11 in *śloka* No. 351. The author has stressed over the placement of malefic planets in malefic signs in the 8th house as that may cause widowhood to the female.

अस्तगाः पापखेटाश्चेत्पापर्क्षे विधवा भवेत्
क्रूरेष्टमे च विधवा पापक्षेत्रे विशेषतः ।।

Jyotiṣatattvaprakāśa, p. 311

If malefics fall in malefic sign in 7th house, the native becomes widow or malefics are in the 8th from ascendant, then also the female becomes widow and that very malefic is placed in the 8th in malefic sign, then the native becomes widow.

The author of *Jyotiṣārṇava Navanītama* mentions a few important combination for loss of spouse in *ślokas* 90-95. The contents of the *ślokas* are applicable in the horoscope of a female that she may suffer widowhood if these combinations are present in her birth chart.

दारेशे नीचराशिस्थे शुक्रे रन्ध्राधिपसंयुते
अष्टादशे त्रयस्त्रिंशे वत्सरे दारनाशनं ।।

Jyotiṣārṇava Navanītama Ch.II P. 95

The native will lose her spouse in his 28th or 33rd year if the 7th lord in debility while Venus is in the 8th from the ascendant.

मदेशेंऽशराशिस्थे व्ययेशे मदराशिगे
वत्सरेकोनविंशाख्ये दारनाशं विनिर्दिशेत् ।।

Jyotiṣārṇava Navanītama Ch.II P. 95

Should the 7th lord be in the 8th house while the 12th lord is in the 7th house, the subject will lose her spouse at the age of 19.

पापमध्यगते शुक्रे जामित्रेशेऽथवा पुनः
जामित्रे पापमध्ये जायारिष्टं वदेद् बुधः ||202

Jyotiṣārṇava Navanītama Ch.II P. 90

The learned speak of early death of spouse in case Venus is hemmed between malefic heavenly bodies while in addition the 7th house or its lord is also similarly placed.

लग्नेशे नीचराशिस्थे द्यूनेशे निधनंगते
चत्वारिंशत्रु वर्षे कलत्रस्य मृतिर्भवेत् ||223

Jyotiṣārṇava Navanītama Ch.II P. 95

The subject will lose her spouse at the age of 24 if the lord of the ascendant is in debility and ill disposed while the 7th lord is in the 8th house under malefic aspects.

Many more *ślokas* from various classical works may also be quoted here to illustrate the planetary combinations for widowhood. However, let us summarise all combinations of widowhood, which are mentioned by sages and have been found most authentic.

Planetary Combinations For Widowhood

1. If the lord of the 7th house falls in the 8th house with 8th lord and is conjoined with malefics or aspected by malefics.
2. If the Sun is conjoined with 7th lord and the 8th lord aspects them with *Rāhu* in the 7th house.
3. If Mars occupies the 8th house with the lord of the 8th house and the *lagna* falls in malefic *navāṁśa.*
4. Conjunction of Mars, *Rāhu*, and Saturn in the 8th or 7th house will give early widowhood.

5. If the 7th house is owned by a malefic planet and is occupied by Mars and Saturn together or Mars and Saturn join 8th house with malefic lord of the 7th house, same results will appear soon after marriage.
6. If the 7th house and its lord are hemmed between malefics and are devoid of conjunction or aspect of benefics.
7. Mars if placed in the 7th or 8th house adversely and is not *Yogakāraka*, one should think of widowhood provided other combinations confirm it.
8. If *Rāhu* falls in the sign of Mars and occupies *Troikas*.
9. If there is mutual exchange between the 7th and 8th lord under the aspect of malefics.
10. If the lords of the 6th and 8th are associated in the 6th or 12th house, the loss of husband will take place soon after marriage.
11. If Moon is associated with malefics or hemmed between malefics, one may become widow. If the 7th and 8th houses are afflicted by malefics if reckoned from Moon, one will lose her husband.
12. The lord of the *lagna* and the 7th lord are conjoined with malefics along with Venus.
13. If three malefics are conjoined in the 7th house, the female may be the cause of death of her husband and mostly due to her extramarital affair.
14. If the 7th lord Mercury is posited in the 8th house with malefics or under affliction or placed under *pāpakartarī Yoga*, the female may manage the death of her husband or he may die due to her.
15. If *Ketu* joins the 7th and Mars occupies 8th or 12th house with malefics or Mars is afflicted, the

female will become widow. Similarly if Mars joins 7th and *Ketu* is afflicted in the 8th with malefics, she will lose her husband.

16. If Moon occupies *Rāhu*, Venus conjoins Mars, and malefics occupy the 8th house, the native will lose life partner.
17. If Saturn occupies the ascendant and Mars joins the 8th or 12th house with malefics, one will become widow.
18. If Mars joins 7th or 8th and the Sun joins the ascendant, there is a possibility of widowhood.
19. If Moon is posited in the ascendant and Mars joins the 7th or 8th and any of Mars or Moon is aspected by 8th lord, the native will lose the spouse.
20. If Mercury and Saturn join the 7th house together, one will be involved in carnal activities and will lose her life partner as well.
21. If lord of the 7th house occupies the Troikas or any of the lord of Troikas join the 7th house but 8th lord should join the 7th house and any of the combination is under the aspect of malefic or associated with malefics, one will lose her husband.

Our Observations Regarding The Subject

If we program the computer with all these combinations and apply to the practical horoscopes of widows, only 10% accuracy will be seen. This is so because astrological aphorisms that is the planetary combinations as mentioned in classical works can not be applied verbatim. Scholars must use their intelligence to understand the planetary configuration and the action resulting into loss of the husband. The correct application of the appropriate rules of astrology will certainly enhance the confidence to foretell such a shivering and disastrous truth of widowhood. The 8th house indicates the span of married life whereas the 7th house represents all about husband. Jupiter indicates *saubhāgya* of a female and Mars is the significator of husband. In one way or the other, Moon and Venus signify spouse. The blending of these planets and houses with their relationships with the concerning *Bhāvas* will reveal the truth.

It is easy to predict widowhood with the 7th or 8th house afflicted by Mars, Saturn or nodes. But many times it is not so easy. If there is no planetary affliction of the 7th house or 8th house or the female is not *maṅgalī* or when Jupiter lends its aspect over the 7th house or Jupiter occupies the 7th or 8th house, widowhood is not suspected but in practical study of horoscope, we have observed that this is not true. It is believed that Jupiter's placement in the 8th house or its aspect over the 8th house gives rise to *akhaṇḍa saubhāgya* yoga. In many cases, I have found in the horoscope of few widows that Jupiter occupied the 8th house or aspected the 8th house. In the horoscope of Beena and Manju, Jupiter's placement in the 8th house can not be overlooked. This needs very keen study whether the placement of Jupiter in the 8th house will save widowhood or not? Whether *aṣṭama guru* will bless the female with *akhaṇḍa saubhāgya*. If Jupiter owns the 7th house and joins the 8th house in Martian sign Aries and is aspected by Mars, widowhood can not be saved by *aṣṭama guru*. Similarly, if Jupiter is retrograde in 8th in inimical sign, that may cause widowhood even if it is not aspected by Mars, Saturn or *Rāhu*. I have explained various planetary combinations for widowhood with the help of various illustrations. I am surprised that many females suffered loss of their husband when Jupiter's sub-period or major period is operative over them. I will try to conclude a few thought-provoking observations regarding widowhood in concluding paragraph of this paper.

A Scientific Analysis And Practical Cases Of Early Widowhood

Widowhood within 5 months after marriage (No *kuja doṣa*)

Case 3.1: (Horoscope No. 1)

She was born in Cancer ascendant. *Yogakāraka* Mars occupies the 5th house Scorpio under retrograde motion under argotic *navāṁśa*. The 7th house is aspected by 7th lord Saturn who obtains debilitation in the 10th house and the lord of the 6th and 9th house Jupiter occupies the 3rd house. Apparently this appears to be quite a good horoscope for marriage due to aspect of Jupiter and Saturn, the lords of the 7th and 9th house respectively. Here the aspect of retrograde Mars on the 8th house is extremely adverse for the life of husband. I have tried to establish that the placement of Mars in the 5th house for the female natives may cause widowhood. She got married on June 24th, 1994 during sub-period of Mercury in the major period of Sun. Jupiter and *Ketu* are only 1^0 apart. The *Bhāgyādhipati* Jupiter falls close over the axis of *Rāhu* and *Ketu*. She lost her husband in the sub-period of Mercury in the major period of Sun on November 4th, 1994. I have explained repeatedly in my writings that one should not be married during *daśā bhukti* of those planets who indicate adversity, miseries, widowhood, separation and mishappenings in married life. Mostly we have found that the adversity took place in the lives of those whose marriage took place during negative vibrations of planets.

Case : 3.1 *Horoscope No. : 1*

Date	: 02.06.1969	Time	: 10:00:00
Place	: Mainpuri	Lat 27°:14′	Long 79°:01′
Ayanāmśa	: 23:25:47	Sidereal Time	: 02:27:57

Pln	**Degree**	**Rāśi**	**Nakṣatra**	**Pad**
Asc	20:01:22	Can	Aśleṣā	2
Sun	18:01:54	Tau	Rohiṇī	3
Mon	11:13:36	Sag	Mūlā	4
Mar(R)	16:03:10	Sco	Anurādhā	4
Mer(R/C)	12:21:32	Tau	Rohiṇī	1
Jup	02:49:07	Vir	U Phālgunī	2
Ven	03:19:13	Ari	Aśvinī	1
Sat	10:33:05	Ari	Aśvinī	4
Rah(R)	03:41:21	Pis	U Bhādrapadā	1
Ket(R)	03:41:21	Vir	U Phālgunī	3

Lagna Chart

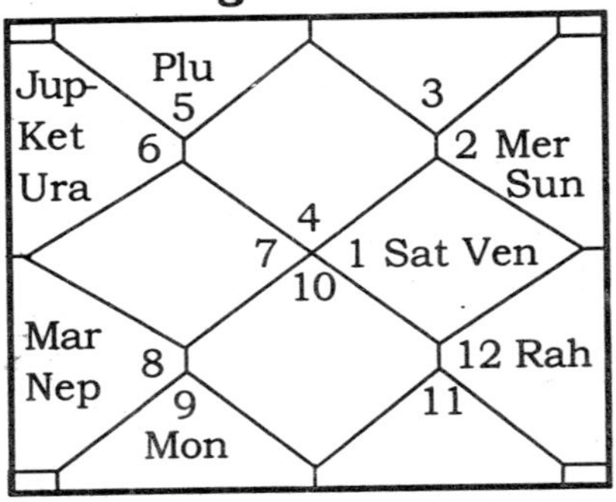

Navāmśa Chart

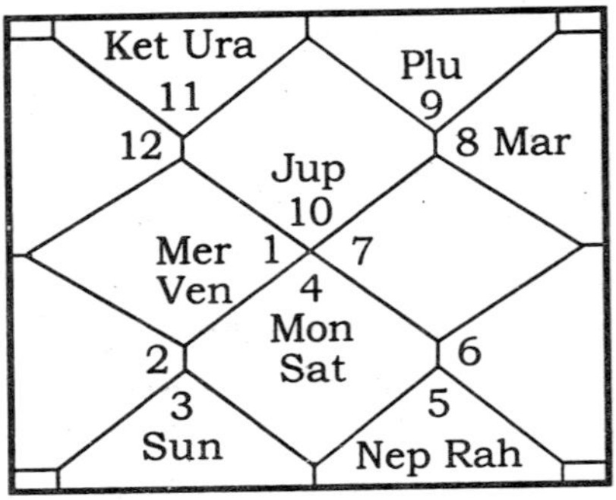

Balance of Vimśottarī Daśā of **Ketu 1Y 1M 8D**

Name of Event	Date of Event	Major Period	Sub Period
Marriage	24.6.1994	Sun	Mercury
Widowhood	04.11.1994	Sun	Mercury

In the present case, as soon as the sub-period of Saturn in the major period of Sun began on May 16th, 1993, the marriage took place on June 24th, 1994 and within 5 months after marriage, her husband was crushed in a road accident. In this horoscope Mars and Saturn both aspect the 12th house which is 7th from *lagna* lord Moon. The aspect of Mars over the 8th house is damaging for the life of husband. The 2nd house is 8th from 7th and indicates the death of husband. The 8th house also indicates family life as well. Therefore, the marriage and widowhood both took place during the major period of Sun.

Widowhood took place on November 4th, 1994 in the major period of Sun in the sub-period of Mercury. Mercury is the lord of the 7th house as reckoned from *lagna* lord Moon. Here Mercury is combust and falls in inimical constellation of *Rohiṇī* and obtains *navāṁśa* of Mars. Therefore, the husband expired during sub-period of Mercury in the major period of Sun.

If we see the horoscope carefully, Mars and Saturn are responsible for widowhood, Saturn gets debilitated, i.e., falls in Martian sign Aries. There are only Jupiter and *Ketu* who fall in Saturn's *navāṁśa* whereas Venus and Mercury both fall in Martian *navāṁśa* Aries. Mars also falls in its own argotic *navāṁśa*. Therefore, the planets who are under the influence of Mars can bring widowhood in their *daśā bhukti*. These are Venus and Mercury. Mercury is the 8th lord from Mars and joins the 7th whereas Mercury is 7th lord from *lagna* lord Moon and joins 6th. Therefore, sub-period of Mercury in the major period of Sun, from where it is second lord, resulted in widowhood.

SUICIDE OF HUSBAND WITHIN 3 YEARS (NO *kuja doṣa*)

Case 3.2 – (Horoscope No. 2)

The native is a daughter of a multi millionaire MP. Her marriage took place during Venus-Rahu period (March 3rd, 1993 to November 3rd, 1996) on March 6th, 1996 with a good looking, smart boy. Father-in-law was a very strict person. He scolded her husband on March 8th, 1999 due to a failure of the undertaking. The shock was so deep that her husband committed suicide on the same day when she was passing through Venus-Jupiter *daśā* November 3rd, 1996 to January 3rd, 2000. Thus she suffered widowhood just after three years of her marriage date at just 23 years of age. She was also blessed with a son on April 8th, 1998. Father of the widow girl got a serious shock and tried for her second marriage. Finally, she got married again on December 8th, 2000 in Venus-Saturn *daśā-bhukti*. This girl is also not *maṅgalī*. Even then, she suffered an early widowhood due to following planetary combinations.

1. *Ketu* occupies the 8th house, which is as bad as Mars in the 8th house. Saturn aspects the 8th house, *Ketu* and Venus in addition to *lagna* and *lagna* lord Mercury.
2. She was born in *jyeṣṭhā nakṣatra* 3rd *pada*. The husband was eldest and the husband was also born in *jyeṣṭhā nakṣatra*. Husband and wife will suffer heavily by death of either of them, if both are born in *jyeṣṭhā nakṣatra*.
3. Jupiter occupies the 7th house in own sign Pisces. Whenever Jupiter falls in watery sign in the 7th house, it brings disasters to conjugal life.
4. Mars who is the 8th lord, falls in the 9th house from *lagna* but in the 8th house from debilitated Moon. Thus Mars in 8th from Moon and *Ketu* in the 8th from *lagna* caused the early widowhood.

Case : 3.2 *Horoscope No. : 2*

Date	: 23.02.1976	Time :	20:20:00
Place	: Harda Khas	Lat 22°:22′	Long 77°:08′
Ayanāmśa	: 23:21:39	Sidereal Time :	06:09:03

Pln	**Degree**	**Rāśi**	**Nakṣatra**	**Pad**
Asc	08:34:02	Vir	U Phālgunī	4
Sun	10:35:32	Aqu	Satabhiṣā	2
Mon	26:29:55	Sco	Jyeṣṭhā	3
Mar	27:15:22	Tau	Mṛgśirā	2
Mer	15:15:35	Cap	Śrāvaṇa	2
Jup	29:37:22	Pis	Revatī	4
Ven	11:17:39	Cap	Śrāvaṇa	1
Sat(R)	03:28:41	Can	Puṣya	1
Rah(R)	22:02:48	Lib	Viśākhā	1
Ket(R)	22:02:48	Ari	Bharanī	3

Lagna Chart

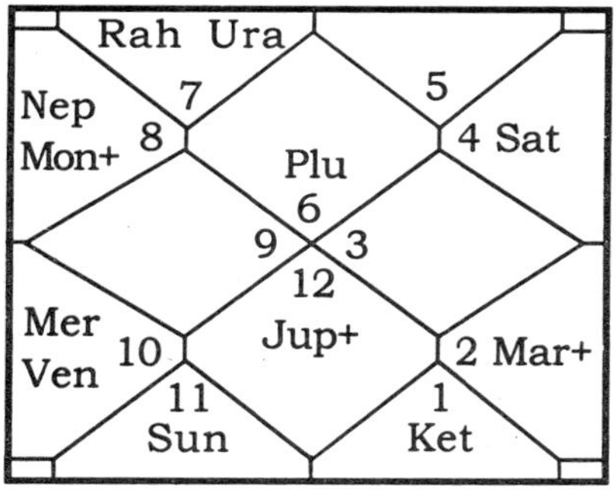

Navāmśa Chart

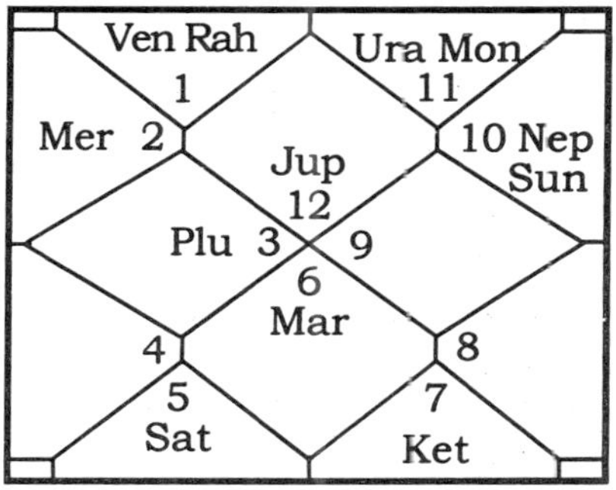

Balance of Vimśottarī Daśā of **Mercury 4Y 5M 17D**

Name of Event	Date of Event	Major Period	Sub Period
Marriage	06.03.1996	Venus	Rahu
Widowhood	08.03.1999	Venus	Jupiter
2nd Marriage	08.12.2000	Venus	Saturn

5. The 7th lord Jupiter and the 2nd lord Venus both obtain argotic *navāṁśa* which caused first marriage and resulted into second marriage as well. Hence Jupiter and Venus both are *māraka* for Virgo ascendant.
6. Moon-Mars opposition or conjunction is adverse for marital happiness. Similarly, Mars Jupiter and Saturn-Mars opposition and conjunction as aspected on each other spoils conjugal bliss.

LOSS OF HUSBAND IN LESS THAN A YEAR (Not *maṅgalī*)

Case 3.3 (Horoscope No. 3)

I am illustrating a case of a native who got married on May 8th, 1996 and lost her husband on April 17th, 1997 under very tragic circumstances. She was in advance way of family when her husband expired within a few minutes after coming back from his office. In this horoscope, we find that Mars is posited in the 10th house with *yogakāraka* Venus. The 7th lord Moon joins the 9th house under no malefic aspect. Why did she become the victim of misfortune resulting into her widowhood within one year of her marriage? This is a complicated case in which even a competent astrologer may not be able to predict early widowhood. Following observations may help us to astrologically justify the death of her husband.

1. Death of husband is governed by the 8th house in a female nativity. The lord of the 8th house, the Sun occupies the 11th house in Martian sign Scorpio and Saturn's *nakṣatra anurādhā*. The Sun is under mutual aspect with Saturn who falls in Mars *nakṣatra mṛgaśirā*. The mutual aspect of Sun and Saturn is always adverse and produces malefic effect. Hence both Sun and Saturn occupy the *nakṣatra* of Saturn and Mars respectively which is a damaging factor in regard to the matters connected with 8th house, i.e., longevity

of husband, as Sun owns the 8th and Saturn owns the 2nd.

2. The 7th lord Moon joins the 9th house in inimical sign Virgo. The Moon is shifted in the 8th house and obtains Saturn's *navāṁśa*.
3. The lord of *lagna* retrograde Saturn obtains inimical *navāṁśa* of Sun and 4th and 11th lord Mars falls in Saturn's *navāṁśa* Aquarius. Thus opposition of Mars and Saturn in *navāṃsā* is present indicating a disaster in marriage.
4. Conjunction of Moon and Venus in *navāṁśa* chart is also adverse for long lasting marital happiness.
5. *Kāraka* of *saubhāgya*, Jupiter, falls over the axis of *Rāhu* and *Ketu* and falls in inimical *navāṁśa* Virgo. However, close conjunction of Venus and Mars in *Svāti nakṣatra* and placement of two planets in Saturn's *navāṁśa* caused widowhood. The marriage of the female took place during *Rāhu Rāhu daṣā Bhukti* on May 8th, 1996 and the husband expired during *Rāhu* Jupiter period on April 17th, 1997 which indicates the adversity of close affliction of Jupiter with *Rāhu* may cause such problem provided other negative indications are found in the birth chart of a female.

It is essential to look into *Bhāva cālita* chart without making any mistake in this birth chart. The 7th lord Moon who occupies the 9th house is shifted in the 8th house, that indicates early death of her husband during *Rāhu* Jupiter *daṣā bhukti*. Jupiter is the lord of the 3rd and 12th house and joins the 12th house with *Rāhu*. Placement of Jupiter over the axis of *Rāhu* and *Ketu* is certainly adverse for longevity of husband. Conjunction of Venus and Mars in *svāti nakṣatra*, which is ruled by *Rāhu*, is also adverse because Jupiter is closely associated with *Rāhu*. As soon as Jupiter's sub-period in *Rāhu*

Case : 3.3 *Horoscope No. : 3*

Date	: 29.11.1972	Time :	11:00:00
Place	: Bareilly	Lat 28°:20′	Long 79°:24′
Ayanāmśa	: 23:28:58	Sidereal Time :	15:20:24

Pln	**Degree**	**Rāśi**	**Nakṣatra**	**Pad**
Asc	13:51:14	Cap	Śrāvaṇa	2
Sun	13:37:04	Sco	Anurādhā	4
Mon	00:57:28	Vir	U Phālgunī	2
Mar	15:20:49	Lib	Svāti	3
Mer(R/C)	06:35:46	Sco	Anurādhā	1
Jup	16:58:28	Sag	Pūrvāṣāḍha	2
Ven	12:16:25	Lib	Svāti	2
Sat(R)	24:25:20	Tau	Mṛgśirā	1
Rah(R)	24:10:00	Sag	Pūrvāṣāḍha	4
Ket(R)	24:10:00	Gem	Punarvasu	2

Lagna Chart

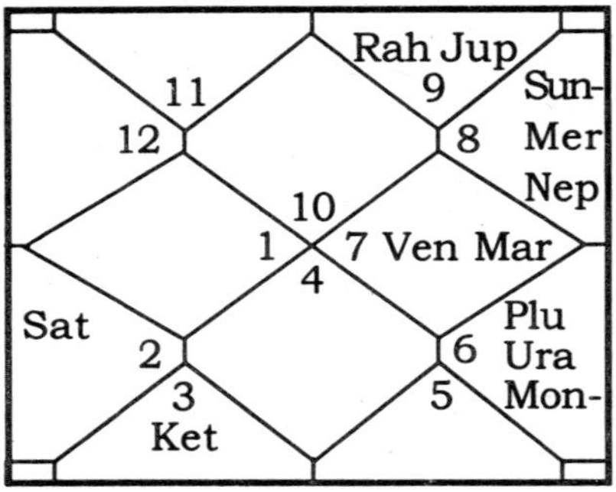

Navāmśa Chart

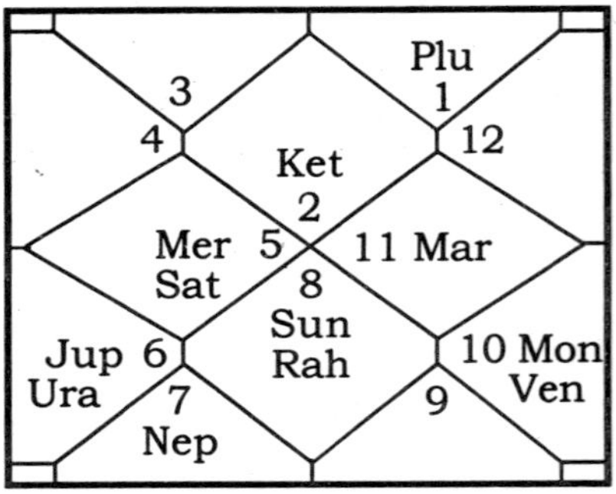

Balance of Vimśottarī Daśā of **Sun 4Y 0M 25D**

Name of Event	Date of Event	Major Period	Sub Period
Marriage	08.5.1996	Rahu	Rahu
Widowhood	17.4.1997	Rahu	Jupiter

started, she suffered the biggest tragedy in loss of her husband.

ACCIDENTIAL LOSS OF HUSBAND DUE TO AIRCRASH (No *kuja doṣa*) widowhood within 4 ¼ years

Case 3.4 – (Horoscope No. 4)

She was an extremely charming girl and got married with a very smart, active, handsome, energetic, loving and caring man around 23 years of age on October 5th, 1973 during *Rāhu*-Jupiter *daśā bhukti*. The husband was working as a Pilot Officer in Indian Airforce. I have pointed out again and again that the placement of Jupiter in the 7th house is damaging for married life and life partner. In this birth chart marriage took place in the sub-period of Jupiter who owns the 8th and 5th house. The plane of her husband crashed on March 2nd, 1978 and that brought the greatest sorrow of widowhood during *Rāhu* – Mercury *daśā bhukti*. The astrological reasons may be analysed as under—

1. The 8th house in a female nativity covers the longevity of husband and *Rāhu* occupies the 8th house under the malefic aspect of Mars and Saturn. This combination alone is powerful enough to bring widowhood.
2. The lord of the 8th house Jupiter joins the 7th house and 7th lord Saturn is afflicted due to placement over the axis of *Rāhu* and *Ketu*.
3. Mercury is the lord of the 2nd house and is associated with Venus and Sun in the 3rd house. Mercury obtains *navāṁśa* of its debilitation and becomes a *mārakeśa* in this birth chart. That is the reason why Mercury *bhukti* which is 8th from *Rāhu*, the *daśā* lord, brought widowhood. Mercury is 7th lord from *Rāhu* and joins the 8th house. Therefore *Rāhu*-Mercury period is extremely adverse for her.

Case : 3.4 *Horoscope No. : 4*

Date	: 07.11.1950	Time	:	01:41:00
Place	: Delhi	Lat 28°:39′		Long 77°:13′
Ayanāmśa	: 23:10:13	Sidereal Time	:	04:21:45

Pln	**Degree**	**Rāśi**	**Nakṣatra**	**Pad**
Asc	15:15:51	Leo	P Phālgunī	1
Sun	20:40:36	Lib	Viśākhā	1
Mon	07:25:07	Vir	U Phālgunī	4
Mar	07:15:06	Sag	Mūlā	3
Mer(C)	23:48:10	Lib	Viśākhā	2
Jup	04:43:39	Aqu	Dhaniṣṭhā	4
Ven(D)	18:53:04	Lib	Svāti	4
Sat	05:32:53	Vir	U Phālgunī	3
Rah(R)	04:21:33	Pis	U Bhādrapadā	1
Ket(R)	04:21:33	Vir	U Phālgunī	3

Lagna Chart

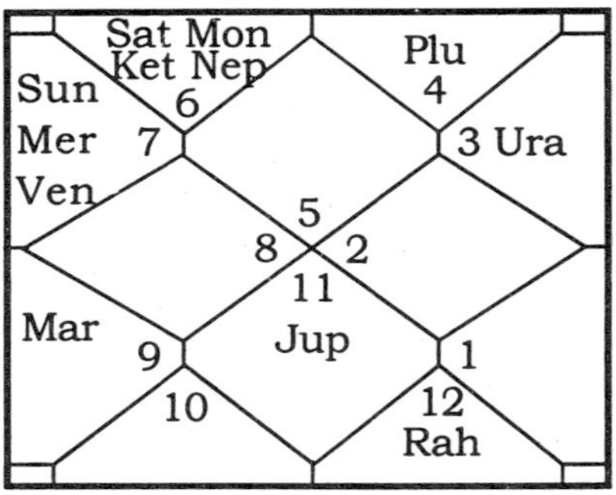

Navāmśa Chart

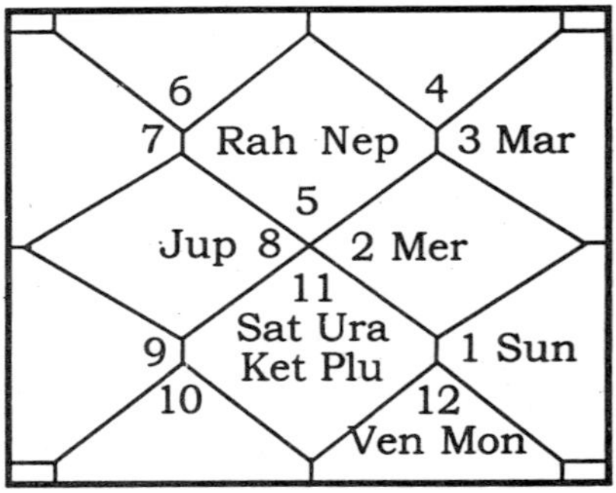

Balance of Vimśottarī Daśā of **Sun 1Y 1M 28D**

Name of Event	Date of Event	Major Period	Sub Period
1st Marriage	05.10.1973	Rahu	Jupiter
Widowhood	02.03.1978	Rahu	Mercury
2nd Marriage	29.09.1979	Rahu	Ketu

4. She got married again on September 29th, 1979. First son from first husband was born on March 2nd, 1978. The second son was born from second husband on December 17th, 1980.

SUICIDE OF HUSBAND AFTER 15 YEARS (NO *kuja doṣa*)

Case 3.5 - (Horoscope No. 5)

Let me illustrate another case of an extremely talented female Class I officer and posted as DGM in Development Authority. She is not a *maṅgalī* but she lost her husband after nearly 15 years of her marriage. The husband was an architect engineer and always suffered from mental depression and committed suicide on December 4th, 2000 during sub-period of Venus in the major period of Moon. The combinations of loss of husband are—

1. The 7th lord Moon falls in the last *pāda* of *Aśvanī* whereby its dispositor is Mars.
2. The *yogakāraka* Venus is under deep combustion and is associated with inimical Sun in the 8th house. The 8th house governs length of life of husband. Both Sun and Venus obtain the *navāṁśa* of Venus where 8th lord Sun is debilitated.
3. Mars and Saturn are placed in the 10th and 1st house respectively and aspect each other. Mars owns the 4th house and its affliction means the matters connected with the happy home of husband and wife will be damaged. Affliction or mutual aspect of Mars and Saturn always plays a negative role in married life.
4. The matters should be taken into consideration from 7th house, 7th lord and *kāraka* Mars as well. Here the 7th lord is Mars and Mars is posited in the 7th from Moon under the aspect of retrograde Saturn.

Case : 3.5 *Horoscope No. : 5*

Date	: 07.09.1963	Time	: 15:30:00
Place	: Allahabad	Lat 25°:27′	Long 81°:50′
Ayanāmśa	: 23:20:42	Sidereal Time	: 14:30:24

Pln	**Degree**	**Rāśi**	**Nakṣatra**	**Pad**
Asc	01:42:47	Cap	Uttarāṣāḍha	2
Sun	20:42:58	Leo	P Phālgunī	3
Mon	09:40:06	Ari	Aśvinī	3
Mar	03:21:45	Lib	Citrā	4
Mer(R)	11:46:55	Vir	Hastā	1
Jup(R)	24:47:55	Pis	Revatī	3
Ven(D)	22:59:38	Leo	P Phālgunī	3
Sat(R)	24:37:39	Cap	Dhaniṣṭhā	1
Rah(R)	25:21:41	Gem	Punarvasu	2
Ket(R)	25:21:41	Sag	Pūrvāṣāḍha	4

Lagna Chart

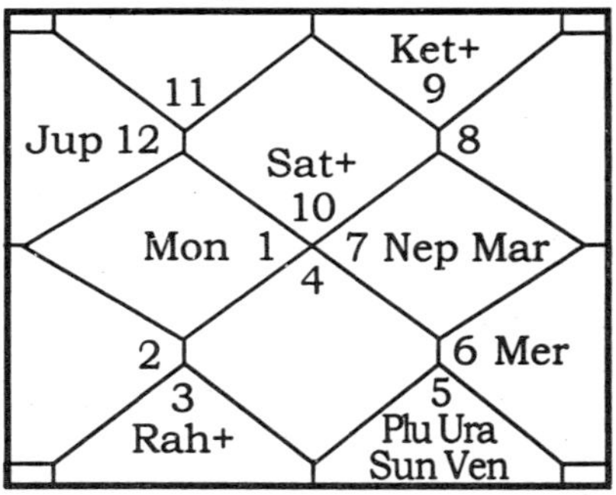

Navāmśa Chart

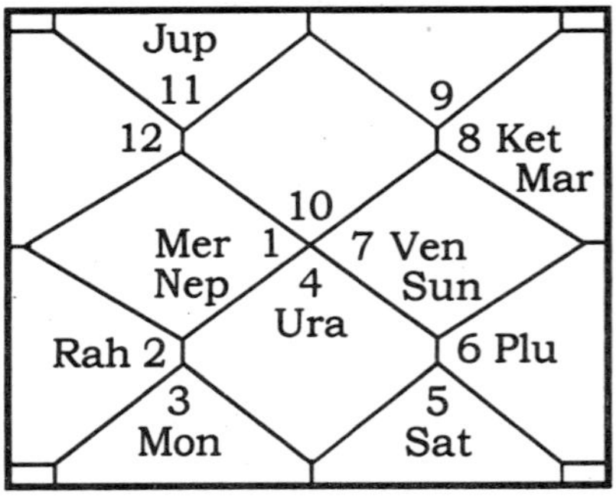

Balance of Vimśottarī Daśā of **Ketu 1Y 11M 2D**

Name of Event	Date of Event	Major Period	Sub Period
Marriage	10.02.1986	Sun	Moon
Widowhood	04.12.2000	Moon	Venus

5. Let us take the sign occupied by Mars as ascendant. It is Libra here and Mars happens a *māraka* for Libra ascendant. The 7th and 2nd lord Mars is heavily afflicted by 4th and 5th lord retrograde Saturn. Thus the matters of the 7th house have been damaged. 4th house should also be taken into consideration. From Mars, the 4th house is occupied by retrograde Saturn and is also aspected by Mars. Thus, the happiness of conjugal bliss has been hampered. This also shows that the married life of 15 years was also miserable.

Loss Of Husband And Young Daughter In A Road Accident (No *kuja doṣa*)

Case No. – 3.6 (Horoscope No. 6)

She is a very charming, extremely fair and pretty woman with sharp features, impressive overall personality. She is very bold, courageous and intelligent. She got married with a promising IPS officer on January 30th, 1975 at 18 years of age. Her life partner who was IG Police, expired in a road accident on July 26th, 2002 when she was passing through the sub-period of Moon in the major period of Moon from February 2nd, 2002 to December 2nd, 2002.

It is very difficult to judge her widowhood in this horoscope and why this fatal incident occurred during the sub-period of Moon in the major period of Moon. Moon is placed in *Jyeṣṭhā nakṣatra* and in the sign of its debilitation and is also aspected by Mars and is associated with Saturn and *Rāhu*. Thus the Moon is heavily afflicted. Therefore, soon after the beginning of the major period of Moon, she suffered tragic death of her husband.

Jupiter in the 8th house gives rise to *saubhāgya yoga* but retrograde Jupiter does not do so. It

Case : 3.6 *Horoscope No. : 6*

Date	: 26.01.1957	Time	:	09:09:44
Place	: Unnao	Lat 26°:32′	Long 80°:30′	
Ayanāmśa	: 23:15:42	Sidereal Time	:	17:22:24

Pln	**Degree**	**Rāśi**	**Nakṣatra**	**Pad**
Asc	23:43:21	Aqu	P Bhādrapadā	2
Sun	12:40:17	Cap	Śrāvaṇa	1
Mon	20:34:13	Sco	Jyeṣṭhā	2
Mar	05:15:20	Ari	Aśvinī	2
Mer	19:08:08	Sag	Pūrvāṣāḍha	2
Jup(R)	08:23:08	Vir	U Phālgunī	4
Ven	23:22:00	Sag	Pūrvāṣāḍha	4
Sat	18:28:53	Sco	Jyeṣṭhā	1
Rah(R)	03:12:51	Sco	Viśākhā	4
Ket(R)	03:12:51	Tau	Kṛtikā	2

Lagna Chart

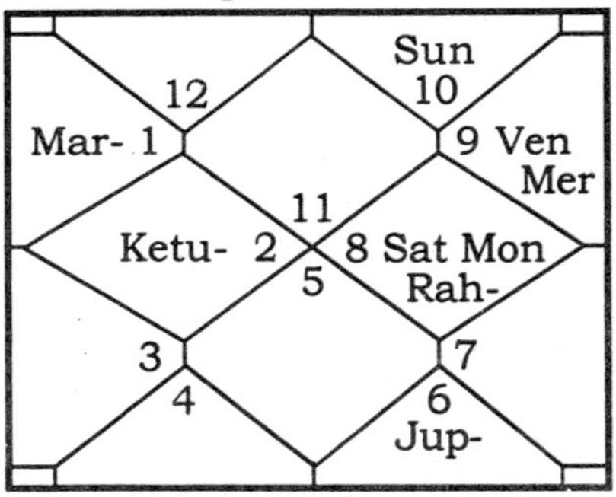

Navāmśa Chart

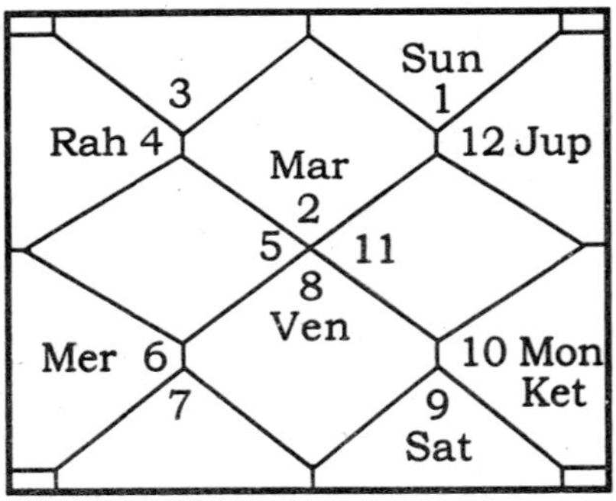

Balance of Vimśottarī Daśā of **Mercury 12Y 0M 8D**

Name of Event	Date of Event	Major Period	Sub Period
Marriage	30.01.1975	Ketu	Saturn
Widowhood	26.07.2002	Moon	Moon

curtails the life of husband. There is mutual exchange between 8th lord Mercury and 11th lord Jupiter. She got married with IPS officer on January 30th, 1975 during *ketu* saturn *daṣā bhukti*.

She is well qualified and has done M.Sc. in Bio-chemistry. She therefore got good job of gazetted level in place of her husband on November 15th, 2002. Moon is the 6th lord and its placement in the 10th house has given her the service of her choice in police department.

Thus, *Jyeṣṭhā* borns suffer either divorce or loss of husband during Moon or Mercury *daśā bhukti*.

Indications For Accidental Death Of Husband

The 8th house indicates happiness of married life and husband in a female nativity whereas 8th from 8th, i.e., 3rd house governs the demise of husband. Here retrograde Jupiter falls in the 8th house and Mars joins 3rd from *lagna* under no benefic aspect. Mars is placed in *Aśvinī nakṣatra* ruled by *Ketu* and Jupiter is also placed in *Maghā nakṣatra* ruled by *ketu*. Moreover, Venus occupies the 11th house of its enemy Jupiter and is hemmed between enemies, Sun, Moon and Saturn giving rise to *pāpakartari yoga*. Venus also obtains *navāṁśa* of Mars and mutual exchange is also there between Mars and Venus. These factors are responsible for tragic accident of husband.

The 7th lord Sun occupies 12th in Capricorn and obtains *navāṁśa* of Mars. Sun receives the malefic aspect of Saturn. Thus the 7th house, 4th house (sweet home) and the 8th house are badly damaged in one or the other way and that caused the accidental death of her husband.

Rule: If a female is born in *Jyeṣṭhā nakṣatra*, she may suffer tragedy of her married life during Moon or Mercury *daśā bhukti.* Retrograde Jupiter in the 8th house becomes a malefic and does not save widowhood particularly if malefics are placed in the 8th from Jupiter.

WIDOWHOOD WITHIN TWO MONTHS OF MARRIAGE (*aṣṭama maṅgalī*) Husband Crushed By A Train
Case 3.7 – (Horoscope No. 7)

This is the horoscope of another unfortunate girl. She was born in Aries ascendant with debilitated Saturn and exalted Sun. In fact combination of Saturn and Sun denies happiness of marriage provided this combination has anything to do with 7th house. Mars occupies the 8th house under retrograde motion in own sign. Here Moon is hemmed between two first rate malefics. She got married on April 27th, 1999 during Saturn-Venus period. Here 7th and 2nd lord Venus is *mārakeśa* for Aries ascendant and is associated with *Rāhu* and obtains inimical *navāṁśa* of Jupiter. She suffered widowhood on June 27th, 1999 just after two months when her husband was crushed under train. Marriage of the native was performed during sub-period of Venus which happens a killer for Aries ascendant and its placement in the 12th house is further bad, as it falls over the axis of nodes and is aspected by retrograde Jupiter. This period of *mārakeśa* Venus killed her husband. Marriages should not be performed in such *māraka* period or under those periods which indicate adversities. She lost her mother around 12 years of age on October 19th, 1981, lost her father on April 4th, 1993. After the loss of husband, she is working as teacher in a small school to meet her both ends. It is not out of place to mention that she had done M.A., B.Ed., before her marriage.

Case : 3.7 *Horoscope No. : 7*

Date	: 02.05.1969	Time :	06:04:00
Place	: Lucknow	Lat 26°:50′	Long 80°:54′
Ayanāmśa	: 23:25:42	Sidereal Time :	20:36:37

Pln	**Degree**	**Rāśi**	**Nakṣatra**	**Pad**
Asc	27:38:03	Ari	Kṛtikā	1
Sun	18:00:27	Ari	Bharanī	2
Mon	15:22:26	Lib	Svāti	3
Mar(R)	23:12:17	Sco	Jyeṣṭhā	2
Mer	08:23:59	Tau	Kṛtikā	4
Jup(R)	03:21:36	Vir	U Phālgunī	3
Ven	17:09:40	Pis	Revatī	1
Sat(C)	06:50:06	Ari	Aśvinī	3
Rah(R)	06:12:44	Pis	U Bhādrapadā	1
Ket(R)	06:12:44	Vir	U Phālgunī	3

Lagna Chart

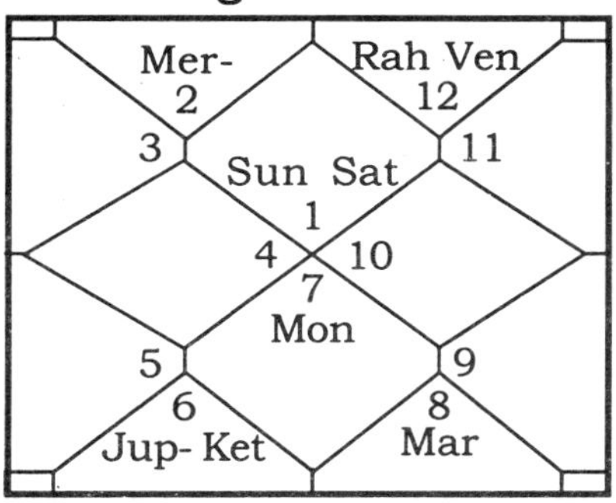

Navāmśa Chart

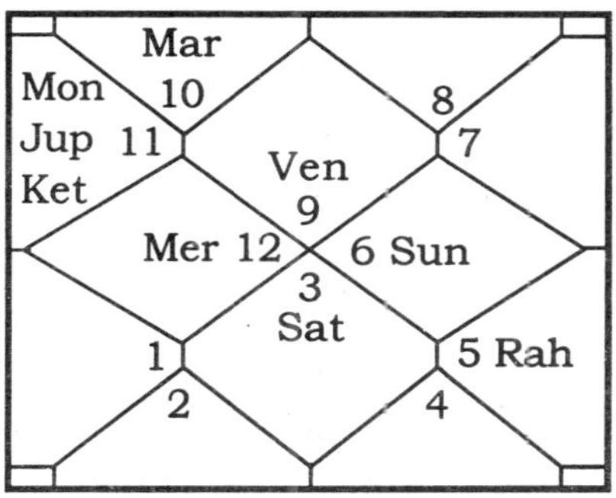

Balance of Vimśottarī Daśā of **Rahu 6Y 2M 28D**

Name of Event	Date of Event	Major Period	Sub Period
Marriage	27.04.1999	Saturn	Venus
Widowhood	27:06.1999	Saturn	Venus

Venus falls in Saturn's constellation *uttarā bhādrapadā* where Moon falls in *Rāhu* constellation *svāti* and Moon is placed under *pāpakartari yoga*. Saturn is debilitated and Venus and Saturn are 12th from each other. Thus, during this period Saturn and its dispositor were quite active during the concerned *daśā bhukti* which resulted into the death of her life partner. Following aphorisms hold good for the planetary combinations in this present case.

Loss Of Husband Within 1 Year After Marriage

Case 3.8 – (Horoscope No. 8)

She was an exceptionally beautiful, very fair girl of outstanding merits of features and figure. She got married in May 1972 at 17 years of age with a Mechanical Engineer. During the sub-period of Mars in the major period of Mars, she was in a family way in advance stage. Around May 1973, when she was undergoing the sub-period of *Rāhu* in the major period of Mars, she pressurised her husband to go somewhere alongwith her. The husband agreed and they went to a hill. Both of them stayed at a very pleasant place. She was extremely happy as this trip happened just before delivery. After spending some time there, her husband started the jeep and tried to reach her just to avoid a few hundred feets of walk for his wife, due to her pregnancy. The jeep went out of his control and toppled hundreds of feets down. The husband immediately expired.

In this birth chart, the 8th house is occupied by the lord of *lagna* Venus, malefic *Rāhu* and Moon. The 8th house indicates life of husband, this combination is aspected by Jupiter and *Ketu* from 2nd house. In this horoscope, Jupiter and Mercury both are retrograde, 2nd house is occupied by retrograde Jupiter and 2nd lord Mercury is also

It is believed that placement of Jupiter in the 8th house gives rise to *akhaṇḍa saubhāgya yoga* irrespective of its being malefic or benefic for the particular ascendant. In this horoscope Jupiter is the lord of 4th and 7th house and joins the 8th. Many so-called astrologers foretold her to be blessed with *saubhāgya yoga* due to placement of Jupiter in the 8th house. But it did not happen so because her husband died after 6 years of marriage and that too during the major period of Jupiter. It should be carefully noted that the lord of the 7th house if placed in martian sign in the 8th house and receives the aspect of Mars, she will definitely loose her husband in early-married life. This is a classical case of widowhood where the rules are applicable absolutely.

Husband Shot Himself After Seeing Physical Involvement Of His Wife With Another Person

Case 3.10 – (Horoscope No.10)

She was born in Leo ascendant with Mars in the 7th house. The 7th lord Saturn is also placed in the sign of Aries, Mars obtains *navāṁśa* of Saturn. She was married with a very handsome IPS officer on June 4th, 1964 during Moon-Jupiter period. She invited her lover on February 28th, 1982 when her husband was out of station. Somehow as her husband had certain doubts regarding her relations with the other person, he came back around midnight and was deeply shocked to find his doubts confirmed. He committed suicide on the same night.

In the birth chart *yogakāraka* Mars is posited in the 7th house and *Ketu* in the 8th house. I find that *Ketu* must be attached an importance equal to Mars. Here *Ketu* in the 8th and Mars in the 7th show

Case : 3.10 *Horoscope No. : 10*

Date	: 24.05.1941	Time	: 11:32:18
Place	: Varanasi	Lat 25°:20′	Long 83°:00′
Ayanāmśa	: 23:02:16	Sidereal Time	: 03:40:06

Pln	**Degree**	**Rāśi**	**Nakṣatra**	**Pad**
Asc	05:35:20	Leo	Maghā	2
Sun	09:37:54	Tau	Kṛtikā	4
Mon	18:04:19	Ari	Bharanī	2
Mar	12:21:27	Aqu	Satabhiṣā	2
Mer	28:33:17	Tau	Mṛgśirā	2
Jup(C)	06:25:27	Tau	Kṛtikā	3
Ven(C)	18:52:10	Tau	Rohiṇī	3
Sat(C)	26:55:52	Ari	Kṛtikā	1
Rah(R)	06:56:37	Vir	U Phālgunī	4
Ket(R)	06:56:37	Pis	U Bhādrapadā	2

Lagna Chart

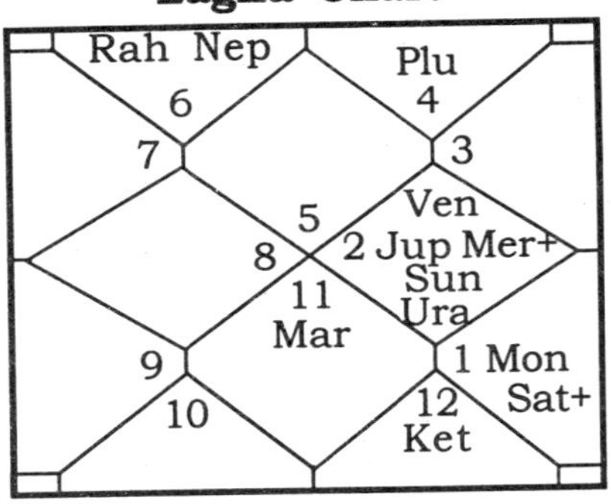

Navāmśa Chart

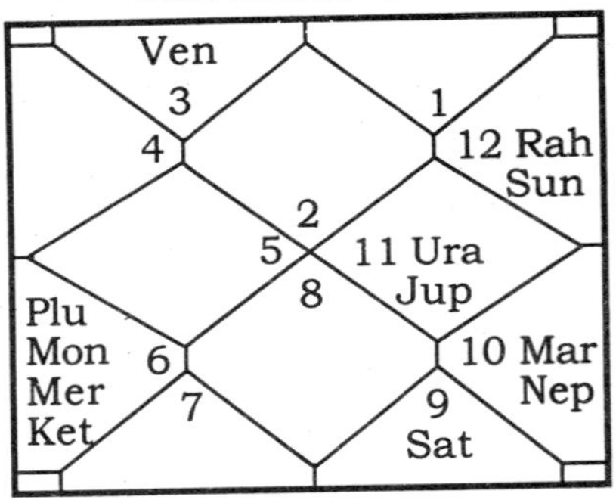

Balance of Vimśottarī Daśā of **Venus 12Y 10M 21D**

Name of Event	Date of Event	Major Period	Sub Period
Marriage	04.06.1964	Moon	Jupiter
Widowhood	28.2.1982	Rahu	Jupiter

widowhood. Sages have also mentioned that malefic in the 7th causes widowhood. The 8th house is hemmed between first rate malefics Mars and Saturn. Mars obtains *navāṁśa* of Saturn and the 7th lord Saturn falls in the *navāṁśa* of Jupiter in the 8th house from *navāṁśa lagna*. Thus Jupiter, the 8th lord caused widowhood in its own *bhukti* in the major period of *Rāhu*.

Suffered Widowhood Within One And Half Year As Husband Was Killed By His Own Wife

Case 3.11 – (Horoscope No. 11)

The lord of the 7th house Mars in Scorpio joins the 7th house itself in association with 2nd and 5th lord Mercury and *Ketu*. Saturn occupies the 10th house and there is mutual aspect between Mars and Saturn. She was deeply involved with a muslim boy. Marriage could not be possible with that boy as she was Hindu. Due to utmost pressure of parents, she got married in October 1987 (Jupiter) with a handsome engineer boy. She was blessed with a daughter in October 1988 (Jupiter) and soon after she diplomatically, cleverly and intelligently managed the murder of her husband in January 1989. Here 5th lord Mercury is placed with 7th lord Mars. This is also a *Madan Gopal Yoga* which makes one adulterous. Mercury provides her negative intelligence and *Ketu* further enhanced the intensity of Mars. Mutual aspect between Mars and Saturn further aggravates the intensity of Mars. In *Bhāva Kautūhalam, Jīvanāha* mentions in *chapter* 9 that the placement of Mercury in the 7th house makes one adulterous and she kills her husband if Mercury is afflicted. The Woman native śloka '14' mentions a critical condition of placement of Mercury in the 7th house in Virgo only. In other *ślokas* as mentioned earlier, three malefics in the 7th house

Case : 3.11 *Horoscope No. : 11*

Date	: 02.11.1965	Time	:	19:42:00
Place	: Aligarh	Lat 27°:54′		Long 78°:04′
Ayanāmśa	: 23:22:30	Sidereal Time	:	22:10:50

Pln	Degree	Rāśi	Nakṣatra	Pad
Asc	23:19:48	Tau	Rohiṇī	4
Sun	16:34:27	Lib	Svāti	3
Mon	00:03:26	Aqu	Dhaniṣṭhā	3
Mar	27:51:24	Sco	Jyeṣṭhā	4
Mer	07:04:43	Sco	Anurādhā	2
Jup(R)	07:37:19	Gem	Ārdrā	1
Ven	03:10:44	Sag	Mūlā	1
Sat(R)	17:13:41	Aqu	Satabhiṣā	4
Rah(R)	11:35:24	Tau	Rohiṇī	1
Ket(R)	11:35:24	Sco	Anurādhā	3

Lagna Chart

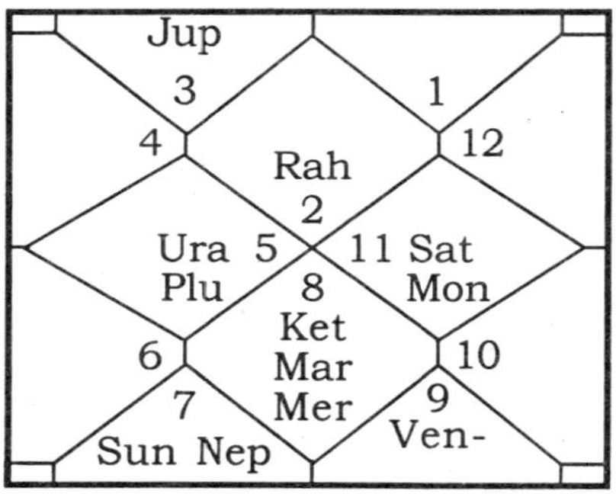

Navāmśa Chart

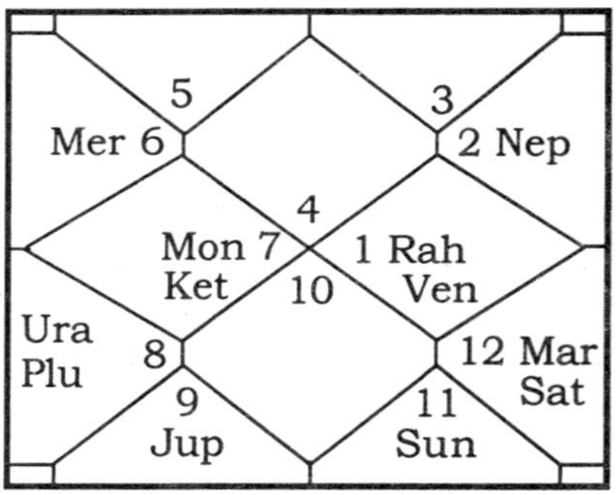

Balance of Vimśottarī Daśā of **Mars 3Y 5M 19D**

Name of Event	Date of Event	Major Period	Sub Period
Marriage	October, 1987	Jupiter	Jupiter
Widowhood	January, 1989	Jupiter	Jupiter

are extremely bad, such woman kills her husband and goes to her lover. In this case, three malefics Mars, *Ketu* and Mercury are associated in the 7th house. These are aspected by Rāhu. How appropriate sages have mentioned and according to concerning *śloka*, she should have killed her husband to marry her lover. This may be noted that she got married in the sub-period of Jupiter in the major period of Jupiter running from April 23rd, 1987 to June 1st, 1989. Here Jupiter is a malefic as it is 8th and 11th lord, occupies the 2nd house under retrograde motion and aspects *lagna* lord Venus in the 8th house. Retrograde Jupiter is always bad for female nativities if it is posited in or aspects the 8th house. The husband was killed by her in the same *daśā bhukti*. Jupiter falls in *ārdrā nakṣatra* and in Gemini sign and as it is 8th from 7th house and its lord, it killed her husband in its *daśā bhukti*. The 2nd house indicates death of the husband being 8th from 7th.

Loss Of Husband After Two Years Of Marriage In A Road Accident

Case 3.12 – (Horoscope No. 12)

Here Mars is placed in the 7th house in Scorpio. Thus she is a strong *maṅgalī* girl. Jupiter occupies the *lagna*, thus there is mutual aspect between Jupiter and Mars. Her father was Chairman of UPSEB and consulted me about the matching of horoscope with a doctor boy. He was not *maṅgalī*. I strongly advised against the proposal. Many astrologers of Varanasi advised for the marriage because *kuja doṣa* was neutralised by Jupiter's mutual aspect, according to them. Mr. Chairman did not give any importance to my observation that *kuja doṣa* gets enhanced by Jupiter's association or aspect. The native was married on February 9th, 1974 during Ketu-Moon *daśā bhukti*. The husband was very handsome and

Case : 3.12 *Horoscope No. : 12*

Date	: 16.02.1954	Time :	11:36:00
Place	: Calcutta	Lat 22°:30′	Long 88°:20′
Ayanāmśa	: 23:13:15	Sidereal Time :	21:42:07

Pln	**Degree**	**Rāśi**	**Nakṣatra**	**Pad**
Asc	13:30:54	Tau	Rohiṇī	2
Sun	03:49:06	Aqu	Dhaniṣṭhā	4
Mon	16:01:43	Can	Puṣya	4
Mar	10:20:32	Sco	Anurādhā	3
Mer	21:31:40	Aqu	P Bhādrapadā	1
Jup	23:14:59	Tau	Rohiṇī	4
Ven(C)	07:58:57	Aqu	Satabhiṣā	1
Sat	16:07:52	Lib	Svāti	3
Rah(R)	00:29:49	Cap	Uttarāṣāḍha	2
Ket(R)	00:29:49	Can	Punarvasu	4

Lagna Chart

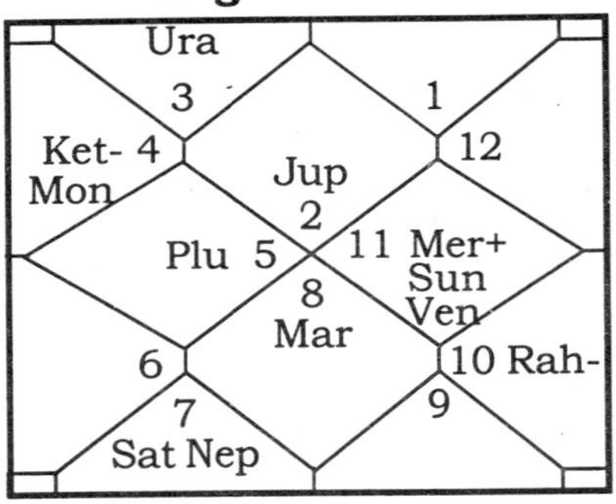

Navāmśa Chart

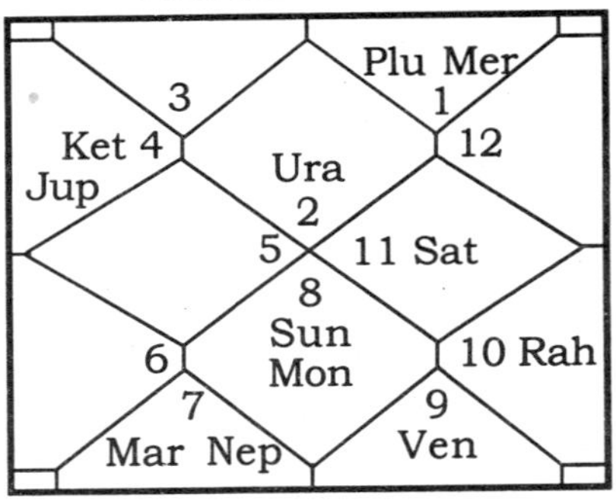

Balance of Vimśottarī Daśā of **Saturn 0Y 10M 27D**

Name of Event	Date of Event	Major Period	Sub Period
Marriage	09.02.1974	Ketu	Moon
Widowhood	16.03.1976	Ketu	Jupiter

smart doctor who got crushed by the car on March 16th, 1976. Thus she suffered widowhood during sub-period of Jupiter and in the major period of Ketu. According to Acharya H.N. Katwe, if Saturn is just behind Mars, then it is damaging and makes one strong *maṅgalī*. The 8th house from *lagna* is occupied by *Rāhu*. Malefics in the 8th house are bad for long lasting married life.

Loss Of Husband Within Ten Months Of Marriage In An Air Crash

Case 3.13 – (Horoscope No. 13)

For Libra ascendant, position of Mars must be carefully examined as Mars owns 2nd and 7th house and thus it possesses the strength to kill the native. Mars falls in the 8th house, so either the marriage will be delayed and she will lead a miserable life or will be separated or loose her husband or may meet with untimely and unnatural end of her life depending upon the various other factors. Jupiter is the lord of the 8th and 4th house and it is placed in the 2nd house under retrograde motion and it is aspecting 8th house as well.

In the present case of a lady producer of AIR, the affliction of the 7th lord Mars may be noted as it falls in the 8th house under the mutual aspect with Saturn. Thus the 7th, 8th and 2nd houses are under the influence of Mars and Saturn. Sun also obtains *navāṁśa* of Saturn. These combinations delayed her marriage though she was extremely beautiful and charming, till 34 years of age. She was married on March 11th, 1961 during Moon-*Rāhu* period. Once she had gone to airport to see off her husband and saw that the plane caught fire within few seconds after taking off. Widowhood was cursed on her within 10 months of her marriage on January 10th, 1962 during sub-period of Jupiter and

Case : 3.13 *Horoscope No. : 13*

Date	: 06.03.1927	Time	:	21:15:00
Place	: Ambala	Lat 30°:19′		Long 76°:49′
Ayanāmśa	: 22:50:07	Sidereal Time	:	07:45:47

Pln	**Degree**	**Rāśi**	**Nakṣatra**	**Pad**
Asc	00:04:12	Lib	Citrā	3
Sun	22:14:38	Aqu	P Bhādrapadā	1
Mon	02:36:38	Ari	Aśvinī	1
Mar	13:49:06	Tau	Rohiṇī	2
Mer(R)	04:15:35	Pis	U Bhādrapadā	1
Jup(C)	18:17:02	Aqu	Satabhiṣā	4
Ven	17:10:33	Pis	Revatī	1
Sat	14:43:21	Sco	Anurādhā	4
Rah(R)	11:22:42	Gem	Ārdrā	2
Ket(R)	11:22:42	Sag	Mūlā	4

Lagna Chart

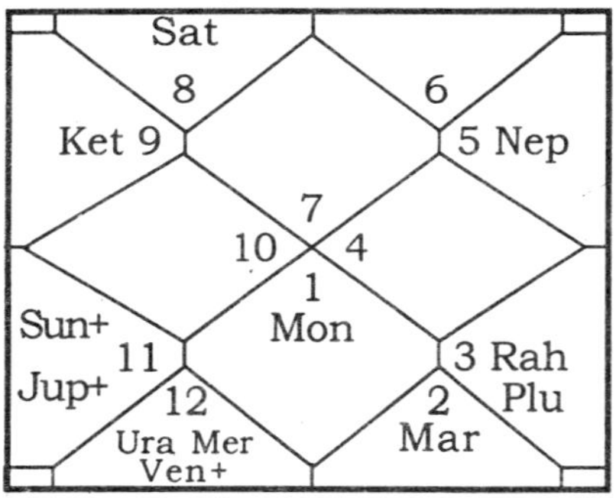

Navāmśa Chart

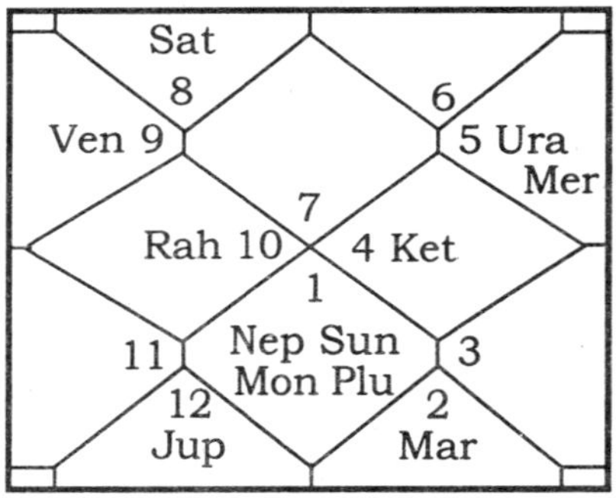

Balance of Vimśottarī Daśā of **Ketu 5Y 7M 16D**

Name of Event	Date of Event	Major Period	Sub Period
Marriage	11.03.1961	Moon	Rahu
Widowhood	10.01.1962	Moon	Jupiter

in the major period of Moon. The ascendant, Mars, Saturn and Moon have gained strength by obtaining vargottama *navāṁśa.* The 2nd and 7th lord Mars in the 8th, Saturn in the 2nd resulted in widowhood. Saturn has further reduced her happiness of conjugal life as it is placed in the sign of Mars and in own constellation *anurādhā.* The 4th house should also be judged for confirmation. Here Saturn the 4th lord has been damaged due to mutual aspect of Mars. The 4th house has further spoiled the happiness of home as it is under *pāpakartari yoga.*

It may be carefully noted that placement of Mars in the 8th house in Taurus for female nativities will result into accidental death of husband. The possibility of widowhood will be further strengthened if malefic aspects of Mars or Saturn is identical to 8th or 2nd house.

HUSBAND WAS KILLED BY CRIMINALS AFTER 8 YEARS OF MARRIAGE UNDER MYSTERIOUS CIRCUMSTANCES (NO *kuja doṣa*)

Case 3.14 – (Horoscope No. 14)

She was leading a very happy and prosperous married life with her loving, caring and accommodating husband. The husband was an Industrialist and multimillionaire. Certain criminals demanded a huge sum of money. He refused to give money inspite of repeated threats. That resulted into his murder on the evening of November 18th, 1999 (Thursday). The native was in hospital in labour-pain to deliver the child. There was difference of only a few hours in the murder of her husband and delivery of the son. None had the courage to tell her about this great tragic killing of her husband. She was informed only the next day just before final departure of the body of her husband for cremation.

She was born in Scorpio ascendant. There is no

Case : 3.14 *Horoscope No. : 14*

Date	: 12.08.1968	Time :	14:45:00
Place	: Jhansi	Lat 25°:27′	Long 78°:34′
Ayanāmśa	: 23:25:04	Sidereal Time :	11:52:49

Pln	**Degree**	**Rāśi**	**Nakṣatra**	**Pad**
Asc	24:16:21	Sco	Jyeṣṭhā	3
Sun	26:17:16	Can	Aśleṣā	3
Mon	14:44:16	Pis	U Bhādrapadā	4
Mar(C)	10:53:24	Can	Puṣya	3
Mer(C)	01:27:25	Leo	Maghā	1
Jup	17:03:09	Leo	P Phālgunī	2
Ven	10:51:41	Leo	Maghā	4
Sat(R)	02:06:36	Ari	Aśvinī	1
Rah(R)	17:14:30	Pis	Revatī	1
Ket(R)	17:14:30	Vir	Hastā	3

Lagna Chart

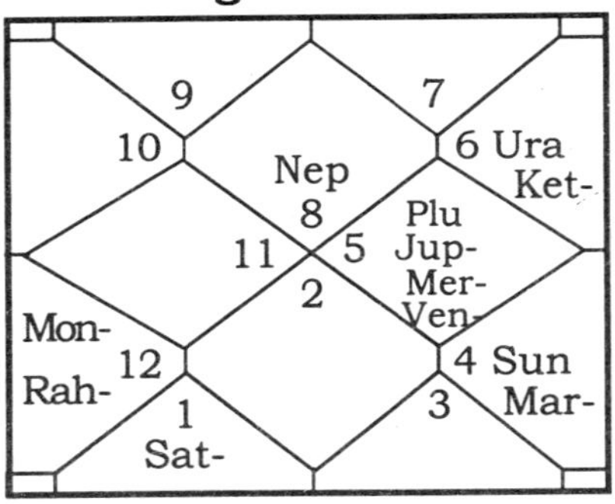

Navāmśa Chart

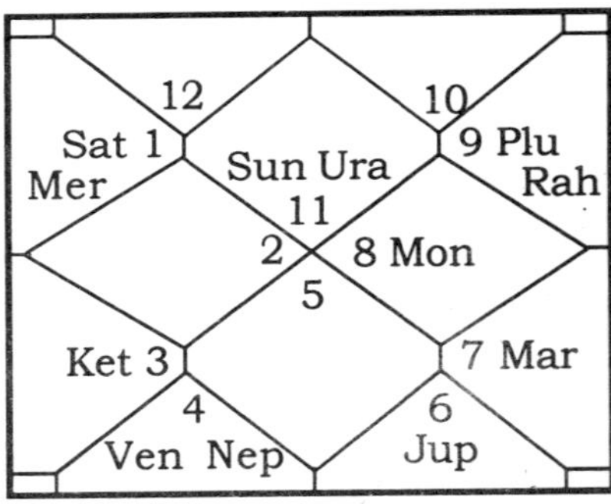

Balance of Vimśottarī Daśā of **Saturn 2Y 8M 29D**

Name of Event	Date of Event	Major Period	Sub Period
Marriage	1990	Ketu	Moon
Widowhood	18.11.1999	Venus	Moon

planet in the 7th or 8th house which may indicate widowhood or any such tragedy. It is not easy to foretell about the murder of her husband by looking into her birth chart.

1. In *Bhāva* Chart, the *lagna* lord Mars falls in the 8th house and obtains *navāṁśa* of the 7th lord Venus. This is certainly adverse for the life of husband.
2. The 7th and 8th lords Venus and Mercury occupy 10th house under *pāpakartari yoga*. Therefore the matters of the 7th and 8th house have been spoiled.
3. The lord of 8th house Mercury obtains *navāṁśa* of Mars in association with debilitated Saturn and that too under mutual aspect between malefic Mars, Saturn and Mercury. Thus the 8th lord Mercury is heavily afflicted by Mars and Saturn. Therefore, it resulted into the murder of husband. There may be other reason for loss of husband. How can we explain the murder of her husband by examination of the chart of the female?
4. The 8th lord Mercury falls in a fiery sign Leo and fiery *navāṁśa* Aries. Mercury falls in *Ketu's nakṣatra maghā*. *Ketu* also acts like Mars. Moreover Mercury is hemmed between Mars and *Ketu* in *Rāśi* chart as well as *Bhāva chart*. In *navāṁśa*, Mercury obtains Mars *navāṁśa* and is aspected by Mars and is associated with malefic Saturn. Thus 8th lord Mercury is under the heavy affliction of Mars, Saturn and *Ketu*. Violent planets, fiery sign and 8th lord indicate the assassination of husband.
5. The assassination of her husband took place on November 18th, 1999 when sub-period of Moon and major period of Venus was under operation. From Venus-Moon is 12th lord and occupies the 8th house from Venus. Moon also obtains

navāṁśa of Mars due to being in debilitation. Moon is posited in Saturn's *nakṣatra uttarā bhādrapadā* over the axis of *Rāhu* and *Ketu*. Moon is closely associated with *Rāhu*, therefore Moon will act like *Rāhu*. As soon as sub-period of Moon came under operation on October 27th, 1999 to December 2nd, 1999, the planning of killing was done and executed exactly on November 18th, 1999.

Loss Of Husband In A Road Accident

Case 3.15 – (Horoscope No. 15)

She is beautiful daughter of an IAS Officer. She was working in a five star hotel as Assistant Manager. During the year 1990 very handsome and smart boy saw her and proposed for marriage. The boy was class I IES officer in Railways. The proposal came to me. I saw that *Rāhu* and Mars were placed in the 8th house in close conjunction in Aquarius. I was not happy with this match but the parents of the girl could not refuse the proposal. I advised *Viṣṇu Pratimā Vivāha* because the marriage was inevitable. Certain other remedies for prevention of widowhood were also suggested. The marriage took place on February 27th, 1991 during Moon-*Rāhu daśā bhukti*. She was blessed with a son soon after marriage and was leading extremely happy married life with her loving, caring, accommo-dating and handsome life partner. But her son expired when he was hardly an year old and the whole family was doomed into dark. Later on she was blessed with another son, but the black clouds were still roaming around her. The husband left such a nice job and started family business. There was a turn over of hundred crores a year. He lost all his money and property due to one very bad incident of kidnapping of his father. The family of

Case : 3.15 *Horoscope No. : 15*

Date	: 29.12.1969	Time :	20:27:00
Place	: Baraut	Lat 29°:06′	Long 77°:15′
Ayanāmśa	: 23:26:20	Sidereal Time :	02:37:33

Pln	**Degree**	**Rāśi**	**Nakṣatra**	**Pad**
Asc	22:40:39	Can	Aśleṣā	2
Sun	14:17:37	Sag	Pūrvāṣāḍha	1
Mon	18:14:28	Leo	P Phālgunī	2
Mar	17:01:26	Aqu	Satabhiṣā	4
Mer	03:52:18	Cap	Uttarāṣāḍha	3
Jup	08:33:18	Lib	Svāti	1
Ven(C)	08:01:19	Sag	Mūlā	3
Sat(R)	08:38:29	Ari	Aśvinī	3
Rah(S)	20:46:00	Aqu	P Bhādrapadā	1
Ket(S)	20:46:00	Leo	P Phālgunī	3

Lagna Chart

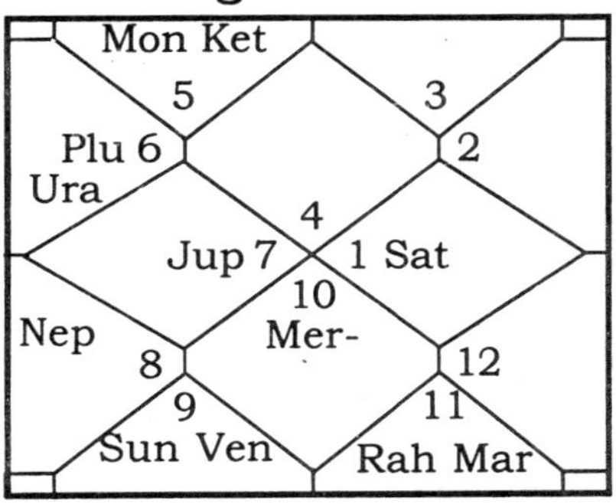

Navāmśa Chart

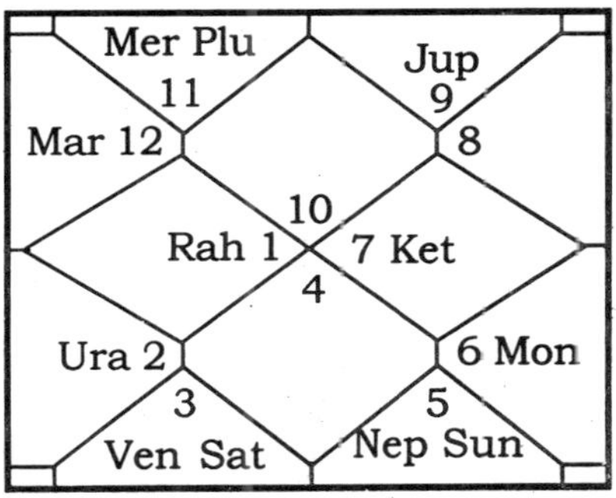

Balance of Vimśottarī Daśā of **Venus 12Y 7M 20D**

Name of Event	Date of Event	Major Period	Sub Period
Marriage	27.02.1991	Moon	Rahu
Widowhood	09.08.2001	Mars	Saturn

multimillionaire went into deep grief and setbacks. Her husband was forced to join private job to meet both ends. He was picking up well. The female native planned to visit Jaipur with her son and husband. They were going from Delhi to Jaipur and there is six lane, extremely good road, where there was no possibility of accident. The planets brought the biggest calamity in her life when head on collision with a Tata Siera took place on August 9th, 2001 during sub-period of Saturn in the major period of Mars. Her husband expired on the spot and she received multiple fractures in her body. Incidentally she got the best treatment in Apollo Hospital of Delhi for about six months. At present, she is staying with her parent–in-laws and leading a maladious and lonely life of a widow. She faced the biggest misery and in flash of a second blossoms of her life were crushed and everything went into endless dark, during Mars-Saturn period.

Now let us analyse her horoscope. There is mutual exchange between Mars and Saturn. Mars is placed in the 8th house in Aquarius and Saturn in Aries in the sign of debilitation in the 10th house. Here 7th and 8th lord Saturn occupies Martian sign. *Yogakāraka Mars* is closely associated with *Rāhu*. This is a strong indication of widowhood. There is strong belief among astrologers that aspect of Jupiter over Mars neutralises or cancels the *kuja doṣa*. Here Jupiter aspects the 8th house. Mars and *Rāhu*, who join the 8th house and the 7th and 8th lord Saturn. If Jupiter cancelled the *kuja doṣa* why she suffered a tragic death of her husband? It is also believed that the placement of Mars in Leo or Aquarius anywhere in the birth chart does not give rise to *kuja doṣa*. This is stated in the *ślokas* mentioned earlier.

In this case, we clearly see Mars joins 8th house in Aquarius and is also aspected by Jupiter. The aspect of Jupiter has strengthened the 7th and 8th lord Saturn. Why did she suffer widowhood? if *kuja doṣa* was cancelled and Jupiter's aspect over Mars and Saturn nullifies such adversity. I, therefore, opine that the placement of Mars in Aquarius or Leo does not cancel *kuja doṣa* and the aspect of Jupiter or Moon over Mars (as that can be seen in the case as Jupiter and Moon both aspect Mars), does not cancel *kuja doṣa* of any kind. In my experience, the *kuja doṣa* gets enhanced due to aspect or conjunction of Moon and Jupiter.

In this horoscope, there is mutual exchange between 4th and 6th lord also as 4th lord Venus joins 6th and 6th lord Jupiter joins 4th. This is an adverse combination which indicates loss of happiness, prosperity, property and peace.

Placement of the 12th lord Mercury in the 7th house is also adverse as it is aspected by *mārakeśa* and debilitated Saturn. Let me explain that the loss of husband can take place during *daśā bhukti* of 7th and 8th lord or planets placed therein or during the period of occupants or lord of 2nd house or otherwise during the period of Jupiter, if it is retrograde or afflicted and has a concern with the life of husband. I believe that Jupiter is the *kāraka* of *suhāga,* i.e., the life of husband where Mars is the significator of husband.

Loss Of Husband Due To Massive Heart Attack

Case No. 3.16 (Horoscope No. 16)

This horoscope belongs to a most charming, captivating and attractive doctor who had a love-marriage with a smart ENT surgeon. They were leading a very happy married life. Suddenly her

Case : 3.16 *Horoscope No. : 16*

Date	: 23.10.1955	Time	:	20:34:00
Place	: Mainpuri	Lat 27°:14		Long 79°:01′
Ayanāmśa	: 23:14:39	Sidereal Time	:	22:25:05

Pln	**Degree**	**Rāśi**	**Nakṣatra**	**Pad**
Asc	26:34:20	Tau	Mṛgśirā	1
Sun	06:11:19	Lib	Citrā	4
Mon	02:30:18	Cap	Uttarāṣāḍha	2
Mar	13:15:53	Vir	Hastā	1
Mer	19:58:46	Vir	Hastā	3
Jup	03:43:47	Leo	Maghā	2
Ven	19:58:32	Lib	Svāti	4
Sat	27:42:05	Lib	Viśākhā	3
Rah(S)	25:18:02	Sco	Jyeṣṭhā	3
Ket(S)	25:18:02	Tau	Mṛgśirā	1

Lagna Chart

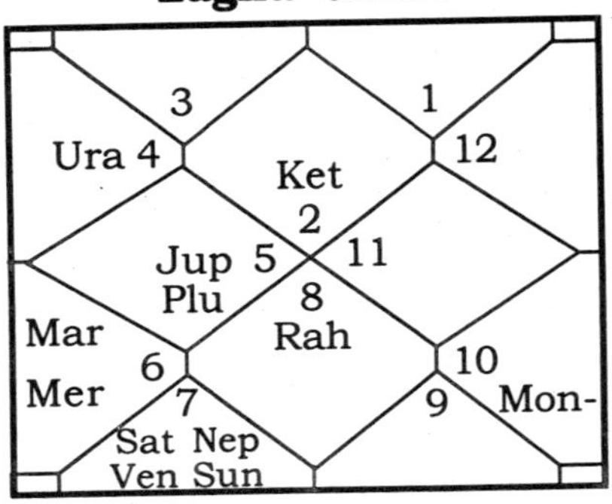

Navāmśa Chart

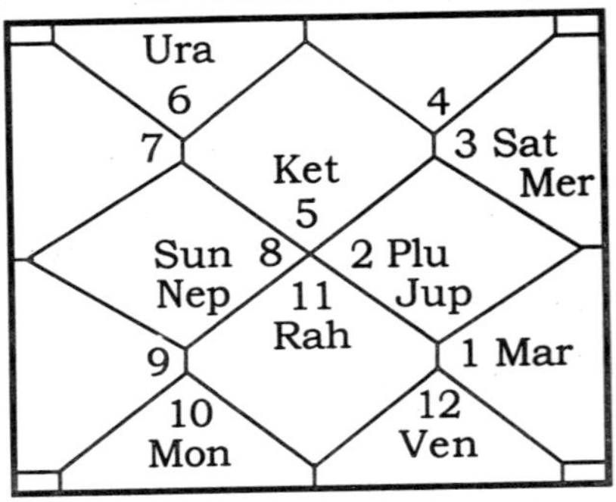

Balance of Vimśottarī Daśā of **Sun 3Y 4M 14D**

Name of Event	Date of Event	Major Period	Sub Period
Marriage	17.05.1981	Rahu	Saturn
Widowhood	04.11.1996	Jupiter	Saturn

husband met with a massive heart-attack. She got married in 1981 and she lost her husband on November 5th, 1996 during Jupiter-Saturn period. It may be noted that Saturn is *yogakāraka* and joins the 7th house, 12th and 7th lord Mars occupies the 5th in association with 5th lord Mercury. The aspect of Mars over the 8th house, conjunction of *Rāhu*, Venus and Saturn in the 7th house is responsible for loss of her husband. 7th lord Mars is conjoined with the Mercury who is *mārakeśa*. Here the affliction of 4th house can also be seen. 8th lord Jupiter occupies the 4th house and 4th lord Sun is debilitated in the 6th and is hemmed between Mars, Saturn and *Rāhu* giving rise to *pāpakartari yoga*. In *bhāva* chart, Saturn and Sun conjoin in the 6th house. Jupiter's aspect also over the 8th could not save widowhood and the death of husband took place in major period of Jupiter in the sub-period of Saturn. Here we can see that the placement of Mars in the 5th house is almost as adverse as Mars in the 7th or 8th house. She had a love marriage on May 17th, 1981 during *Rāhu* Saturn *daṣā bhukti* and blessed with two female children on February 20th, 1984 and October 12th, 1987 respectively.

Husband Expired In An Air Crash After Six years Of Marriage

Case No. 3.17 (Horoscope No. 17)

This is the horoscope of Maneka Gandhi, wife of Sanjay Gandhi and daughter-in-law of Smt. Indira Gandhi, late PM of India. She was born in Cancer ascendant. Mars who is a *yogakāraka*, occupies the 8th house under mutual aspect of Jupiter and Sun. She was born in Aries-Moon sign and *Aśvinī- nakṣatra* which comes under *Mūla*. This sign is of Mars and

Case : 3 17 *Horoscope No. : 17*

Date	: 26.08.1956	Time	:	04:10:00
Place	: A.F.C.	Lat 28°:37′		Long 77°:12′
Ayanāmśa	: 23:15:21	Sidereal Time	:	02:05:26

Pln	**Degree**	**Rāśi**	**Nakṣatra**	**Pad**
Asc	15:51:56	Can	Puṣya	4
Sun	09:24:43	Leo	Maghā	3
Mon	29:55:51	Pis	Revatī	4
Mar(R)	28:52:50	Aqu	P Bhādrapadā	3
Mer	06:01:57	Vir	U Phālgunī	3
Jup(C)	16:43:25	Leo	P Phālgunī	2
Ven	23:43:11	Gem	Punarvasu	2
Sat	03:27:41	Sco	Anurādhā	1
Rah(R)	10:10:05	Sco	Anurādhā	3
Ket(R)	10:10:05	Tau	Rohiṇī	1

Lagna Chart

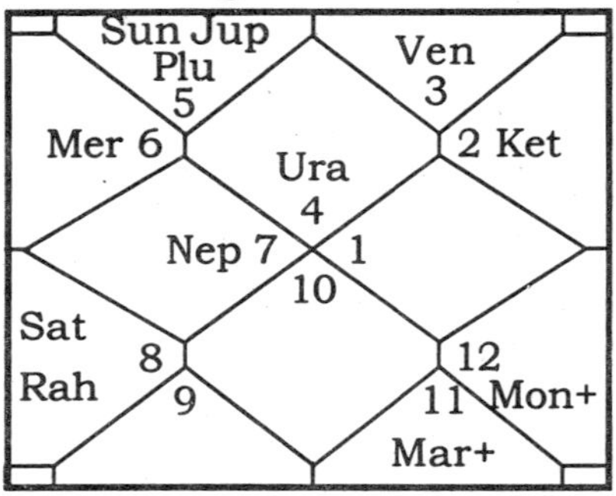

Navāmśa Chart

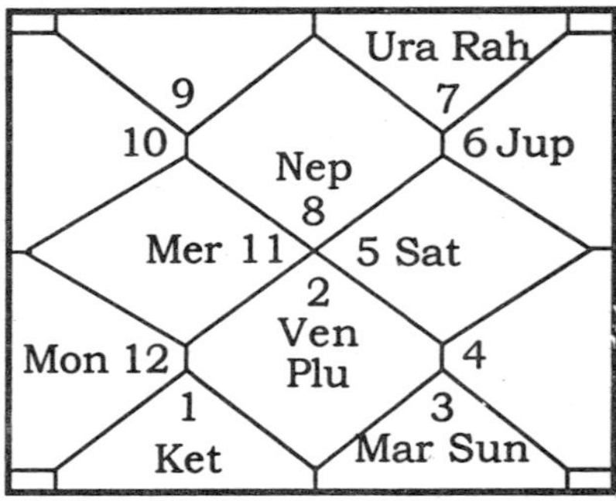

Balance of Vimśottarī Daśā of **Mercury 0Y 1M 1D**

Name of Event	Date of Event	Major Period	Sub Period
Marriage	29.09.1974	Venus	Jupiter
Widowhood	23.06.1980	Venus	Mercury

Mars occupies 8th house in square position with Saturn. She lost her husband on June, 23rd, 1980 when she was passing through the sub-period Mercury in the major period of Venus. She had also been blessed with a son who is her biggest support to depend on. Here we can also see that 4th lord Venus occupies the 12th house which further confirms the adverse probabilities of conjugal life.

Husband Committed Suicide Immediately After Marriage

Case No. 3.18 – (Horoscope No. 18)

This is the horoscope of Rekha, famous film actress. She has always been appreciated for her talent in the field of acting. In real life, she could not get happiness of her married life and suffered widowhood soon after her marriage with Mukesh Agarwal. She also remained involved with famous personalities of film industry from time to time. What made her widow? Why did her husband Mukesh Agarwal committed suicide? Lord of *lagna* Jupiter occupies the 8th house in its sign of exaltation. As I said earlier, aspect of Jupiter or its placement in the 8th house gives long life to husband. In this horoscope, 8th house and exalted Jupiter is aspected by Mars and Saturn both. Mars aspects the 7th house where *Ketu* is posited. Venus is hemmed between Mars, *Rāhu* and Saturn giving rise to *pāpakartari yoga*. This snatched the happiness of conjugal life. Mars is shifted in the 2nd house in *Bhāva* chart. From there also, Mars aspects the 8th house, here there is mutual aspect between Mars and Jupiter in *bhāva* chalit. Therefore, *akhaṇḍa saubhāgya yoga* is converted into *vaidhavya yoga*. Presence of *Ketu* in the 7th house is as bad as that of Mars. If 8th house is occupied by benefic and aspected by malefic like Mars and Saturn, one looses

Case : 3.18 *Horoscope No. : 18*

Date	: 10.10.1954	Time :	11:00:00
Place	: Madras	Lat 13°:05′	Long 80°:18′
Ayanāmśa	: 23:13:47	Sidereal Time :	12:04:20

Pln	**Degree**	**Rāśi**	**Nakṣatra**	**Pad**
Asc	02:28:31	Sag	Mūlā	1
Sun	23:09:00	Vir	Hastā	4
Mon	25:23:26	Aqu	P Bhādrapadā	2
Mar	29:41:08	Sag	Uttarāṣāḍha	1
Mer	18:05:06	Lib	Svāti	4
Jup	04:28:27	Can	Puṣya	1
Ven	02:39:53	Sco	Viśākhā	4
Sat	15:48:16	Lib	Svāti	3
Rah(R)	16:21:54	Sag	Pūrvāṣāḍha	1
Ket(R)	16:21:54	Gem	Ārdrā	3

Lagna Chart

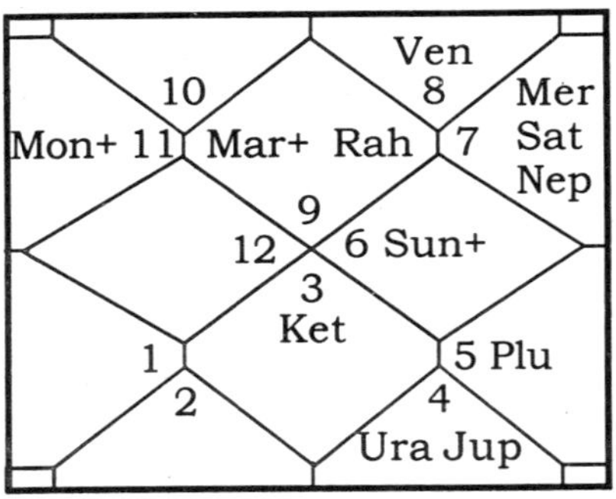

Navāmśa Chart

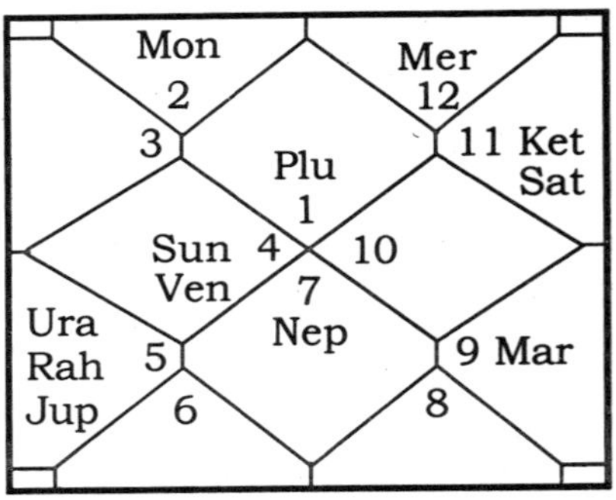

Balance of Vimśottarī Daśā of **Jupiter 9Y 6M 11D**

Name of Event	Date of Event	Major Period	Sub Period
Marriage	1988	Mercury	Venus
Widowhood	02.10.1989	Mercury	Sun

her husband. Here 7th lord Mercury is conjoined with exalted Saturn in the 11th house. 7th lord Mercury obtains *navāṁśa* of its debilitation. In the *ślokas* mentioned earlier, it has been clearly mentioned, if 7th lord Mercury gets debilitated or afflicted or placed in the 8th house, the female will kill her husband and whole family will be destroyed. Here killing means the source of death of her husband. It is well known that her husband Mukesh Agarwal committed suicide by hanging himself by *dupatta* of Rekha. In fact she misbehaved and tortured him a lot as per newspaper and magazines. Since Mukesh loved Rekha to the degree of insanity, he could therefore not bear the shock given to him by Rekha and killed himself. Thus Rekha was the actual cause of suicide by Mukesh Agarwal.

Husband Killed By A Human Bomb

Case – 3.19 (Horoscope No. 19)

This horoscope belongs to Mrs. Sonia Gandhi, who became wife of late Mr. Rajiv Gandhi, former Prime Minister of India on February 25th, 1968 in Jupiter-Ketu period. The tragic killing of her husband Mr. Rajiv Gandhi on May 21st, 1991 (Saturn-*Rāhu*) shocked the whole world. At that time she was running in the 45th year of age and her life completely changed. From the position of a queen, she just became the widow of a former PM. She kept herself away from Indian politics as she had paid a heavy cost for the same. She was running under the sub-period of *Rāhu* in the major period of Saturn when Rajiv Gandhi was killed. The lord of the 7th and 8th house joins the ascendant under the aspect of malefic Mars from the 6th house. It is retrograde Saturn in the ascendant who obtains *navāṁśa* of Mars. It will not be out of place to mention that she

Case : 3.19 *Horoscope No. : 19*

Date	: 09.12.1946	Time	: 21:30:00
Place	: Turin	Lat 45°:04′	Long 07°:40′
Ayanāmśa	: 23:06:40	Sidereal Time	: 02:42:00

Pln	**Degree**	**Rāśi**	**Nakṣatra**	**Pad**
Asc	29:29:23	Can	Aśleṣā	4
Sun	24:05:17	Sco	Jyeṣṭhā	3
Mon	10:08:54	Gem	Ārdrā	2
Mar(C)	01:11:18	Sag	Mūlā	1
Mer	03:21:06	Sco	Anurādhā	1
Jup	23:01:13	Lib	Viśākhā	1
Ven	24:02:57	Lib	Viśākhā	2
Sat(R)	15:26:07	Can	Puṣya	4
Rah(R)	18:40:26	Tau	Rohiṇī	3
Ket(R/C)	18:40:26	Sco	Jyeṣṭhā	1

Lagna Chart

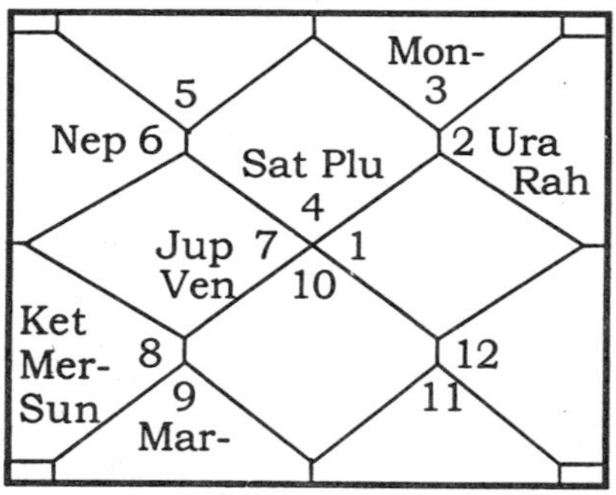

Navāmśa Chart

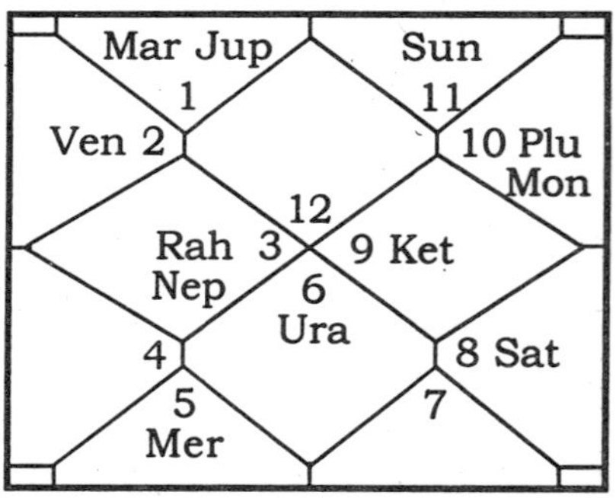

Balance of Vimśottarī Daśā of **Rahu 13Y 3M 18D**

Name of Event	Date of Event	Major Period	Sub Period
Marriage	25.02.1968	Jupiter	Ketu
Widowhood	21.05.1991	Saturn	Rahu

was running under Saturn-*Rāhu* period whereas Rajiv Gandhi was running under *Rāhu*-Saturn *daśā bhukti* and Mrs. Indira Gandhi who was killed on October 31st, 1984, was running under Saturn *Rāhu daśā bhukti*. *Lagna* Moon falls in *Rāhu's nakṣatra Ārdrā* and it is hemmed between first rate malefics Saturn and Mars giving rise to *pāpakartari yoga*. Jupiter's aspect over the 8th house and *lagna* lord Moon could not save widowhood. Hemming of Moon between malefics and aspect of Mars over Moon is always damaging for long lasting conjugal life. In *bhāva chalit*, Mars is shifted in the 5th house and the aspect of Mars over the 8th house also kills the husband provided other planetary set-up also supports.

Loss Of Husband In An Accident After Three Years Of Marriage

Case No. 3.20 - (Horoscope No. 20)

This is the horoscope of very beautiful and rich female who was married to a business magnet on May 22nd, 1989 during Moon-Mercury *daśā bhukti* and lost her husband in the sub-period of Mars in the major period of Jupiter. In her horoscope, Mars and Rahu join the 8th house in Capricorn. 8th lord Saturn occupies 12th house. Conjunction of *Rāhu* and Mars in the 8th house has strong indication of widowhood. Mars and *Rāhu* are shifted in the 9th house in *Bhāva Calit*. Here Mars and Saturn aspect each other and Saturn aspects 7th lord Jupiter. It may be noted that when 7th lord occupies the sign ruled by Mars or Saturn and is aspected by Mars or Saturn, widowhood is possible. *Rāhu* and Mars in the 8th house surely cause widowhood. All these combinations are present in this birth chart which

Case : 3.20 *Horoscope No. : 20*

Date	: 28.09.1971	Time :	23:00:35
Place	: Farrukhabad	Lat 27°:23′	Long 79°:35′
Ayanāmśa	: 23:27:56	Sidereal Time :	23:16:15

Pln	**Degree**	**Rāśi**	**Nakṣatra**	**Pad**
Asc	08:24:08	Gem	Ārdrā	1
Sun	11:28:00	Vir	Hastā	1
Mon	23:35:29	Sag	Pūrvāṣāḍha	4
Mar	20:48:45	Cap	Śrāvaṇa	4
Mer(C)	03:30:39	Vir	U Phālgunī	3
Jup	09:04:30	Sco	Anurādhā	2
Ven(C)	20:04:23	Vir	Hastā	4
Sat(R)	12:58:44	Tau	Rohiṇī	1
Rah	19:46:50	Cap	Śrāvaṇa	3
Ket	19:46:50	Can	Aśleṣā	1

Lagna Chart

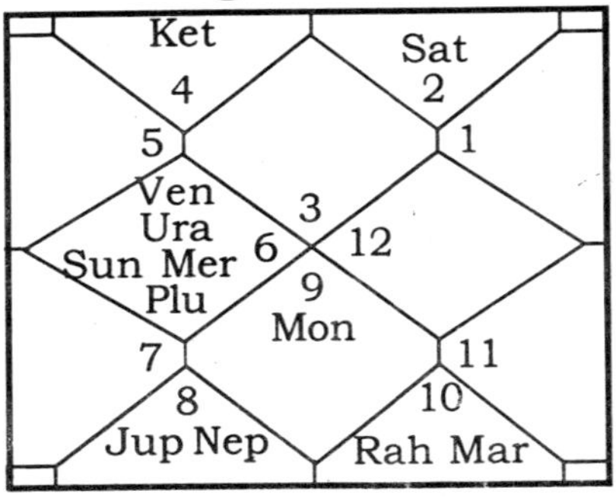

Navāmśa Chart

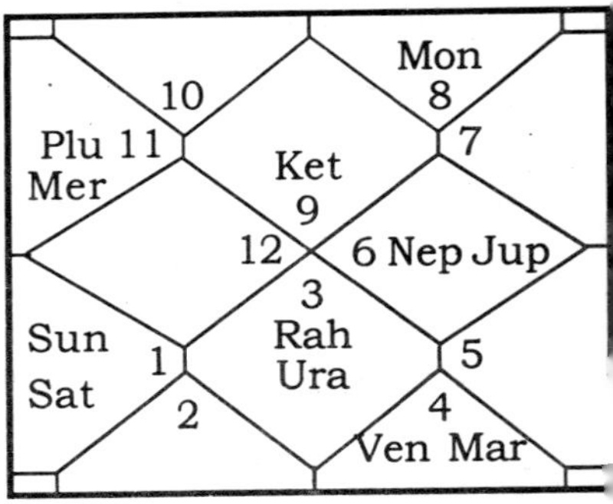

Balance of Vimśottarī Daśā of **Ven 4Y 7M 10D**

Name of Event	Date of Event	Major Period	Sub Period
Marriage	22.05.1989	Moon	Mercury
Widowhood	07.05.1992	Mars	Mars

resulted into early widowhood during Mars Mars *daśā bhukti* on May 7th, 1992.

Husband Crushed By A Truck In Less Than A Month After Marriage At 20 Years Of Age

Case 3.21 – (Horoscope No. 21)

This is the irony of misfortune that she suffered intense tragedy and terrible plight of widowhood just after 24 days of her marriage. She got married decently on November 23rd, 1987 during sub-period of Venus in the major period of Mercury and suffered the tragic death of her life partner on December 17th, 1987 just after 24 days of her marriage.

The husband had gone for the morning walk and there was lot of fog. The truck driver could not see him. As a result, he was crushed badly by the truck and expired on the spot. He was a teacher in a private school at Sitapur. The wife proved *pati-hantā* for him. In this horoscope, retrograde Saturn who owns the 6th house occupies the 7th house under retrograde motion. *Rāhu* occupies the 8th house in Aries and is aspected by Mars and *Ketu* from the 2nd house. We have repeatedly opined that if *Rāhu*, *Ketu*, Moon or Saturn are placed in Martian sign in the 7th or 8th and are under mutual aspect with Mars, widowhood occurs. The 7th lord Jupiter is a *bādhaka* and *mārakeśa* for this ascendant and is deep combust. The birth took place on the day of *amāvasyā*. It is believed that the female becomes widow if she is born on *amāvasyā*. In this horoscope, 7th lord Jupiter is exalted in the 11th house with its lord Moon, ascendant and 10th lord Mercury and 12th lord Sun, Jupiter aspects its own 7th house, but still due to deep combustion and being a *bādhaka* and *mārakeśa*, killed her husband within

Case : 3.21 *Horoscope No. : 21*

Date	: 05.08.1967	Time	:	09:20:00
Place	: Sitapur	Lat 25°:11′	Long 80°:52′	
Ayanāmśa	: 23:24:07	Sidereal Time	:	06:05:32

Pln	**Degree**	**Rāśi**	**Nakṣatra**	**Pad**
Asc	07:51:04	Vir	U Phālgunī	4
Sun	18:39:07	Can	Aśleṣā	1
Mon	06:14:30	Can	Puṣya	1
Mar	14:53:08	Lib	Svāti	3
Mer	00:34:49	Can	Punarvasu	4
Jup(D)	21:19:47	Can	Aśleṣā	2
Ven	20:16:52	Leo	P Phālgunī	3
Sat(R)	18:57:28	Pis	Revatī	1
Rah(R)	07:59:05	Ari	Aśvinī	3
Ket(R)	07:59:05	Lib	Svāti	1

Lagna Chart

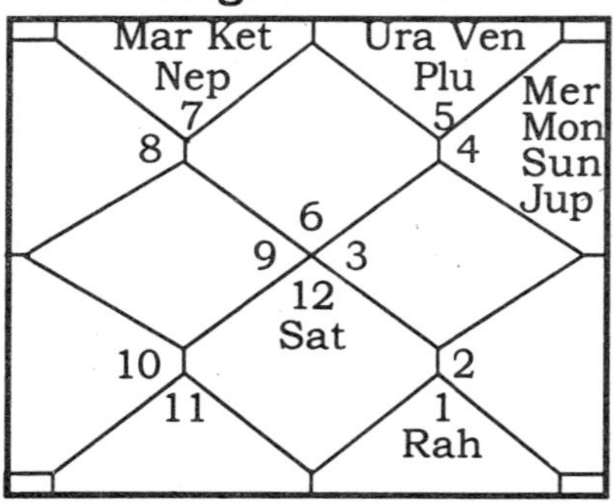

Navāmśa Chart

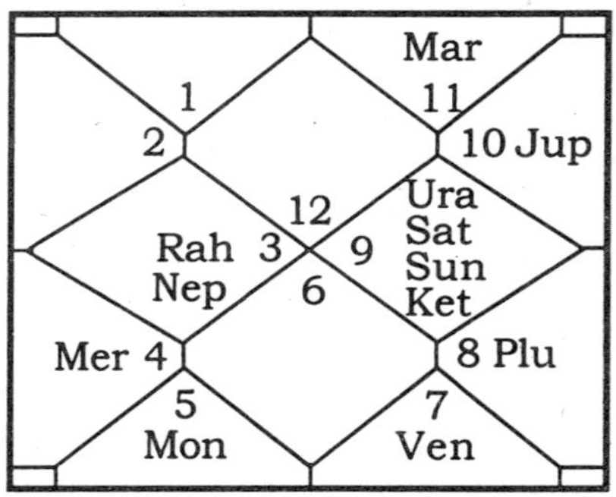

Balance of Vimśottarī Daśā of **Saturn 14Y 10M 8D**

Name of Event	Date of Event	Major Period	Sub Period
Marriage	23.11.1987	Mercury	Venus
Widowhood	17.12.1987	Mercury	Venus

24 days after marriage. Mars and *Ketu* are also *mārakeśa* for this ascendant as Mars is 8th and 3rd lord, placed in 2nd house in conjunction with Ketu. 2nd house is 3rd from 7th house and indicates husband's death. Venus is the lord of the 2nd house and is 2nd from 7th Jupiter and *mahādaśā* lord Mercury. Therefore, she lost her husband during Mercury-Venus period. It may be noted that Venus, if placed in Leo or conjoined with Sun or Moon or hemmed between them, will curtail conjugal bliss to a great extent.

Evil Combinations In A Nutshell

1. *Rāhu* in 8th house in fiery sign Aries of Mars and aspected by Mars.
2. 8th lord Mars over the axis of nodes.
3. 7th lord Jupiter is deeply combust, *bādhaka* and *mārakeśa* and obtains *navāṁśa* of debilitation.
4. Retrograde Saturn owns the 5th and 6th and joins the 7th house in Jupiter's sign and *navāṁśa.*
5. 2nd lord Venus occupies 12th house in inimical sign Leo which curtail marital happiness.
6. The birth took place on *amāvasyā* which also gives rise to widowhood, if other combinations also confirm.

Husband Collapsed On A New Year Day

Case No. 3.22 – (Horoscope No. 22)

She was very charming and attractive female who got married on December 5st, 1961 at 23 years of age during sub-period of Mercury in the major period of Venus. She was blessed with two beautiful daughters. The husband suddenly collapsed on January 1st, 1969 during sub-period of Venus in the major period of Sun. She was born in *maghā nakṣatra* 4th pada which

Case : 3.22 *Horoscope No. : 22*

Date	: 14.03.1938	Time :	08:30:00
Place	: Rawalpindi	Lat 33°:38′	Long 73°:08′
Ayanāmśa	: 22:59:53	Sidereal Time :	19:16:49

Pln	**Degree**	**Rāśi**	**Nakṣatra**	**Pad**
Asc	05:40:16	Ari	Aśvinī	2
Sun	29:53:09	Aqu	P Bhādrapadā	3
Mon	02:49:37	Leo	Maghā	1
Mar	08:18:00	Ari	Aśvinī	3
Mer(C)	05:15:50	Pis	U Bhādrapadā	1
Jup	26:23:35	Cap	Dhaniṣṭhā	1
Ven(C)	09:09:44	Pis	U Bhādrapadā	2
Sat(C)	13:04:28	Pis	U Bhādrapadā	3
Rah(R)	06:27:49	Sco	Anurādhā	1
Ket(R)	06:27:49	Tau	Kṛtikā	3

Lagna Chart

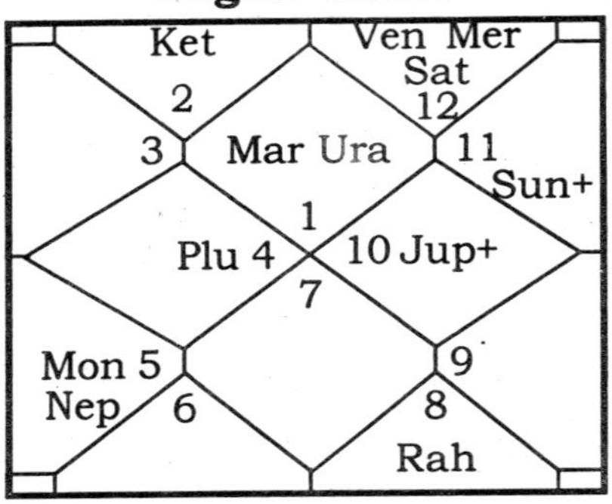

Navāmśa Chart

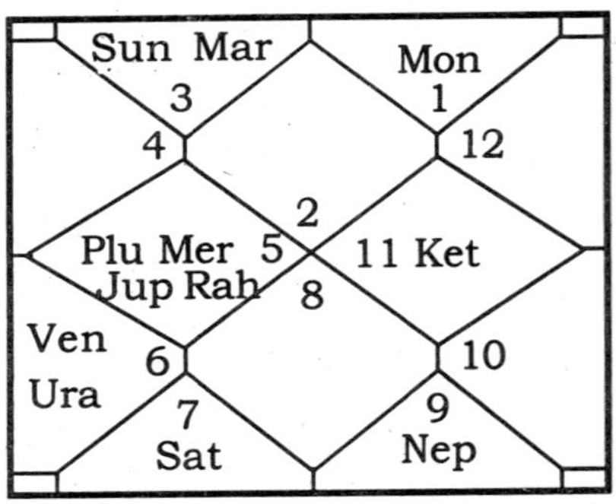

Balance of Vimśottarī Daśā of **Ket 5Y 6M 5D**

Name of Event	Date of Event	Major Period	Sub Period
Marriage	05.12.1961	Venus	Mercury
Widowhood	01.01.1969	Sun	Venus

is a *nakṣatra* of *mūlā*. Here *Rāhu* occupies the 8th house and Mars joins the ascendant and aspects *Rāhu*. It has been observed that if *Rāhu* joins the 8th house in Martian sign Aries, widowhood comes quite early because it is a fiery sign. If *Rāhu* joins 8th house in Scorpio Martian sign and is aspected by Mars, widowhood comes in between the 6th and 11th year after marriage depending on other planetary combinations. 7th lord Venus occupies the 12th house in its sign of exaltation, i.e., Venus is associated with Mercury and Saturn, 8th lord Mars is hemmed between Saturn and *Ketu*. 8th house from Moon is afflicted which resulted into widowhood in Sun - Venus period on January 1st, 1969. Venus is the lord of the 2nd and 7th house, i.e., the *mārakeśa* and joins 2nd from Sun. This becomes a *māraka* for husband, 2nd house is 8th from 7th, therefore, its lordship is always adverse if other planetary combinations confirm widowhood.

If 8th lord Mars joins ascendant or the 7th house and malefic like *Rāhu*, *Ketu* or Saturn occupies the 8th, widowhood will certainly be there, as in the present case.

Loss Of Husband Due To Massive Heart Attack

Case No. 3.23 – (Horoscope No. 23)

This horoscope belongs to a charming, innocent and very simple girl who got married to a lecturer of Physics on November 24th, 1968. The marriage was ceremonised at Allahabad at a very high scale, almost entire city was decorated by colourful lights, flowers and perfumes. Her father very enthusiastically celebrated the marriage of his most loving, caring and affectionate daughter which took place on November 24th, 1968 during Mars-Venus *daśā bhukti*. She faced unending miseries, problems, tensions,

Case : 3.23 *Horoscope No. : 23*

Date	: 20.07.1948	Time :	20:29:00
Place	: Faizabad	Lat 26°:46′	Long 82°:08′
Ayanāmśa	: 23:08:08	Sidereal Time :	16:20:43

Pln	**Degree**	**Rāśi**	**Nakṣatra**	**Pad**
Asc	03:16:28	Aqu	Dhaniṣṭhā	3
Sun	04:37:52	Can	Puṣya	1
Mon	29:15:08	Sag	Uttarāṣāḍha	1
Mar	08:50:36	Vir	U Phālgunī	4
Mer	14:51:37	Gem	Ārdrā	3
Jup(R)	27:01:31	Sco	Jyeṣṭhā	4
Ven	01:51:52	Gem	Mṛgśirā	3
Sat	29:18:30	Can	Aśleṣā	4
Rah(R)	17:43:11	Ari	Bharanī	2
Ket(R)	17:43:11	Lib	Svāti	4

Lagna Chart

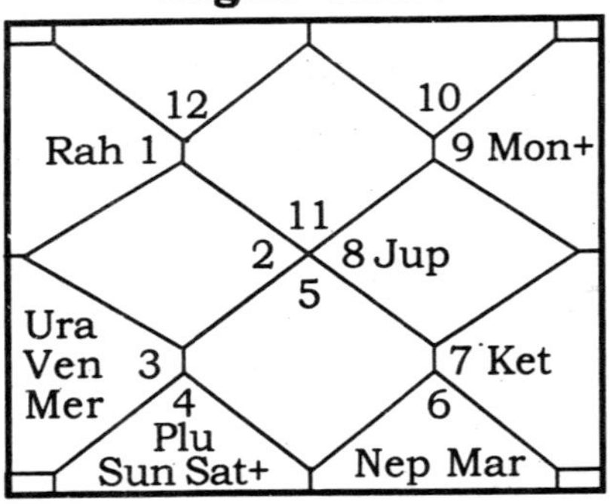

Navāmśa Chart

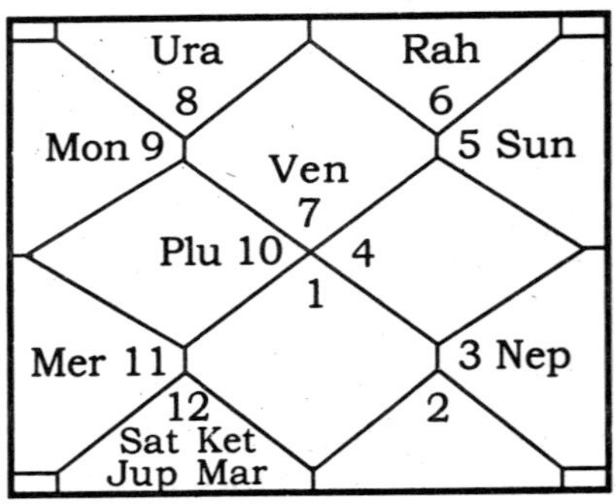

Balance of Vimśottarī Daśā of **Sun 4Y 10M 1D**

Name of Event	Date of Event	Major Period	Sub Period
Marriage	24.11.1968	Mars	Venus
Widowhood	07.11.1997	Jupiter	Venus

frustrations, distress, despair, dissatisfaction, humiliation just after reaching her home of in-laws. They were so harsh with her that she was beaten badly whenever tears appeared in her eyes. All jewellery and garments were snatched from her. She stayed with her husband for one month but she was unable to recognise him because they were never together for that one month. She was forced to sleep in the storeroom or veranda during winters on the ground.

Any way after coming back to her parents after one month, she cried continuously for three days. As a result of that, her father received unbearable shock and expired. Whole family was shattered and doomed into mourns. Her father believed in astrology a lot. Horoscope of both were matched by one famous astrologer of Lucknow, even then this tragedy took place. Her father died at an early age whereas many astrologers predicted a long life of 76 years of age. All went wrong and whole family started to disbelieve astrology. She remained separated from her husband for seven years or so. We suggested her *vrata* on Tuesdays, donation for *maṅgala*, recitation of Vedic m antras for *maṅgala* and reading of *maṅgala stotra* etc.

At around 28 years of age in 1976, her husband visited her making her astonished. However, she started living with her husband thereafter. Effect of Mars can be seen in this case. The marriage took place at 21 years of age but the conjugal bliss was absent till 28 years of age. She hardly enjoyed marriage for 21 years and suddenly her husband expired on November 7th, 1997 during Jupiter Venus *daśā bhukti*, which is invariably bad. Many a times, it has been found in many cases that the death of husband takes place in major or sub-period of

2nd lord. 2nd house is 8th from 7th and indicates the death of husband. Sub-period lord Venus is the lord of 7th house as reckoned from Jupiter and is placed in the 8th house and from there, Jupiter falls in the sign of Mars and is retrograde in the 10th house in *jyeṣṭhā nakṣatra*.

In this horoscope, Mars falls in the 8th house and Saturn and Sun join in the 6th house. 7th house is placed under strong *pāpakartari yoga*, 8th house is joined by Mars and aspected by Saturn. *Rāhu* who is 8th from 8th house, i.e., in the 3rd house, falls in aries and is aspected by Mars and Saturn both. This resulted into sudden loss of her husband and lonely life thereafter.

Thus, she faced immense miseries of married life inspite of 34½ matching points of *aṣṭakūṭa* and balance of *kuja doṣa*. That's why I have always emphasized that it is not only matching points and matching *kuja doṣa* which matters. There must be matching of planets and *bhāvas* as well. Why Mars and Moon should be considered for happy married life? Why 7 other planets and *bhāvas* should not be taken into account?

Husband Expired Due To Severe Stomach Problem

Case No. 3. 24 – (Horoscope No. 24)

She got married with an Engineer around 16th year of her age during Venus–Venus period. She suffered sudden loss of her husband around forty-five years of age during Moon–Saturn period on October 22nd, 1969. She is not *maṅgalī* either from *lagna* or Moon or Venus. She enjoyed lot of fortune of all kinds of luxury, vehicles, servants, ornaments etc. The conjunctions of the lords of both the triangles, Mercury and Saturn in the ascendant made her very fortunate. However, the placement of the 2nd and 7th

Case : 3.24 *Horoscope No. : 24*

Date	: 09.11.1924	Time :	05:35:00
Place	: Chandausi	Lat 28°:06′	Long 77°:50′
Ayanāmśa	: 22:48:14	Sidereal Time :	08:27:54

Pln	**Degree**	**Rāśi**	**Nakṣatra**	**Pad**
Asc	09:39:47	Lib	Svāti	1
Sun	23:31:04	Lib	Viśākhā	2
Mon	24:52:34	Pis	Revatī	3
Mar	15:13:46	Aqu	Satabhiṣā	3
Mer(C)	01:47:44	Sco	Viśākhā	4
Jup	28:32:30	Sco	Jyeṣṭhā	4
Ven	14:48:24	Vir	Hastā	2
Sat(C)	13:41:22	Lib	Svāti	3
Rah(R)	25:56:12	Can	Aśleṣā	3
Ket(R)	25:56:12	Cap	Dhaniṣṭhā	1

Lagna Chart

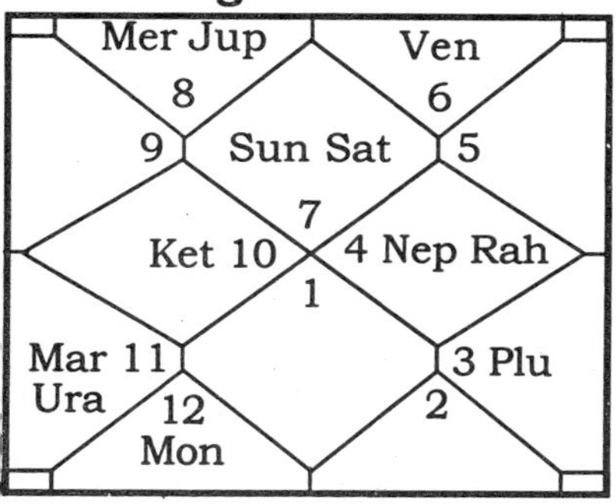

Navāmśa Chart

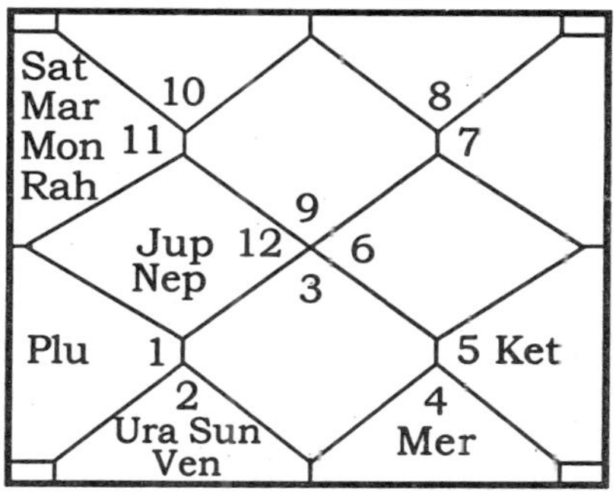

Balance of Vimśottarī Daśā of **Mercury 6Y 6M 12D**

Name of Event	Date of Event	Major Period	Sub Period
Marriage	Nov., 1940	Venus	Venus
Widowhood	22.10.1969	Moon	Saturn

lord Mars in the 5th house is really very adverse. The death of husband took place during Moon–Saturn *daśā bhukti.* Saturn is 8th from Moon and is afflicted due to conjunction with the Sun. Mars aspects 8th house and Saturn aspects 7th house. This can be noted that widowhood took place during *yogakāraka* Saturn's sub-period who is exalted in the ascendant and has given rise to *Śasa Mahāpuruṣa Rāja Yoga.*

It is a tough exercise to time widowhood. It is not essential at all that it will take place during *daśā bhukti* of concerning planets only. If Mars is responsible for widowhood, it may come around 21 to 28 years or 42 to 49 years of age. If Saturn is responsible, widowhood may come around 31 to 36 years or 54 years. Many combinations are there for widowhood after 7, 10, 15, 20 years of marriage. After approximate age, *daśā bhukti* will help in timing widowhood.

Loss Of Husband During Stomach Operation

Case No. 3.25 – (Horoscope No. 25)

She was the first child of her parents. The birth took place in *jyeṣṭhā nakṣatra,* fourth *pāda.* Her mother expired soon after her birth. She got married around 21 years of age. The married life was miserable. The husband was quite smart, good looking and attractive. Many girls were involved with him. She lost her husband on January 23rd, 1969 during operation of stomach.

For Libra ascendant, Mars is the worst planet and here Mars occupies the ascendant in association with the 9th lord Mercury. *Rāhu* occupies the 8th house and is aspected by Mars and Saturn. Birth has taken place on new Moon day, i.e., *amāvasyā.* The lord of the ascendant joins the 12th house under

Case : 3.25 *Horoscope No. : 25*

Date	: 26.11.1927	Time :	05:20:00
Place	: Bareilly	Lat 28°:20′	Long 79°:24′
Ayanāmśa	: 22:50:42	Sidereal Time :	09:23:18

Pln	**Degree**	**Rāśi**	**Nakṣatra**	**Pad**
Asc	21:27:55	Lib	Viśākhā	1
Sun	09:52:40	Sco	Anurādhā	2
Mon	27:19:10	Sco	Jyeṣṭhā	4
Mar(C)	28:24:34	Lib	Viśākhā	3
Mer	20:02:38	Lib	Viśākhā	1
Jup	00:49:51	Pis	P Bhādrapadā	4
Ven	23:15:53	Vir	Hastā	4
Sat(C)	16:27:22	Sco	Anurādhā	4
Rah	25:53:12	Tau	Mṛgśirā	1
Ket	25:53:12	Sco	Jyeṣṭhā	3

Lagna Chart

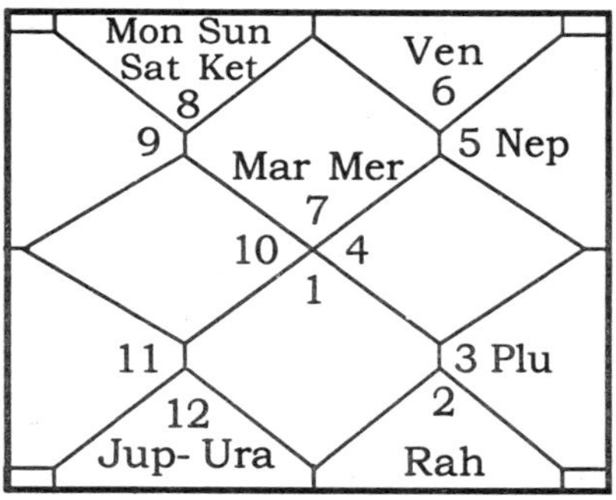

Navāmśa Chart

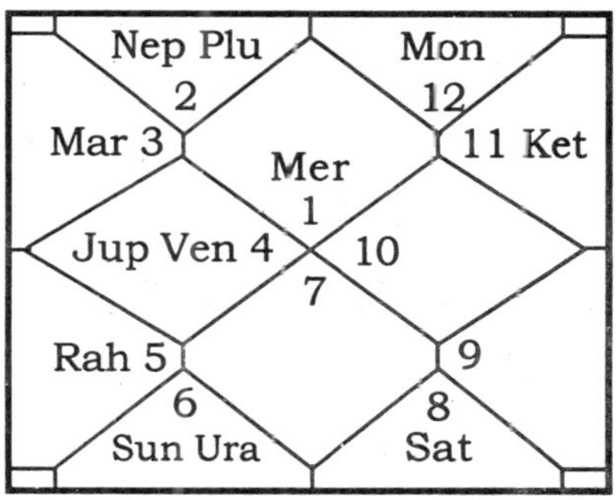

Balance of Vimśottarī Daśā of **Mercury 3Y 5M 0D**

Name of Event	Date of Event	Major Period	Sub Period
Marriage	04.04.1947	Venus	Rahu
Widowhood	23.01.1969	Moon	Saturn

debilitation and 12th lord Mercury occupies the ascendant under affliction by Mars.

We have observed that the major period of Moon is very adverse for *jyeṣṭhā* borns. She underwent the curse of widowhood on January 23rd, 1969 during major period of Moon and sub-period of Saturn. Saturn heavily afflicts the 2nd house, and the Moon and thus both happen a *mārakeśa* for her husband. She was blessed with one daughter and two sons and expired on May 30th, 2001 after leading so lonely life of more than 32 years.

Here placement of *Rāhu* in the 8th house and aspect of Mars, Saturn, Sun, Moon and *Ketu* over there, resulted into widowhood around 41 years of age. She suffered a lot thereafter.

Death Of Husband Due To Massive Heart Attack

Case No. 3.26 – (Horoscope No. 26)

She got married on June 24th, 1982 at 18 years of age during sub–period of *Ketu* in the major period of *Rāhu*. Her husband was a man of outstanding personality. He was very kind-hearted, helping and judicious. On August 6th, 1993 her husband expired due to a massive heart attack. She faced the biggest tragedy in loss of husband at 29 years of age when there were many dreams to be blossomed. But the sudden widowhood crushed her dreams miserably and ruined her life.

Placement of Mars in the 5th house should be held responsible for the curse of widowhood. The ascendant is under *pāpakartari yoga*. In this case again, the Jupiter could not save widowhood though it aspects the 8th house. The lord of the 8th house Sun occupies the 6th house in close association with *Rāhu* and Venus. There is mutual exchange between 5th lord Venus and 6th lord Mercury. 8th house is

Case : 3.26 *Horoscope No. : 26*

Date	: 18.06.1964	Time :	20:55:05
Place	: Lucknow	Lat 26°:50′	Long 80°:54′
Ayanāmśa	: 23:21:20	Sidereal Time :	14:36:16

Pln	**Degree**	**Rāśi**	**Nakṣatra**	**Pad**
Asc	02:32:34	Cap	Uttarāṣāḍha	2
Sun	04:02:19	Gem	Mṛgśirā	4
Mon	23:40:14	Vir	Citrā	1
Mar	07:28:05	Tau	Kṛtikā	4
Mer(C)	23:39:39	Tau	Mṛgśirā	1
Jup	22:09:35	Ari	Bharanī	3
Ven(R/D)	06:05:55	Gem	Mṛgśirā	4
Sat(R)	11:40:23	Aqu	Satabhiṣā	2
Rah(R/C)	08:40:46	Gem	Ārdrā	1
Ket(R)	08:40:46	Sag	Mūlā	3

Lagna Chart

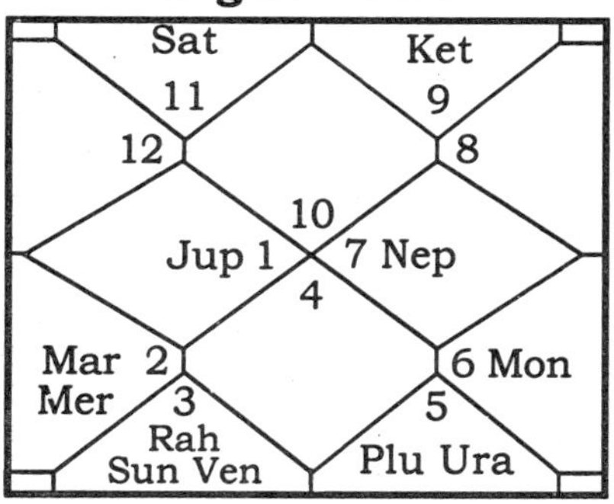

Navāmśa Chart

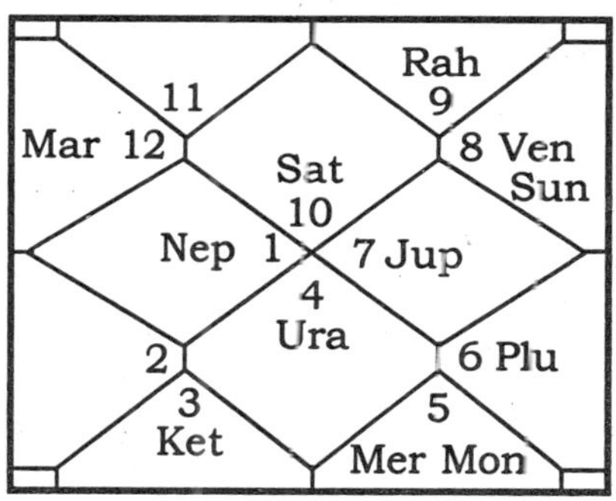

Balance of Vimśottarī Daśā of **Mars 6Y 9M 26D**

Name of Event	Date of Event	Major Period	Sub Period
Marriage	24.06.1982	Rahu	Ketu
Widowhood	06.08.1993	Jupiter	Saturn

aspected by retrograde Saturn from 2nd house and Mars from 5th house. Thus, the 8th house which rules the span of married life, is heavily afflicted because the 8th lord Sun is closely associated in the 6th house over the axis of nodes and the 8th house is aspected by first rate malefics like Mars and Saturn.

The husband expired on August 6th, 1993 in the sub-period of Saturn in the major period of Jupiter. Saturn owns the 2nd house and it becomes stronger malefic as it becomes retrograde. Jupiter who is the 12th and 3rd lord, is a malefic for Capricorn ascendant. Thus, the joint aspect of 12th and 3rd lord Jupiter, *lagna* and 2nd lord retrograde Saturn and 4th and 11th lord Mars over the 8th house resulted into the tragedy. It may be noted that Jupiter is the lord of the 2nd house as reckoned from 2nd and therefore, sub-period of Saturn in the major period of Jupiter snatched the pleasure of conjugal bliss and the pleasant company of her most loving and caring life partner.

Loss Of Husband Due To Massive Heart Attack

Case No. 3.27 - (Horoscope No. 27)

The father of the female native was a minister. He ceremonised her marriage around 22 years of age in November 1967 with a high-class research scholar and Professor in Geology. The husband made certain most valuable researches in India on Himalaya Mountain. The government still gets millions of rupees every month as an outcome of the researches he made on Himalaya. He was expected to get any award like Nobel Prize or so in due course of time. It was heaviest misfortune that her husband suddenly received a severe and massive heart attack and expired when he was forty years old, leaving behind

Case : 3.27 *Horoscope No. : 27*

Date	: 27.09.1945	Time	: 00:30:00
Place	: Bareilly	Lat 28°:20′	Long 79°:24′
Ayanāmśa	: 23:05:39	Sidereal Time	: 23:38:18

Pln	**Degree**	**Rāśi**	**Nakṣatra**	**Pad**
Asc	14:13:22	Gem	Ārdrā	3
Sun	10:10:43	Vir	Hastā	1
Mon	17:56:29	Tau	Rohiṇī	3
Mar	17:34:30	Gem	Ārdrā	4
Mer(C)	05:31:27	Vir	U Phālgunī	3
Jup(C)	13:45:04	Vir	Hastā	2
Ven	09:25:32	Leo	Maghā	3
Sat	00:18:34	Can	Punarvasu	4
Rah(R)	11:19:18	Gem	Ārdrā	2
Ket(R)	11:19:18	Sag	Mūlā	4

Lagna Chart

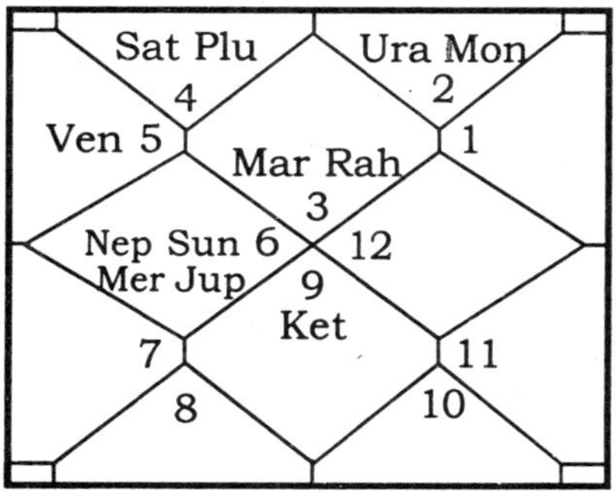

Navāmśa Chart

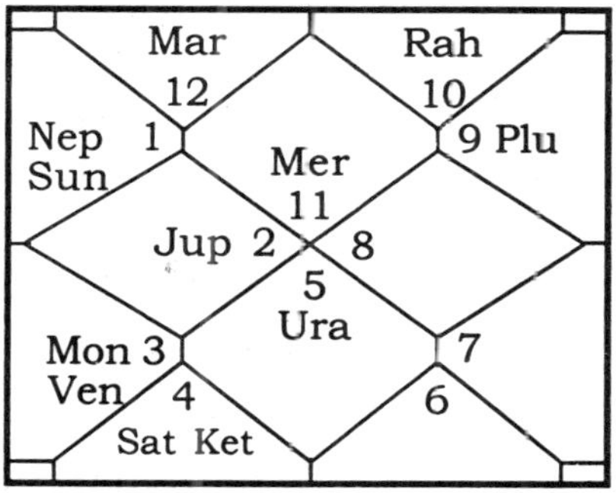

Balance of Vimśottarī Daśā of **Moon 4Y 0M 16D**

Name of Event	Date of Event	Major Period	Sub Period
Marriage	November, 1967	Rahu	Ketu
Widowhood	19.07.1982	Jupiter	Ketu

his two daughters and a son. The female suffered the tragic death of her husband around 37 years of age during sub-period of *Ketu* in the major period of Jupiter.

The lord of the 8th house Mars is conjoined with *Rāhu* in the ascendant. Saturn and Mars both aspect the 8th house and *Rāśi* lord Venus occupies Leo sign which is always adverse. 7th and 8th house are heavily afflicted by Mars and Saturn. It may be noted that Mars is the lord of the 6th house and Saturn aspects the 8th house alongwih the aspect of *mārakeśa* Jupiter on the 8th house which snatched the life of her husband at an early age.

The widowhood occurred in the Jupiter-*Ketu* period. Here the Jupiter is the lord of the 8th house and *mārakeśa* for Gemini ascendant and it is also combust and *bādhakādhipati*. *Ketu* joins the 7th house. Thus, Jupiter and *Ketu* both became *mārakeśa* for husband and this *daśā* of Jupiter-*Ketu* resulted into this biggest tragedy of her life.

We had forewarned for this tragedy as we were in close contact. It may be noted that Mars obtains *navāṁśa* of Jupiter in whose *daśā* she suffered widowhood. This is a rule of astrology that widowhood may take place during close *daśā bhukti* of that planet which indicates this tragedy.

Suffered Loss Of Husband After Eighteen Years of Marriage

Case No. 3.28 – (Horoscope No. 28)

Mrs. Indira Gandhi made history in politics. She was Prime Minister of India for a long time and was honoured for her merits, extraordinary intelligence, aggressive politics, immense courage and unaccountable achievements all over the globe. She was married to Feroz Gandhi during *Rāhu* Saturn

Case : 3.28 *Horoscope No. : 28*

Date	: 19.11.1917	Time :	23:11:00
Place	: Allahabad	Lat 25°:27′	Long 81°:50′
Ayanāmśa	: 22:42:52	Sidereal Time :	03:01:01

Pln	**Degree**	**Rāśi**	**Nakṣatra**	**Pad**
Asc	27:21:18	Can	Aśleṣā	4
Sun	04:07:29	Sco	Anurādhā	1
Mon	05:34:55	Cap	Uttarāṣāḍha	3
Mar	16:22:29	Leo	P Phālgunī	1
Mer(C)	13:13:43	Sco	Anurādhā	3
Jup(R)	15:00:07	Tau	Rohiṇī	2
Ven	21:00:18	Sag	Pūrvāṣāḍha	3
Sat	21:47:14	Can	Aśleṣā	2
Rah	09:18:38	Sag	Mūlā	3
Ket	09:18:38	Gem	Ārdrā	1

Lagna Chart

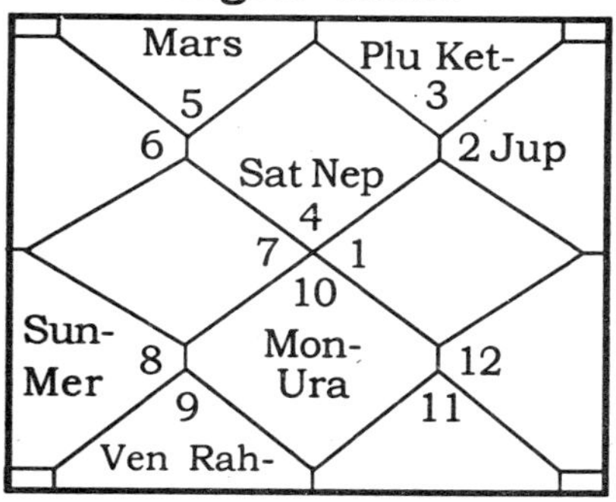

Navāmśa Chart

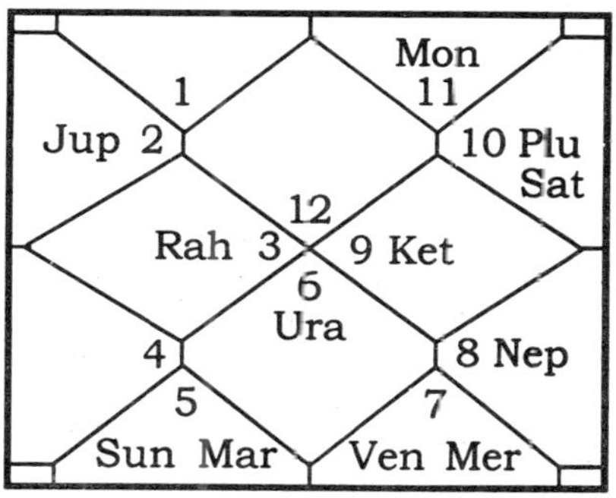

Balance of Vimśottarī Daśā of **Son 1Y 11M 26D**

Name of Event	Date of Event	Major Period	Sub Period
Marriage	26.03.1942	Rahu	Saturn
Widowhood	09.09.1960	Jupiter	Mercury
Death	31.10.1984	Saturn	Mars

period. She lost him and suffered the terrible plight of widowhood on September 9th, 1960 in the sub-period of Mercury in the major period of Jupiter. *Yogakāraka* Mars occupies the 2nd house and aspects the 8th whereas Saturn is 7th and 8th lord and joins the ascendant. From *lagna* lord Moon, Saturn is 7th and Mars is in 8th and *Ketu* is in 6th. *Daśā* lord and 7th lord Saturn obtains own *navāṁśa* and Mars is 8th from there, in *navāṁśa* chart as well. The widowhood could take place during the major period of Jupiter and sub-period of Mercury. Mercury who is posited in the sign of Mars, Scorpio and is aspected by Mars as well. From major *daśā* lord Jupiter, Mercury owns the 2nd house and it is posited in the 7th house. Thus, Mercury becomes the killer of her husband as reckoned from major period lord Jupiter.

Mrs. Indira Gandhi was assassinated on October 31st, 1984 in the major period of Saturn in the sub-period of Mars. Even in this horoscope, aspect of *bhāgyādhipati* Jupiter over 7th house could not save widowhood.

Sudden Loss of Husband Due to Tetanus

Case No. 3.29 – (Horoscope No. 29)

She had a love marriage with a teacher on January 16th 1968 during the sub-period of Moon in the major period of Mars. I have repeatedly said that the marriage should not take place during *daśā bhukti* of that planet which is going to create disaster in married life, otherwise havoc will take place certainly. *Rāhu* obtains *vargottama navāṁśa*. The placement of *Rāhu* in Aries or Scorpio under the aspect or association of Mars in 7th or 8th house, certainly gives rise to widowhood. Her husband suffered from septic and at that time strict curfew was continuing due to riots following assassination

Case : 3.29 *Horoscope No. : 29*

Date	: 27.05.1949	Time :	13:50:00
Place	: Delhi	Lat 28°:39′	Long 77°:13′
Ayanāmśa	: 23:08:53	Sidereal Time :	05:47:07

Pln	**Degree**	**Rāśi**	**Nakṣatra**	**Pad**
Asc	04:00:47	Vir	U Phālgunī	3
Sun	12:33:21	Tau	Rohiṇī	1
Mon(C)	05:44:26	Tau	Kṛtikā	3
Mar(C)	26:59:02	Ari	Kṛtikā	1
Mer(R/C)	23:24:12	Tau	Mṛgśirā	1
Jup(R)	08:57:11	Cap	Uttarāṣāḍha	4
Ven	23:14:01	Tau	Rohiṇī	4
Sat	06:45:02	Leo	Maghā	3
Rah(R)	02:00:17	Ari	Aśvinī	1
Ket(R)	02:00:17	Lib	Citrā	3

Lagna Chart

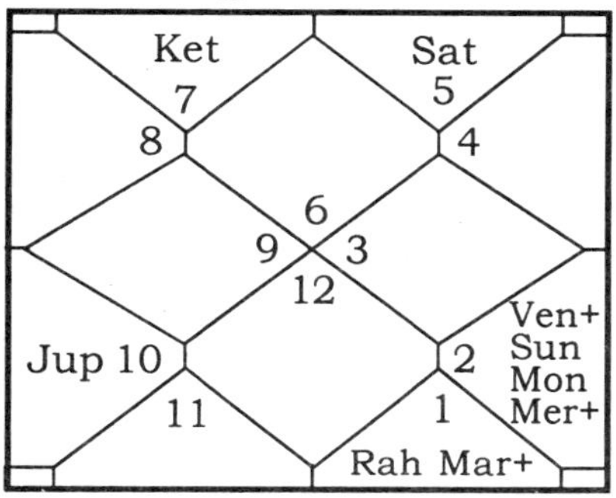

Navāmśa Chart

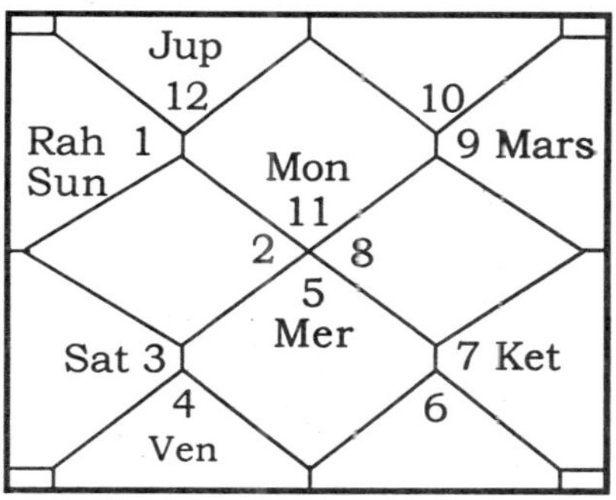

Balance of Vimśottarī Daśā of **Sun 1Y 11M 0D**

Name of Event	Date of Event	Major Period	Sub Period
Marriage	16.01.1968	Mars	Moon
Widowhood	05.11.1984	Rahu	Moon

of Mrs. Indira Gandhi. In spite of best efforts, he could not be hospitalized and expired on November 5th, 1984 when she was passing through Rahu-Moon period. Rahu occupies the 8th house and is associated with Mars. Moon is heavily afflicted due to conjunction with inimical Venus and Sun and is also aspected by malefic Saturn. Therefore, subperiod of Moon in the major period of Rahu resulted into plightful demise of her husband. In this horoscope, 9th house is very strong and aspected *kendrādhipati* Jupiter as well. The husband was a simple instructor. He had purchased many acres of land at a very cheap rate, just in few thousand rupees in Ghaziabad. Due to her good fortune, many big organisations and factories established around that land and the cost of land multiplied thousands of time. By God's grace, she is playing in billions of rupees and she is a leading land lady of Ghaziabad and now she has become a colonizer.

Husband Expired Within Two Months Of Marriage

Case No. 3.30 – (Horoscope No. 30)

In this horoscope, the combination of widowhood is strongly present due to placement of Mars in 8th house in Saturn's sign Aquarius. 8th lord Saturn is retrograde and joins the 11th and Mars and Saturn aspect each other and afflict the 8th house. This clearly signifies early widowhood and almost no marital happiness. She got married during sub-period of Moon in the major period of *Rāhu* on June 5th, 1993. Within 2 months, in same *daśā bhukti*, her husband expired. Association of *Rāhu* and Moon in the 7th house can be seen. The death of husband took place during sub-period of Moon in the major period of *Rāhu*. Affliction of 4th house is also there as 4th lord Venus joins the 6th house in inimical sign under *pāpakartari yoga*.

Case : 3.30 *Horoscope No. : 30*

Date	: 24.11.1971	Time	:	22:55:00
Place	: —	Lat 28°:15′		Long 76°:36′
Ayanāmśa	: 23:28:04	Sidereal Time	:	02:43:27

Pln	**Degree**	**Rāśi**	**Nakṣatra**	**Pad**
Asc	23:38:16	Can	Aśleṣā	3
Sun	08:18:31	Sco	Anurādhā	2
Mon	26:07:53	Cap	Dhaniṣṭhā	1
Mar	16:42:26	Aqu	Satabhiṣā	4
Mer	00:10:22	Sag	Mūlā	1
Jup	20:29:18	Sco	Jyeṣṭhā	2
Ven	01:04:22	Sag	Mūlā	1
Sat(R)	09:39:33	Tau	Kṛtikā	4
Rah	14:11:10	Cap	Śrāvaṇa	2
Ket	14:11:10	Can	Puṣya	4

Lagna Chart

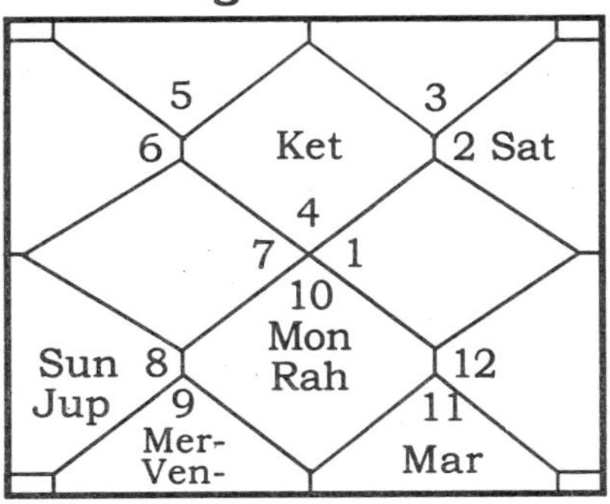

Navāmśa Chart

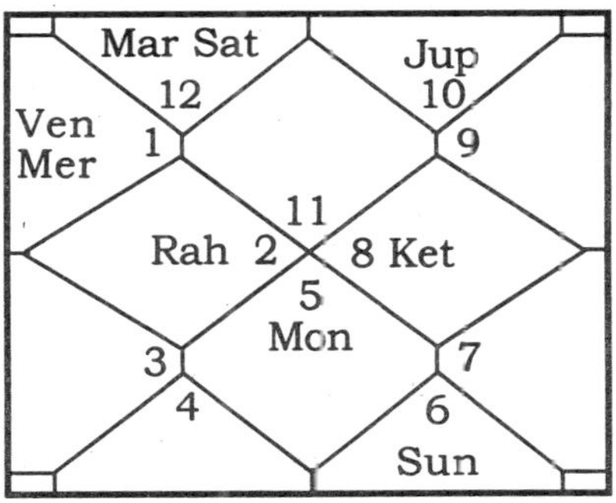

Balance of Vimśottarī Daśā of **Mars 5Y 6M 11D**

Name of Event	Date of Event	Major Period	Sub Period
Marriage	05.06.1993	Rahu	Moon
Widowhood	27.07.1993	Rahu	Moon

In our society, it is generally presumed that *maṅgalī* girl suffers widowhood, if she gets married with a non-*maṅgalī* boy. It is absolutely wrong. Mars does play a vital role in giving rise to various adversities in marriage and conjugal bliss like all other malefics. There are various other factors and planetary combinations which cause widowhood, even if the husband is also *maṅgalī*.

In *case No. 3.1* she lost her husband within 5 months of marriage. She is not *maṅgalī* because *yogakāraka* Mars occupies the 5th house. *Bhāgyādhipati* Jupiter aspects 7th, 9th and 11th house but even then Jupiter could not save widowhood. In this horoscope birth took place in the first *pada* of *mūlā nakṣatra*. Mars aspects 8th house, Saturn aspects 12th and 7th. *Bhāgyādhipati* Jupiter falls close over the axis of *Rāhu* and *Ketu*. *Ketu* is only one degree apart from Jupiter. Thus the lord of the house of fortune is heavily afflicted.

In *case No. 3.2* Jupiter occupies own sign Pisces in the 7th house. It is believed that Jupiter in the 7th brings all kinds of happiness, prosperity and long life to husband if it occupies the 7th house. She is not *maṅgalī* as Mars joins the 9th house. Why did she suffer widowhood within 3 years of marriage? It happened due to her birth in *Jyeṣṭhā nakṣatra*. In fact she was married to a boy who was also born in *Jyeṣṭhā nakṣatra*. She was married in Venus-*Rāhu* period and suffered widowhood in Venus-Jupiter period. Here Jupiter has formed *Haṁsa Māhāpuruṣa Rāja Yoga*. It is 7th lord and placed in 7th, even then caused widowhood in its *bhukti*. Here Venus and Jupiter both are *mārakeśa*. Let me hasten to add that Jupiter–Venus or Venus-Jupiter brings havoc in the life if at least one is adversely placed.

In Case No. 3.3, she is not *maṅgalī* as Mars joins the 10th house with 10th lord Venus, there is no affliction of the 7th or 8th house. The lord of the ascendant Saturn is well placed in *Trikoṇa*, then why did she suffer widowhood within 10 months of marriage? She got married during *Rāhu-Rāhu* period and lost her husband during *Rāhu*-Jupiter. It was really a tough job to foresee widowhood in this case. Saturn and Mercury both are retrograde. Sun and Saturn who own the 8th and 2nd house respectively, aspect each other and fall in the constellation of Mars and Saturn respectively. This is fatal for husband because 8th house indicates happiness of married life and 2nd house indicates family life and death of husband. More over lord of 6th and 9th house Mercury and the lord of 8th Sun are conjoined in the 11th under *pāpakartari yoga*. Mars and Saturn are 6th and 8th from each other. Mars aspects *lagna* and *lagna* lord both. Saturn aspects the 7th, the 8th lord Sun, 6th and 9th lord Mercury and the 2nd house. Venus and Mars are conjoined in *svāti nakṣatra* and they are closely associated within 3^0. *Rāhu* afflicted Jupiter adversely and that brought such an early widowhood to the native.

In *Case No. 3.4,* fifth and eighth lord Jupiter occupies the 8th house. She is not *maṅgalī*. *Yogakāraka* Mars occupies the 5th house. She lost her husband in air crash within 4½ years of marriage in *Rāhu*-Jupiter period. Here the placement of Mars in the 5th house and joint aspect of Saturn and Mars over the 8th house and *Rāhu* is responsible for her widowhood. Here the 8th lord Jupiter joins 7th and 7th lord Saturn is afflicted due to its placement over the nodes and aspect the 8th house.

In this *Case No. 3.5*, she is not *maṅgalī* as Mars joins the 10th house, 7th or 8th house is also not afflicted. Jupiter aspects the 7th house, 9th house and 11th house. Here 9th lord Mercury is exalted in the 9th house. Jupiter occupies own sign Saturn occupies *lagna* in own sign, 7th lord Moon is placed in Aries and in 1st pada of *Aśvinī nakṣatra* and is aspected by malefic Mars. The 7th house is under the adverse influence of Mars who becomes the 8th lord if reckoned from Moon. Mutual aspect between Saturn and Mars is also adverse for family life. She lost her husband during Moon-Venus *daśā bhukti*.

In *Case No. 3.6*, she suffered widowhood during sub-period of Moon in major period of Moon. Because Moon falls in *jyeṣṭhā nakṣatra* in 10th house. She is not *maṅgalī*. 7th lord Sun is placed in 12th house and aspected by Saturn. Here Jupiter occupies the 8th house which indicates long life and *akhaṇḍa saubhāgya* but she lost her husband at the age of 45 because retrograde Jupiter is malefic in the 8th house especially for Aquarius ascendant. Here Jupiter is *mārakeśa* and retrograde. Jupiter should be treated like malefic Mars. Due to the birth in *jyeṣṭhā* and placement of Moon in the sign of Mars under heavy affliction of *Rāhu* and Saturn. She suffered widowhood. We have seen that if Moon falls in the sign of Mars and is aspected by Mars and if it is also associated with malefics, one will suffer widowhood.

In all these cases, which are illustrated here, the females are not *maṅgalī* from ascendant. The affliction of 7th or 8th house is also not present and even there is no indication of loss of husband at the preliminary judgement. But almost all these females suffered early widowhood. We have also come across the observation that Jupiter does not always save widowhood. By chance in all the illustrations except a few, either it was the major period of Jupiter or the sub-period of Jupiter which resulted into widowhood. We have mentioned that Jupiter in a female horoscope indicates *saubhāgya*. If Jupiter owns malefic houses, *trikas* or it is adversely placed and if it is retrograde and has anything to do with the 7th or 8th house either by occupation or aspect, that will intensify the chances of widowhood.

The 5th house is a triangle but if Mars is placed there, widowhood may come in evidence. This is very bad disposition of Mars in the horoscope of any female.

In case of horoscope nos. 1, 4, 16, 24, 26 we have seen that position of Mars in the 5th has brought great disaster in their lives and made them widow. These are few important points to be taken a serious view of, while examining the life of husband, i.e., the *saubhāgya*. These are in addition to general combination which are given in various classical works and are stated in the beginning.

If Moon falls in the sign of Mars, i.e., in Scorpio or Aries and birth constellation is that of *Mūla*, i.e. *jyeṣṭhā or aśvinī*, if Mars is so placed in the birth chart that Moon may receive full aspect of Mars, widowhood may take place. If Moon is associated with Mars or there is mutual aspect between Moon and Mars, the possibility of widowhood becomes stronger, provided any of the Moon or Mars own *trikas* or are related with the concerning houses or signs. If so, the death of husband can take place during Moon's, Mercury's, *Ketu's* or Mars *daṣā bhukti* as the case may be. If Saturn, *Rāhu* or *Ketu* also get associated with this planetary combination, the curse of widowhood will appear soon in life.

If Jupiter falls in the 7th house identical to Cancer, Scorpio or Pisces, one should not think of happy and everlasting conjugal life. In fact placement of Jupiter in the 7th house in fiery sign, i.e. Aries, Leo or Sagittarius is encouraging for lasting happiness. Retrograde Jupiter in the 7th or 8th house should be examined like Mars. In case No. 2, Jupiter and Pisces in the 7th house caused widowhood in the 3rd year of marriage. In case No. 4, Jupiter in Aquarius in the 7th, resulted into early widowhood after four and half years. If Jupiter owns 7th and joins 8th under mutual aspect with Mars, early widowhood will take place. Similarly, if 8th lord Jupiter is placed in the 7th house and Mars aspects 7th or 8th house, widowhood will appear soon after marriage. Therefore, any kind of high and favourable results should not be expected if Jupiter joins 7th or 8th house.

If one finds difficulty to judge whether the combination will really make the female widow, he should examine the 4th house and its lord. The placement of 4th lord in *trikas* (6th, 8th or 12th) or the placement of lords of *trikas* in 4th will strengthen the probabilities of widowhood. Placement of *Ketu* should be examined just like Mars. If *Ketu* and Mars both afflict 7th and 8th house, the widowhood will come soon after marriage.

If 7th lord falls in *trikas* over the axis of nodes, that is also adverse for the married life and longevity of spouse. We have made observation that if Mars simply occupies the 7th house and is aspected by *lagna* lord or the *lagna* is aspected or owned by Jupiter, death of husband will not take place. If *lagna* is placed under *pāpakartari yoga* and Mars is retrograde in the 7th house, that will bring separation but definitely not widowhood. If the ascendant and 7th house are hemmed between Sun and Saturn in a way that Sun is aspected by Saturn, the happiness of married life is denied generally. If the *lagna* lord is weak, the marriage may be completely denied.

In various cases, it has been found that if Mars and Saturn aspect each other and one of them owns the 7th house, serious problems in marriage appear but if Mars is 7th lord and occupies own sign or the sign of Saturn and is aspected by Saturn, widowhood will be the outcome.

If 7th lord Jupiter is placed in 8th house and aspected by 8th lord Mars, the widowhood will appear after a few years of marriage. The worst combination for widowhood may be the joint influence of Saturn, Mars and *Rāhu* over the 8th house. For a long life of husband, Mars and *Ketu* should not occupy 7th and 8th house respectively. If the 7th lord is placed in the 6th or 8th house under *pāpakartari yoga*, such havocs are bound to come. We have found that the placement of 7th lord in the 6th may give rise to separation if afflicted and if 7th lord occupies the 8th house under affliction, the loss of spouse generally appears.

It is believed that Jupiter's aspect or association with Mars appreciably neutralizes or reduces *kuja doṣa*. It is also believed that the conjunction or mutual aspect of Moon and Mars will nullify the *kuja doṣa* if Mars occupies any of the sensitive houses. Our humble opinion is not in favour of this view. In our various articles and books, we have tried to illustrate and proved the fact that Jupiter's aspect and association with Mars enhances the *kuja doṣa*. Similarly, the intensity of *kuja doṣa* gets multiplied if Moon is associated with Mars or has mutual aspect with Mars.

It is also believed that if Jupiter aspects the 7th house, all adversities regarding marital happiness get nullified. In our humble observation of hundreds of horoscopes, we can support this view. In various horoscopes, aspect of Jupiter in 7th house caused widowhood in its own *daśā bhukti*. Retrograde Jupiter in the 7th house, if owns *upchaya* or *trikas* is more adverse. We have made an attempt to explain the role of Jupiter in the 8th house earlier in the concluding paragraphs of the subject.

Many times, we generally examine the *rāśi* chart and *navāṁśa* chart but I always emphasise on *bhāva* chart as well. If ascendant lord Mars occupies 9th house and gets shifted in 8th house and is aspected by any malefic, widowhood should be predicted. Placement of Mars in 7th or 8th house tends the female towards widowhood. If the lord of the ascendant is strong, widowhood will be prevented. If 9th and 7th house are also strong but Mars, Saturn, *rāhu* or *ketu* are adversely placed in the 7th or 8th or there is any combination of loss of husband, the intensity will be heavily reduced and widowhood will not take place. We therefore, opine to examine the strength of ascendant which is of foremost important. Secondly, the strength of 9th house, thirdly the strength of 7th house should be judged to reach the final conclusion. In many horoscopes, strong combinations of loss of life partner are present but widowhood was prevented because the ascendant and other concerning houses were quite strong and well fortified.

It is believed, due to classical aphorisms that *kuja doṣa* gets nullified if Mars falls in Leo or Aquarius anywhere in the horoscope. We do not support this view at all. In the horoscope of Mrs. Maneka Gandhi, *yogakāraka* Mars joins 8th in Aquarius. Jupiter and Mars aspected each other, even then she suffered loss of husband at 24 years of age on 23rd June of 1980. In case Nos. 15 and 30, Mars joins Aquarius in 8th, even then, they suffered terrible sorrow and grief of early widowhood. I believe that placement of Mars in any sign in 8th is worst for longevity of husband.

If Mars occupies the ascendant or the 2nd house in association with *Rāhu* and *Ketu*, widowhood may take place around 36th to 45th year of age. If many malefics occupy the 7th house or if Mars and *Ketu* conjoin in the 7th house or if Mars joins the 7th and Ketu joins 8th, the female becomes the cause of death, suicide, accident or murder of her husband.

A common belief in our society, among our families prevails that if the girl is *maṅgalī*, she is likely to suffer heavily after marriage. On the contrary, it is also accepted that non *maṅgalī* girls will have high degree of conjugal bliss. Mrs. Sonia Gandhi is not *maṅgalī* but she suffered a lot when her husband Mr. Rajiv Gandhi was killed on May 21st, 1991. She has also faced so many violent deaths in her family. Here the lord of *lagna* Moon who joins the 12th house, is under the mutual aspect with Mars. The lord of 7th and 8th house joins the ascendant under the aspect of Mars. If Saturn and Mars are 8th and 6th from each other, and the ascendant is weak and any of them owns 6th house, such marital disaster is bound to come. If 7th or 8th house is aspected by Mars and Saturn both, similar adversities will appear.

If *Rāhu* or *Ketu* are placed in the 8th house, Mars and Saturn aspect 8th house from anywhere, widowhood will surely be there. Similarly, the conjunction of Mars and *Rāhu* gives rise to widowhood under peculiar circumstances. If Moon is afflicted in one way or the other or it is placed under *pāpa-kartari yoga*, problems in married life will arrive. If Moon is placed in the sign of Mars and aspected by them, the loss of husband may take place. If Moon is placed anywhere in Scorpio or Aries in *aśvinī* or *jyeṣṭhā* and is aspected by Mars as well, the probability of widowhood becomes stronger.

Each case has different configuration of planets and the whole horoscope should be examined carefully. In one horoscope, placement of Mars and Saturn, Mars and *Rāhu* or Mars and *Ketu* in the 8th house can result in widowhood while in other horoscope, it may not do so if the ascendant and 9th house are strong and well fortified. We therefore, suggest to examine *navāṁśa* chart and *bhāva* chart as well before finally reaching any conclusion. If the affliction of the concerning houses are heavier, ascendant is weak and 9th house is also not well disposed, the loss of husband will take place at an early age. If affliction is less and the ascendant and 9th house are strong, the widowhood will not take place before 40 years of age. It is essential to know whether there is any specific and strong combination of widowhood in the birth chart. If such combination is present, the appropriate *daśā bhukti* should be worked out only after overall judgment of the birth chart. Many preventive measures may also be observed from early life, if the combinations of disaster are found present in the horoscope. If the remedial measure selected by us are appropriate and suitable, the curse of widowhood can certainly be converted into ever lasting happy married life.

त्येजेदेकं कुलस्यार्थे ग्रामस्यार्थे कुलं त्यजेत् ।
ग्रामं जनपदस्यार्थे आत्मार्थे पृथिवीं त्यजेत् ।।

Sacrifice a person in order to save a family;
for saving a village, sacrifice a family;
sacrifice a village to save a nation
and for saving yourself, sacrifice
even the whole earth.

Chapter-4

TIMING WIDOWHOOD

Once, my astrological guru told me that after a thorough examination and careful judgement of the horoscope, one can foretell all events of life correctly upto ninety-nine percent. However, the timing of events is really a tough exercise and it is not possible to time each and every event correctly and precisely. In fact, there are so many missing links in astrology, which I believe, have been burnt in the fire of Nalanda University. It was Allauddin Khilji who destroyed invaluable treasure of knowledge of various subjects when he invaded India. As the record of history reveals that this fire was burning for nearly six months, it can be imagined how many manuscripts, books and literature were present in Nalanda which was the first and foremost university of India.

Like all other aspects of life, it is really tough to tell the time of widowhood too with fine accuracy. We have *viṁśottarī daśā system, aṣṭottarī daśā* and transits of planets including *aṣṭaka varga* with us to help in timing events. Apart from *viṁśottarī* and *aṣṭottarī*, there are so many other *daśā* systems like *kālacakra daśā*, Gemini *daśā*, *cara daśā* and *gatyātmaka daśā* systems, which are not much in use. We will confine ourselves to *viṁśottarī daśā* system only and transits. It will not be out of place to mention that only those events can take place in life, which are indicated by the lords of major and sub-period during particular course of time. It depends on our knowledge, experience and intelligence that how appropriate use of astrological rules, we make in making accurate prediction and observations. Transits of planets can only help in fine-tuning of time of the events indicated by *daśā bhukti* during that period.

We will attempt sincerely and honestly, to work out the time of widowhood of a few cases for the benefit of our readers. However, before that, let us look at few aphorisms from classics.

क्रूर मृत्यौ मश्त्युयो मन्नवांशे वैधव्यं स्यात्तद्दशान्तर्दशादौ

1. It means that the widowhood takes place during *daśā bhukti* of the *navāṁśa* lord occupied by the lord of the 8th house provided malefics occupy the 8th house.
2. It is not at all essential that widowhood will take place during the *daśā bhukti* of Mars, Saturn or *Rāhu* if these planets are responsible for causing widowhood. It may take place during the period of 2nd lord or the planet occupied by 2nd house as 2nd house is 8th from 7th and governs death of husband. The sub-period lord may be 2nd from the major *daśā* lord responsible for widowhood or the sub-period will be of 7th or 8th lord from *mahādaśā* lord or the planet posited there or may bring such disasters during their *bhukti*. The planets occupying or aspecting or making relationship with the 2nd house of 2nd lord, 8th house of 8th lord may bring widowhood, or death of the spouse. 8th house is actually 2nd from 7th. The 2nd house is 8th from 7th house and indicates death of husband. So the 8th and 2nd house should be examined for the judgement of

widowhood in the horoscope of a female. Acharya Mukund Ballabh writes in his great classic *Phalita Mārtaṇḍa* under *Strī Jātaka chapter* as *śloka* 18:-

क्रूरेऽष्टमे विधवता निधने खरेंऽशे यस्य स्थितो वयसि तस्य समे प्रदिस्ठा ।
सत्स्वर्थगेषु मरणं स्वयमेव तस्याः कन्यालिंगो हरिषु चाल्पसुतत्वामन्दौ ।।

If malefic is placed in the 8th house from *lagna* in the horoscope of a woman, the widowhood will take place during the major or sub-period of the *navāṁśa* lord occupied by the malefic occupant of the 8th house. If a benefic is placed in the 2nd house (benefic by nature, placement and lordship, such benefic should be free from malefic aspect or association) the woman will die in front of her husband, i.e., she will obtain *akhaṇḍa saubhāgya*. Acharya Mukund Ballabh further writes in *śloka* 20 of *Phalita Mārtaṇḍa*

रन्ध्रे मिश्रबले शुभाशुभखगैरालोकिते वा युते
दाम्पत्योः समकालमृत्युमखिलज्योतिर्विदः संविदुः।
एकस्थौ मृदुलग्नपौ च यदि वा लग्नस्थिते कामपे
कामस्थे तनुपे शुभग्रहयुते मृत्युस्तयोस्तुल्यतः

The husband and wife will die together if the 8th house in a female horoscope is strong and it is aspected or associated with benefics and malefics. If lord of 7th and *lagna* are conjoined or there is mutual exchange between lord of 1st house and 7th house and in addition to that 7th lord is associated with benefics or a benefic, the death of wife and husband will be together. This is said by all astrologers.

क्रूरेऽष्टमे विधवता निधनेश्वरांशे
यस्य स्थितो वयसि तस्य समे प्रदिष्टा।
सत्स्वर्थगेषु मरणं स्वयमेव तस्याः
कन्यालिगो हरिषु चाल्पसुतत्वमन्दोः।।43।।

Chapter 16 *Jātaka Pārijāta*, Volume II

If malefic occupies the 8th house, the wife dies during the *daśā bhukti* of *navāṁśa* lord of that malefic. If benefics occupy the 2nd house, she will not suffer widowhood. On the contrary, she will die prior to her husband. If Moon falls in Taurus, Virgo, Leo or Scorpio, there will be few children only.

3. Widowhood may come during *daśā bhukti* of the *navāṁśa* lord of the planet occupied by 8th house or the lord of the 8th house. First, the planet responsible for widowhood may be worked out. The *navāṁśa* lord of that planet may create such havoc during their *daśā bhukti*. Find out the *navāṁśa* lord of the planet, which is the worst malefic and responsible to cause widowhood. Find out the *sarvāṣṭaka varga* points in the sign occupied by him. That will be the age during which widowhood may occur.
4. Subtract the longitude of the ascendant or ascendant lord from the longitude of the 7th lord, when Jupiter will transit over the point so obtained, widowhood or divorce may come in evidence. However, the transit should only be used when *daśā bhukti* is indicating widowhood strongly. The use of transit is to make the prediction more precise and to time the event correctly within a shorter span.
5. It is generally believed that the combination of Jupiter and Venus in the ascendant or 7th house will bestow lot of good fortune in respect

of life partner but it is not so in true sense. Generally, Venus-Jupiter *daśā bhukti* creates problems in married life, if at least one of these planets own malefic houses. If the longitude of Venus is less than the longitude of Jupiter and both fall in the constellation of a malefic or obtain *navāṁśa* of a malefic planet, there will be loss of spouse.

6. Placement of Mars with Sun, *Ketu* or *Rāhu* either in the ascendant or in 7th, 8th or 12th house may bring loss of life partner.
7. If the lord of the 7th house is conjoined with Saturn and is aspected by Mars, one will suffer widowhood provided Moon and *Rāhu* join 6th house in addition to that.
8. If the combination of widowhood is present with strong Mars under the aspect of Saturn, early widowhood is likely.

Any *yoga* regarding widowhood should be examined properly before final conclusion. We will be discussing here the art of timing widowhood. It is a tough task. I believe that one may be successful in timing widowhood if he is well versed with the rules and observation regarding this mishappening of life. Here the cases are from different walks of life and all cases have different configuration for working of the time of widowhood. If we study the *daśā bhukti* which caused widowhood and why did it do so, I strongly believe there will be precise accuracy in our foretelling time of widowhood. These cases have been examined and explained here:-

Case 4.1 – (Horoscope No.1-*vide* p.134)

Marriage - June 24th, 1994 at 25 years of age during Sun-Mercury *daśā bhukti*.

Widowhood – November 4th, 1994 after 4½ months of marriage during Sun-Mercury *daśā bhukti.*

Mercury is under the influence of Mars. It is combust and falls in inimical constellation of Moon. The 2nd house which indicates marriage and death of husband is owned by Sun. The 2nd house from Sun is owned by Mercury who is heavily afflicted by Mars. Moreover Mercury obtains *navāṁśa* of Mars, therefore, during the *bhukti* of Mercury in the major period of Sun, she suffered loss of husband.

Case 4.2 – (Horoscope No.2-*vide* p.137)

Marriage – March 6th, 1996 at 20 years of age during Venus-*Rāhu daśā bhukti*

Widowhood – March 8th, 1999 in Venus-Jupiter *daśā* bhukti

According to the *śloka* quoted above, *Ketu* who joins the 8th house falls in the *navāṁśa* of Venus. Therefore, in major period of Venus, widowhood took place when sub-period of Jupiter was operating. Jupiter is 7th lord under *vargottama navāṁśa.* It cannot be believed that she suffered widowhood in Venus-Jupiter period. Jupiter is placed under *pāpa-kartari yoga.* Moon falls in *jyeṣṭha nakṣatra* and is aspected by Mars. This combination is responsible for widowhood. Here Jupiter is 8th lord from Mars and 2nd lord from Moon. Therefore, Jupiter's sub-period killed her husband. It may be noted that if Jupiter joins 7th house in a watery sign under affliction, adversity may appear soon after marriage.

Case 4.3 – (Horoscope No.3-*vide* p.140)

Marriage – May 8th, 1996 during *Rāhu-Rāhu daśā bhukti.*

Widowhood – April 17th, 1997 during *Rāhu*-Jupiter *daśā bhukti.*

This is a typical case of widowhood. She got married on May 8th, 1996 in *Rāhu-Rāhu* period and *Rāhu* is placed in 12th house with 12th lord Jupiter. Her husband expired on April 17th, 1997 during *Rāhu* Jupiter *daśā bhukti*. *Rāhu* obtains *navāṁśa* of Mars, Jupiter is 7th lord from Moon and joins the 4th house as reckoned from Moon. Jupiter is certainly a malefic for Capricorn ascendant and as soon as Jupiter's sub-period in *Rāhu* began, the husband suddenly lost his life. If Jupiter is afflicted in the horoscope of a female, the adversity may come in major or sub-period of Jupiter. Here afflicted Jupiter aspected the 8th house and caused the tragedy within 10 months after marriage.

Case 4.4 – (Horoscope No.4-*vide* p.142)

Marriage – October 5th, 1973 *Rāhu*-Jupiter period
Widowhood – March 2nd, 1978 *Rāhu*-Mercury period
Second marriage – September 29th, 1979
First son – March 1st, 1975
Second son – October 17th, 1980

Jupiter occupies the 7th house in Aquarius. Here Jupiter is forming *kendra trikoṇa Rāja Yoga*. She suffered widowhood 4½ years after marriage during *Rāhu*-Mercury period. *Rāhu* joins the 8th house and Mercury is 8th from *Rāhu* and owns 7th house from *Rāhu* and 11th house from ascendant. Here Mercury obtains *navāṁśa* of debilitation, it is combust too. Seeing the position of Mars in 5th and *Rāhu* in the 8th and Saturn in the 2nd house, the widowhood may be expected within 36 to 45 years of age. If the marriage could be avoided during *Rāhu*-Jupiter period, it was quite possible to save widowhood. Here I want to say that planets which indicate loss of husband, will not essentially cause widowhood during their *daśā bhukti*. *daśā bhukti* of those planets may not come in life at all. The widowhood may appear during the *daśā bhukti* of those planets which show the possibility of adversity due to affliction, conjunction or aspect by malefics and during *daśā* of planets which are related to the concerning houses as well. *Navāṁśa* chart should certainly be examined carefully. In the present case, *Rāhu* in 12th, Mercury in 8th under debilitation in *navāṁśa* chart shows adverse results because Mercury is 2nd lord from *navāṁśa lagna*. In *Rāśi* chart, *Rāhu* and Mercury are in *khaḍaṣṭaka* position and Mercury is 2nd lord which also shows the death of husband as it is 8th from 7th. Mercury is 8th from *Rāhu*.

Case 4.5 – (Horoscope No.5-*vide* p.144)

Marriage – February 10th, 1986 during Venus-Jupiter *daśā bhukti*.

Widowhood – December 4th, 2000 during Moon-Venus *daśā bhukti*.

One daughter – June 29th, 1992

7th lord Moon falls in *aśvinī* in Aries and the moon is aspected by its dispositor Mars. Mutual aspect between Mars and Saturn is also responsible for this great tragedy. The death of husband took place in the sub-period of Venus in the major period of Moon. Venus is the lord of 2nd and 7th house as reckoned from 7th lord Moon and Venus is adversely placed in the 8th house in Leo with Sun. Sun and Venus are placed in *pūrva phālgunī* constellation and in the same *navāṁśa* of Libra where the Sun obtains its debilitation.

I believe that the position of the 2nd lord from *lagna* should be considered as it is 8th from the 7th house and rules death of husband as well. Similarly, the position 2nd lord from the position of 7th

lord is also very inauspicious. Mars is the *kāraka* of widowhood and Jupiter is the *kāraka* of husband. So, examine the ascendant, the position of 7th lord as *lagna*, Mars and Jupiter, to reach to the final conclusion. Here Venus sub–period caused widowhood. Venus is 8th from ascendant and ascendant lord. From 7th lord Moon, Venus is the lord of 2nd and 7th house and joins the 5th house in Leo. From Jupiter, Venus is the lord of 8th and 3rd house. From Mars, Venus is the 8th lord and joins the 11th house with Sun in Leo. Thus, Venus becomes *māraka* for husband from all angles. The widowhood came during the major period of Moon because Moon occupies the Aries and is aspected by Mars and Saturn. This is the strong indication of widowhood. Widowhood was possible in Moon–Mars *daśā bhukti* or in Moon–Venus *daśā bhukti*. Placement of retrograde Jupiter in own sign Pisces, in 3rd house and its aspect over the 7th and 9th house resulted in the conjugal bliss for about 15 years.

Case 4.6 – (Horoscope No.6-*vide* p.146)

Marriage – January 30th, 1975 during *Ketu*-Saturn *daśā bhukti*.

Widowhood – July 26th, 2002 during Moon-Moon *daśā bhukti*.

Birth of first daughter – April 13th, 1978

Birth of second daughter – July 3rd, 1985

Here Moon is placed in *jyeṣṭha nakṣatra* in 10th house in Scorpio under debilitation. Moon receives the adverse aspect of Mars as well. Moon and Mars are in *khaḍaṣṭaka* position. Therefore, widowhood took place when she was running under sub-period of Moon in the major period of Moon. Moon is 7th lord as reckoned from 7th lord Sun. From Mars-Moon is 4th lord and joins the 8th house in conjunction with *Rāhu* and Saturn. From Jupiter, Mars is placed in the 8th house and Mars is the dispositor of Moon, therefore, the affliction of Moon is maximum as regards to loss of husband.

Case 4.7 – (Horoscope No.7-*vide* p.149)

Marriage April 27th, 1999 during Saturn-Venus *daśā bhukti*

Widowhood – June, 27th, 1999 during Saturn-Venus *daśā bhukti*

Widowhood took place during Saturn-Venus *daśā bhukti*. Venus is lord of 2nd and 7th house from ascendant and joins the 12th house under exaltation with *Rāhu*. Placement of 2nd lord in the 12th house with malefic may cause widowhood in *daśā bhukti* of that planet. Here 7th lord Venus is afflicted by *Rāhu* in the12th house. Venus owns 3rd and 7th house from its own position. Retrograde Mars occupies the 8th house and Venus is 12th and 7th lord from there and is afflicted by *Rāhu*. Venus is 10th and 2nd lord as reckoned from Jupiter and falls in 7th house over the axis of *Rāhu* and *Ketu*. Thus, Venus becomes the *māraka* for husband. In this case, the marriage should have been avoided during *Rāhu*–Venus *daśā bhukti*.

Case 4.8 – (Horoscope No.8-*vide* p.151)

Marriage – in the 17th year during Mars-Mars *daśā bhukti*.

Widowhood – in 18th year during Mars-*Rāhu daśā bhukti*.

The *lagna* and 6th lord Venus joins the 8th house in association with inimical Moon and *Rāhu* and is aspected by Saturn and inimical Jupiter. 7th lord Mars occupies own sign Aries in 12th house under mutual aspect with Saturn. Widowhood took place during sub-period of *Rāhu* in the major period of Mars. From the ascendant, 7th lord Mars joins the 12th house and is aspected by Saturn, this indicates severe harm or loss of husband.

From Jupiter-Moon Venus and *Rāhu* are conjoined in the 7th house and are aspected by 8th lord Saturn. Jupiter is afflicted due to conjunction with *Ketu* and due to mutual aspect with *lagna* lord Venus. 8th house indicates pan of married life and it is owned by Jupiter who occupies the 2nd house and falls over the axis of *Rāhu* and *Ketu*. Therefore, she suffered widowhood during the major period of Mars who is most heavily afflicted and adversely placed under mutual aspect with Saturn. *Rāhu* is placed in 8th from *lagna* and 7th house from Jupiter. Therefore, the husband expired in the accident when the sub-period of Mars in major period of *Rāhu* was operative over her.

Case 4.9 – (Horoscope No.9-*vide* p.154)

Marriage – March 7th, 1979 during Jupiter-Mercury *daśā bhukti*

Widowhood – March 19th, 1985 during Jupiter-Mars *daśā bhukti*

A son born on February 20th, 1980 and a daughter on February 18th, 1982.

Jupiter is 4th and 7th lord and occupies Martian sign Aries. 8th lord Mars occupies the 2nd house and has mutual aspect with Saturn. This is a classical case when she suffered widowhood when sub-period of Mars was operating over her in the major period of Jupiter. If 7th lord is placed in 8th house and 8th lord aspects the same, widowhood may take place during their *daśā bhukti*. From 7th lord Jupiter-Mars is 7th and from Mars, Jupiter is 7th.

Thus, Jupiter-Mars *daśā bhukti* will cause widowhood is indicated from all angle.

Case 4.10 – (Horoscope No.10-*vide* p.156)

Widowhood – February 28th, 1982 during *Rāhu* Jupiter *daśā bhukti*

Yogakāraka Mars occupies the 7th house and *Ketu* occupies the 8th house. Jupiter is the 8th lord and is afflicted in the 10th house. Jupiter obtains *navāṁśa* of Saturn who is *mārakeśa* for Leo ascendant. There is mutual exchange between Mars and Saturn in this horoscope. *Rāhu* is placed in the 8th house from mars, i.e., 2nd from ascendant. Jupiter is the 8th lord from ascendant and 7th lord from *Rāhu*. Therefore, her husband committed suicide on February 28th, 1982 when the sub-period of Jupiter in the major period of *Rāhu* was running. For Leo ascendant, Jupiter is a malefic, therefore, the widowhood took place in Jupiter's sub–period. Jupiter-*Rāhu* both obtains *navāṁśa* of Saturn who is *mārakeśa* for husband. Therefore, *daśā bhukti* of *Rāhu*-Jupiter proved disastrous for her.

Case 4.11 – (Horoscope No.11-*vide* p.158)

Marriage – October 87 during Jupiter-Jupiter *daśā bhukti*

Widowhood – January 89 during Jupiter-Jupiter *daśā bhukti*

Strong indication of widowhood is present in this horoscope as Moon-*Ketu*-Mercury are present in 7th house. The Saturn aspects this combination. Such a serious affliction of 7th house by Mars, *Ketu*, Mercury and Saturn will certainly cause very early widowhood. The marriage took place in Jupiter-Jupiter *daśā bhukti* and widowhood also took place during the same bhukti. Here retrograde Jupiter who is the lord of the 8th house is placed in the 2nd house under the aspect of malefic Mars and inimical Venus. The Jupiter becomes a *mārakeśa* for husband. Therefore, the husband died in the fire accident in the sub-period of Jupiter in the major period of Jupiter. From 7th lord Mars, Jupiter is placed in the 8th house and that automatically becomes a *maraka* for husband. In *navāṁśa* chart, Mars and Saturn are conjoined in the 8th house and 12th from the position of the *lagna* lord Venus. In *navāṁśa* chart, lord of the 8th house is Jupiter. Mars and Saturn obtain *navāṁśa* of Jupiter, therefore, Jupiter becomes killer for husband from all angles.

Case 4.12 – (Horoscope No.12-*vide* p.160)

Marriage – February 9th, 1974 during *Ketu* – Moon *daśā bhukti*

Widowhood – March 16th, 1976 during *Ketu*–Jupiter *daśā bhukti*

Mars occupies the 7th house of its own and 8th and 11th lord Jupiter who is placed in the ascendant, aspects the 7th house and Mars. Widowhood took place in the sub-period of Jupiter in the major period of *Ketu*. Jupiter is the lord of the 8th house and is aspected by Mars. Therefore, the accidental death of her husband took place in the sub-period of Jupiter in the major period of *Ketu*. It is a rule that *navāṁśa* lord of the malefic placed in the 8th house may give rise to widowhood. Here *Rāhu* is the dispositor of Jupiter and *Rāhu* obtains the *navāṁśa* of Jupiter as well. Therefore, Jupiter's sub-period was fatal for her husband. *Ketu* also acts like Mars and its aspect over the 8th house shows widowhood during its own major period. In case there is lesser adversity in regard to span of married life, probability of widowhood could be in the major period of Venus in the sub–period of Jupiter or Mars.

Case 4.13 – (Horoscope No.13-*vide* p.162)

Marriage – March 11th, 1961 during Moon – *Rāhu daśā bhukti*

Widowhood – January 10th, 1962 during Moon – Jupiter *daśā bhukti*

One of the worst combination of widowhood is present in this birth chart. It may be noted that 2nd and 7th lord Mars occupies the 8th house and this is sufficient to give rise to widowhood to any female. Here Saturn occupies the 2nd house. There is mutual aspect between Saturn and Mars, so widowhood was destined to her soon after marriage. Moon occupies the 7th house in martian sign and falls in *Aśvinī nakṣatra.* From Moon, Saturn is placed in the 8th house under the aspect of Mars. Moon, Mars and Saturn obtain *vargottama navāṁśa.* 3rd and 6th lord Jupiter who is a malefic for Libra ascendant joins the 5th house in Aquarius in association with Sun. Jupiter is combust and is shifted in the 6th house with Sun. From ascendant Jupiter is the 3rd lord and is dispositor of *Ketu.* From Moon-Jupiter is the 12th lord and is placed in malefic sign in combustion in the constellation of *Rāhu.* Here the dispositor of Mars that is the 8th lord Venus falls in the sign and *navāṁśa* of Jupiter. Therefore, Jupiter's sub-period in the major period of Moon has given the biggest tragedy of loss of husband within 10 months after marriage. Here again we see very early widowhood is indicated to the female. In such case the planets placed in the

8th house and *navāṁśa* lord of that or *navāṁśa* lord of the 8th lord may cause widowhood. If Mars or Saturn indicates widowhood, then the *navāṁśa* or the constellation obtained by the same is also important while examining the time of loss of husband.

Case 4.14 – (Horoscope No.14-*vide* p.164)

Marriage – 1990 during *Ketu*-Moon *daśā bhukti*

Widowhood – November 18th, 1999 during Venus-Moon *daśā bhukti*

Two daughters

Venus is the lord of the 7th and 12th house who is a malefic for Scorpio ascendant. Venus falls in Leo in association with Jupiter and Mercury and sub-period lord Moon is 8th from there. Even in *bhāva* chart, Moon and Venus are in *khaḍaṣṭaka* position. Moon falls over the axis of *Rāhu* and *Ketu* and obtains *navāṁśa* of its debilitation. Major period lord Venus obtains *navāṁśa* of Moon. Moon falls in Saturn's *nakṣatra Uttarā Bhādrapadā* whereas Saturn is debilitated in 6th house under *vargottama navāṁśa*. In *bhāva* chart, Mars is shifted in the 8th house, Mars obtains *navāṁśa* of Venus. Therefore, it was the major period of Venus which resulted into her widowhood. On the other hand Mars falls in the sign of Moon and Moon obtains *navāṁśa* of Mars, therefore, when the sub-period of Moon was running, her widowhood took place.

Case 4.15 – (Horoscope No.15-*vide* p.167)

Marriage – February 27th, 1991 during Moon-*Rāhu daśā bhukti*

Widowhood – August 9th, 2001 during Mars-Saturn *daśā bhukti*

First son expired, second son alive

A combination of widowhood is very strongly present in this birth chart as *Rāhu* and Mars occupy the 8th house which is 7th from *lagna* lord Moon. 7th lord, debilitated Saturn aspects the 7th house and 9th lord Jupiter. 12th lord Mercury occupies the 7th house under Saturn's aspect. It is said that the *kuja doṣa* gets nullified if Moon and Jupiter aspect Mars but we have not found this correct in our observation regarding number of cases. In this horoscope *Rāhu* and Mars occupy the 8th house under the aspect of benefic Jupiter and *lagna* lord Moon but she suffered widowhood on August 9th, 2001 after about 10 years of her marriage during Mars Saturn *daśā bhukti*. Mars is *yogakāraka* for Cancer ascendant but its close conjunction with *Rāhu* in the 8th house in Saturn's sign Aquarius resulted into widowhood in its major period. Had Mars not been a *yogakāraka* here, the widowhood would have come earlier? Sub–period lord is Saturn who is placed in martian sign Aries under debilitation. 8th lord Mars also occupies Saturn's sign, therefore sub-period of Saturn is strong enough to bring widowhood to her. *Rāhu* who occupies the 8th house, joins the *navāṁśa* of Mars. Therefore, the widowhood resulted into the major period of Mars. In *navāṁśa* chart, Mars and Saturn both aspect each other and indicate accidental death of her husband in their *daśā bhukti*. Her husband died in a road accident due to extreme loss of blood while going from Delhi to Jaipur.

Case 4.16 – (Horoscope No.16-*vide* p.170)

Marriage – May 17th, 1981 during *Rāhu*-Saturn *daśā bhukti*

Widowhood – November 4th, 1996 during Jupiter-Saturn *daśā bhukti*

First daughter - February 20th, 1984
Second daughter - October 12th, 1987

She is very charming, smart, intelligent, dynamic, dashing and diligent doctor of Gynaecology in a Medical College. She has received various awards, appreciations, and certificates for her meritorious performance. She had a love marriage on May 17th, 1981. She was enjoying immense happiness, love, care, prosperity and emotional feelings in her family life with her children and husband. Suddenly on November 4th, 1996, her husband suffered a massive heart attack when he was shifting from one house to another in the Medical College campus. Here 8th lord is Jupiter who aspects the 8th house, even then the loss of her husband could not be saved at such an early age. She suffered this tragedy during the major period of Jupiter in sub-period of Saturn, Jupiter is the 8th lord and is aspected by malefic Saturn. Jupiter is also 8th from Moon, therefore, the husband died in the major period of Jupiter. Saturn, *Rāhu* and Venus are placed in the 7th house and *Rāhu* obtains *navāṁśa* of Saturn. Moreover, Saturn is 2nd lord as reckoned from Jupiter, therefore, sub-period of Saturn resulted into this biggest tragedy of her life. *Rāhu* occupies the 7th house and falls in *Jyeṣṭha nakṣatra* in Scorpio sign. This is bad for husband's longevity. It may be noted that planets placed in the 7th house if falls in *Jyeṣṭhā*, *Dhaniṣṭhā* or *Aśleṣā*, that will curtail happiness in married life. Here affliction of 7th house by *Rāhu* and Saturn resulted into late marriage and early widowhood. Aspect of Mars over 8th house is responsible for early widowhood as it owns 7th and aspects 8th.

I have mentioned earlier that for timing widowhood, position of planets should be reckoned from Mars as Mars is the *kāraka* of widowhood. Jupiter is 7th lord from Mars and is placed in 12th house from Mars, under the aspect of 6th and 7th lord Saturn as reckoned from Jupiter. Therefore, she was miserably trapped by the hands of misfortune of loss of her life partner during the sub-period of Saturn in the major period of Jupiter.

Case – 4.17 – (Horoscope No.17-*vide* p.172)

Marriage – September 29th, 1974 during Venus–Jupiter *daśā bhukti*

Widowhood – June 23rd, 1980 during Venus-Mercury *daśā bhukti*

Son – March 13th, 1980 during Venus – Mercury *daśā bhukti*

This is the horoscope of Mrs. Maneka Gandhi, wife of late Mr. Sanjay Gandhi. She got married on September 29th, 1974 in sub-period of Jupiter in the major period of Venus. She lost her husband in a plane crash on June 23rd, 1980 during Venus Mercury *daśā bhukti.* Venus is placed in the 12th house in Gemini. Venus is 8th from 7th and 8th lord Saturn and *Rāhu* as well. *Rāhu* obtains *navāṁśa* of Venus and Venus obtains its own *navāṁśa.* Mars who is placed in the 8th house, obtains *navāṁśa* of Mercury. Therefore, widowhood came in the sub-period of Mercury in the major period of Venus. Moreover, Mercury is 8th as reckoned from Mars and Venus is 8th as reckoned from 7th lord Saturn. Thus, the widowhood is clearly indicated in the sub-period of Mercury in the major period of Venus. It is not essential that Mars or Saturn will cause widowhood though they are placed in the 8th house and Saturn owns 8th house too.

Case – 4.18 – (Horoscope No.18-*vide* p.174)

Marriage – 1988 during Mercury-Venus *daśā bhukti.*

Widowhood – October 2nd, 1989 during sub-period of Sun in the major period of Mercury.

She is a famous film actress of Indian cinema. She got married with Mr. Mukesh Agarwal after a long lasting courtship and after about a year, her husband committed suicide due to misbehaviour of Rekha with him. He was a business tycoon but he loved his wife so much that he could not bear the negative attitude of his wife. Here *lagna* lord Jupiter occupies 8th house in its sign of exaltation Cancer and is aspected by Mars and Saturn both in *rāśi* chart as well as *bhāva* chart. Here Jupiter obtains *navāṁśa* of the Sun. therefore, she suffered widowhood in the sub-period of Sun in the major period of Mercury who is the 7th lord and obtains *navāṁśa* of its debilitation. It may be noted that *Ketu* is placed in the 7th house and Mars aspects 7th and 8th house and *lagna* lord Jupiter. Conjunction of Mars and *Rāhu* in the ascendant is strong indication of widowhood especially due to aspect of 2nd lord Saturn. *Ketu* is placed in the 7th house in the sign of Mercury, therefore, Mercury will give adverse effect of *Ketu* during its major period. Moreover, Mercury is 8th lord from 8th lord Moon and Sun is 8th from Moon. Mercury falls in the *Svāti* constellation, which is ruled by *Rāhu*. Mercury obtains *navāṁśa* of debilitation, that is Mercury falls in Jupiter's *navāṁśa*, therefore, it becomes a killer of husband. Moon and Jupiter both are planets of emotions who are involved here in giving rise to widowhood to Rekha. This is the reason that her husband got a severe emotional set back and committed suicide. Here again, we see that the indications of widowhood are present in this horoscope because Mars and *Rāhu* are conjoined in the ascendant aspected by Saturn and ascendant lord occupies the 8th house which is aspected by Saturn and Mars both. 6th lord Venus occupies the 12th house in Martian sign under *pāpakartari yoga*. However, at the time of widowhood, *daśā bhukti* of none of these planets who are involved in causing widowhood, was running. Therefore, for any events of life sub-period and major period may be different from those planets who are indicating a particular event, good or bad. If we keep it in mind, we will definitely be benefited in timing events of life.

Case 4.19 – (Horoscope No.19-*vide* p.176)

Marriage – February 25th, 1968 during Jupiter-Ketu *daśā bhukti*

Widowhood – May 21st, 1991 during Saturn-*Rāhu daśā bhukti*

Mrs. Sonia Gandhi, wife of Rajiv Gandhi, lost her husband during Saturn-*Rāhu* period. Saturn is 7th and 8th lord and is worst malefic for Cancer ascendant. Mars also aspects Saturn. Saturn is retrograde and is 8th lord from Moon as well. *Lagna* lord Moon occupies 12th house and is shifted in 11th house from where Mars is 8th. *Rāhu* falls in Moon's *nakṣatra Rohiṇī* and Moon falls in *Rāhu's nakṣatra Ārdrā*. Moon is hemmed between Saturn and *Rāhu* giving rise to *pāpakartari yoga*. Therefore, sub-period of *Rāhu* in the major period of Moon was extremely bad as Saturn is 8th lord from Moon and joins 2nd house.

As reckoned from Mars, Saturn is in 8th house and *Rāhu* is in the 6th house. From Jupiter, *Rāhu* is 8th and Saturn is 10th, therefore Saturn obtains *navāṁśa* of Mars and *Rāhu* is 8th from there, therefore sub-period of *Rāhu* in the major period of Saturn resulted into the loss of her husband.

Many times it becomes difficult to interpret correct *daśā bhukti* for timing widowhood. In this case Saturn obtains *navāṁśa* of Mars, therefore, tragedy was possible in Mars bhukti in Saturn but a careful evaluation of the horoscope reveals that the widowhood took place in the sub-period of *Rāhu* and not in the sub-period of Mars as per the reasons explained above.

Case 4.20 – (Horoscope No.20-*vide* p.178)

Marriage – May 22nd, 1989 during Moon-Mercury *daśā bhukti*

Widowhood – May 7th, 1992 during Mars-Mars *daśā bhukti*

She is a beautiful and very rich woman whose marriage was ceremonised on May 22nd, 1989 during sub–period of Mercury in the major period of Moon. The husband was murdered due to personal enemity on May 7th, 1992 just after three years of marriage, during Mars-Mars *daśā bhukti*.

Mars and *Rāhu* occupy the 8th house with and fall in Saturn's sign Capricorn. This shows early widowhood. For timing widowhood correctly, one should examine sub-period of planets responsible for widowhood during the major period of the same planet in which the marriage took place and especially when the major period lord is adversely placed and playing a role to cause widowhood.

Here *Rāhu* is placed in the 8th house with Mars and Moon. Therefore, major period of Mars and sub-period of Mars, indicate widowhood in its *daśā bhukti*. The 8th lord Saturn is placed in the 12th house under retrogration and aspects 7th lord Jupiter who occupies the 6th house in Martian sign Scorpio. Here the 8th lord Saturn damaged the 7th house and its lord Jupiter. *Rāhu* and Mars damaged the 8th house, i.e., the house of longevity of husband. Therefore, the husband was killed during sub-period of Mars in the major period of Mars.

Placement of 7th lord Jupiter in Martian sign Scorpio in the 6th house and the placement of *Rāhu* with Mars in the 8th house and placement of 8th lord Saturn under debilitated *navāṁśa* in Aries shows that her husband will be killed soon after marriage.

Case 4.21 – (Horoscope No.21-*vide* p.180)

Marriage – November 23rd, 1987 during sub-period of Venus in the major period of Mercury.

Widowhood – December 17th, 1987 during sub-period of Venus in the major period of Mercury.

We have tried to illustrate the correctness of aphorisms mentioned by our sages in various classical works. In the early pages of this *chapter*, we have referred the *śloka* of *Phalita Mārtaṇḍa* that the death of husband will take place during the major or sub-period of the *navāṁśa* occupied by the malefic occupant of the 8th house. In this horoscope, *Rāhu* occupies the 8th house in Aries under the mutual aspect of 8th and 3rd lord Mars. *Rāhu* obtains *navāṁśa* of Mercury, therefore, widowhood took place in the major period of Mercury. Lord of the 2nd house is Venus who is placed in inimical sign Leo in the 12th house. Moreover, Mars and *Ketu* are the dispositor of Venus and Venus obtains own *navāṁśa* in the 8th house in *navāṁśa* chart. This horoscope indicates very early widowhood immediately after marriage. Therefore, marriage and widowhood took place in the same *daśā bhukti* of Mercury-Venus. The lord of 2nd house resulted into marriage but due to severe affliction of 2nd house and its lord, the husband was crushed by a truck just after 24 days of her marriage. 8th and 2nd house indicate loss of husband. The influence of Mars, *Ketu* and *Rāhu* on the 8th house and the placement of the 6th lord Saturn in the 7th house under retrograde motion is extremely adverse for conjugal bliss and life of her husband. In such cases, where the combination of loss of husband are present, there must be proper matching of horoscopes by the competent astrologers. Selection of *muhūrta* for marriage is best prevention. Dr. B.V. Raman has emphasized a lot on the proper selection of time (muhurta) which saves widowhood, divorce and other adversities.

Case 4.22 – (Horoscope No.22-*vide* p.182)

Marriage – December 5th, 1961 during sub-period of Mercury in the major period of Venus.

Widowhood – January 1st, 1969 during sub-period of Venus in the major period of Sun

Children – One son and two daughters

This lady was born in Aries ascendant with Mars in the ascendant. *Rāhu* occupies 8th house in martian sign and is aspected by Mars as well. Here *Rāhu* obtains the *navāṁśa* of Sun and at the time of widowhood, major period of Sun was running. Venus is the lord of the 2nd and 7th house and hence it becomes a *mārakeśa* and its placement in the 12th house in the sign of exaltation with Saturn and Mercury is adverse especially because Venus obtains *navāṁśa* of its debilitation. Therefore, sub-period of Venus in the major period of Sun brought widowhood to her on January 1st, 1969. It may also be noted that she was born in *Maghā nakṣatra* 1st *pada* which is an adverse *mūla* and Venus is also 8th from Moon alongwith Saturn and debilitated Mercury. Mars in the *lagna* in Aries and *Rāhu* in the 8th house in Scorpio are indicating widowhood within 10 years of marriage in a general way. Marriage took place on November 5th, 1961 during Venus- Mercury *daśā bhukti.* Venus *daśā* ended on September 18th, 1963 so the widowhood could have come in the subsequent major period of the Sun. Ultimately, she lost her husband in an accident on January 1st, 1969 during Sun-Venus period. Both are in *dvidvādaśa* position in *rāśi* chart. Thus it could be the sub–period of Venus who is the strong *mārakeśa* for her husband in various ways. Venus is 8th from Moon and Sun is 7th from there. From Mars, Venus is the lord of 2nd and 7th house and joins the 12th house. From Jupiter, Sun is the lord of the 8th house and joins 2nd house. Mars and *lagna* both fall in *aśvinī nakṣatra* and are 3^0 apart. Jupiter is debilitated and falls in the *nakṣatra* of Mars, that is *dhaniṣṭhā*. Jupiter obtains Sun's *navāṁśa*. This confirms the possibility of widowhood within a period of 9 and 10 years of marriage.

Case 4.23 – (Horoscope No.23-*vide* p.184)

Marriage – November 24th, 1968 during the sub-period of Venus in the major period of Mars.

Widowhood – November 7th, 1997 during the sub-period of Venus in the major period of Jupiter

Children – Two daughters and a son.

This is the horoscope of a charming female who was married at 20 years of age on November 24th, 1968 during Mars-Venus *daśā bhukti*. She faced lot of miseries in her conjugal life. She remained separated from her husband for 7 years after her marriage due to various undesirable activities of mother-in-law. After the days of her misery, she enjoyed conjugal bliss of high order for 20 years and lost her husband suddenly due to a massive heart attack on November 7th, 1997 during major period of Jupiter and sub-period of Venus. Now again applying the same formula that malefic Mars occupies the 8th house in inimical sign Virgo and obtains *navāṁśa* of Jupiter, therefore, widowhood took place during Jupiter's major period.

Moreover, Jupiter is the lord of 2nd house and occupies *jyeṣṭhā nakṣatra*. Therefore, Jupiter is strong enough to cause the death of her spouse. Venus is 7th lord and 12th lord from Jupiter and is 8th from radical location of Jupiter in the *rāśi* chart as well as in *navāṁśa* chart. Therefore, such a great tragedy of loss of her husband took place in the sub–period of Venus in the major period of Jupiter. Both are the best benefics and Venus happens to be a *yogakāraka* for Aquarius ascendant. Moreover, Jupiter and Venus occupy quadrant and triangle respectively. This may mislead to find out the correct time of such a tragedy which is strongly indicated in her birth chart. Therefore, the rules and aphorisms as given in classical works must be applied carefully for accuracy and correctness in the observation.

It is easy to find out major period lord who will bring the widowhood. From there, examine the position of 2nd and 7th lord and also from *lagna*, the position of 2nd and 7th lord should be judged. If the 7th lord is placed in 12th house under affliction, that may bring such tragedy. It is immaterial whether the concerning planet is a *yogakaraka* or it is *svakṣetrī*, exalted or debilitated. The careful examination of the birth chart with sincere application of *navāṁśa* chart to work out the period of widowhood is most essential. We can say with confidence that without considering *navāṁśa* chart, correct time of widowhood cannot be worked out.

Case 4.24 – (Horoscope No.24-*vide* p.187)

Marriage – During the sub-period of Venus in the major period of Venus.

Widowhood – October 22nd, 1969 during the sub-period of Saturn in the major period of Moon.

She lost her husband on October 22nd, 1969 in the sub-period of Saturn in the major period of Moon. She was hardly 45 years old at the time of this unbearable tragedy of her life. She was born in *revatī nakṣatra* which belongs to *mūla*. Mars happens to be a *mārakeśa* for Libra ascendant and its placement in the fifth house is very adverse for long lasting happiness of married life. Aspect of Mars over the 8th house, 8th and *lagna* lord Venus and 12th house is very adverse. Mars and Venus are in *khaḍaṣṭaka* position. 7th house is receiving the aspect of Sun and Saturn and 8th house is receiving the aspect of Mercury and Jupiter. In this horoscope, Mars should be held responsible for loss of her husband at 45th years of age. Mars obtains *navāṁśa* of Saturn. Therefore, the tragedy occurred during the sub-period of Saturn. *Lagna* and 8th house Venus is debilitated in 12th house and falls in *Hastā nakṣatra*, which is ruled by Moon. Venus is also aspected by Moon. Therefore, the death of the husband took place in the major period of Moon and the sub-period of Saturn on October 22nd, 1969. Here *saubhāgya kāraka* Jupiter falls in the sign of Mars in Scorpio in *jyeṣṭhā nakṣatra* in Moon *navāṁśa*. Jupiter is shifted in the 3rd *bhāva* chart and from there it aspects the 7th house. However, even Jupiter's aspect over 7th or 9th house could not protect the life of her husband. The ascendant is hemmed between benefics like Jupiter, Venus and Mercury. Therefore, she enjoyed the happiness of her married life for about 29 years as she was married at the age of 16 years and suffered the tragedy of loss of her husband at 45 years of age. She lived for 17 years thereafter when she suffered cardiac arrest on August 19th, 1986 in the sub-period of Saturn in the major period of *Rāhu*.

Case 4.25 – (Horoscope No.25-*vide* p.189)

She was the first child of her parents. The birth took place in *Jyeṣṭhā nakṣatra*, fourth pada. Her mother expired soon after her birth. She got married in 21st years of her age. The married life was miserable. The husband was quite smart, good looking and attractive. Many girls were involved with him. She lost her husband on January 23rd, 1969 during stomach operation.

For Libra ascendant, Mars is the worst planet and here Mars occupies the ascendant in association with the 9th lord Mercury. *Rāhu* occupies the 8th house and is aspected by Mars and Saturn. Birth has taken place on new Moon day, i.e., Amāvasyā. The lord of the ascendant joins the 12th house under debilitation and 12th lord Mercury occupies the ascendant under affliction by Mars.

We have observed that the major period of Moon is very adverse for *Jyeṣṭhā* borns. She underwent the curse of widowhood on January 23rd, 1969 during major period of Moon and sub-period of Saturn. Saturn heavily afflicts the 2nd house and the Moon and thus both happen *mārakeśa* for her husband. She was blessed with one daughter and two sons and expired on May 30th, 2001 after leading lonely life for more than 32 years.

Here placement of *Rāhu* in the 8th house and aspect of Mars, Saturn, the Sun, the Moon and Ketu over there, resulted into widowhood around 41st years of her age. She suffered a lot thereafter.

Case 4.26 – (Horoscope No.26-*vide* p.191)

Marriage – June 24th, 1982 during sub-period of *Ketu* in the major period of *Rāhu*.

Widowhood – August 6th, 1993 during sub-period of Saturn in the major period of Jupiter.

Children – A daughter and a son

She suffered widowhood on August 6th, 1993 due to a massive heart attack to her husband during Jupiter-Saturn *daśā bhukti.* Here Mars occupies the 5th house in association with Mercury under mutual aspect with Saturn. Saturn occupies 2nd in aquarius under retrograde motion and Mars falls in the 5th house, both Mars and Saturn aspect 8th house. Mars should be mainly held responsible for her early widowhood at 29 years of age. Mars obtains *navāṁśa* of Jupiter, therefore, it was Jupiter's major period to cause widowhood.

The 2nd house is owned and occupied by retrograde Saturn and Saturn also obtains its own *navāṁśa.* Therefore, sub-period of Saturn in the major period of Jupiter resulted into loss of her husband.

Case – 4.27 – (Horoscope No.27-*vide* p.193)

Marriage – November 1967 during *Rāhu-Ketu daśā bhukti*

Widowhood – July 19th, 1982 during Jupiter-*Ketu daśā bhukti*

She is wife of a Geology professor and suffered widowhood on July 19th, 1982 due to massive heart attack to her husband during Jupiter-*Ketu daśā bhukti.* 11th and 6th lord Mars is conjoined with *Rāhu* in the ascendant. Aspect of Mars on 7th and 8th house and on the 7th lord Jupiter and ascendant lord Mercury is most undesirable. 7th lord Jupiter is aspected by Mars and Saturn both and obtains inimical *navāṁśa* of Venus. Here placement of *Ketu* in the 7th house, the aspect of Mars and Saturn over 7th lord Jupiter and 8th house is strongly indicating early widowhood. Mars is mainly responsible for widowhood. 7th lord Jupiter is aspected by Mars and Saturn, Mars obtains *navāṁśa* of Jupiter, and therefore, the death of husband took place during major period of Jupiter. *Ketu* occupies the 7th house under the aspect of Mars and *Ketu* falls in own *nakṣatra mūla*, whereas *Rāhu* and Mars both falls in *Ārdrā* constellation, ruled by *Rāhu*. Thus *Ketu* becomes a strong malefic in the 7th house. The sub-period of *Ketu* in the major period of Jupiter resulted into widowhood on July 19th, 1982.

For timing widowhood, lord of the *navāṁśa* of Mars must be taken into consideration where Mars is playing a vital role in killing the husband of the female. See whether *navāṁśa* lord is the same in whose *daśā* marriage took place or it belongs to the planet of subsequent major period in case clear and early widowhood is indicated and Mars obtains any of the *navāṁśa* as mentioned above, widowhood may take place during the same. If malefics are placed in the 8th house, the *navāṁśa* lord of that planet may bring widowhood during their *daśā bhukti*. Sub period may belong to the lord or occupant of the 2nd house and if Jupiter is not well fortified and falls in martian sign Aries or Scorpio and is aspected by Mars, the widowhood may come during Jupiter *mahādaśā*. The aspect of Jupiter over seventh or eighth house may delay widowhood but can not prevent it. If there is no planet in the 8th house, the *navāṁśa* lord of the worst malefic should be examined. *Navāṁśa* lord of the 8th house may also cause widowhood. *Nakṣatra* lord of the planet should also be taken into consideration like *navāṁśa* lord and if both are identical, widowhood will take place in *daśā bhukti* of that planet.

Malefics placed in 7th house in the *nakṣatra* of malefic planets like *Ketu*, *Rāhu*, Mars and Saturn may also kill her husband during their *daśā bhukti*. If the concerning planet falls in the *nakṣatra* of Mūla's, the widowhood may come during their *daśā bhukti*. If we can work out the lord of major period responsible for this tragedy, one should try to find out whether lord of 2nd and 8th house from that planet and ascendant indicates the widowhood during period of *navāṁśa* of *nakṣatra* lord. This requires lot of patience, careful judgement, vast experience and deep knowledge of the subject.

Case 4.28 – (Horoscope No.28-*vide* p.195)

Marriage – March 26th, 1942 during *Rāhu*-Saturn *daśā bhukti*

Widowhood – September 9th, 1960 during Jupiter-Mercury *daśā bhukti*

Mrs. Indira Gandhi suffered widowhood on September 9th, 1960 during Jupiter-Mercury *daśā bhukti*. Saturn is 7th and 8th lord falls in ascendant and obtains own *navāṁśa*. *Rāhu* and *Ketu* are placed in *mūla* and *ardrā* constellation, i.e., there is mutual exchange of their *nakṣatras*. The 7th and 8th lord Saturn, who falls in own *navāṁśa*, falls in *aśleṣā nakṣatra*. Mercury falls in *anurādhā nakṣatra*, i.e., there is mutual exchange of *nakṣatras* between Mercury and Saturn. Therefore, it was the sub-period of Mercury, in which 7th lord falls, which caused the death of her husband. Jupiter occupies the 11th house as 6th and 9th lord and aspects the 7th house. Jupiter obtains *vargottama navāṁśa*. *Ketu* and *Rāhu* are shifted in 11th and 5th house respectively. Thus, *Ketu* afflicts Jupiter and obtains *navāṁśa* of Jupiter as well. Therefore, Jupiter's major period resulted in her widowhood in the sub-period of Mercury who is the lord of the 7th house from Jupiter as placed from there under combustion and affliction in inimical sign. Thus Jupiter-Mercury period, who are also *khaḍaṣṭaka* in *navāṁśa* chart, resulted into death of husband.

Note: We have discussed here the established horoscope of Mrs. Indira Gandhi of Cancer ascendant. We had rectified her time of birth and discussed that horoscope with Leo ascendant at various places. According to that, the judgement of widowhood is very precise and accurate because Mercury is the lord of 2nd house and Jupiter is lord of 8th house in whose *daśā bhukti* she suffered loss of her husband.

Case 4.29 – (Horoscope No.29-*vide* p.197)

Marriage – January 16th, 1968 during Mars-Moon *daśā bhukti*

Widowhood – November 5th, 1984 during *Rāhu*-Moon *daśā bhukti*

She is a lecturer in an intermediate college. Her husband was also a teacher. He suffered from septic and unfortunately, there was very strict curfew in Delhi at that time, due to assassination of Mrs. Indira Gandhi. Inspite of best efforts, he could not be hospitalized for proper treatment and expired on November 5th, 1984. Her everything was lost but she became a multimillionaire. Her husband had purchased very cheap land for the purpose of agriculture in 1972 or so. Later on, that area was declared as industrial area of Ghaziabad. Many factories and industries were laid down around that land. The cost of the land increased leaps and bounds. However, she lost her husband on November 5th, 1984 during *Rāhu*-Moon period. Mars and *Rāhu* occupy 8th house which is a clear indication of widowhood.

Here *Rāhu* obtains *vargottama navāṁśa* in Aries, which is ruled by Mars. Therefore, her husband died when she was running under the last phase of the major period of *Rāhu*. The 2nd lord Venus obtains *navāṁśa* of Moon and Jupiter occupies the 12th house. *Rāhu* and Mars both are placed in fiery sign. *Saubhāgya kāraka* Jupiter is debilitated and falls in the *Śrāvaṇa*, the *nakṣatra* of Moon, which is 7th lord from Jupiter. Therefore, sub-period of Moon in the major period of *Rāhu* resulted into her widowhood on November 5th, 1984. I have observed that the lord of the *navāṁśa* occupied by the constellation lord in which the lord of the 2nd house falls, may cause widowhood during its *bhukti*. Moreover, the *navāṁśa* lord occupied by the 2nd lord may also cause death of husband during its sub-period. Here 2nd lord Venus obtain *navāṁśa* of Moon whose *bhukti* killed her husband.

Case 4.30 – (Horoscope No.30-*vide* p.199)

Marriage – June 5th, 1993 during *Rāhu*-Moon *daśā bhukti*

Widowhood – July 27th, 1993 during *Rāhu*-Moon *daśā bhukti*

She got married on June 5th, 1993 and suffered widowhood in the sub-period of Moon in the major period of *Rāhu*. Mars occupies the 8th house in Saturn's sign and *Rāhu* occupies the 7th house with Moon. Both are placed in aquarius and capricorn respectively. There is mutual aspect between Mars and Saturn. 7th and 8th lord Saturn, who is retrograde is aspected by Mars, Jupiter and inimical Sun. *Rāhu* falls in the 7th house in *rāśi* chart in Moon's *nakṣatra śrāvaṇa* and Moon conjoins with *rāhu* and falls in Mars *nakṣatra dhaniṣṭhā*. Therefore, Moon is under the influence of Mars and *Rāhu*. Conjunction of two planets like Moon and *Rāhu* gives bad results during their *daśā bhukti*. Here 7th lord Saturn falls in *anurādhā nakṣatra* ruled by Saturn, thus there is mutual exchange between *nakṣatras* of Saturn and Sun. Adversity has been further enhanced due to aspect between Saturn and Sun. Thus, 7th lord Saturn is heavily afflicted due to the inimical aspect of Sun and Mars and placement in *kṛttikā nakṣatra* and as it obtains *navāṁśa* of Jupiter in association with Mars. Thus Saturn is heavily afflicted and spoiled the results of 7th house as it aspects the 8th house and occupant of 8th house Mars mutually. Therefore, the combination of widowhood is clearly present. Jupiter-Mercury and Venus fall in the *nakṣatra* of *Mūla's* in which Jupiter, who is *saubhāgya kāraka* falls in *jyeṣṭhā nakṣatra* and Scorpio sign under the mutual aspect with Saturn. So *saubhāgya* has been heavily damaged. Here *Rāhu* falls in *saubhāgya nakṣatra* ruled by Moon and therefore has given rise to widowhood during the sub-period of Moon in own's major period on July 27th, 1993. Here Moon is the *karmic* control planet also and its placement in the seventh house in the *nakṣatra* of Mars caused widowhood during its bhukti.

Case 4.31 – (Horoscope No. 31)

Marriage – October 7th, 1992 during Jupiter-Jupiter *daśā bhukti*

Widowhood – August 28th, 2003 during Jupiter-Sun *daśā bhukti*

This is the most recent case in which I foretold about her widowhood about three months earlier. She is a beautiful wife of an area manager of a famous pharmaceutical company. I told her hus-

Case : 4.31 *Horoscope No. : 31*

Date	: 18.10.1972	Time :	11:45:00
Place	: Kanpur	Lat 26°:27′	Long 80°:19′
Ayanāmśa	: 23:28:52	Sidereal Time :	13:23:36

Pln	**Degree**	**Rāśi**	**Nakṣatra**	**Pad**
Asc	14:24:08	Sag	Pūrvāṣāḍha	1
Sun	01:29:13	Lib	Citrā	3
Mon	03:43:12	Aqu	Dhaniṣṭhā	4
Mar(C)	17:43:00	Vir	Hastā	3
Mer	19:39:32	Lib	Svāti	4
Jup	09:15:35	Sag	Mūlā	3
Ven	21:29:38	Leo	P Phālgunī	3
Sat(R)	26:53:40	Tau	Mṛgśirā	2
Rah(R)	27:44:14	Sag	Uttarāṣāḍha	1
Ket(R)	27:44:14	Gem	Punarvasu	3

Lagna Chart

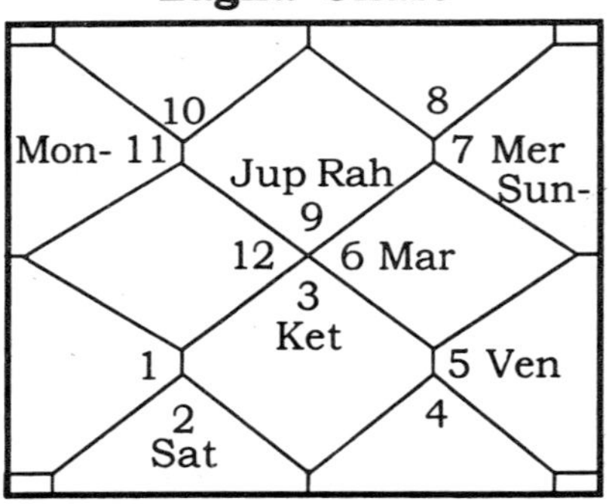

Navāmśa Chart

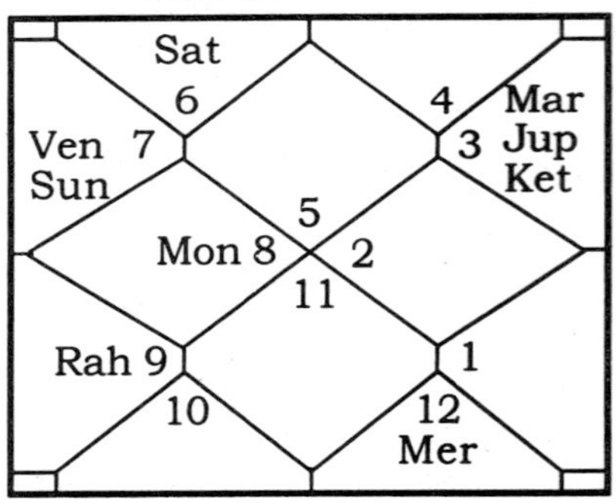

Balance of Vimśottarī Daśā of **Mars 1Y 6M 17D**

Name of Event	Date of Event	Major Period	Sub Period
Marriage	07.10.1992	Jupiter	Jupiter
Widowhood	28.08.2003	Jupiter	Sun

band that Mars will be coming very near to earth on August 28th, 2003 and *Rāhu* will also be entering into the sign of Mars Aries on August 28th, 2003 and a week on either side of this date will be very critical for his life. I advised against rash driving, any kind of hectic action, impulsive reaction and inimical activities towards criminals. I also advised that his wife must also observe Tuesday *vrata* and must recite *aṅgāraka stotra* and Vedic *mantra* of Mars etc. However, he ignored all that. In fact people have lost faith in astrological prediction and for that, various so called imperfect astrologers who are not well conversant with this science, are mostly responsible. People are misguided by them and their predictions fail miserably. Therefore, general people go to astrologers to listen only that their future is bright, full of prosperity, happiness, wealth, popularity, power, pelf and innumerable achievements as well as full of success. They discard them if there is any negative forecast. I strongly believe that any honest astrologer will speak anything only after confirmation from various angles after being confident of his observation. Any way in the above case, her husband was coming back to Lucknow on August 28th, 2003 by his own new car. He had collision with a strong tree probably due to being somewhat in sleep. He died on the spot itself. The female of this case informed all this to me on August 29th, 2003 about this biggest misery of her life which was foreseen by me earlier. Her voice was full of tears, grief and sorrow, which pained me a lot.

In this horoscope Jupiter occupies Sagittarius ascendant and is shifted in 12th house in *bhāva* chart. *Ketu* occupies the 7th house and Venus is shifted from 9th to 8th, Mars from 10th to 9th, Mercury and Sun from 11th to 10th, Moon is shifted from 3rd to 2nd. Here the Jupiter's location influencing 7th or 8th house could not save her widowhood. Here Mars is 8th from 8th lord Moon and it is placed in inimical sign Virgo. The 2nd and 8th houses indicate husband's death in one or other way. The lord of 2nd house Saturn aspects the lord of the 8th house Moon. *Lagna* lord Jupiter is shifted in the 12th house in Martian sign Scorpio, Mars and Saturn both in *bhāva* chart influence each other. Placement of *Ketu* in the 7th house is also undesirable. 7th lord Mercury obtains *navāṁśa* of debilitation. Jupiter, Mars, *Ketu* conjoins inimical *navāṁśa* Gemini. Mars and Saturn both aspect each other and these are negative factors for longevity of husband. Worst of them is the placement of Mars in the 8th house from 8th lord Moon and Moon is also placed in *dhaniṣṭhā nakṣatra* 4th Pada. Mars is placed in *Hastā nakṣatra*. Thus, there is mutual exchange of Moon and Mars and Mars is 8th from Moon in *rāśi* as well as *navāṁśa* chart. The marriage took place in the sub-period of Jupiter in the major period of Jupiter. How to work out the time of widowhood, first see if early widowhood is indicated as in the present case. Since the marriage took place in the sub-period of Jupiter in the major period of Jupiter, one should examine other sub-periods of Jupiter, which may bring widowhood. The Sun falls in *citrā*, Moon falls in *dhaniṣṭhā* and Saturn falls in *mṛgaśirā nakṣatra*, therefore, the adverse effect of Mars will come during sub-period of Sun. Since the sub-period of Sun comes prior to Moon and Mars, therefore, the biggest tragedy came in the sub-period of Sun in the major period of Jupiter. From 8th lord Moon, Sun is the 8th lord as well who obtains debilitation sign under *vargottama navāṁśa*. The tragedy took place when Mars was transiting over 8th lord Moon and Saturn was transiting over the axis of *Rāhu* and *Ketu* in the 7th house from *lagna*. *Rāhu* and *Ketu* were transiting over radical Saturn. On the same day, *Rāhu* entered in Aries and *Ketu* in Libra and Mars was very close to earth and that resulted in loss of her husband.

Case 4.32 – (Horoscope No. 32)

Marriage – October 7th, 1992 during *Rāhu-Ketu daśā bhukti*

Death – August 28th, 2003 during Jupiter-Saturn *daśā bhukti*

This is the horoscope of the husband of the above female. Mars, Sun and Mercury are placed in the 7th house but Mercury is shifted in 6th. Jupiter aspects ascendant owned by him. 2nd lord Saturn occupies its debilitation sign under *vargottama navāṁśa*. In *navāṁśa* chart, Saturn and Mars both conjoin in 8th house in Aries. The native is strong *mangali* and 7th house, Sun and Mars are aspected by 2nd lord Saturn. The tragedy took place during the major period of Jupiter and sub-period of Saturn. Here Jupiter as *lagna* lord occupies 9th house and aspects *lagna*. Jupiter also obtains *navāṁśa* of exaltation but it became *māraka* for him as Jupiter falls in *mrityuanśa*. From Jupiter, Saturn is 7th and 6th lord, thus Saturn becomes a *mārakeśa*. In *bhāva* chart, Saturn is 8th from Jupiter. Therefore, unnatural death of his life came during the sub-period of Saturn in the major period of Jupiter. Saturn is *mārakeśa* from *lagna* as well as *mahādaśā* lord Jupiter. Placement of the 12th and 5th lord Mars with 7th lord Mercury with 9th lord Sun in 7th house clearly indicates love marriage. Saturn is shifted

Case : 4.32 *Horoscope No. : 32*

Date : 11.07.1968 Time : 18:05:00

Place : Raurkela Lat 22°:16′ Long 85°:01′

Ayanāmśa : 23:24:59 Sidereal Time : 13:33:00

Pln	**Degree**	**Rāśi**	**Nakṣatra**	**Pad**
Asc	18:49:09	Sag	Pūrvāṣāḍha	2
Sun	25:49:40	Gem	Punarvasu	2
Mon	14:42:42	Cap	Śrāvaṇa	2
Mar(C)	20:07:05	Gem	Punarvasu	1
Mer	05:03:52	Gem	Mṛgśirā	4
Jup	10:47:13	Leo	Maghā	4
Ven(C)	01:38:31	Can	Punarvasu	4
Sat	01:31:58	Ari	Aśvinī	1
Rah(R)	20:03:32	Pis	Revatī	2
Ket(R)	20:03:32	Vir	Hastā	4

Lagna Chart

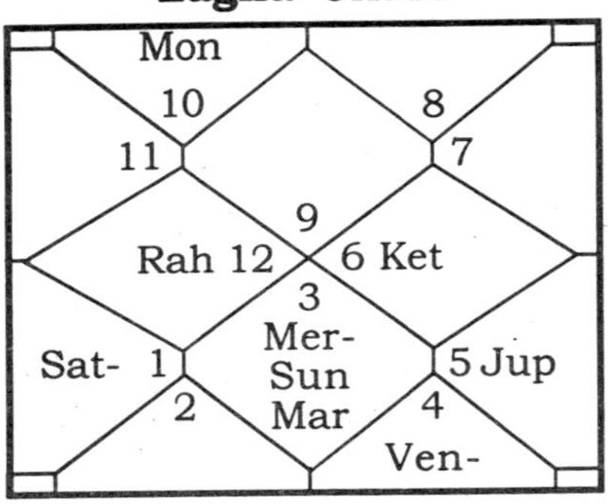

Navāmśa Chart

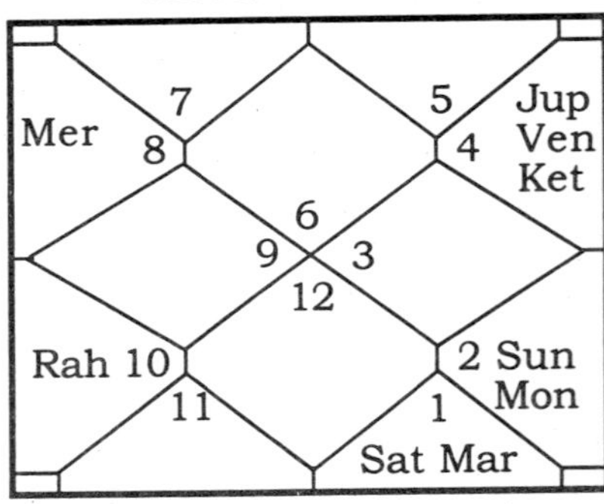

Balance of Vimśottarī Daśā of **Moon 6Y 5M 18D**

Name of Event	Date of Event	Major Period	Sub Period
Marriage	07.10.1992	Rahu	Ketu
Death	28.08.2003	Jupiter	Saturn

in the 4th house and Mars is placed in the 7th house, both are in square from each other. Saturn happens 8th from radical Jupiter in *bhāva* chart and that becomes *mārakeśa* from various angles. Therefore, accidental loss of life took place during Jupiter-Saturn period on August 28th, 2003.

Case 4.33 (Horoscope No. 33)

Marriage - June 1971 during Venus-*Ketu daśā bhukti*

Widowhood – February 24th, 1996 during *Rāhu-Rāhu daśā bhukti*

Children – A son and a daughter

She was born in Libra ascendant with Mars and *Ketu* in the 12th house. Mars aspects the 7th house as its owner and *yogakāraka* Saturn aspects the 8th house. Thus the 7th and 8th houses are afflicted by malefics. The 7th and 2nd lord Mars is closely associated with *Ketu*, with a difference of only 1° between them, in the 12th house. Both fall in the 2nd *pada* of Hastā *nakṣatra*. Here Moon falls in *Ketu's nakṣatra maghā* which belongs to *mūla*. Thus there is mutual exchange of *nakṣatra* of Moon and *Ketu*. Opposition and exchange of the inimical Sun and Saturn is also adverse because both fall over the axis of Moon. However, Moon and Mercury are shifted in 10th and 4th house respectively. Jupiter who falls in *dhaniṣṭhā nakṣatra* aspects Mars and 8th house. Mars happens *māraka* for Libra and Jupiter is also a malefic and like *mārakeśa* for Libra ascendant as Jupiter, here, owns the 3rd and 6th house. Therefore, the aspect of debilitated Jupiter over the 8th house and Mars could not save widowhood though delayed the same.

Her husband expired on February 24th, 1996 due to some dreaded and perilous disease when she was passing through *Rāhu daśā bhukti*. *Rāhu* falls in

Case : 4.33 *Horoscope No. : 33*

Date	: 03.03.1950	Time	: 23:10:00
Place	: Karnal	Lat 29°:41′	Long 76°:59′
Ayanāmśa	: 23:09:37	Sidereal Time	: 09:31:38

Pln	**Degree**	**Rāśi**	**Nakṣatra**	**Pad**
Asc	22:28:43	Lib	Viśākhā	1
Sun	19:25:19	Aqu	Satabhiṣā	4
Mon	09:57:44	Leo	Maghā	3
Mar(R)	15:26:39	Vir	Hastā	2
Mer	00:11:21	Aqu	Dhaniṣṭhā	3
Jup	27:51:00	Cap	Dhaniṣṭhā	2
Ven	12:10:42	Cap	Śrāvaṇa	1
Sat(R)	23:10:02	Leo	P Phālgunī	3
Rah(R)	14:17:25	Pis	U Bhādrapadā	4
Ket(R)	14:17:25	Vir	Hastā	2

Lagna Chart

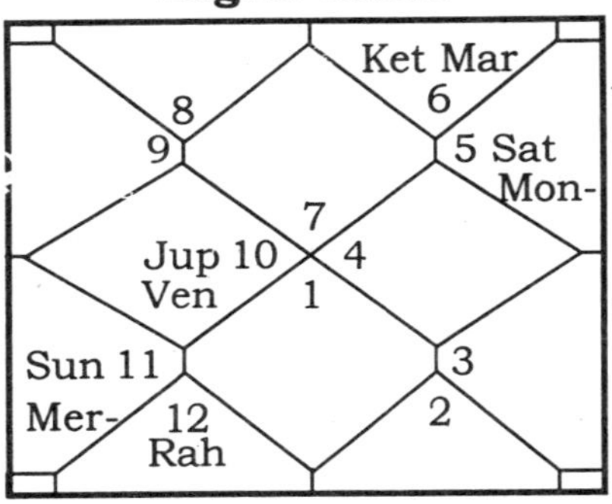

Navāmśa Chart

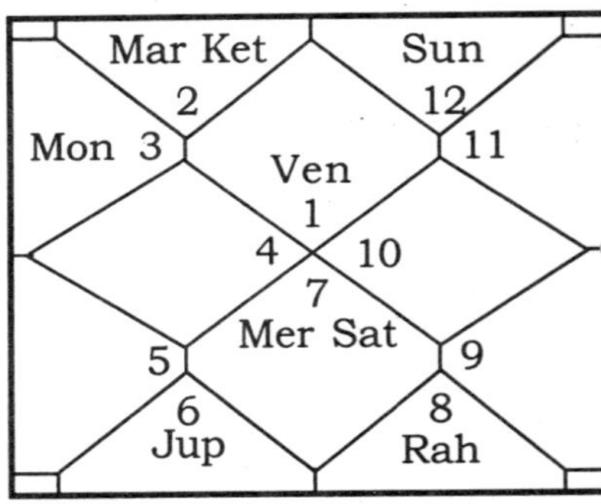

Balance of Vimśottarī Daśā of **Ketu 1Y 9M 7D**

Name of Event	Date of Event	Major Period	Sub Period
Marriage	June, 1971	Venus	Ketu
Widowhood	24.02.1996	Rahu	Rahu

uttarabhādrāpadā nakṣatra which is ruled by Saturn and Saturn is associated with Moon from where *Rāhu* is 8th. *Rāhu* obtains *navāṁśa* of Mars and that is in the 8th house from *navāṁśa lagna*. Thus the placement of *Rāhu* in Saturn's *nakṣatra* and Mars *navāṁśa* snatched all happiness of her conjugal bliss by killing her husband. It may be noted that the lord of ascendant in the 8th house obtains *navāṁśa* of *mārakeśa* Mars. This is also an adverse indication for the life of her husband. *Rāhu* who is placed 8th from *lagna* lord Venus in *navāṁśa* of Mars, clearly indicates widowhood during the sub-period of *Rāhu* in the major period of *Rāhu*. For Libra ascendant, please do note, if the 8th lord or the planet placed in the 8th house fall in the *navāṁśa* of Mars or Saturn, widowhood may take place during *daśā bhukti* of *Rāhu* or *Ketu*, if these obtain *navāṁśa* of Mars and are *khaḍaṣṭaka* from *lagna* lord in *navāṁśa* chart, provided the combination of loss of spouse is present.

Case 4.34 – (Horoscope No. 34)

Marriage – June 1971 during Venus-Jupiter *daśā bhukti*

Date of death – February 24th, 1996 during Mars-*Rāhu daśā bhukti*

Children - A son and a daughter

This is the horoscope of the husband whose horoscope is mentioned in case No. 33 above. Mars and Saturn are placed in 7th house in Leo whereas 2nd and 11th lord Jupiter occupies 12th house under debilitation in association with *yogakāraka* Venus. The native is born in the last *pada* of *revatī nakṣatra* which belongs to *mūla*. He expired during Mars-*Rāhu daśā bhukti* on February 24th, 1996, who are respectively placed in 7th and 2nd house. The 7th and 2nd occupants indicate death of the native as a

Case : 4.34 *Horoscope No. : 34*

Date	: 01.12.1949	Time :	12:40:00
Place	: Karnal	Lat 29°:41′	Long 76°:59′
Ayanāmśa	: 23:09:21	Sidereal Time :	16:57:12

Pln	**Degree**	**Rāśi**	**Nakṣatra**	**Pad**
Asc	14:26:19	Aqu	Satabhiṣā	3
Sun	15:36:47	Sco	Anurādhā	4
Mon	27:53:26	Pis	Revatī	4
Mar	25:39:38	Leo	P Phālgunī	4
Mer(C)	20:50:03	Sco	Jyeṣṭhā	2
Jup	06:55:50	Cap	Uttarāṣāḍha	4
Ven	02:22:05	Cap	Uttarāṣāḍha	2
Sat	25:31:38	Leo	P Phālgunī	4
Rah(R)	22:13:40	Pis	Revatī	2
Ket(R)	22:13:40	Vir	Hastā	4

Lagna Chart

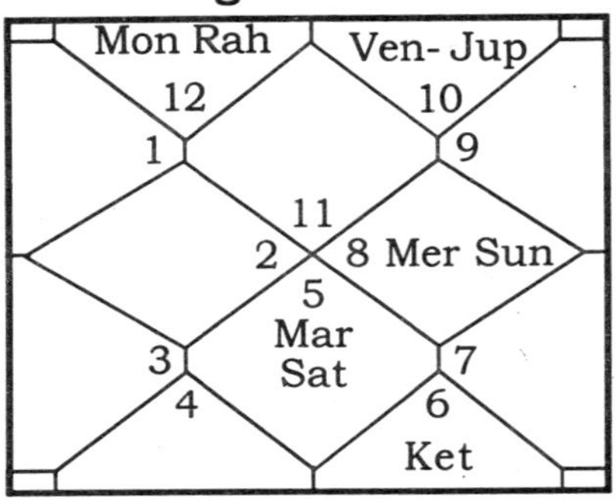

Navāmśa Chart

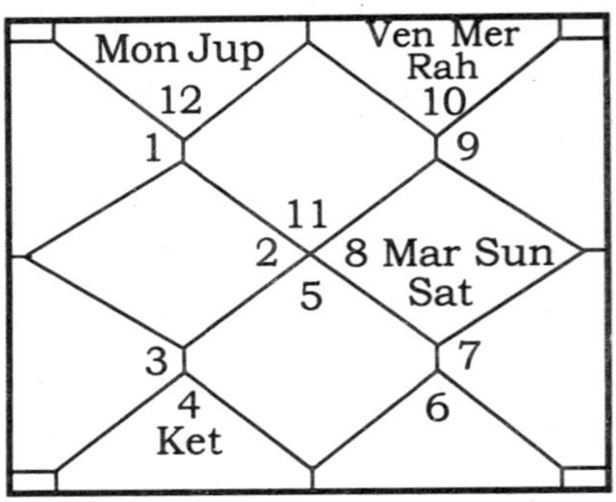

Balance of Vimśottarī Daśā of **Mercury 2Y 8M 8D**

Name of Event	Date of Event	Major Period	Sub Period
Marriage	June, 1971	Venus	Jupiter
Death	24.02.1996	Mars	Rahu

principle. Thus, Mars-*Rāhu* period who are 6th and 8th from each other resulted into the death of the native during their *daśā bhukti*.

In this example and in the example of case No. 32, Mars occupies the 7th house and it is believed most often that the Mars in 7th house will kill the spouse and not to self. This is not so as we have seen and illustrated two cases of husband alongwith their widows. In both these cases, Mars signifies death of self and not of wife.

A careful judgement and sincere analysis of the horoscope is required before reaching to any conclusion. It is not at all essential that if husband and wife both are *maṅgalī*, there can not be loss of spouse. It should be properly examined whether widowhood is present in the horoscope of a female? Similarly, horoscope of husband should also be judged carefully if he has a short life. The females who have combinations of early widowhood should never be married with the persons with short span of life. The ascendant, 6th and 8th houses must be strong in the horoscope of their husbands. Proper matching of horoscopes by the competent astrologers must essentially be done and there should be no compromise in matching. Question arises whether widowhood can be saved if there are very strong and vital indications of loss of spouse. Widowhood can not be saved especially when the horoscope of the husband is weak for longevity. However, widowhood can certainly be prevented in reasonable number of cases if proper matching of horoscopes is there and there is a selection of most suitable *muhūrta* of marriage.

Conclusion

We have discussed so many cases here in respect to foretelling widowhood and its time period. There can mainly be four reasons for widowhood to take place in early life.

1. Accidental death of husband.
2. Death due to any dreaded disease like Cancer, heart attack, brain haemorrhage or the like.
3. Suicide and
4. Murder

The reason of death of husband can also be worked out. However, though it is most essential but quite difficult to work out the time of the death of the husband precisely.

We have made an honest and sincere effort to work out the time of loss of husband. It is not at all essential that a girl having strong *kuja doṣa* will suffer from widowhood certainly. We have illustrated number of cases where *kuja doṣa* is not present in the birth chart of the girl and she suffered very early widowhood. There is a prominent role of Mars, Saturn, *Rāhu* and *Ketu* in giving rise to curse of widowhood. If these planets adversely influence the 7th or 8th or both of these houses identical to malefic signs, associations and aspects, the female is likely to suffer widowhood.

A man having Mars in the 8th house may result in his accidental death but this position will not damage the life of wife or his conjugal bliss but in case of a female, Mars in the 8th house, may result in the death of her husband. A man having Mars in the 8th house should never be got married with a female having Mars in the 7th or 8th house or having malefics there, otherwise that promote the possibility of widowhood.

If Mars, Saturn or other malefics occupy the 8th house, in evil signs or with evil aspects, widowhood may take place during the *daṣā bhukti* of *navāṁśa* lord of the malefic occupant of the 8th house or the lord of the 8th house. The 2nd house also deals the death of husband as it is 8th from the 7th house. The death of life partner may take place during the *daśā bhukti* of the lord of the 2nd house or *navāṁśa* or *nakṣatra* lord of the 2nd house. It is simple to find out the major period lord during which widowhood is likely to appear. If early widowhood is indicated, the widowhood should take place in the same major period in which marriage took place provided those planets have any thing to do with the loss of husband and indicate their role in befalling widowhood on the concerning female.

After finding out the lord of major period in which widowhood is likely to take place, workout the worst malefic responsible for the death of husband. The death may take place during the *navāṁśa* lord of that planet or during the sub-period of the lord of the 2nd or 8th house as reckoned from the lord of major period, worked out first as explained above.

Mars is the significator of widowhood and Jupiter is *kāraka* of *saubhāgya yoga.* If Jupiter is a malefic for a particular ascendant or it is afflicted or Jupiter falls in *jyeṣṭhā* or *aśvinī* constellation, the widowhood may come during the sub-period of Jupiter. We have observed that in nearly 50% of cases, widowhood took place during the major or sub-period of Jupiter. The death of the husband may also take place during the major or sub-periods of nodes, i.e., *Rāhu* and *Ketu. Daśā bhukti* of *Rāhu*-Saturn or Saturn-*Rāhu* is also adverse. The planets placed in the 7th, 8th or 2nd even in the 6th or 12th house may befall widowhood.

After working out the major and sub-period of widowhood, application of transit further precise the worst span of time for a female to be cursed by the biggest tragedy of her widowhood. We want to draw the attention of our readers that transits should never be applied before working out the *daśā bhukti.* Reasonable number of the females who received the curse of widowhood, were born in the constellation of *mūlās,* e.g., *jyeṣṭhā, aśvinī, revatī, maghā, aśleṣā* and *mūlā* etc. If Moon falls in these *nakṣatra* and is aspected by malefics like Mars, widowhood may come during the sub-period of Moon or *nakṣatra* lord or sign lord occupied by the Moon or during the *daśā bhukti* of the malefic planet who afflicts such a Moon.

Thus, the period of widowhood should be arrived at on the basis of principles, as discussed here and also in the explanation of timing of widowhood of various cases.

सुवर्णपुष्पां पृथिवीं चिन्वन्ति पुरुषास्त्रयः ।
शूरश्च कृतविद्यश्च यश्च जानाति सेवितुम् ॥

Only those who are courageous, learned and human can acquire wealth and prosperity from this golden flowers yielding earth.

Chapter-5

WIDOWHOOD AND MISCONCEPTIONS ABOUT JUPITER

Jupiter is the best benefic among all planets. Association or aspect of Jupiter can minimise most of the adversities and can also rule out many negative indications. We expect that of advantages, prosperity, power, popularity, property, promotions, peace, wealth, happiness, children, education, success, fortune and conjugal bliss of a high degree.

Jupiter is not so benevolent in regard to marital harmony according to our humble observations of natal horoscopes. Jupiter may be benefic for one ascendant while it may be a malefic for the other. If Jupiter is a malefic for a particular ascendant, there will be loss of conjugal bliss, if it has to do anything with the houses related to marriage and marital harmony. Here in this *chapter*, I will confine myself to the negative effect of Jupiter regarding the span of married life.

Placement of Jupiter in the 7th house brings various kinds of problems in marriage especially if Jupiter happens a malefic for that ascendant. In watery signs Cancer, Scorpio and Pisces in the 7th house, Jupiter creates havoc in regard to marital harmony. This is a general belief that Jupiter in the 7th house gives a decent and happy married life and the spouse would be good looking, having high moral values in life. Though this is true at various places but this does not hold good in all cases. The aspect of Jupiter over the 7th or 8th house in a female nativity gives a long span of married life. This belief too, does not hold good everywhere. It is also an accepted truth that Jupiter's period will be bestowing auspicious and benefic results to the native. However, I have found that Jupiter does not save widowhood or separation, even if it is posited in the 7th or 8th house or lends aspect over there, in a female horoscope in particular. If the combinations of widowhood are present in a birth chart, the widowhood may take place even during the sub-period or major period of Jupiter, as the case may be. It has been mentioned in various scripts that the placement or aspect of Jupiter over the 7th or 8th house rules out the possibilities of widowhood.

The 7th house governs husband and the 8th house rules the marital happiness, *saubhāgya* and life of husband in a female birth chart. Looking at Jupiter's location in the 8th house under retrograde motion in Virgo in the horoscope of wife of a senior IPS officer, I had once opined a long life for her husband. She was not having any kind of *kuja doṣa* either from ascendant or from Moon. On August 26th, 2002 I was shocked when I heard that her husband and young daughter died in a road accident on the spot itself. This tragedy with the beautiful woman took place around her 45th year of age. This tragic event for once broke my confidence in astrology. I took out more than ten dozen horoscopes of females who had suffered early loss of their spouse. I observed that around 50% of them entered into the marital disaster of widowhood during the major or sub-period of Jupiter and in most of the cases, Jupiter either lended its aspect over the 7th or 8th house or it was placed there only.

I will try to explain my humble observation with the help of few illustrations that Jupiter is not always good and Saturn is not always bad. It is believed and a few Sanskrit scripts also mention that *kuja doṣa* gets cancelled or is nullified if Jupiter or Moon aspect Mars or are associated with that. In my observations of more than hundreds of birth chart, I do not find myself in a position to support this view. I have examined innumerable charts showing close relationship of Mars-Jupiter or Mars-Moon where killings, suicides, separation, litigation and widowhood took place. We have explained all this in our book *Predicting Marriage*, in length. Here I intend to deal with the role of Jupiter in saving or causing widowhood. At various places, Jupiter makes one fortunate to enjoy *saubhāgya*. On the contrary, in various cases Jupiter gives rise to widowhood during its *daṣā bhukti* and does not save widowhood inspite of its aspect over the concerning houses.

Jupiter is the significator of *saubhāgya yoga* whereas Mars is the significator of husband and the Sun rules the activities, education, profession, influence and impression of the husband. However, Mars and Jupiter certainly play a prominent role as far as loss of husband is concerned particularly in young age. Affliction of Jupiter is very adverse even in the 7th or 8th house. One should not be misguided even if Jupiter is exalted or placed in own sign giving rise to *Haṁsa Mahāpuruṣa Rājayoga* in the 7th house.

Let me illustrate few cases where Jupiter played a negative role in causing loss of husband, untimely:-

Case No. 5.1 (Horoscope No.2-*vide* p.137)

The birth took place when Virgo ascendant was rising with Jupiter in Pisces in the 7th house. She is the daughter of a multimillionaire business man who believed a lot in astrology. Placement of Jupiter in the 7th house in Pisces was appreciated by one and all for her happy and everlasting married life. She is not *maṅgalī* from ascendant but she is *maṅgalī* from Moon. Her marriage was ceremonised at a very large scale on March 6th, 1996 during sub-period of *Rāhu* in the major period of Venus, after proper matching of birth charts of both. There was compatability of 28 points out of 36 and the boy, as also *candra maṅgalī*. Her husband committed suicide on March 8th, 1999 during sub-period of Jupiter in the major period of Venus. The husband failed in examination and his father scolded him in insulting way and that became the cause of suicide.

In this horoscope, Jupiter occupies its own sign Pisces in the 7th house but that could not save her early widowhood inspite of obtaining *vargottama navāṁśa*. Here Moon falls in *jyeṣṭhā* in Scorpio and is aspected by its dispositor Mars, *Ketu* occupies the 8th house and the Sun joins the 6th giving rise to *pāpakārtari yoga*. Retrograde Saturn aspects the ascendant, the lord of the ascendant Mercury, Venus, the 8th house and *Ketu*. Jupiter suffers *kendrādhipati doṣa* and it is also a *bādhaka* for Virgo ascendant. In *navāṁśa*, the 7th lord Jupiter is under mutual aspect with 8th lord Mars and these all combinations resulted into early widowhood of this girl around 23 years of age.

Case No. 5.2 (Horoscope No.4-*vide* p.142)

The birth chart belongs to the wife of an Airforce Officer who suffered widowhood within 4½ years of marriage inspite of the placement of the 5th and 8th lord Jupiter in the 7th house. She was choosen, out of one hundred girls by her husband as she was extremely beautiful and charming. Jupiter's presence in the 7th house was appreciated by one and all at the time of her marriage. She got married on October 5th, 1973 during sub-period of Jupiter in the major period of *Rāhu*. She faced the biggest tragedy on March 2nd, 1978 when, the aeroplane her husband was piloting, crashed in front of her eyes, immediately after taking off. *Rāhu's* major period and Mercury's sub-period was operative over her at that time.

Here Jupiter obtains *navāṁśa* of Mars and falls in the constellation of Mars, *dhaniṣṭhā*, Mars joins the 5th house in Jupiter's sign Sagittarius and aspects the 8th house and that created the tragedy. Jupiter is also responsible to cause early widowhood.

Case No. 5.3 (Horoscope No.11-*vide* p.158)

She is a beautiful female who enjoyed all kinds of luxury and wealth during her college and university days. She loved a muslim boy but ultimately marriage with him could not take place due to family traditions. She ultimately got married with a scientist around October 1987 during sub-period of Jupiter in the major period of Jupiter. Her husband expired in a fire accident within 15 months after marriage in January 1989. Thus, she got married and suffered widowhood during Jupiter-Jupiter *daśā bhukti*. There are various combinations in the birth chart for widowhood. Mars-*Ketu* and Mercury occupy the 7th house and these are under mutual aspect with Saturn who is posited in the 10th. Moon is associated with Saturn and aspected by Mars and Jupiter. It is strongly believed that the aspect or placement of

Jupiter in the 7th or 8th house gives rise to *akhaṇḍa saubhāgya yoga,* i.e., the wife will die in front of her husband. In this horoscope, Jupiter is placed in the 2nd house in Gemini under retrograde motion under the aspect of 2nd and 12th lord Mars. In *bhāva calita* chart, Jupiter is shifted in the ascendant. In either cases, Jupiter lends aspect over the 8th or 7th house but widowhood could not be saved. Here Jupiter obtains own *navāṁśa.*

The 8th house indicates the span of married life that is the life of husband. Here Jupiter falls in *Rāhu's* constellation *ārdrā* as 8th and 11th lord and receives the malefic aspect of evil Mars. Thus Jupiter is afflicted heavily as it falls over the axis of nodes. Since early widowhood is indicated to her, therefore, it resulted in Jupiter-Jupiter *daśā bhukti* which is the same *daśā* in which the marriage took place. I therefore, humbly opine that Jupiter's influence over the 7th or 8th house in a female nativity should not be wrongly interpreted for high hopes to save widowhood. For Leo ascendant, Jupiter is a malefic and if it is placed even in the 7th house under the aspect of any malefic, that may make one widow during the period of its influence.

Case No. 5.4 (Horoscope No.9-*vide* p.154)

The lady got married on March 7th, 1979 with a handsome, and smart doctor. She was blessed with a son on February 20th, 1982. She had a quarrelsome nature whereas her husband was quite peace-loving. The husband committed suicide on March 19th, 1985 after knowing about her physical relationship with other man. At the time of widowhood, she was running under the sub-period of Mars in the major period of Jupiter. She was born under Virgo ascendant with 6th lord Saturn, 7th lord Jupiter occupies the 8th house in Aries and 8th lord Mars aspects Jupiter in the 8th house.

The 7th and 8th lord Jupiter and Mars aspects each other identical to 8th and 2nd house. It is believed that Jupiter's placement in the 12th, 7th, 2nd, 4th, 8th and 11th house gives high moral character and saves widowhood. In the present case, Jupiter's presence in the 8th house could neither bless her with high degree of moral character nor it could save widowhood. I humbly opine that we should not expect too much from benefic Jupiter.

This is certainly true that it is only Jupiter who can bless a female with *akhaṇḍa saubhāgya yoga.* But it is not at all true that Jupiter's influence on the concerning houses always saves widowhood. I have tried to illustrate the same here that high hopes from Jupiter for each and every ascendant is misleading in respect of long life of husband, high degree of conjugal bliss and for moral character.

Case No. 5.5 (Horoscope No.16-*vide* p.170)

This is the horoscope of a famous gynaelcologist of UP who is very famous for her talent and merits in the field of medicine. She had a love marriage with a E.N.T. Surgeon on May 17th, 1981. Her husband expired on November 4th, 1996 due to massive heart-attack when she was under the influence of major period of Jupiter and sub-period of Saturn. Here Jupiter is the 8th and 11th lord. Thus, it is a malefic for Taurus ascendant. Jupiter aspects the 8th house alongwith Mars. The Jupiter is the 8th lord and is aspected by malefic Saturn. From Jupiter, Saturn is 7th lord and Jupiter is the 8th lord. Here Jupiter aspects over the 8th house, could not save widowhood. On the other hand, joint aspect of Mars-Jupiter and Saturn over the 8th house in the *bhāva calita* resulted into the biggest tragedy of loss of husband during Jupiter-Saturn period.

Case No. 5.6 (Horoscope No.23-*vide* p.184)

She got married on Nov. 24th, 1968 during *Rāhu*-Moon period. She remained separated from her husband for 8 years after marriage due to misbehaviour of her mother-in-law. She suffered widowhood on November 7th, 1997 during sub-period of Venus in the major period of Jupiter. Here Jupiter is the lord of the 2nd and 11th house. It is placed in Martian sign Scorpio. Jupiter is the dispositor of Mars, therefore, the effect of Mars has come during the major period of Jupiter. The lord of ascendant Saturn and 7th lord Sun are conjoined in the 6th house. From where, Saturn aspects the 8th, 12th and 3rd house giving rise to loss off husband. Venus and Jupiter are 6th and 8th from each other in *rāśi* and *navāṁśa* both. Sub-period of Venus in the major period of Jupiter caused widowhood. It is a rule that malefic planet placed in the 8th house, if indicates widowhood, the same will come in evidence during the major or sub-period of the *navāṁśa* lord occupied by the malefic planet who has joined 8th house. Here the planet posited in the 8th house is Mars, who is solely responsible for widowhood. Mars obtains *navāṁśa* of Jupiter and sub-period lord Venus joins the 8th house from *daśā* lord Jupiter in the birth and *navāṁśa* both. Venus becomes 7th and 12th lord if recknoed from *daśā* lord Jupiter. Therefore, sudden setback of the unexpected demise of her husband took place during major period of Jupiter and sub-period of Saturn. This is the sole reason of the emphasis on the *navāṁśa* chart. This helps a lot not only in timing events but it also helps in making very accurate observations regarding all aspects of marriage.

Case No. 5.7 (Horoscope No.26-*vide* p.191)

She got married on June 24th, 1982 at 18 years of age and suffered widowhood on August 6th, 1993 at 29 years of age during the sub-period of Saturn in the major period of Jupiter. The Jupiter, Mars and Saturn aspect the 8th house which governs widowhood. Here again Jupiter's aspect over the 8th house could not save widowhood. Here Jupiter occupy the Martian sign Aries and is 8th from 7th lord Moon. Jupiter is also aspected by malefic and retrograde Saturn. Jupiter is a malefic for Capricorn ascendant. Retrograde Saturn occupies the 2nd house in own sign and aspects the 8th house, 2nd house indicates death of husband as it is 8th from 7th. The 8th house indicates span and happiness of married life. Thus, Saturn in the 2nd who is 6th from 2nd lord Moon and aspects the 8th house caused loss of husband due to massive heart attack in its *bhukti* during the major period of Jupiter. I have always tried to prove that Mars in the 5th house is maladroit for females and may cause widowhood. Here Mars who aspects the 8th house and obtains *navāṁśa* of Jupiter also indicates widowhood during the course of major period especially when Mars is the dispositor of Jupiter. These points may be noted carefully where Mars plays a vital role giving rise to such tragedy.

Case No. 5.8 (Horoscope No.3-*vide* p.140)

This poor girl who lost her parents before her marriage and was serving in a school to meet her both ends. She got married on May 8th, 1996 during *Rāhu-Rāhu* period and suffered loss of husband within 1 year of her marriage on April 17th, 1997 during sub-period of Jupiter in the major period of *Rāhu*. Here Jupiter occupies the 12th house in association with *Rāhu* and aspects the 8th house. The *Rāhu* obtains *navāṁśa* of Mars and is associated closely with *Rāhu*. In other words, *saubhāgya kāraka* Jupiter falls over the axis of *Rāhu* and *Ketu*. Therefore, sub-period of Jupiter in the major period of Rāhu resulted into massive heart attack to her husband. That ruined her life as she was cursed for widowhood within a few months after her marriage.

Case No. 5.9 (Horoscope No.28-*vide* p.195)

Mrs. Indira Gandhi, the former Prime Minister of India, suffered widowhood on September 9th, 1960 during major period of Jupiter and the sub-period of Mercury. Here Jupiter aspects the ascendant lord Moon and the 7th house. Mars also aspects Moon in *bhāva calita* and vice-versa. *Ketu* is shifted in the 11th house and conjoins with Jupiter. Ketu obtains *navāṁśa* of Jupiter and both are *khaḍaṣṭaka* in *navāṁśa* chart. Jupiter is the lord of the 6th and 9th house and Mercury is 12th lord from Ascendant and 2nd lord from major period lord Jupiter, who is placed in the 7th house from Jupiter as well. Mercury is posited in the sign of Mars as well as under the aspect of Mars and Jupiter. Therefore, she suffered loss of her husband during major period of Jupiter in the sub-period of Mercury.

Case No. 5.10 (Horoscope No.27-*vide* p.193)

She suffered widowhood on July 19th, 1982 during Jupiter–*Ketu daśā bhukti*. Jupiter is the lord of 10th and 4th house and placed in 4th house under the adverse aspect of Mars and Saturn. Here Jupiter is 7th lord aspected by Mars and Saturn. Both Mars and Saturn aspect 8th house as well. Here Mars is associated with *Rāhu* who has killed her husband when she was 37 years of age. Mars obtains *navāṁśa* of Jupiter in whose major period her husband died.

Ketu is placed in the 7th house of Jupiter and Sagittarius is under the aspect of Mars. Therefore, *Ketu* who is a killer for her husband gives rise to widowhood during its own sub-period in the major period of Jupiter. Here *navāṁśa* lord of Mars is Jupiter who created the havoc in its own *mahādaśā.*

Case No. 5.11 – (Horoscope No.12-*vide* p.160)

She is the daughter of the Chairman of the biggest government organisation of India after Railways. She is very charming, pretty and innocent. She got married on February 9th, 1974 during *Ketu*-Moon period. The marriage took place inspite of my repeated warnings, with a doctor. She suffered loss of her husband on March 16th, 1976 as he was crushed by car in a road accident during sub-period of Jupiter in the major period of *Ketu.* Jupiter is 8th lord and falls in Taurus ascendant and is aspected by malefic Mars. *Ketu* is posited in the 2nd house in *dvirdaśā* position. Jupiter's aspect over 7th house and Mars could not prevent widowhood. Widowhood took place during Jupiter's sub-period in the major period of *Ketu.* Here Jupiter is the 8th lord and also is the *navāṁśa* lord of Venus who occupies the 8th house in *navāṁśa* chart. Here it may be noted that 8th lord Jupiter lends its aspect over the 7th house and obtains *navāṁśa* of its exaltation even then, the widowhood took place during sub-period of Jupiter in the major period of *Ketu* within 2½ years of her marriage. Therefore, any misconception of false hopes should never be there about Jupiter in regard to everlasting conjugal bliss.

Case No. 5.12 – (Horoscope No.13-*vide* p.162)

This radio producer entered into wedlock at 34 years of age on March 11th, 1961 during Moon-*Rāhu daśā bhukti.* Just after 10 months, her husband expired in a plane crash soon after take off on Jan. 10th, 1962 during sub-period of Jupiter in the major period of Moon. Jupiter is a malefic for Libra ascendant. It is placed in the 5th house with Sun and is shifted in the 6th house. Moon is placed in the 7th house in Martian sign Aries and 7th lord Mars occupies the 8th house. *Yogakāraka* Saturn occupies the 2nd house under mutual aspect with Mars. However, sub-period of Jupiter killed her husband because Jupiter is the *navāṁśa* lord of the 8th house Venus. Here Jupiter obtains own *navāṁśa,* even then it could not protect widowhood at least in own *daśā.* It may be noted that she was born in *aśvinī nakṣatra* and in the sign of Mars - Aries and Moon is the dispositor of Mars, so it resulted into widowhood into its own major period and Jupiter is 12th lord from Moon and that is afflicted in various ways as mentioned above. Therefore, Jupiter brought widowhood in its *bhukti.*

Case No. 5.13 - (Horoscope No.10-*vide* p.156)

She was the wife of an IPS officer. She was quite charming, beautiful and had an impressive personality. Her husband committed suicide on February 28th, 1982 during *Rāhu*-Jupiter period. *Rāhu* is placed in the 2nd house and Jupiter is placed in the 10th house in Taurus in association with Venus, Sun and Mercury. Jupiter is the 8th lord and is aspected by Mars. Therefore, Jupiter's sub-period forced her husband to commit suicide. Jupiter is 7th lord from major period lord *Rāhu* and this house is hemmed between 1st rate malefics Mars and Saturn. Thus, the 8th from *lagna* and 7th from major period lord *Rāhu* is Pisces and that is placed under *pāpakartari yoga.* Jupiter is combust and is placed with inimical Venus and Mercury, therefore,

Jupiter's sub-period in the major period *Rāhu* created such circumstances that she was caught red-handed in adultery, unfaithfulness and disloyalty towards her husband and as a result of which, husband committed suicide.

Case No. 5.14 – (Horoscope No.25-*vide* p.189)

She got married on April 4th, 1947 at 20 years of her age and suffered widowhood during Moon-Saturn period. Moon is posited in the 2nd house in *jyeṣṭhā nakṣatra* and is conjoined with Sun, Saturn and *Ketu.* Many times, persons born in *jyeṣṭhā nakṣatra* suffer a lot during the major or sub-period of Moon especially if the widowhood is indicated to them. I know a few female nativities who were born in *jyeṣṭhā nakṣatra* and they suffered widowhood during Mars *daśā bhukti.* Here Saturn joins the 2nd house in martian sign Scorpio and obtains vargottama *navāṁśa.* Here Moon is the dispositor of Mars and Mars happens a killer for Libra, therefore, Moon gives effects like Mars and Moon is posited in 2nd with inimical Saturn and Ketu. Therefore, Saturn's sub-period in the major period of Moon, resulted in sudden loss of husband due to ulcer in stomach. Here Moon and Saturn both are heaily afflicted because these are placed over the axis of *Rāhu* and *Ketu* in the 2nd house, which is 8th from 7th showing untimely death of husband. Birth took place in *Jyeṣṭhā nakṣatra* and the husband was also *Jyeṣṭha* (eldest) in the family which resulted into the tragedy. Therefore, sub-period of Saturn finally brought unhappy end of her husband during its course and *bhukti.*

Dozens of cases may also be illustrated to prove the misconceptions about Jupiter in saving widowhood or blessing the native for ever lasting conjugal bliss. These humble observation in regard to role of Jupiter and widowhood, I have expressed only what I have realised and experienced during the study of horoscopes of various females who suffered untimely demise of their husband.

In this regard, I have observed that the widowhood generally comes early or late depending upon the overall planetary positions in the birth chart. If early widowhood is indicated, one should try to examine sub-periods responsible for loss of spouse but major period should be same in which marriage took place or the major period may be just next to that depending upon the remaining course of period. If malefics occupy the 8th house and give rise to widowhood, the same may come during the *daśā bhukti* during the *navāṁśa* lord of planet placed in the 8th house or *navāṁśa* lord obtained by the lord of the 8th house. The widowhood may also come during the *daśā bhukti* of those planets who are afflicted in the 7th house or 8th house or during the *daśā* of the *navāṁśa* lord obtained by the planet who is solely responsible for widowhood.

The 2nd house from ascendant which is 8th from 7th, is also important and its affliction may result in widowhood during its course. The 8th house from ascendant, its lord and planets also play negative role. Females born in *jyeṣṭhā nakṣatra* may suffer widowhood during major or sub-period of Moon and during the *daśā bhukti* obtained by Moon.

Here we have made an honest, sincere, practical endeavour to judge whether Jupiter can prevent widowhood, if it is posited in a favourable position. Jupiter's placement in the 7th house in watery sign is extremely adverse but if Jupiter is the lord of the 8th joins the 7th or Jupiter owns the 7th and joins 8th under the malefic aspect of Mars, widowhood may come in evidence during *daśā bhukti* of Jupiter.

The aspect of Jupiter over the 7th house, 8th house, ascendant etc. does not prevent widowhood if it is indicated by the other planetary combinations in a horoscope. One should also examine whether Jupiter is auspicious or inauspicious for particular ascendant. Many times Jupiter may act as malefic, like Mars such as placement of retrograde Jupiter in the 8th house in inimical sign under malefic aspect. Aspect of Mars over Jupiter and the aspect of Jupiter over Mars destroys the good effect of both. In such cases, Jupiter becomes a malefic and Mars becomes a heavier malefic to harm the female.

I therefore, strongly but humbly opine that we should not have false hopes from Jupiter especially if it is favourably placed in the birth chart, that it will surely prevent widowhood and will bless the native with ever lasting conjugal bliss. On the contrary Jupiter may result into loss of spouse, if adversely placed and afflicted as illustrated here in number of cases.

षड्दोषाः पुरुषेणेह हातव्या भूतिमिच्छता ।
निद्रा तन्द्रा भयं क्रोध आलस्यं दीर्घसूत्रता ।।

He who seeks for wealth, prosperity and fame must avoid six drawbacks, e.g., sleep, lack of concentration, fear, anger and laziness.

Chapter-6

AKHAṆḌA SAUBHAGYA YOGA FOR FEMALES

Loss of husband is more common than the loss of wife. The women who die earlier than their husbands, are fortunate and are said to have attained *akhaṇḍa saubhāgya*. Almost all women desire to be *akhaṇḍa saubhāgyavatī*. One attains it on the basis of *karma* of previous life. The average age of men is less than that of women as per survey. The rate of death of men is certainly higher than women because men have to suffer occupational hazards and do risky works as compared to women. The life of a woman is full of happiness and pride so long her husband is alive. Remaining alive of husband is the honour of a woman. We will make an honest and sincere effort to explain the planetary combination in the horoscope of a woman to attain *akhaṇḍa saubhāgya yoga*.

The combination of *akhaṇḍa saubhāgya yoga* in the horoscope of women is most fortunate for them. Almost one hundred percent of married women have an inner desire to die before their husbands but only a few are fortunate to have their desires fulfilled.

First of all, we shall try to quote a few of important aphorisms as given in various classical texts. Thereafter, we shall be illustrating a few practical cases and verifying of the combination of *akhaṇḍa saubhāgya yoga*.

सौभाग्य सौम्यग्रहे निधनगे मरणं धवाग्रे
स्वस्थैः शुभैर्मरणगैर्हुरितैस्तथैव

Jyotiṣatattva Strījātaka

If benefics are placed in the 8th or benefic are in the 2nd with malefics in the 8th, then the female acquires *Akhaṇḍa Saubhāgya*, i.e., the female will die earlier than her husband.

लग्नादिन्दोः शुभो वा यदि मदनपतिर्द्यूनयायी विषाख्या,
दोषं चैवानपत्यं तदनु च नियतं हन्ति वैधव्यदोषम् ।

Jyotiṣatattva Prakāśa 311

If 7th lord is placed in the 7th from ascendant or from Moon or benefics are placed there, then *viṣākhya doṣa*, curse of barenness, widowhood gets cancelled.

अक्षराणि द्विगुणितानि मात्रा च चतुर्गुणा
एकीकृत्य त्रिभिर्भक्तं शेष ज्ञेयं च लक्षणम्
एकं च पुरुषं हन्ति द्वितीयं नारी तथैव च
शून्ये च पुरुषं ज्ञेयं एवं प्रश्नस्य लक्षणम्

Jyotiṣa Sarvasaṁgraha 73

Double the number of letters in the names of the couple and multiply by 4 the *mātrās*, then add them and divide the resultant by 3, if the remainder is 1 or zero, then the male dies earlier otherwise female dies earlier.

स्त्रीणां जन्मफलं नृयोगमुदितं यत्तत्पतौ योजयेत्
तासां देहशुभाशुभं हिमकराल्लग्नाच्च वीर्याधिकात्
भर्तृसामगुणं गुणं मदगृहाच्छिद्राच्च तेषां मृतिं
सौम्यासौम्यबलाबलेन सफलं सञ्चिन्त्य सर्वं वदेत्

Phalitamārtanḍa Strījātaka Ch. 368

All auspicious *yoga* present in the horoscope of a woman will give good results to her husband and should be understood thus. Physical pleasure and comfort in the horoscope should be studied from the ascendant or Moon, whichever is stronger. Merits and demerits of the husband should be examined from the 7th house and his death from the 8th house.

Mantreśvara writes in the *śloka* 15 of *chapter* 6th in the great classical work *Phaladīpikā* that the female having *mahābhāgya yoga* in her horoscope will be blessed with *akhaṇḍa saubhāgya.*

महाभाग्ये जातः सकलनयनानन्दजनको, वदान्यो विख्यातः
क्षितिपतिरशीत्यायुरमलः ।
वधूनां योगेऽस्मिन् सति धन सुमांगल्य सहिता, चिरं
पुत्रैः पौत्रैः शुभमुपगता स्म सुचरिता ।।15।।

Phaladīpikā page 69, *Ch.* 6.

The person with *mahābhāgya yoga* will be immensely popular in the public, will be very generous in giving gifts and will possess a very high reputation. She will be a ruler of the earth, will have a life span of 80 years and will be of spotless character. A female born with this *yoga* will be exceedingly fortunate and possess sweet manners and *akhaṇḍa saubhāgya.*

Mantreśvara defines *mahābhāgya yoga* as under:-

ओजेष्वर्केन्दुलग्नान्यजनि दिवि पुमांश्चेन्महाभाग्ययोगः
स्त्रीणां तद्व्यत्यये स्याच्छशिनि सुरगुरोः केन्द्रगे केसरीति ।
जीवान्त्याष्टारिसंस्थे शशिनि तु शकटः केन्द्रगे नास्ति लग्ना
च्चन्द्रे केन्द्रादिगेऽर्कादधमसमवरिष्ठाख्ययोगाः प्रसिद्धाः ।।14

Phaladīpikā Ch. 6,

Mahābhāgya yoga is caused in the case of a male if the birth is during the day (between sunrise and sunset), if the ascendant, Sun, Moon is in odd signs. *Mahābhāgya yoga* will arise in the case of a female if the birth is during the night time (after sunset and before sunrise) when the ascendant, the Sun, the Moon are in even signs.

तुंगस्था गगनाटना शुभकरा रन्ध्रे सपापे वधु
वैधव्यं समुपैति पापभवते पापग्रहालोकिते ।
रन्ध्रे शांशपतौ खले च विधवा निःसंशयं भामिनी
सौम्ये रन्ध्रगतैः समेति तरुणी प्रागेव मृत्युं पतेः ।। 27 ।।

Jātaka Pārijāta, Ch. 16 Part II

Even if all benefics occupy their sign of exaltation but if malefic occupy the 8th house in the malefic sign and that is aspected by any evil planet, the female suffers widowhood. If the *navāṁśa* occupied by the 8th lord is owned by a malefic, the widowhood is certain. If benefics occupy the 8th house, the female will die before her husband.

यदा शुभाः क्रूरखगा विलग्ने द्वितीयगः शोभनखेचरस्तु ।1
सा भर्तुरग्रे म्रियते च नारी गोसिंहकर्केन्दुगतेऽल्पपुत्रा
स्त्रीराशितो भवति चेद्विषमो नृराशिर्नारी मृता यद
सखेऽपि समे पुमांसम् ।। 2

Sugama Jyotiṣa, Ch. 4

if malefics and benefics fall in the ascendant, benefics falls in the 2nd house, then female dies earlier than her husband. If Moon falls in Taurus, Leo and Cancer in a female nativity, she has few number of sons. If the sign of husband is an odd number if reckoned from the sign of a wife, the wife will die prior to her husband. If the number is even, the husband will die before his wife.

Combinations For Obtaining Akhaṇḍa Saubhagya

On the basis of practical application of the above-mentioned aphorisms, which are taken from various classical texts, I have observed that a female can attain *akhaṇḍa saubhāgya* only if the 9th house is well fortified or strong in addition to these combinations of benefic and malefic planets, as given in *ślokas*. This may be summarized as under:

1. If benefics are placed in the 8th house, the female dies before her husband. If malefics occupy the 8th lord, the strong benefics join the second, the female will die prior to her husband.
2. If a strong benefic or the lord of the 7th join the 7th house from the ascendant or Moon, the combination of widowhood gets cancelled automatically.
3. If benefics occupy the 2nd house, the malefics and benefics both join the ascendant, the female will expire before her husband.
4. If the birth of a female takes place during night and the ascendant, Moon and the Sun falls in even signs, the female dies before her husband.
5. The seventh house should be well fortified but the ascendant should be weak or its lord should be placed adversely. The second or 8th house or both should be occupied by benefics, well fortified. However, if 8th house is weak or afflicted, the 2nd house should essentially be well disposed by the influence of benefic placed. *akhaṇḍa saubhāgya yoga* will be effective only if the 9th house is strong and its lord is well placed or the 9th house is occupied by the *Kendra* lords and benefics. If the 9th house is weak or afflicted in the horoscope of a female, she may not attain *saubhāgya* or *māṅgalya*

inspite of the presence of other benefic combinations of planets in her horoscope. Therefore, first of all, the strength should be examined while making judgement whether the death of wife will take place before her husband, i.e., whether she will attain *akhaṇḍa saubhāgya.*

Case No. 6.1 (Horoscope No. 35)

Great Kalpana Chawla, the first Indian born woman to venture into space, born in small town of India, Karnal, she got her schooling in the Tagore School. She completed her high school from Bal Niketan in 1976. after completing her school education, she joined the B.Sc. in Aeronautical Engineering in Punjab Engineering College at Chandigarh. She appeared in GRE and TOEFL examination, which are the qualifying, and eligibility tests for study in foreign countries. She went to America and joined M.S. postgraduate degree course in Aerospace Engineering in the University of Texas at Arlington in August 1984. in 1988 She got her Ph.D from this subject in the University of Colorado. Seeing her competence in the subject and keen desire for research and specialization, she received special grant and scholarship from the University of Colorado to pursue her Ph.D programme. Incidentally, this was also the beginning of a love affair with an American pilot in 1984 to John Piere Harrison and she got married during Venus-Venus *daśā bhukti.* She joined NASA in 1988 and took American citizenship in 1993. Her first voyage into space was from 19th November to 5th December on Columbia STS-87 as Prime Robotic Arm Operator.

In early 1995, she applied for the position of a civilian scientist in NASA for the voyage of American spaceship, Columbia. The ensuing voyage of Columbia

Case : 6.1 *Horoscope No. : 35*

Date	: 17.03.1962	Time	: 10:00:00
Place	: Karnal	Lat 29°:41′	Long 76°:59′
Ayanāmśa	: 23:19:33	Sidereal Time	: 21:15:02

Pln	**Degree**	**Rāśi**	**Nakṣatra**	**Pad**
Asc	09:59:06	Tau	Kṛtikā	4
Sun	02:46:52	Pis	P Bhādrapadā	4
Mon	17:54:25	Can	Aśleṣā	1
Mar	10:29:01	Aqu	Satabhiṣā	2
Mer	09:05:03	Aqu	Satabhiṣā	1
Jup	04:44:21	Aqu	Dhaniṣṭhā	4
Ven	14:39:26	Pis	U Bhādrapadā	4
Sat	14:47:29	Cap	Śrāvaṇa	2
Rah	24:10:42	Can	Aśleṣā	3
Ket	24:10:42	Cap	Dhaniṣṭhā	1

Lagna Chart

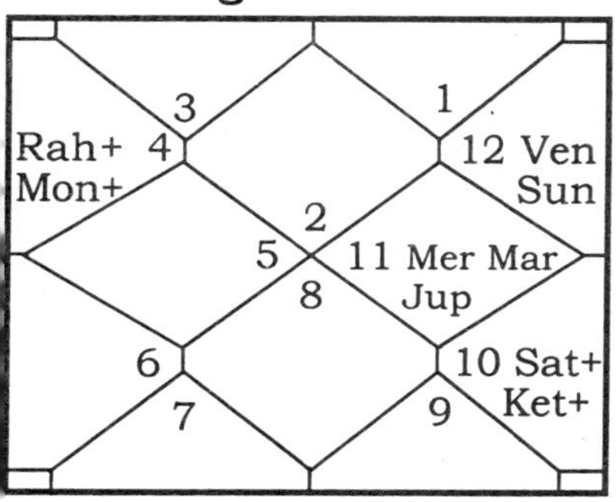

Navāmśa Chart

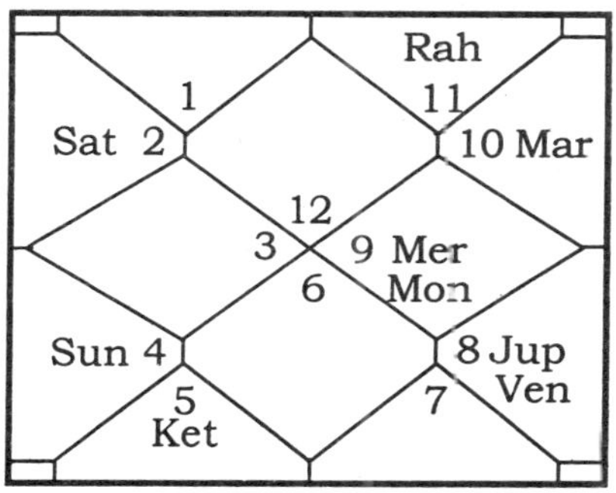

Balance of Vimśottarī Daśā of **Mercury 15Y 5M 0D**

Name of Event	Date of Event	Major Period	Sub Period
Marriage	1984	Venus	Venus
Death	01.02.2003	Venus	Mercury

was contemplated to take off in July 2002 for which selection of astronauts was done in January 2002. It was a matter of great pride that Kalpana Chawla was again or selected as mission specialist on the space shuttle Columbia STS-107 tentatively scheduled to take off in July 2002 and with this rare event in the history of space mission, she became the first woman in the world to venture into space twice, the Pride of India, as Kalpana Chawla. Unfortunately, we lost her on the tragic explosion of Columbia space shuttle STS-113 on 1st February 2003. She had almost completed her voyage and her shuttle was about to land on the earth after just 16 minutes if the explosion would not have taken place.

The loss of Mrs. Kalpana Chawla is certainly irrecoverable. However we are concerned with the combinations of *akhaṇḍa saubhāgya yoga* present in her horoscope. She was born in Taurus ascendant. *Yogakāraka* Saturn is conjoined with *Ketu* in the 9th house but both are shifted in the 10th house. She was born in *aśleṣā nakṣatra* last *pada*, which is of *mūlā*. Lord of *lagna* Venus is exalted in the 11th house and is associated with 4th lord Sun. The combination of *lagna* lord Venus and 4th lord Sun is certainly splendid with prosperous and happy wife. However, 5th and 2nd lord Mercury occupies the 10th house with 12th and 7th lord Mars and 8th and 12th lord Jupiter in Aquarius sign. Aquarius is an airy sign. Thus the combination of 12th and 8th lord Jupiter and Mars is present in the 10th house with 2nd lord Mercury. This combination shows that Mrs. Kalpana Chawla was extremely intelligent, dynamic and dashing lady who was blessed with immense courage and enthusiasm. Professionally she was highly placed due to strong

10th house. 10th and 9th lord Saturn is very strong in *ṣaḍabala*. In *bhāva* chart, 5 planets occupy the 10th house and *ādhi yoga* has also been formed. Moreover, *karmic* planets are associated with *Rāhu* and *Ketu*, therefore, the strength of *karmic* control planets has been largely enhanced. Moon and Saturn are *karmic* control planets and are placed 7th from each other. This is supposed to be strongest *rājayoga*. Apart from that, strong *sapta graha mallika rājayoga* is also present. Both the triangle lords are conjoined in the 10th in *bhāva chart* in association with 8th and 11th lord Jupiter, 7th and 12th lord Mars which shows unaccountable success in profession. In this horoscope, *lagna* lord Venus is exalted, Moon and Saturn fall in own. Mars obtains *navāṁśa* of its exaltation and 10th lord *yogakāraka* Saturn obtains *navāṁśa* of Venus, the lord of the *lagna*. These all combinations made her a woman of worldwide fame. Fag end of the major period of Venus when the sub-period of Mercury was running over her, resulted into her tragic death in space on February 1st, 2003. It will not be out of place to mention that Madam Kalpana Chawla had expressed her prime ambition a few days ago that she wanted to die in space only. She was a true patriot and almighty fulfilled her last ambition on February 1st, 2003 as she breathed last there in space.

She was running under the sub-period of Mercury who is *mārakeśa* for Taurus ascendant and is heavily afflicted due to conjunction of another *mārakeśa* Mars who is inimical to Mercury. Mercury obtains *mrityuanśa* and Venus who's *mahādaśā* was running, obtains the *navāṁśa* of Mars. Saturn was transiting in the ascendant and was aspecting 7th and 12th lord Mars, 8th lord Jupiter, 2nd and 5th lord

Mercury, radical Moon, *Rāhu* and 3rd house, and 7th house. Mars was transiting into 7th house and was aspecting the ascendant, Mercury, Mars and Jupiter, i.e., transiting Saturn and Mars were aspecting *mārakeśa* planets both Mercury and Mars. This is very adverse and critical combination for death especially as *Rāhu* and *Ketu* were conjoined with Saturn and Mars respectively. Moon and Sun were transiting in *śrāvaṇa nakṣatra* over the axis of *Rāhu* and *Ketu*. Moon and Sun was facing radical Moon and *Rāhu* and was crossing *Ketu* and Saturn on the black day of her death.

Here we are concerned with her death as *saubhāgyavatī* female. The 7th lord Mars occupies the 10th house who is strong in *digbala* and obtains 1.2 *ṣaḍabala*. 2nd lord Mercury is conjoined with Jupiter and 2nd house is aspected by Jupiter and that indicates comparatively long life to her husband. *Lagna* is unaspected by any benefic planets but is aspected by malefic Mars. *Lagna* lord Venus is associated with inimical Sun and obtains *navāṁśa* of *mārakeśa* Mars. 8th house is also afflicted as its lord Jupiter is associated with Mars and Mercury and is placed under *pāpakartari yoga*. Moreover, 8th lord Jupiter and *lagna* lord Venus obtains *navāṁśa* of Mars under the aspect of Saturn. This is certainly indicating short and unnatural end of her life. let us examine the 9th house where *yogakāraka* Saturn is placed in own sign Capricorn. In *Bhāva* chart Saturn is shifted in the 10th house, it is the second strongest planet as it obtains 1.33 *ṣaḍabala*. Thus 9th house is strong, 8th house is afflicted, 7th and 2nd house is well fortified and 9th house also happens to be quite powerful. Therefore, she had a death of *saubhāgyavatī* female though her tragic death is not only a very heavy loss of India or USA but it's a loss of an intellectual, dynamic, outstanding, and meritorious female astronaut of the world wide fame. Such great soul are rarely born on this earth.

Case No. 6.2 (Horoscope No. 36)

Marriage – November 24th, 1989 during Moon Saturn period.

Death – May 27th, 1993 during Moon Venus period.

This is the case of the daughter of my elder sister who always secured the first position in school, college and University. She was working as a Probationary Officer in a nationalized bank and had outstanding records.

She was married on November 24th, 1989 during sub-period of Saturn in the major period of Moon. Here Saturn is *yogakāraka* and joins the 2nd house. She died due to breast cancer on May 27th, 1993 during sub-period of Venus in the major period of Moon before her husband at 34 years of age. However, though she died within 4 years of marriage she attained *akhaṇḍa saubhāgya*. Here Mars is a malefic planet and is a *mārakeśa* for Libra. Ascendant joins the 8th house under retrograde motion whereas Saturn is a *yogakāraka* for Libra *lagna* and joins the 2nd house in Martian sign Scorpio under full aspect of Mars. Benefic Jupiter, Mercury and Sun are shifted in the 2nd house, thus the 2nd house is well disposed and 8th house is heavily afflicted with presence of Mars. She was born in *grand mūlā*, i.e., in the first quarter of *mūlā nakṣatra*. Mars occupies the 8th house in Taurus, the sign of Venus. Venus is debilitated and combust and joins the 12th house over the axis of nodes. Thus the major period of Moon and the sub-period of Venus became *māraka* for her. We find that the

Case : 6.2 *Horoscope No. : 36*

Date	: 18.10.1958	Time	: 08:22:00
Place	: Lucknow	Lat 26°:50′	Long 80°:54′
Ayanāmśa	: 23:16:58	Sidereal Time	: 09:59:58

Pln	**Degree**	**Rāśi**	**Nakṣatra**	**Pad**
Asc	29:24:01	Lib	Viśākhā	3
Sun	00:56:36	Lib	Citrā	3
Mon	12:44:09	Sag	Mūlā	4
Mar(R)	08:48:21	Tau	Kṛtikā	4
Mer(C)	09:31:42	Lib	Svāti	1
Jup	14:55:14	Lib	Svāti	3
Ven(C)	24:44:08	Vir	Citrā	1
Sat	28:09:13	Sco	Jyeṣṭhā	4
Rah(R)	29:05:33	Vir	Citrā	2
Ket(R)	29:05:33	Pis	Revatī	4

Lagna Chart

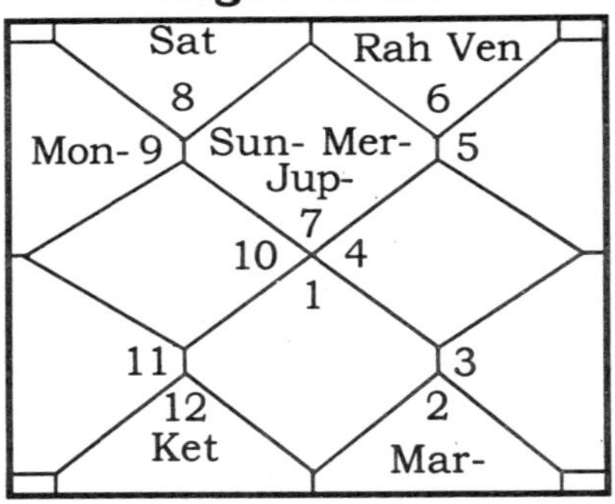

Navāmśa Chart

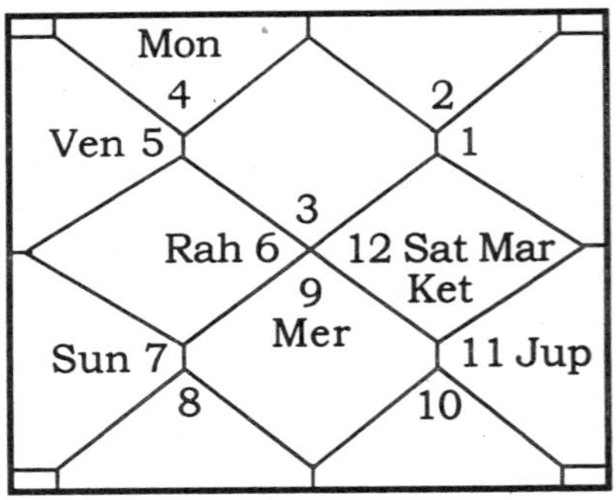

Balance of Vimśottarī Daśā of **Ketu 0Y 3M 23D**

Name of Event	Date of Event	Major Period	Sub Period
Marriage	24.11.1989	Moon	Saturn
Death	27.05.1993	Moon	Venus

2nd house is well disposed and strong whereas the 8th house is heavily afflicted by malefics, therefore, she attained *akhaṇḍa saubhāgya*. In *bhāva* chart, Mars is shifted in the 7th house. The 7th house is strong that is the life of the husband is longer than the life of woman in question because *lagna* lord is weak, combust and afflicted in the 12th house in debilitation and obtains inimical *navāṁśa*.

The female who attains *akhaṇḍa saubhāgya* must have strong 7th house, afflicted or weak ascendant, strong 9th house in particular. In this horoscope, 9th house is quite strong as 9th lord Mercury is associated with Jupiter and Jupiter also aspects the 9th house, therefore, 9th house is well-disposed and quite strong. The ascendant is hemmed between Saturn, *Rāhu* and debilitated Venus. Thus the ascendant is weak. 6th and 12th lords Jupiter and Mercury joins ascendant. This further reduces the strength of ascendant. in *bhāva* chart, 7th lord Mars is placed in the 7th house, thus the husband had to live longer. Since she was born in *mūla*, as the Moon is placed in *mūla nakṣatra*, therefore, she died during the major period of Moon and in the sub-period of Venus as *lagna* and Venus both are afflicted and Venus is 8th lord. The persons who are born in any *nakṣatra* of *mūla* and especially in grand *mūla*, suffer heavily during the major or sub-period of Moon.

Case No. 6.3 (Horoscope No. 37)

Marriage – February 7th, 1979 during Venus – Jupiter *daśā bhukti*.

Death – Sep. 2nd, 2003 during Mars – *Rāhu daśā bhukti*.

She got married on February 7th, 1979 during sub-period of Jupiter in the major period of Venus. The

Case : 6.3 *Horoscope No. : 37*

Date	: 29.09.1957	Time :	18:01:15
Place	: Karnal	Lat 29°:41′	Long 76°:59′
Ayanāmśa	: 23:16:11	Sidereal Time :	18:11:11

Pln	**Degree**	**Rāśi**	**Nakṣatra**	**Pad**
Asc	10:46:38	Pis	U Bhādrapadā	3
Sun	12:49:28	Vir	Hastā	1
Mon	28:25:34	Sco	Jyeṣṭhā	4
Mar	10:11:06	Vir	Hastā	1
Mer	25:47:31	Leo	P Phālgunī	4
Jup(C)	17:32:39	Vir	Hastā	3
Ven	24:35:04	Lib	Viśākhā	2
Sat	16:14:52	Sco	Anurādhā	4
Rah	17:45:31	Lib	Svāti	4
Ket	17:45:31	Ari	Bharanī	2

Lagna Chart

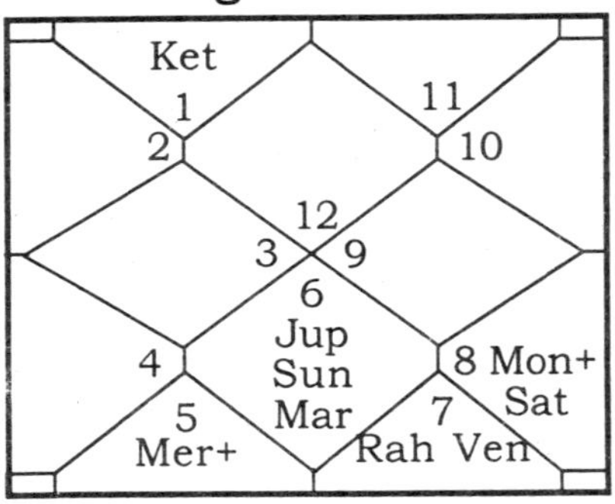

Navāmśa Chart

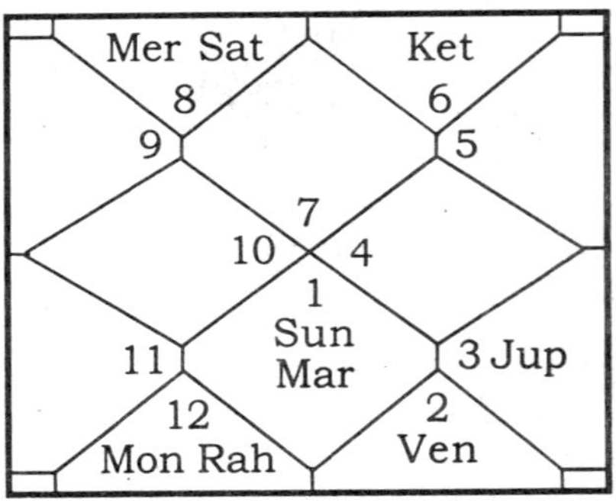

Balance of Vimśottarī Daśā of **Mercury 2Y 0M 2D**

Name of Event	Date of Event	Major Period	Sub Period
Marriage	07.02.1979	Venus	Jupiter
Death	02.09.2003	Mars	Rahu

8th house is occupied by *svakṣetrī* Venus in association with *Rāhu* and lord of 2nd house and lord of *lagna*, Mars and Jupiter are placed in the 7th house with 6th lord Sun. Jupiter aspects the ascendant which is owned by Jupiter as well. Mars aspects the 2nd house, which is owned by, Mars itself. The 7th house is placed under *śubha kartari yoga*, 2nd lord Mars obtains own *navāṁśa*. In *bhāva* chart, 7th lord Mercury is shifted in the 7th house. Thus, the 7th house is well disposed due to association of *lagna* lord Jupiter. The 2nd house is also strong as its lord Mars occupies own *navāṁśa* and falls in Moon's *nakṣatra hasta*. The 8th house and its lord are hemmed between Mars and Saturn, i.e. placed under *pāpakartari yoga*. But the 7th and 2nd house are strong. *Bhāgyādhipati* Mars occupies 7th house but it is combust and *lagna* lord Jupiter is also combust and afflicted. This clearly indicates that she will die at an early age in front of her husband and that her husband will be alive. 2nd lord Mars obtains own *navāṁśa* and joins 7th house whereas *Rāhu* is associated with 8th lord Venus in the 8th house. She expired due to sudden heart failure during the sub-period of *Rāhu* in the major period of Mars when Saturn was transiting in the 8th house from radical Moon. It may be noted that she was born in the last *pada* of *jyeṣṭhā nakṣatra*, which proved fatal for her. She expired when she was nearly 44 years of age and both of her two children, a son and a daughter were unsettled and unmarried. Since 8th lord Mars is conjoined with *lagna* lord Jupiter and the 7th lord Mercury in the 7th house and that indicates *akhaṇḍa saubhāgya yoga* though at an early age. 9th lord Mars joins 7th house in association with *lagna* lord Jupiter. Thus the 9th house is strong, Moon obtains *nīca* bhang as 5th lord joins 9th house and adds strength to the 9th house. Saturn obtains *vargottama navāṁśa* in own constellation *anurādhā* in the 9th house. This has further added strength to the 9th house. The *lagna* and 8th house are weak. Therefore, she attained *saubhāgya yoga* leaving her husband and children behind.

Case No. 6.4 (Horoscope No. 38)

Death – August 15th, 2003 during Mercury Saturn *daśā bhukti*

This is the horoscope of one of our near relative who lived upto 74 years of age and also attained *akhaṇḍa saubhāgya*. She was a pious lady completely dedicated to her husband. They never quarrelled and there was never any difference of opinion between them on any aspect of life. The biggest tragedy of her life was that though she was blessed with 3 sons, they expired one after another due to liver problem. Here 12th lord Jupiter joins the 5th house in Taurus under retrograde motion and is aspected by Mars, Mercury, Sun and Venus. The 7th house is well disposed as its lord Moon occupies the ascendant. The 7th lord Moon is aspected by Jupiter, which indicates long life of husband. This is a clear indication of *akhaṇḍa saubhāgya yoga*. The 2nd house is aspected by Mars and Saturn both. Saturn is the *lagna* lord, therefore, *lagna* becomes weak and 7th house becomes strong. She expired after a long suffering of cancer on August 15th, 2003 during the sub-period of Saturn in the major period of Mercury. Saturn is 2nd lord and becomes a *mārakeśa* due to its placement in the 12th house. Saturn obtains *navāṁśa* of Mercury and Mercury obtains *navāṁśa* of its debilitation. Therefore, tail-end of major period of Mercury

Case : 6.4 *Horoscope No. : 38*

Date	: 07.12.1929	Time :	10:03:00
Place	: Moradabad	Lat 28°:50′	Long 78°:45′
Ayanāmśa	: 22:52:31	Sidereal Time :	14:49:52

Pln	**Degree**	**Rāśi**	**Nakṣatra**	**Pad**
Asc	05:36:55	Cap	Uttarāṣāḍha	3
Sun	21:43:36	Sco	Jyeṣṭhā	2
Mon	27:11:20	Cap	Dhaniṣṭhā	2
Mar	20:37:14	Sco	Jyeṣṭhā	2
Mer(C)	27:02:56	Sco	Jyeṣṭhā	4
Jup(C)	18:00:28	Tau	Rohiṇī	3
Ven	06:59:34	Sco	Anurādhā	2
Sat	07:55:20	Sag	Mūlā	3
Rah(R)	18:46:01	Ari	Bharanī	2
Ket(R)	18:46:01	Lib	Svāti	4

Lagna Chart

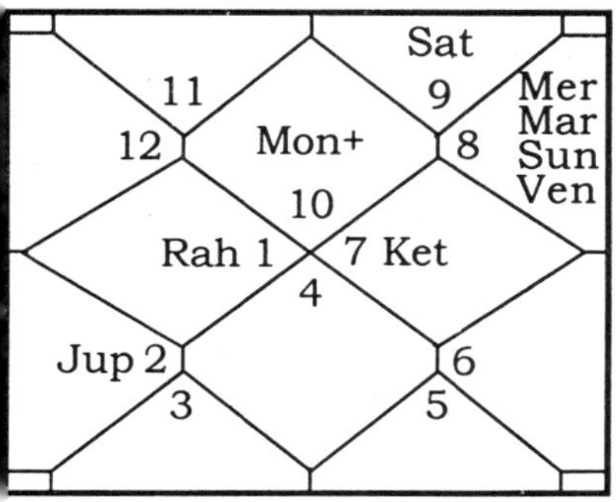

Navāmśa Chart

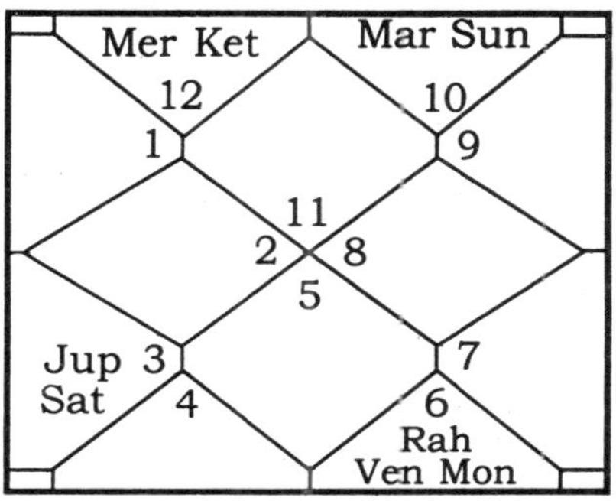

Balance of Vimśottarī Daśā of **Mars 4Y 11M 21D**

Name of Event	Date of Event	Major Period	Sub Period
Marriage	18.06.1955	Jupiter	Saturn
Death	15.08.2003	Mercury	Saturn

resulted into her death as *saubhāgyavatī* on August 15th, 2003.

Case No. 6.5 (Horoscope No. 39)

Marriage – August 17th, 1957 during Moon – Saturn *daśā bhukti*

Death – May 17th, 2002 during Jupiter – *Rāhu daśā bhukti*

She was the most ideal and simple woman who dedicated her life for prosperity, happiness and elevation of her husband in various ways. I often used to say that her husband is the luckiest man in respect of life partner. Unfortunately cancer was diagnosed to her in the month of July 1998. I had written in her's life reading, her husband's as also her children's that she will suffer from any incurable disease in the year 1998 and may not live beyond July 24th, 2002. She suffered a lot due to cancer of her ovaries and uterus etc. and ultimately expired on May 17th, 2002 cared by her husband during the sub–period of *Rāhu* in the major period of Jupiter. Here *Rāhu* is placed in the 12th house and Jupiter occupies the 8th house. Therefore, major period of Jupiter and sub-period of *Rāhu* ended her life but she attained *akhaṇḍa saubhāgya*. Here direct Jupiter occupies the 8th house in Sagittarius and obtains the friendly *navāṁśa* of Sun. Jupiter's aspect over the 2nd house is also encouraging placement giving long life to her husband. Jupiter's placement in 8th house if unafflicted and well disposed, gives rise to *saubhāgya yoga*. *Lagna* lord Venus is afflicted due to conjunction of *Rāhu* and aspect of Saturn. Thus the *lagna* is weak, 7th lord Mars who is debilitated in 3rd, obtains *nīca bhang rājayoga* and aspects 7th house of its own, in *bhāva* chart, making the 7th house strong. The 8th house indicates *māngalya*, so she was fortunate to be

Case : 6.5 *Horoscope No. : 39*

Date	: 06.03.1948	Time :	10:10:00
Place	: Hapur	Lat 28°:43′	Long 77°:47′
Ayanāmśa	: 23:07:48	Sidereal Time :	20:46:26

Pln	**Degree**	**Rāśi**	**Nakṣatra**	**Pad**
Asc	01:41:50	Tau	Kṛtikā	2
Sun	22:23:57	Aqu	P Bhādrapadā	1
Mon	01:09:10	Cap	Uttarāṣāḍha	2
Mar(R)	28:26:57	Can	Aśleṣā	4
Mer	28:40:00	Cap	Dhaniṣṭhā	2
Jup	03:23:45	Sag	Mūlā	2
Ven	04:27:25	Ari	Aśvinī	2
Sat(R)	24:07:16	Can	Aśleṣā	3
Rah(R)	23:07:53	Ari	Bharanī	3
Ket(R)	23:07:53	Lib	Viśākhā	1

Lagna Chart

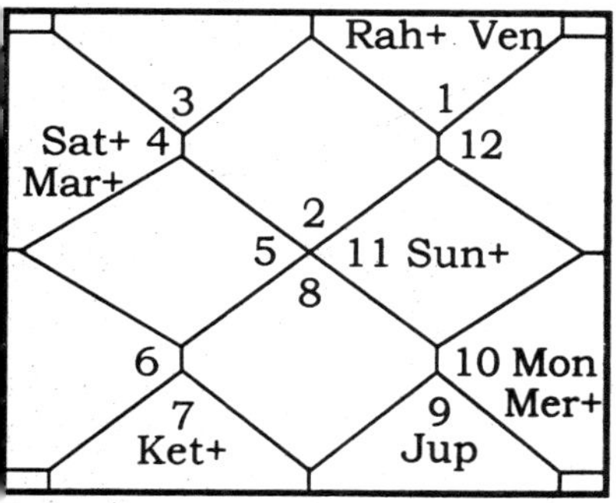

Navāmśa Chart

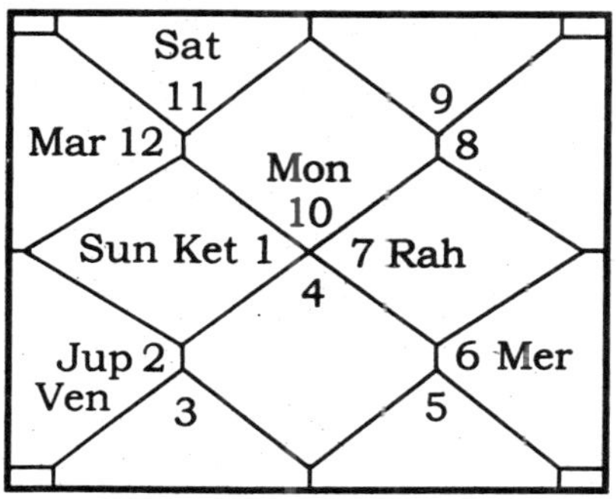

Balance of Vimśottarī Daśā of **Sun 3Y 11M 23D**

Name of Event	Date of Event	Major Period	Sub Period
Marriage	17.08.1957	Moon	Saturn
Death	17.05.2002	Jupiter	Rahu

blessed with *akhaṇḍa saubhāgya*, the 2nd house is well aspected and 7th house is strong. This kind of placement gives rise to *saubhāgya yoga*.

Case No. 6.6 (Horoscope No. 40)

Death – January 22nd, 2003 during Venus – Venus *daśā bhukti*.

Marriage – June 4th, 1969 during Saturn – Venus *daśā bhukti*.

This is the horoscope of wife of an astrologer of worldwide fame, editor and proprietor of various journals and author of various authentic books in astrology, who has always been a great inspirer, assistor, and helper to me as well.

She got married on June 4th, 1969 during the sub-period of Venus in the major period of Saturn. She led a very happy and prosperous life with her husband and was blessed with number of children. She suddenly lost her life on January 22nd, 2003 during sub-period of Venus in the major period of Venus. Thus, Venus played a vital role in her life. Venus is the lord of 3rd and 8th house and joins 2nd and 9th lord Mars. Venus obtains *navāṁśa* of Mars. Thus, the 8th lord Venus is under the influence of Mars and Saturn. *Lagna* lord Jupiter is posited in the 12th house over the axis of *Rāhu* and *Ketu* in association with Moon. In *bhāva* chart, Saturn aspects the Jupiter, Moon and *Rāhu*. Thus, the *lagna* is weak but the 7th house is quite strong as its lord Mercury joins the 10th house with Sun under retrograde motion. Mercury obtains own *navāṁśa*. Sun and Mars are the strongest planet in this birth chart as they obtain 1.78 and 1.24 *śaḍabala* respectively. Mars is the 2nd lord and aspects the 2nd house. Jupiter aspects the 8th house. Thus, the 2nd and 8th house are well fortified but

Case : 6.6 *Horoscope No. : 40*

Date	: 12.01.1951	Time :	11:30:00
Place	: Puri	Lat 19°:48′	Long 85°:52′
Ayanāmśa	: 23:10:26	Sidereal Time :	19:07:10

Pln	**Degree**	**Rāśi**	**Nakṣatra**	**Pad**
Asc	28:16:56	Pis	Revatī	4
Sun	28:02:53	Sag	Uttarāṣāḍha	1
Mon	25:57:35	Aqu	P Bhādrapadā	2
Mar	28:42:56	Cap	Dhaniṣṭhā	2
Mer(R)	08:45:21	Sag	Mūlā	3
Jup	13:42:54	Aqu	Satabhiṣā	3
Ven	12:18:19	Cap	Śrāvaṇa	1
Sat(S)	09:11:28	Vir	U Phālgunī	4
Rah(R)	27:35:58	Aqu	P Bhādrapadā	3
Ket(R)	27:35:58	Leo	U Phālgunī	1

Lagna Chart

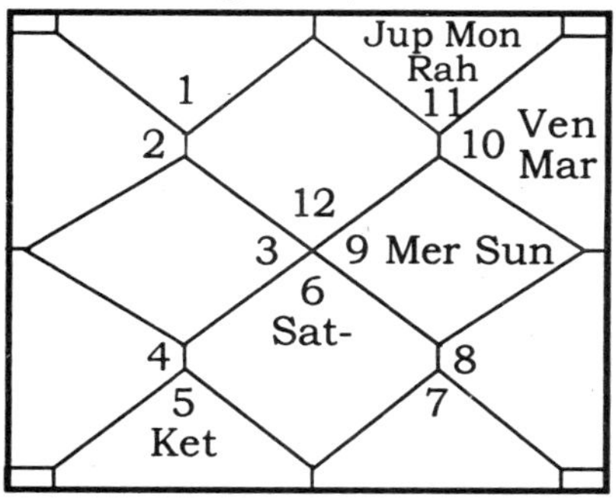

Navāmśa Chart

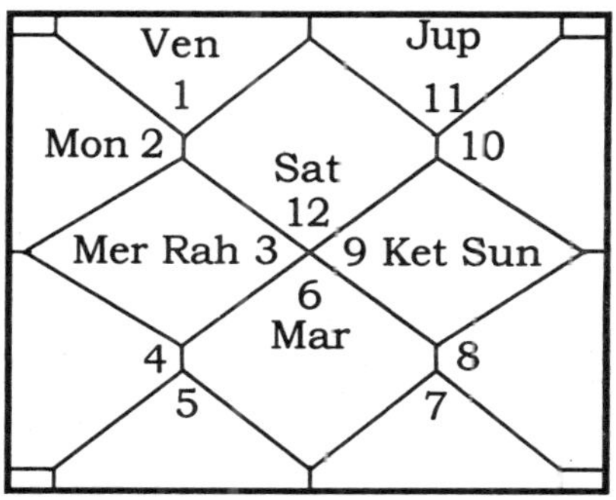

Balance of Vimśottarī Daśā of **Jup 8Y 10M 5D**

Name of Event	Date of Event	Major Period	Sub Period
Marriage	04.06.1969	Saturn	Venus
Death	22.01.2003	Venus	Venus

the 8th and *lagna* lord Venus and Jupiter is afflicted which gave the life span of 52 years. The 9th house must be strong for *akhaṇḍa saubhāgya yoga* as discussed earlier. In this horoscope, 9th lord Mars is placed in the 11th house in exaltation and is associated with 3rd and 8th lord Venus. Thus, the 9th house is well fortified. All planets are hemmed between *Ketu* and *Rāhu*. She led a very pious life. It was the Venus-Venus *daśā bhukti* on January 22nd, 2003 when she breathed last. Venuṣ is the 8th lord and some how it is placed under *pāpakartari yoga* and *śubhakartari yoga* as well. Venus obtains *navāṁśa* of Mars and is associated with Mars. Soon after the beginning of the major period, sub-period of Venus, she left this world for final abode as a *saubhāgyavatī* and fortunate wife. Jupiter and Saturn's aspect on the 8th house gives long life to her husband and affliction of Venus as discussed above, gives middle span of life to her. There is mutual exchange in the *lagna* lord Jupiter and 11th and 12th lord Saturn. In this horoscope, this combination has given rise to *akhaṇḍa saubhāgya yoga* to her and immense success, popularity, prosperity, piousity and wide knowledge, deep understanding, astonishing foresight and extreme simplicity to her husband.

10th and *lagna* lord Jupiter aspects the 8th house and there is no affliction of the 8th house. However the 2nd lord Mars who is exalted in the 11th house is associated with Venus there. This is a powerful combination of everlasting happiness in married life and her long association throughout her life. This combination of Mars-Venus is placed under *śubha kartari yoga*. Placement of the 11th and 12th lord Saturn in the 7th house is not auspicious especially as Saturn falls in the *nakṣatra* of Sun but Saturn obtains the *navāṁśa* of the ascendant, i.e. Pisces. This gives a long life to her husband. The ascendant lord Jupiter falls over the axis of *Rāhu* and *Ketu* obtains *vargottama navāṁśa.* There is mutual exchange in the *navāṁśa* of Jupiter and Saturn and that shows a long life to her husband and *akhaṇḍa saubhāgya yoga.* She expired during the sub-period of Venus in the major period of Sun. Sun is the lord of 6th house and is associated with the 7th lord Mercury and Venus who is the 8th lord occupies the 2nd house as reckoned from Sun. The Sun and Venus are in *dvidvādaśa* position whose major and sub-period ended her life and she attained *akhaṇḍa saubhāgya* at 52 years of age. 9th lord Mars is exalted in the 11th house and is placed under *śubha kartari yoga.* Thus the 9th house is strong. 7th lord Mercury obtains own *navāṁśa, lagna* lord Jupiter who obtains *vargottama navāṁśa,* aspects the 8th house and this aspect is free from affliction. Therefore, this has given *akhaṇḍa saubhāgya yoga* to this ladv.

Case No. 6.7 (Horoscope No. 41)

Marriage – November 27th 1966 during *Rāhu* – Venus *daśā bhukti.*

Death – 1997 during Saturn – Venus *daśā bhukti.*

She attained *akhaṇḍa saubhāgya* in the year 1997 during sub-period of Venus in the major period of Saturn at 57 years of age. The lord of the 2nd and 7th house, Mars is associated with *lagna* lord Venus and *yogakāraka* Saturn is the 7th house. It has been observed by us that placement of Mars in own sign Aries does not cause death to husband, on the contrary, the conjunction of the *lagna* and 7th or the 2nd and 8th house gives rise to *akhaṇḍa saubhāgya yoga* provided it is unafflicted, placed under

Case : 6.7 *Horoscope No. : 41*

Date	: 15.03.1940	Time :	21:00:00
Place	: Jabalpur	Lat 23°:10′	Long 79°:57′
Ayanāmśa	: 23:01:25	Sidereal Time :	08:22:07

Pln	**Degree**	**Rāśi**	**Nakṣatra**	**Pad**
Asc	09:20:38	Lib	Svāti	1
Sun	01:53:04	Pis	P Bhādrapadā	4
Mon	14:05:07	Tau	Rohiṇī	2
Mar	25:33:40	Ari	Bharanī	4
Mer(R/D)	01:45:43	Pis	P Bhādrapadā	4
Jup	22:17:43	Pis	Revatī	2
Ven	14:55:53	Ari	Bharanī	1
Sat	06:25:53	Ari	Aśvinī	2
Rah	27:11:00	Vir	Citrā	2
Ket	27:11:00	Pis	Revatī	4

Lagna Chart

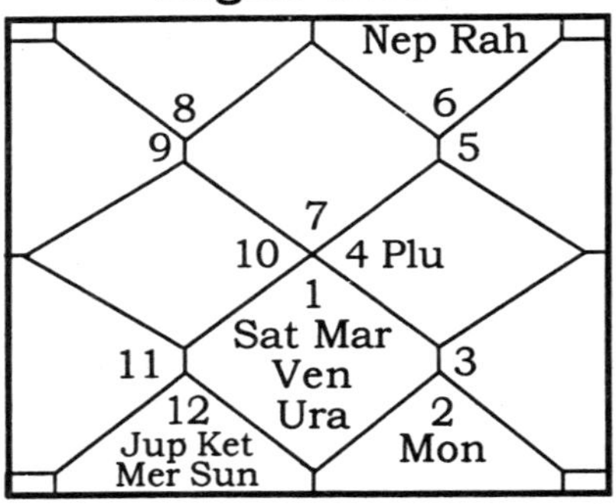

Navāmśa Chart

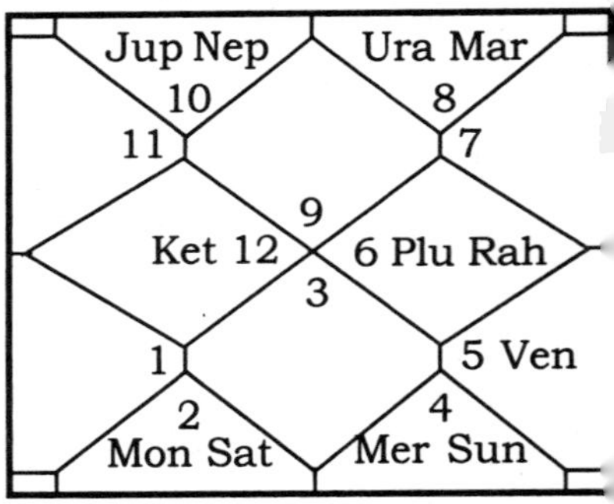

Balance of Vimśottarī Daśā of **Moon 6Y 11M 7D**

Name of Event	Date of Event	Major Period	Sub Period
Marriage	27.11.1966	Rahu	Venus
Death	1997	Saturn	Venus

śubhakartari yoga and well fortified. Here 2nd house is aspected by exalted Moon, *svakṣetrīya* Jupiter and Mars who is the lord of 2nd house as well. Thus the 2nd and 8th house are well disposed and strong. This has given rise to *saubhāgya yoga*. The 12th house from 7th, i.e., the 6th house is afflicted. *Lagna* lord Venus is also placed under *pāpakartari yoga* and obtains *navāṁśa* of the inimical Sun, so her death is indicated earlier than her husband. Venus is 8th lord and Saturn is debilitated in 7th house. From Saturn-Venus is debilitated in 7th house. From Saturn, Venus is 2nd and 7th lord. Thus Venus and Saturn both turned *māraka* for her but made her fortunate to be blessed with *akhaṇḍa saubhāgya*.

Case No. 6.8 (Horoscope No. 42)

Marriage – November 28th 1972 during Sun – Venus *daśā bhukti*.

Death – 1979 during Moon – Saturn *daśā bhukti*.

The woman was suffering from Cancer and expired during the year 1979 during Moon-Saturn *daśā bhukti* at 29 years of age. *Lagna* lord Venus occupied the 8th house over the axis of *Rāhu* and *Ketu* in association with Sun, Saturn and Mercury. Venus is debilitated and combust. Thus the *lagna* becomes weak. The lord of 2nd and 7th house Mars joins the 2nd house in own sign Scorpio. This means that the life of husband is well-fortified but the aspect of Mars over the 8th house and formation of *pāpakartari yoga* around ascendant curtailed her life span. *Lagna* lord Venus who is debilitated, obtains *navāṁśa* of Moon and Moon falls in 3rd house in *rāśi* chart, therefore, Moon becomes a *mārakeśa* for her. The 2nd and 7th lord Mars obtains *navāṁśa* of Saturn in association with Saturn. Moreover, Saturn falls in the 12th house and from

Case : 6.8 *Horoscope No. : 42*

Date	: 17.10.1950	Time	: 07:00:00
Place	: Bagapat	Lat 28°:56′	Long 77°:14′
Ayanāmśa	: 23:10:10	Sidereal Time	: 08:18:53

Pln	**Degree**	**Rāśi**	**Nakṣatra**	**Pad**
Asc	07:09:00	Lib	Svāti	1
Sun	29:56:37	Vir	Citrā	2
Mon	15:28:36	Sag	Pūrvāṣāḍha	1
Mar	21:54:30	Sco	Jyeṣṭhā	2
Mer(C)	19:09:18	Vir	Hastā	3
Jup(R)	04:30:23	Aqu	Dhaniṣṭhā	4
Ven(C)	22:50:34	Vir	Hastā	4
Sat	03:17:16	Vir	U Phālgunī	2
Rah(R)	04:58:58	Pis	U Bhādrapadā	1
Ket(R)	04:58:58	Vir	U Phālgunī	3

Lagna Chart

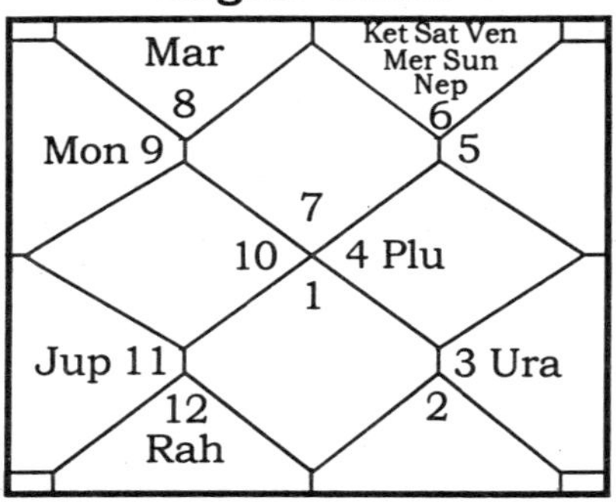

Navāmśa Chart

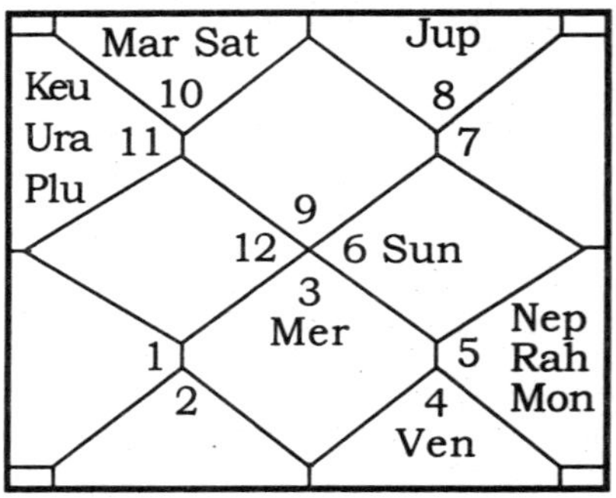

Balance of Vimśottarī Daśā of **Venus 16Y 9M 12D**

Name of Event	Date of Event	Major Period	Sub Period
Marriage	28.11.1972	Sun	Venus
Death	1979	Moon	Saturn

Moon Saturn becomes a *mārakeśa* and she died in the major period of Moon in the sub-period of Saturn in 1979. However, she had a very short span of life of only 29 years but she attained *saubhāgya* of reaching the end of her life journey before her life partner. Let me conclude the observation that the placement of 2nd and 7th lord in own sign in either of these houses, protects the life of the husband and gives *akhaṇḍa saubhāgya* if 12th, 6th or 1st house or their lords are afflicted.

Case No. 6.9 (Horoscope No. 43)

Marriage – June 11th, 1973 during Mars – Mercury *daśā bhukti*

Death – June 2nd, 1995 during Jupiter – Jupiter *daśā bhukti*

The subject belonged to a very rich and famous family of a politician. She was beautiful, lovely and had a love marriage on June 11th, 1973 during Mars-Mercury period. She was blessed with three daughters and a son. Her husband was quite handsome but beautiful women were his weakness as he was always liked and appreciated by such women. After four children were born to the couple, her husband had no interest in her. He had a very powerful concubine. The above woman was an obstacle in their path, and they were charged for the execution of her murder on June 2nd, 1995. There was prominent coverage of this news in all the prestigious newspapers, TV channels of the country. Though she was murdered but still she attained *akhaṇḍa saubhāgya*. Husband and the concubine in question were prosecuted and imprisoned.

In this birth chart, Mars is posited in the 8th house but it is shifted in the 7th. Jupiter aspects

Case : 6.9 *Horoscope No. : 43*

Date	: 23.08.1951	Time :	16:25:00
Place	: Muzaffarnagar	Lat 29°:28′	Long 77°:42′
Ayanāmśa	: 23:11:00	Sidereal Time :	14:09:30

Pln	**Degree**	**Rāśi**	**Nakṣatra**	**Pad**
Asc	24:19:42	Sag	Pūrvāṣāḍha	4
Sun	06:19:12	Leo	Maghā	2
Mon	25:20:37	Ari	Bharanī	4
Mar	10:02:02	Can	Puṣya	3
Mer(R)	20:20:31	Leo	P Phālgunī	3
Jup(R)	20:23:44	Pis	Revatī	2
Ven(R)	23:07:57	Leo	P Phālgunī	3
Sat	07:52:13	Vir	U Phālgunī	4
Rah	16:46:35	Aqu	Satabhiṣā	4
Ket(C)	16:46:35	Leo	P Phālgunī	2

Lagna Chart

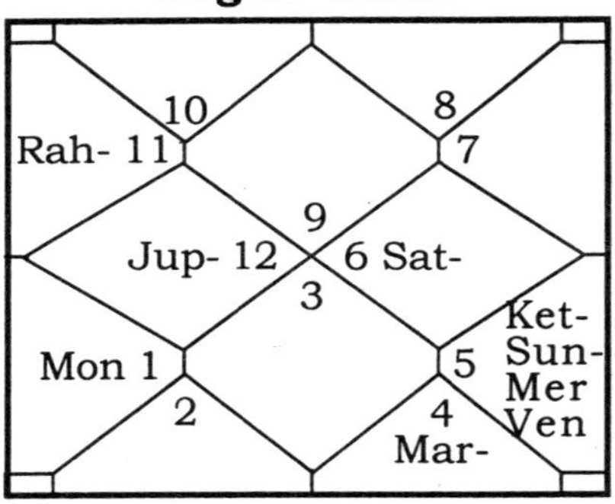

Navāmśa Chart

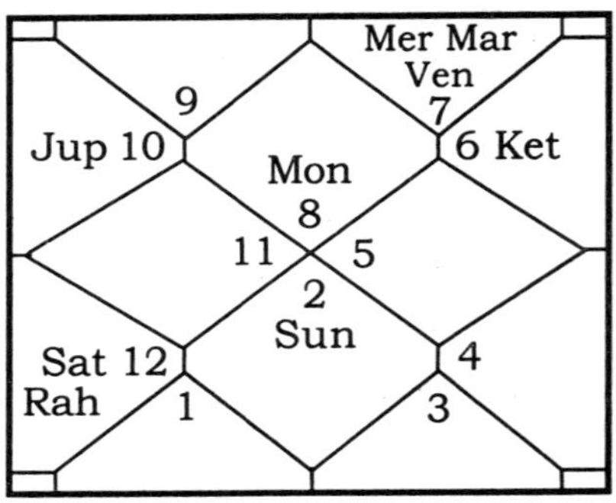

Balance of Vimśottarī Daśā of **Venus 1Y 11M 24D**

Name of Event	Date of Event	Major Period	Sub Period
Marriage	11.06.1973	Mars	Mercury
Death	02.06.1995	Jupiter	Jupiter

the 8th house and 2nd lord Saturn. In *bhāva* chart, Saturn-Jupiter is shifted in 9th and 3rd house respectively. Thus Jupiter aspects the 7th house and 2nd lord Saturn and the 7th lord Mercury, which resulted into *akhaṇḍa saubhāgya.* Placement of Mars in the 8th house caused unnatural death by way of murder. The *bhāgya yoga* of the 9th house should also be strong for obtaining *akhaṇḍa saubhāgya.* 8th lord Moon occupies the 5th house in Martian sign Aries and obtains *navāṁśa* of Mars as well. Saturn is *mārakeśa* for her and obtains *navāṁśa* of Jupiter. Jupiter is shifted in the 3rd house and is dispositor of Saturn as well. Therefore, Jupiter who blessed her with *akhaṇḍa saubhāgya yoga* also became *māraka* for her. Her murder took place on June 2nd, 1995 during sub-period of Jupiter in the major period of Jupiter.

Case No. 6.10 (Horoscope No. 44)

Marriage – 1981 during *Rāhu* – Mars *daśā bhukti*

Death – August 31st, 1997 during Jupiter – *Rāhu daśā bhukti*

Lady Diana Spenser was the wife of Prince Charles of England. I personally believe that she was the most fascinating, charming and captivating woman who won appreciation for her exceptional beauty, slender, physique, outstanding merits and matchless etiquette. The fragrance of flowers spread all over the globe, the amount of love accumulated from *Satayuga* to *Kaliyuga*, attraction like Padminī and simplicity like Mīrā were alloyed together in her. Innumerable persons, whether male or females were great fans of Diana. Almost whole of the world was highly impressed with Diana as she always believed that the greatest happiness is “to love and be loved”. She proved it by divorcing Prince Charles.

Case : 6.10 *Horoscope No. : 44*

Date	: 01.07.1961	Time	:	19:45:00
Place	: Scotland	Lat 57°:00′	Long 05°:00′	
Ayanāmśa	: 23:19:00	Sidereal Time	:	14:23:32

Pln	**Degree**	**Rāśi**	**Nakṣatra**	**Pad**
Asc	01:24:08	Sag	Mūlā	1
Sun	16:23:54	Gem	Ārdrā	3
Mon	02:31:31	Aqu	Dhaniṣṭhā	3
Mar	08:21:40	Leo	Maghā	3
Mer(R/C)	09:51:31	Gem	Ārdrā	1
Jup(R)	11:46:29	Cap	Śrāvaṇa	1
Ven	01:08:21	Tau	Kṛtikā	2
Sat(R)	04:29:37	Cap	Uttarāṣāḍha	3
Rah(R)	04:43:56	Leo	Maghā	2
Ket(R)	04:43:56	Aqu	Dhaniṣṭhā	4

Lagna Chart

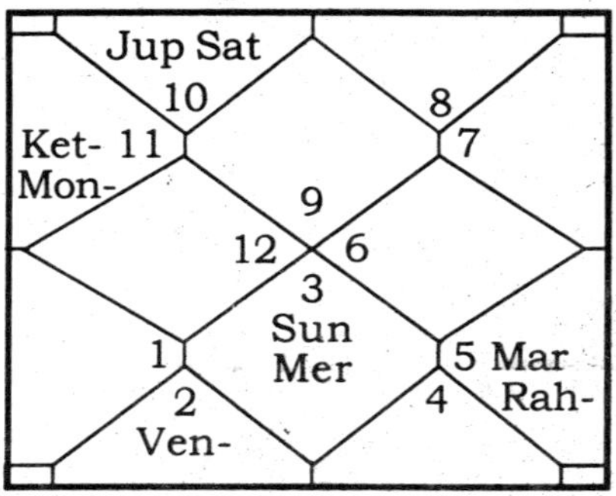

Navāmśa Chart

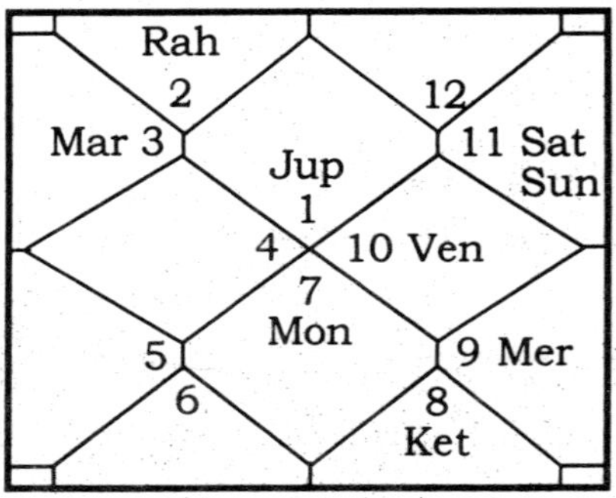

Balance of Vimśottarī Daśā of **Mars 2Y 2M 2D**

Name of Event	Date of Event	Major Period	Sub Period
Marriage	1981	Rahu	Mars
Death	31.08.1997	Jupiter	Rahu

She sacrificed not only royalty but also name, fame, honour, comfort, luxury and lavish life for the sake of her love Dodi Fayed. Earlier, she was married in the year 1981 during *Rāhu* Mars *daśā bhukti*. She was blessed with the son named William on June 21st, 1982 during Jupiter-Jupiter *daśā bhukti* and another son, Harry on Sep. 15th, 1984 during Jupiter-Saturn *daśā bhukti*. She died in a car accident on August 31st, 1997 during sub-period of *Rāhu* in the major period of Jupiter. However, this happened before the divorce with her husband. In this horoscope, the 7th house is well fortified as 9th and 7th lord are conjoined in the 7th house. 2nd house is also well fortified because *lagna* lord Jupiter is conjoined with 2nd lord Saturn in 2nd house under retrograde motion. The aspect of Jupiter and Saturn over the 8th house gave her *akhaṇḍa saubhāgya* but shifting of *Rāhu* in the 8th house in *bhāva chart* and conjunction of 8th lord Moon under the aspect of 12th lord Mars resulted into unnatural and accidental death. Retrograde Jupiter in 2nd house and *Rāhu* in the 8th house in *bhāva* chart caused her sad demise at the age of 36 years during Jupiter-*Rāhu daśā bhukti*. In this case, 7th and 2nd house are strong but the ascendant is weak. The 9th house promotes the 7th house that is of husband. Therefore, she attained *akhaṇḍa saubhāgya*.

Case No. 6.11 (Horoscope No. 45)

Marriage – 1967 during Jupiter – Saturn *daśā bhukti*

Death - 1968 during Jupiter – Mercury *daśā bhukti*

Madhubala, the Anarkali of Indian hearts, was the 2nd wife of Kishore Kumar. The 7th lord Sun occupies the *lagna* in association with 5th and 8th

Case : 6.11 *Horoscope No. : 45*

Date	: 14.02.1933	Time	:	07:00:00
Place	: Delhi	Lat 28°:39′		Long 77°:13′
Ayanāmśa	: 22:55:30	Sidereal Time	:	16:13:21

Pln	**Degree**	**Rāśi**	**Nakṣatra**	**Pad**
Asc	00:23:47	Aqu	Dhaniṣṭhā	3
Sun	01:59:47	Aqu	Dhaniṣṭhā	3
Mon	15:59:00	Vir	Hastā	2
Mar(R)	23:37:56	Leo	P Phālgunī	4
Mer(C)	06:47:54	Aqu	Satabhiṣā	1
Jup(R)	28:15:20	Leo	U Phālgunī	1
Ven	15:20:46	Cap	Śrāvaṇa	2
Sat(C)	16:18:01	Cap	Śrāvaṇa	2
Rah(C)	14:48:16	Aqu	Satabhiṣā	3
Ket	14:48:16	Leo	P Phālgunī	1

Lagna Chart

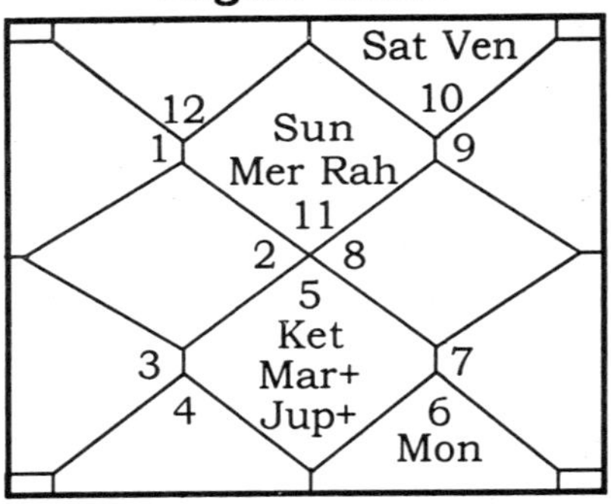

Navāmśa Chart

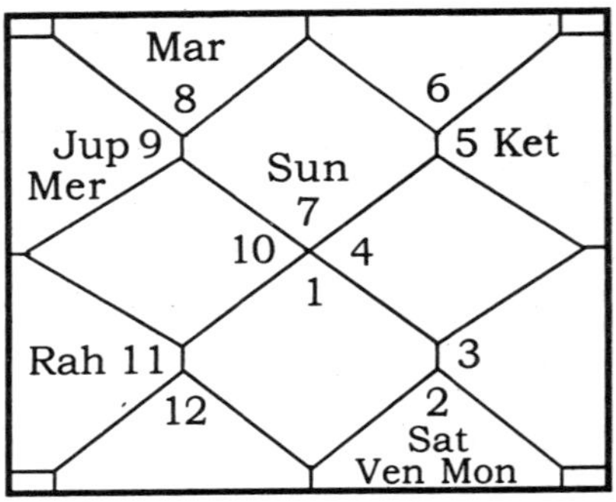

Balance of Vimśottarī Daśā of **Moon 5Y 6M 4D**

Name of Event	Date of Event	Major Period	Sub Period
Marriage	1967	Jupiter	Saturn
Death	1968	Jupiter	Mercury

lord Mercury and *Rāhu*. The 7th house is occupied by 3rd and 10th lord Mars, 11th and 2nd lord Jupiter and *Ketu*. The 9th lord Venus occupies the 12th house in association with 12th lord Saturn. In *Bhāva* chart, Jupiter and Mars are shifted in 8th house and both are retrograde as well. From here Jupiter aspects the 9th lord Venus and *lagna* lord Saturn. Placement of Moon in 8th house has given rise to *viprīta rāja yoga*. Thus the placement of lord of 2nd house in the 7th house under the aspect of 7th lord Sun, has made the 7th house strong. Therefore, such a woman should die before her husband or the husband of such a female should die after her. The 9th house is also well disposed as 9th lord Venus is associated with *lagna* lord Venus and 9th house is aspected by Saturn as well. The 8th house contains Mars, Jupiter and Moon. Here Jupiter gave *akhaṇḍa saubhāgya* and Mars resulted in untimely death due to cancer. To attain *akhaṇḍa saubhāgya*, the 7th house should be stronger than the ascendant. The 2nd house should be aspected or associated by benefics and the 8th house may be joined by malefics, as that will give rise to early death. If the 8th house is also joined by benefics, she will live longer and attain *akhaṇḍa saubhāgya* provided 9th house is well disposed and strong. In the case of Madhubala, 2nd and 7th house are strong and are under the influence of benefic planets whereas the ascendant and 8th house are heavily afflicted and weak. She, therefore, died during the sub–period of Mercury in the major period of Jupiter at 36 years of age in 1968. Jupiter is *mārakeśa* as it owns 2nd and 11th house in association with *Ketu* but obtains own *navāṁśa*. Mercury is 5th and 8th lord and joins the ascendant. Mercury is the lord of 2nd house as reckoned from Jupiter and joins the 7th house from Jupiter under the affliction of *Rāhu* and is combust as well. Therefore, sub-period of Mercury in the major period of Jupiter caused early and tragic death of "Gifted" Madhubala. But her death was honoured with *akhaṇḍa saubhāgya*.

Case No. 6.12 (Horoscope No. 46)

Marriage – 1983 during Saturn – Sun *daśā bhukti*

Death – December 13th, 1985 during Saturn – Mars *daśā bhukti*

Smita Patil was married to Raj Babbar and expired while giving birth to a baby on December 13th, 1985. Lord of the ascendant Jupiter falls in the 6th house in friendly sign. The 2nd house is aspected by its own lord Mars, *lagna* and 10th lord Jupiter, the 5th lord Moon, the 6th lord Sun, 3rd and 8th lord Venus. Thus the 2nd house is well fortified but the ascendant and 8th house are weak and afflicted. 7th lord Mercury is exalted in the 7th house with 9th and 2nd lord Mars. Thus she was fortunate in respect of the matters of the 7th house. It may be clearly seen that the *lagna* is weak, 2nd house and 7th house are strong, the 8th house is afflicted and this is the main planetary configuration which should be judged in a birth chart for examination of *akhaṇḍa saubhāgya yoga*. We have mentioned repeatedly earlier that Mars in the 7th house may cause death to self or husband depending upon various other factors, which we have applied in this work in a number of horoscopes. If the 7th house is weak and afflicted but the ascendant is strong, 9th and 2nd house are either occupied by malefics or influenced by malefic planets, loss of husband should be predicted. On the contrary, if the 7th and 2nd house are strong, 9th house is also well-fortified but the ascendant and 8th house are weak and afflicted, the wife will

Case : 6.12 *Horoscope No. : 46*

Date	: 17.10.1955	Time	: 17:30:00
Place	: Pune	Lat 18°:34′	Long 73°:58′
Ayanāmśa	: 23:14:38	Sidereal Time	: 18:36:43

Pln	**Degree**	**Rāśi**	**Nakṣatra**	**Pad**
Asc	18:25:51	Pis	Revatī	1
Sun	00:05:45	Lib	Citrā	3
Mon	19:28:44	Lib	Svāti	4
Mar	09:20:09	Vir	U Phālgunī	4
Mer(R/C)	22:29:20	Vir	Hastā	4
Jup	02:46:39	Leo	Maghā	1
Ven	12:20:00	Lib	Svāti	2
Sat	27:00:49	Lib	Viśākhā	3
Rah(R)	25:25:15	Sco	Jyeṣṭhā	3
Ket(R)	25:25:15	Tau	Mṛgśirā	1

Lagna Chart

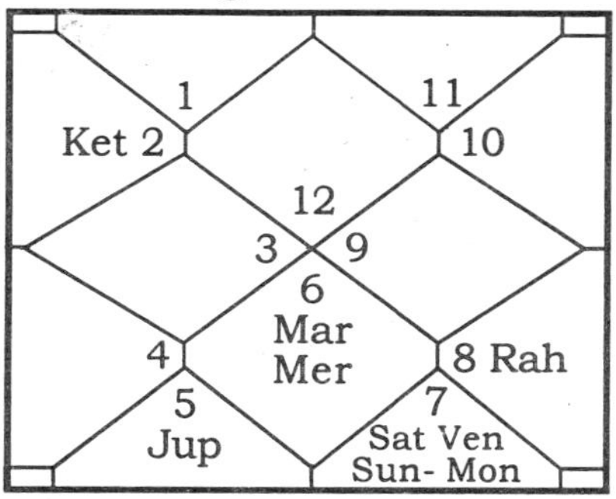

Navāmśa Chart

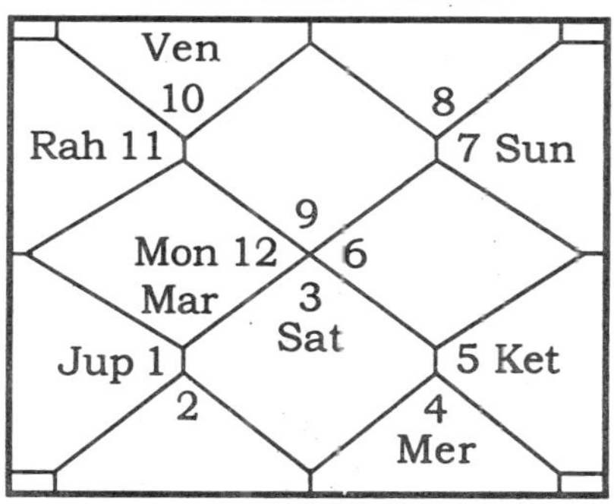

Balance of Vimśottarī Daśā of **Rahu 0Y 8M 13D**

Name of Event	Date of Event	Major Period	Sub Period
Marriage	1983	Saturn	Sun
Death	13.12.1985	Saturn	Mars

predecease her husband but at an early age and her death may be due to some incurable disease like cancer, brain haemorrhage or cardiac arrest or otherwise she may be killed in an accident. The death of the woman may also occur while delivering a child or by suicide. In all such cases where early death of woman takes place, the 8th house will be found afflicted. However, if the death takes place at the advance age as an *akhaṇḍa saubhāgyavatī* female, the 8th will also be occupied or aspected by Jupiter.

We have seen in a number of cases that widowhood took place in spite of the placement or aspect over the 8th house. Jupiter could not prevent widowhood because the 7th and 9th house were weak. A strong 9th house means that the woman is fortunate and if the 9th lord has any relation with the 7th house or 7th lord, she is fortunate in respect of attaining *akhaṇḍa saubhāgya*.

अर्थनाशं मनस्तापं गृहे दुश्चरितानि च ।
वञ्चनं चाऽपमानं च मतिमान्न प्रकाशयेत्।।

A wise man should never disclose to anyone regarding money loss, mental distress, immorality in family, cheating and self-insult.

Chapter-7

BIRTH IN JYEṢṬHĀ NAKṢATRA AND MARITAL DISASTER

The foremost question after the birth of a child is whether the child is born in *mūlā*? The point of birth in *mūla* is very much ignored by the research scholars of astrology though it is one of the important aspect of life. *Mūla śānti* is not sufficient for a boy who is born in *mūlā nakṣatra* but it is also essential to analyse the birth of *mūlā nakṣatra*. A child born in the earlier part of *aśvinī*, *maghā* and *mūlā nakṣatra*, is called to be born in *mūlā* whereas child is born in the last part of *aśleṣā*, *jyeṣṭhā* and *revatī nakṣatra*, is also called to be born in *mūlā*. The nakṣatras of *mūla-aśvinī*, *maghā* and *mūlā* are ruled by *ketu* whose beginning is more adverse. *aśleṣā*, *jyeṣṭhā* and *revatī* are ruled by Mercury whose last part is bad. It means that all *mūlā nakṣatras* are either ruled by *ketu* or by Mercury. It may also be said like that the person born in the last part of the constellation of Mercury or *Ketu*, will be said to be born in *mūlās*. The birth in *mūlās* is adverse and it is harmful for different aspects.

If one is born in the adverse part of *aśleṣā* or *maghā nakṣatra*, it is called *rātri gand*; if the child is born in the adverse part of *jyeṣṭhā* and *mūlā nakṣatra*, it is called *divā gand*; if the child is born in the adverse part of the *revatī* and *aśvinī nakṣatra*, it is called *sandhyā gand*. If the birth of the child took place in the morning or in the evening and there *sandhyā gand* is rising, it will be extremely adverse, i.e., the birth in the last part of *revatī nakṣatra* and early part of *aśvinī nakṣatra* will be extremely bad. If the birth took place in the *rātri gand,* i.e., in *aśleṣā* or *maghā nakṣatra* during night, that is quite adverse. Similarly the birth taken place in *divā gand,* i.e., in *jyeṣṭhā* and *mūla nakṣatra,* is also bad. It means that the birth in *jyeṣṭhā* or *mūlā nakṣatra* is bad only when these *nakṣatras* are rising at day time and the birth took place at that time. Similarly if *revatī* and *aśvinī nakṣatra* are rising and the birth has taken place in *sandhyā gand,* it is harmful. The birth of *sandhyā gand* is more dangerous for the child and the birth in *rātri gand* is more harmful for mother and the birth in *divā gand* is dangerous for father.

Here, I humbly opine that the first 4 ghatīs of *aśvinī, maghā, mūla* are adverse rather than the total duration of the constellation. If the birth is in the last quarter of *jyeṣṭhā* constellation or it is in the first two quarter of *mūlā,* then it is called *aviyukta mūlā.* Birth in this *nakṣatra* is believed to be extremely adverse and the face of the child must not be seen by his father for 8 years. For minimizing the adversities, *śiva arcanā* must be done.

For being precise as well as complete in my writing, I intend to write on *jyeṣṭhā nakṣatra* rather than on all the six constellations of *mūlā.* In English, we call *jyeṣṭhā nakṣatra* as *antares* and *kalb* in Parsi. It starts from 16°40′ to 30°00′ in Scorpio. In this *nakṣatra,* 3 groups stars form a specific design which is clearly visible. The nature of *jyeṣṭhā nakṣatra* is *satvaguḍi,* three-faced, middle-eyed and sharp.

According to sages, we can divide *jyeṣṭhā nakṣatra* into 10 parts, according to its adversities caused to the native.

Part	Degrees	Result
1st part	0.00 – 1.20 (226.40–228.00)	Death of maternal grand-mother or problems equivalent to death
2nd part	1.20 – 2.40 (228.00 – 229.20)	Death of maternal grand-father or equivalent problems
3rd part	2.40 – 4.00 (229.20 – 230.40)	Death of maternal uncle or problems
4th part	4.00 – 5.20 (230.40 – 232.00)	Death of mother of the native.
5th part	5.20 – 6.40 (232.00 – 233.20)	Death of the native.
6th part	6.40 – 8.00 (233.20 – 234.40)	Financial losses, dangers to pets.
7th part	8.00 – 9.00 (234.40 – 236.00)	Adversity to entire family.
8th part	9.20 – 10.40 (236.00 – 237.20)	Dangers to near ones and close relatives.
9th part	10.40 – 12.00 (237.20 – 238.40)	Dangers to father-in-law
10th part	12.00 – 13.20 (238.40 – 240.00)	Natives and his relations have problems.

This is not all, if planets are in certain degrees of *jyeṣṭhā nakṣatra* adversities are only enhanced, such as

Sun - 227° Saturn - 228° *Rāhu* - 231° *Ketu* - 234°

Moon - 233°

Birth in these degrees affects the age of the native. Any work should not be started in these degrees even if planets are favourable. Native must also be very careful in these degrees.

Here, I intend to write only about the birth in *jyeṣṭhā nakṣatra*. I have found that the birth in *jyeṣṭhā nakṣatra* is extremely adverse especially for the happiness of marriage and long lasting married life. This is bad for males and females. It has been observed by the study of inumerable horoscopes of the persons born in *jyeṣṭhā nakṣatra* that they did not have marriage or conjugal bliss. There was difference of opinion and at times it resulted into separation. In few cases, the females born in *jyeṣṭhā nakṣatra* lost their husband and suffered widowhood. If the birth has taken place in *jyeṣṭhā nakṣatra*, 7th house must be properly examined and care should be taken in settling down their marriage. If a girl is born in *jyeṣṭhā nakṣatra*, she must never be married with the boy who is *jyeṣṭhā* or eldest in the family and the marriage of the persons born in *jyeṣṭhā nakṣatra* should not be performed in the month of *jyeṣṭhā*.

Apart from these points, the horoscope of the partner must be examined carefully with regard to conjugal bliss, life of the partner and compatability of views etc. The background of the family should also be taken into consideration before the settlement of the marriage of the persons whose birth have taken place in *jyeṣṭhā nakṣatra*.

Let me illustrate a few cases of the persons of male and female nativities who are born in *jyeṣṭhā nakṣatra*. Here I would like to point out that the birth in the last *pada* of *jyeṣṭhā nakṣatra* or during the last 4 *ghatīs* of *jyeṣṭhā nakṣatra* is not the only sphere where the birth will bring problems in marriage and marital life. But if the birth takes place in any part of the *jyeṣṭhā nakṣatra*, it will bring adversity in marriage.

Case –7.1 (Horoscope No. 47)

She was born in the last part of *jyeṣṭhā nakṣatra* and there was a balance of major period of Mercury for 3 years 3 months 23 days. She is a beautiful and loving girl having serious problems in her eyes. She is quite fair, tall and well educated. She had to compromise for her marriage due to her eye problem. Her eyes were operated four times but the vision remained poor. She was married on May 13th, 2001 during sub-period of Mercury in the major period of Venus with a very ordinary boy, black in complexion having low salary, working as a caretaker in a guest house. He was also having a poor family background and was extremely happy that he got such a nice and good looking wife. Soon after the marriage, differences started taking place and they were separated within 3 months on July 27th, 2001 during the same *daśā bhukti* as it became beyond tolerance for the girl to live under that critical atmosphere full of vulgarity, criticism, scoldings and complaints. I had told the parents of this girl not to marry her at all because she was born in the last *pāda* of *jyeṣṭhā nakṣatra* and the lord of the 7th house Saturn is placed in the 12th house with 12th lord Mercury and 4th and 11th lord Venus. This is definitely a very adverse combination for lasting happiness of married life. The *lagna* is also hemmed in between Mars and Saturn giving rise to *pāpakartari yoga*. Any way, they were not in a position to follow my advice because marital adversity was destined to her.

Case : 7.1 *Horoscope No. : 47*

Date	: 30.07.1974	Time	: 05:30:00
Place	: Delhi	Lat 28°:39′	Long 77°:13′
Ayanāmśa	: 23:30:24	Sidereal Time	: 01:37:51

Pln	**Degree**	**Rāśi**	**Nakṣatra**	**Pad**
Asc	09:45:56	Can	Puṣya	2
Sun	12:57:41	Can	Puṣya	3
Mon	27:22:47	Sco	Jyeṣṭhā	4
Mar	08:00:14	Leo	Maghā	3
Mer	25:08:45	Gem	Punarvasu	2
Jup(R)	23:33:37	Aqu	P Bhādrapadā	2
Ven	17:05:45	Gem	Ārdrā	4
Sat	18:35:15	Gem	Ārdrā	4
Rah	25:01:10	Sco	Jyeṣṭhā	3
Ket	25:01:10	Tau	Mṛgśirā	1

Lagna Chart

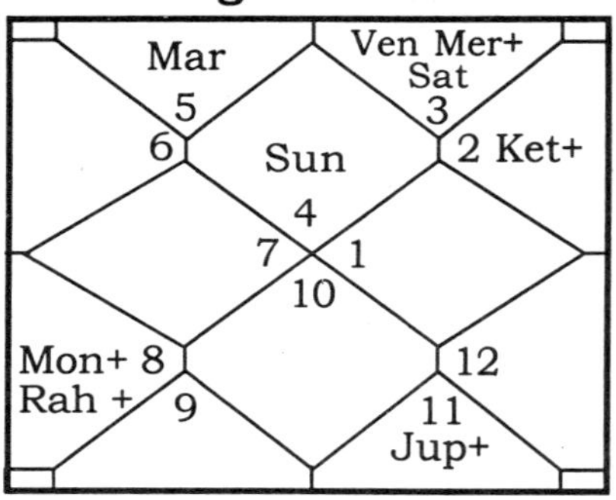

Navāmśa Chart

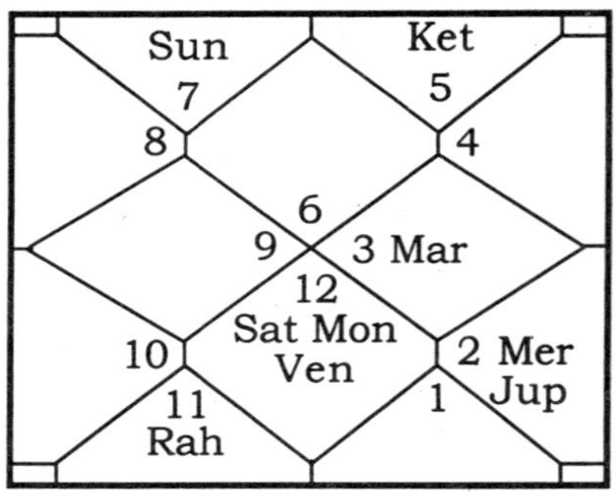

Balance of Vimśottarī Daśā of **Mercury 3Y 4M 2D**

Name of Event	Date of Event	Major Period	Sub Period
Marriage	13.05.2001	Venus	Mercury
Divorce	27.07.2001	Venus	Mercury

Case – 7.2 (Horoscope No. 48)

She was born in Libra ascendant when the 3rd *pāda* of *jyeṣṭhā nakṣatra* was rising. There was balance of Mercury *mahā daśā* at the time of her birth for 4 years 3 months 12 days. In this chart, much adversity is not indicated as such, as the lord of the *lagna* Venus is placed in the 10th house and lord of the 2nd and 7th house Mars is placed in the 11th house though it has shifted in the 12th house in inimical sign. The *lagna* is aspected by Jupiter, *yogakāraka* Saturn is also in the 9th house. The only adversity is that the 7th lord Mars is shifted in the 12th house and is aspected by Jupiter from the 6th house in *bhāva* chart. She got married on February 2nd, 1999 during sub-period of Saturn in the major period of Venus and lived with her husband till May 26th, 2001 and separated thereafter during sub-period of Mercury in the major period of Venus. Her husband was not having any physical relations with her and used to criticize her all the time for her different activities. She did not tell any one that she is facing such problems but one day, she tried to commit suicide. Only thereafter, her parents came to know that she was living with her husband for 15 months without having physical touch. When it became unbearable for her, she tried to finish her life without informing anybody. This happened because she was born in the *Jyeṣṭhā nakṣatra*, almost in the last *pāda*.

Case – 7.3 (Horoscope No. 2-*vide* p.137)

This is the horoscope of a very renowned and rich person. She is a multi-millionaire and got married with a very handsome, smart and decent boy on March 6th, 1996. Her husband committed suicide on March 8th, 1999, i.e., after 3 years of marriage. He had appeared in a competitive examination but could not succeed. The father of the boy scolded him

Case : 7.2 *Horoscope No. : 48*

Date	: 26.08.1974	Time :	10:10:00
Place	: Meerut	Lat 29°:00′	Long 77°:42′
Ayanāmśa	: 23:30:28	Sidereal Time :	08:07:00

Pln	Degree	Rāśi	Nakṣatra	Pad
Asc	04:13:50	Lib	Citrā	4
Sun	09:04:15	Leo	Maghā	3
Mon	26:37:59	Sco	Jyeṣṭhā	3
Mar(C)	25:11:25	Leo	P Phālgunī	4
Mer(C)	17:31:54	Leo	P Phālgunī	2
Jup(R)	20:45:49	Aqu	P Bhādrapadā	1
Ven	20:11:35	Can	Aśleṣā	2
Sat	21:40:18	Gem	Punarvasu	1
Rah(S)	22:39:20	Sco	Jyeṣṭhā	2
Ket(S)	22:39:20	Tau	Rohiṇī	4

Lagna Chart

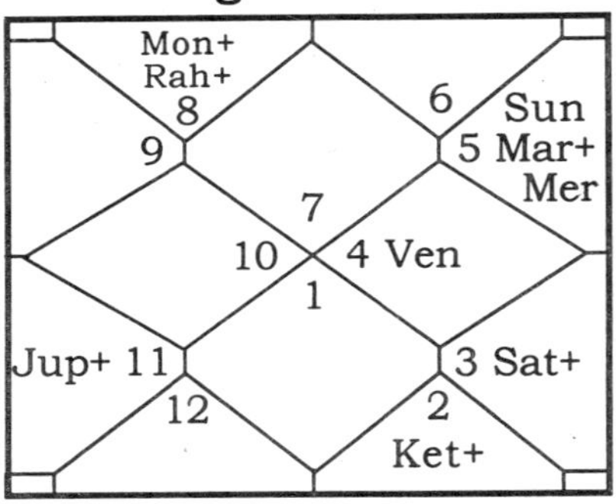

Navāmśa Chart

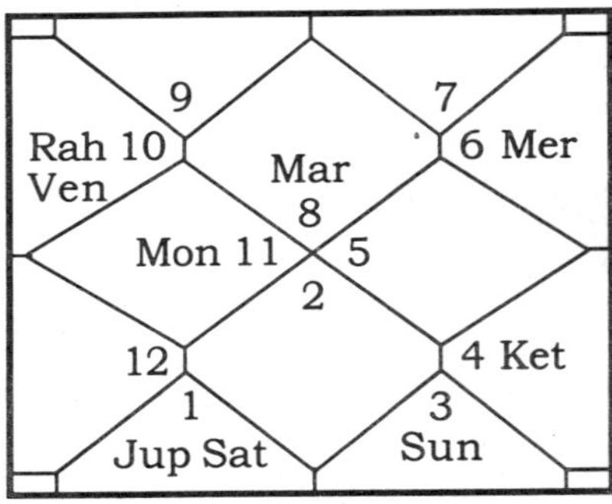

Balance of Vimśottarī Daśā of **Mercury 4Y 3M 15D**

Name of Event	Date of Event	Major Period	Sub Period
Marriage	02.02.1999	Venus	Saturn
Divorce	26.05.2001	Venus	Mercury

indecently. He could not bear the shock and took poison which resulted into end of his life on March 8th, 1999. The native was born in Virgo ascendant and Jupiter is placed in own sign Pisces in the 7th house. The astrologers had told her father that she will lead a very happy and prosperous life as Jupiter has given rise to *Haṁsa Mahāpuruṣa Rāja yoga* in the 7th house. In my articles and in my book *Predicting Marriage and Remedies for Marital Maladies*, I have repeatedly written that Jupiter's placement in the 7th house in watery sign, i.e., in Cancer, Scorpio or Pisces is extremely adverse for conjugal bliss. Here the birth of the girl also took place in the *jyeṣṭhā nakṣatra*, 3rd *pāda*. The girl is not *manglī*. The lord of the *lagna* Mercury is also well placed in the 5th house. Jupiter aspects the *lagna*, the 5th lord Saturn and the 11th lord Moon. It is only *pāpakartari yoga* around the 7th house which has been formed due to the placement of Sun in the 6th house and *Ketu* in the 8th house. That can not cause widowhood. In fact the birth in *jyeṣṭhā nakṣatra* is responsible for the loss of life of her husband. The boy was the eldest son of his father. For the persons born in *jyeṣṭhā nakṣatra*, the marriage with the eldest son of any family is harmful and must not be settled.

Case – 7.4 (Horoscope No. 49)

The native is a highly placed officer in the biggest organization of plastic trade in Asia. The native is handsome, smart, energetic and very dynamic person who rose to these heights due to his extraordinary merits only at the age of 36 years. He is drawing Rs. 40 Lacs per annum. He is born in Taurus ascendant and *yogakāraka* Saturn is placed in the 10th house in own sign giving rise to *Saśa Mahāpuruṣa Rājayoga*. This position of Saturn is responsible for professional elevation. Moon is placed in the 7th house in *jyeṣṭhā*

Case : 7.4 *Horoscope No. : 49*

Date	: 04.12.1964	Time	: 16:32:00
Place	: Delhi	Lat 28°:39′	Long 77°:13′
Ayanāmśa	: 23:21:43	Sidereal Time	: 21:04:02

Pln	**Degree**	**Rāśi**	**Nakṣatra**	**Pad**
Asc	06:22:19	Tau	Kṛtikā	3
Sun	18:58:39	Sco	Jyeṣṭhā	1
Mon(C)	23:22:58	Sco	Jyeṣṭhā	3
Mar	20:23:42	Leo	P Phālgunī	3
Mer	09:44:32	Sag	Mūlā	3
Jup(R)	24:58:58	Ari	Bharanī	4
Ven	18:13:54	Lib	Svāti	4
Sat	05:53:28	Aqu	Dhaniṣṭhā	4
Rah(R)	29:37:20	Tau	Mṛgśirā	2
Ket(R/C)	29:37:20	Sco	Jyeṣṭhā	4

Lagna Chart

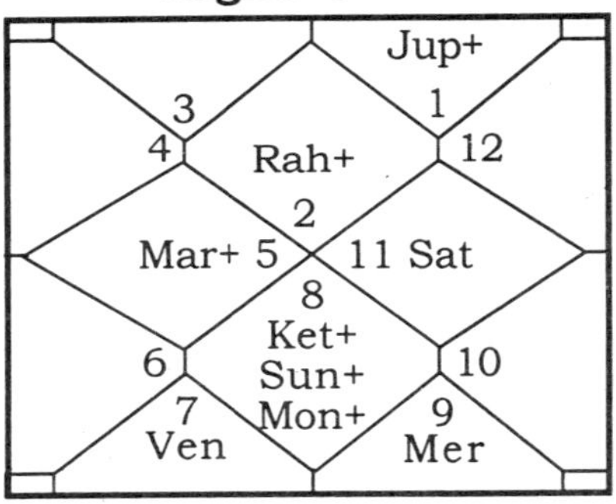

Navāmśa Chart

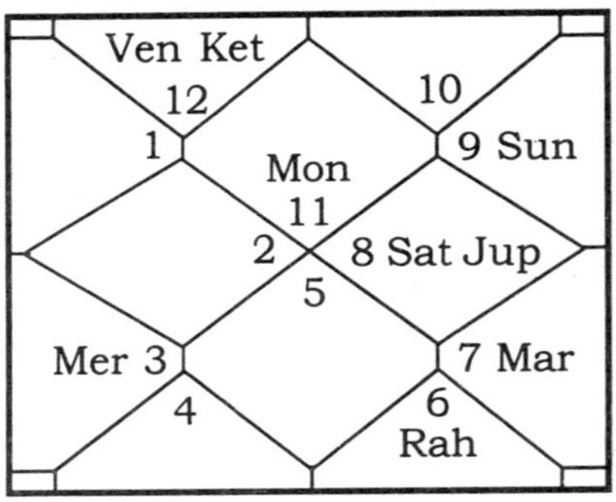

Balance of Vimśottarī Daśā of **Mercury 8Y 5M 7D**

Name of Event	Date of Event	Major Period	Sub Period
1st Marriage	08.11.1987	Venus	Rahu
2nd Marriage	23.08.1997	Venus	Mercury

nakṣatra 2nd *pāda*. Sun and *Ketu* are associated with Moon in the 7th house, hemmed between benefic planets like Venus and Mercury. Moon is the lord of the 3rd house and joins the 7th under the aspect of Mars and Saturn. This combination will curtail marital happiness. The native got married on November 8th, 1987 during Venus-*Rāhu daśā bhukti* with a beautiful girl who made his life hell. The placement of Moon in *jyeṣṭhā nakṣatra* also plays its adverse role. It became impossible for the native to live with her. Ultimately the native divorced his wife and that too with great difficulty. He got married second time on August 23th, 1997 during Venus-Mercury *daśā bhukti*. Here *yogakāraka* Saturn and 7th lord Mars are placed in friendly signs and both are aspecting the 7th house which is owned by Mars. The aspect of Mars and Saturn have not harmed the native so much as much his birth in *jyeṣṭhā nakṣatra*.

Case – 7.5 (Horoscope No. 50)

She got married on October 26th 2000 during Venus-Venus *daśā bhukti*. She was separated within 6 months of marriage in the month of April, 2001. The 7th lord Mercury is placed in the 10th house with Mars and Venus. Jupiter and Saturn both aspect the 10th house, Mars, Mercury and Venus but the Moon is placed in the first *pāda* of *jyeṣṭhā nakṣatra* in the 12th house. There appears no other reason for divorce except *jyeṣṭhā nakṣatra*. She belonged to a poor family and got married with the son of a Chief Engineer. He was quite handsome and smart. Soon after marriage, she created havoc in the family and started to torture her husband and parents-in-law. One fine morning on April 13th, 2001, she went to her mother's place and did not come back. After three weeks, she lodged an FIR that she was being harassed for dowry. The boy and his parents were

Case : 7.5 *Horoscope No. : 50*

Date	: 01.09.1976	Time	: 15:45:00
Place	: Kanpur	Lat 26°:28′	Long 80°:41′
Ayanāmśa	: 23:32:02	Sidereal Time	: 14:20:32

Pln	**Degree**	**Rāśi**	**Nakṣatra**	**Pad**
Asc	28:26:17	Sag	Uttarāṣāḍha	1
Sun	15:33:37	Leo	P Phālgunī	1
Mon	19:08:15	Sco	Jyeṣṭhā	1
Mar	11:43:30	Vir	Hastā	1
Mer	11:48:13	Vir	Hastā	1
Jup	07:07:15	Tau	Kṛtikā	4
Ven	06:04:51	Vir	U Phālgunī	3
Sat	17:16:18	Can	Aśleṣā	1
Rah	11:36:17	Lib	Svāti	2
Ket	11:36:17	Ari	Aśvinī	4

Lagna Chart

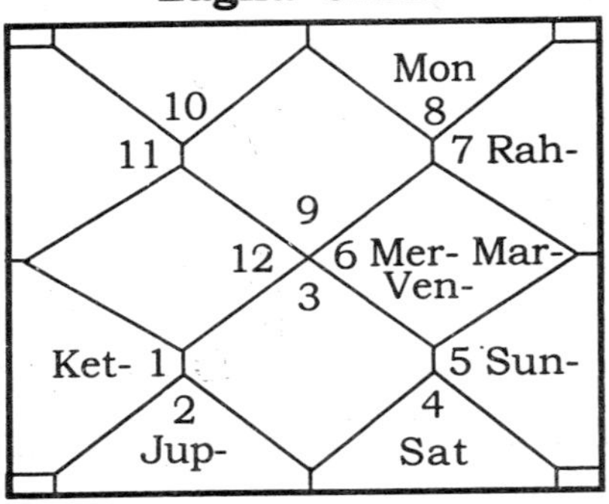

Navāmśa Chart

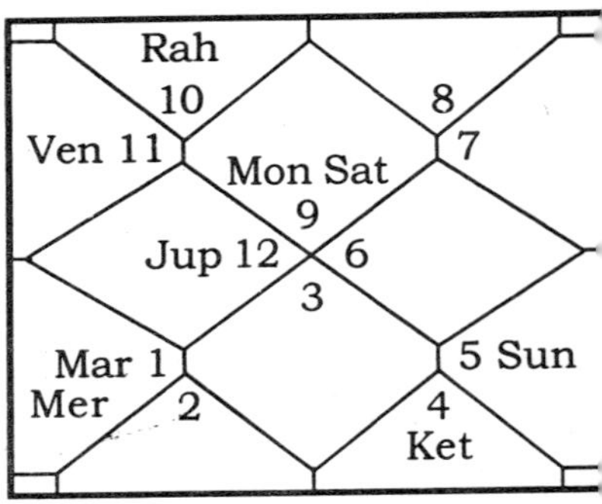

Balance of Vimśottarī Daśā of **Mercury 13Y 10M 6D**

Name of Event	Date of Event	Major Period	Sub Period
Marriage	26.10.2000	Venus	Venus
Divorce	13.04.2001	Venus	Sun

put into serious trouble. Any way due to their influence, bail has been granted to them and thus they could avoid jail. This all happened due to the birth of the girl in *jyeṣṭhā nakṣatra*. Even the aspect of Jupiter over Moon could not curtail the adversity caused by Moon's placement in this most malefic constellation.

Case – 7.6 (Horoscope No. 51)

She was born in Sagittarius ascendant. The 7th lord Mercury is placed in the 7th house with 9th lord Sun and 6th and 11th lord Venus. The combination of Sun, Venus and Mercury in the 7th house is not as harmful as the placement of Moon in the 12th house in Scorpio in *jyeṣṭhā nakṣatra* 4th *pāda*. She is an exceptionally beautiful girl having charming physique but most unfortunate in respect of her conjugal life. The combination of Sun-Mercury is quite powerful in this horoscope in the 7th house. The lord of the 7th house placed in the 7th should not create serious problems in marriage. She got married at 20 years of age during the year 1996 Venus-*Rāhu daśā bhukti*. For almost two years her husband did not touch her at all. He also used to misbehave with her. One day, she came to me and was crying like a child that her life and youth had been ruined. Her husband also came to me at the same time while she was sitting in front of me and started scolding and abusing her and also mishandled her. Due to this critical event, I could not help her at all. She faced this type of miserable life for two more years and thereafter she returned back to her parent's place and divorced her husband during Venus-Saturn *daśā bhukti* as he was impotent, rude and harsh.

Case : 7.6 *Horoscope No. : 51*

Date	: 09.07.1976	Time	:	17:45:00
Place	: Lucknow	Lat 26°:50′		Long 80°:54′
Ayanāmśa	: 23:31:56	Sidereal Time	:	12:48:50

Pln	**Degree**	**Rāśi**	**Nakṣatra**	**Pad**
Asc	06:02:40	Sag	Mūlā	2
Sun	23:51:56	Gem	Punarvasu	2
Mon	27:17:33	Sco	Jyeṣṭhā	4
Mar	07:59:55	Leo	Maghā	3
Mer(C)	16:34:44	Gem	Ārdrā	3
Jup	00:10:55	Tau	Kṛtikā	2
Ven(C)	29:44:10	Gem	Punarvasu	3
Sat	10:27:14	Can	Puṣya	3
Rah(R)	16:52:17	Lib	Svāti	4
Ket(R)	16:52:17	Ari	Bharanī	2

Lagna Chart

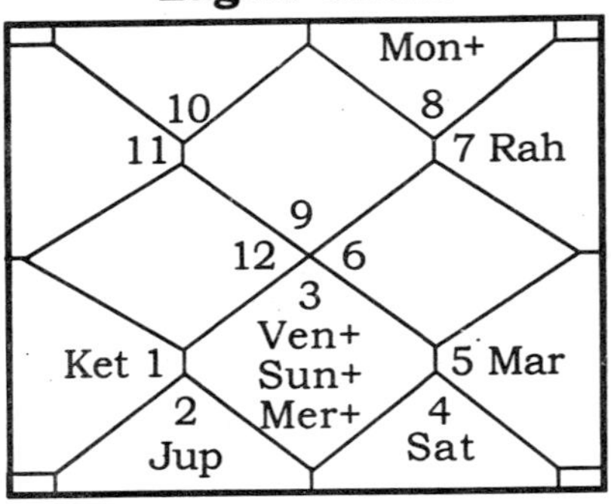

Navāmśa Chart

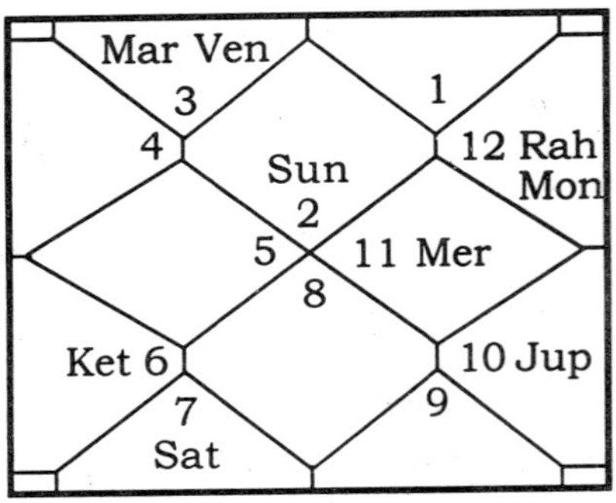

Balance of Vimśottarī Daśā of **Mercury 3Y 5M 12D**

Name of Event	Date of Event	Major Period	Sub Period
Marriage	02.05.1996	Venus	Rahu
Divorce	10.08.2000	Venus	Saturn

Case – 7.7 (Horoscope No. 52)

The native is highly qualified, extremely charming female, born in Aquarius ascendant in *jyeṣṭhā nakṣatra*. Her husband was a Class I officer and she led a happy married life. However, earlier she had an affair and wanted to marry the boy. She was unhappy that her marriage with the person she loved could not materialize. Unfortunately, she was married to the elder brother of the person she loved. All her dreams shattered at that very moment.

Still she led a happy married life till the death of husband. The husband expired in a road accident on July 26th, 2002 during sub-period of Moon in the major period of Moon. Immediately after the transit of Saturn in Gemini, in the 8th house from natal Moon.

7th lord Sun is in the 12th house and Moon is in the *jyeṣṭhā nakṣatra* in 10th house alongwith the aspect of *Rāhu* and Saturn. Mars and Venus have exchanged their *navāṁśa*. This combination clearly indicates the tragedy in the married life which she had. All these combinations as well as, Moon in *jyeṣṭhā nakṣatra* played significant role in causing adversities.

Case – 7.8 (Horoscope No. 53)

She is extremely beautiful lady working as a Class I officer in a bank. She had a love marriage in 1990 with a businessman who was younger than her. She is blessed with one son and one daughter. Her husband is not yet well settled in life. Her husband's elder brother is suffering from Cancer and he is fighting with death at Tata Memorial Hospital in Mumbai. Native proved to be adverse for her elder brother-in-law as she was born in *jyeṣṭhā nakṣatra* in the 4th quarter. Even her married life is also affected. She

Case : 7.7 *Horoscope No. : 52*

Date	: 26.01.1957	Time	:	09:09:00
Place	: Unnao	Lat 26°:32′		Long 80°:30′
Ayanāmśa	: 23:15:42	Sidereal Time	:	17:21:40

Pln	**Degree**	**Rāśi**	**Nakṣatra**	**Pad**
Asc	23:28:13	Aqu	P Bhādrapadā	2
Sun	12:40:15	Cap	Śrāvaṇa	1
Mon	20:33:51	Sco	Jyeṣṭhā	2
Mar	05:15:19	Ari	Aśvinī	2
Mer	19:08:07	Sag	Pūrvāṣāḍha	2
Jup(R)	08:23:08	Vir	U Phālgunī	4
Ven	23:21:58	Sag	Pūrvāṣāḍha	4
Sat	18:28:53	Sco	Jyeṣṭhā	1
Rah(R)	03:12:51	Sco	Viśākhā	4
Ket(R)	03:12:51	Tau	Kṛtikā	2

Lagna Chart

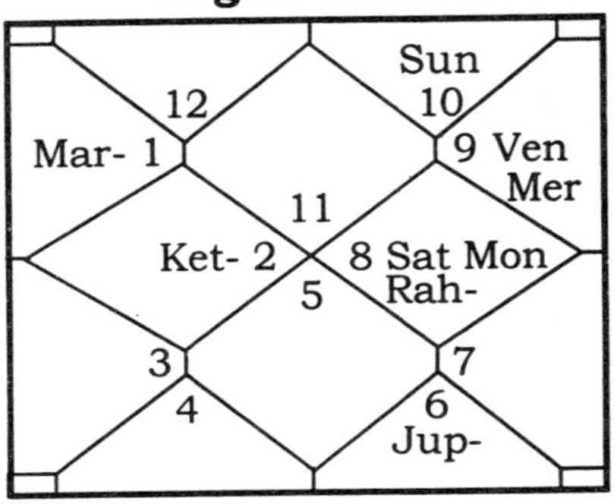

Navāmśa Chart

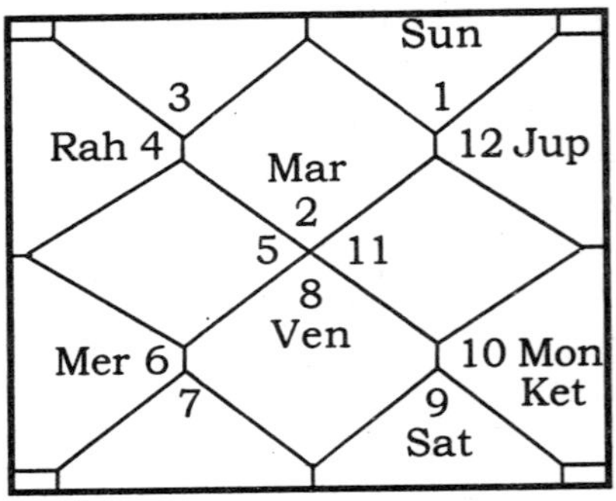

Balance of Vimśottarī Daśā of **Mercury 12Y 0M 11D**

Name of Event	Date of Event	Major Period	Sub Period
Marriage	30.01.1975	Ketu	Saturn
Widowhood	26.07.2002	Moon	Moon

Case : 7.8 *Horoscope No. : 53*

Date	: 20.04.1965	Time	:	12:45:00
Place	: Kanpur	Lat 26°:28′	Long 80°:41′	
Ayanāmśa	: 23:22:02	Sidereal Time	:	02:30:25

Pln	**Degree**	**Rāśi**	**Nakṣatra**	**Pad**
Asc	20:21:49	Can	Aśleṣā	2
Sun	06:37:28	Ari	Aśvinī	2
Mon	27:31:09	Sco	Jyeṣṭhā	4
Mar	15:21:14	Leo	P Phālgunī	1
Mer(R)	18:31:47	Pis	Revatī	1
Jup	06:07:32	Tau	Kṛtikā	3
Ven(D)	08:43:50	Ari	Aśvinī	3
Sat	20:13:35	Aqu	P Bhādrapadā	1
Rah	21:09:08	Tau	Rohiṇī	4
Ket	21:09:08	Sco	Jyeṣṭhā	2

Lagna Chart

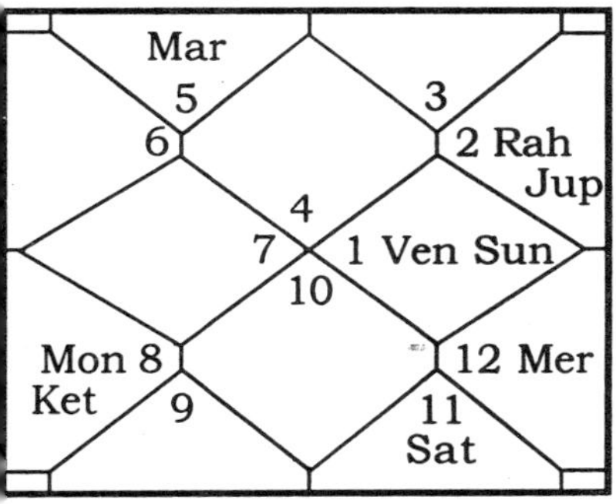

Navāmśa Chart

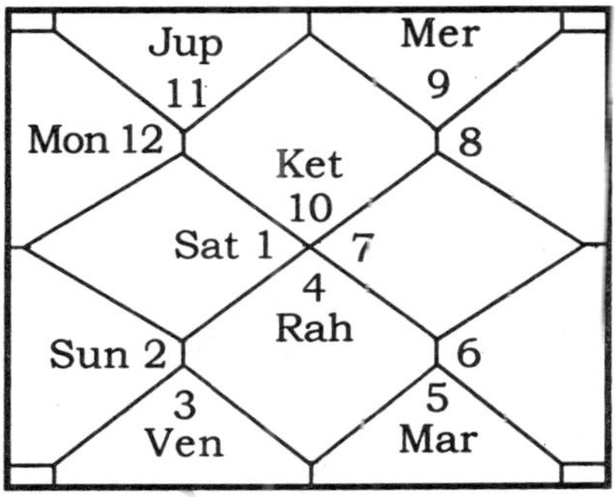

Balance of Vimśottarī Daśā of **Mercury 3Y 1M 29D**

Name of Event	Date of Event	Major Period	Sub Period
Love Marriage	06.11.1990	Venus	Saturn
Divorce	25.12.2002	Moon	Rahu

left her husband on December 25th, 2002 during Moon-*Rāhu daśā bhukti* and now she is living alone.

Ascendant lord Moon gets debilitated in the 5th house alongwith the aspect of malefic Mars and Saturn. Moon is on the axis of *Rāhu* and *Ketu*. Mars and Saturn have mutual aspect with each other. 5th and 9th house signify brother and sister of the husband. 5th house is adversely afflicted and Mercury is debilitated in the 9th house and Mars aspects it. Moon and Mercury are debilitated in 5th and 9th house respectively. This proved to cause cancer for her husband's elder brother as she was born in the *jyeṣṭhā nakṣatra* in the 4th quarter. This means that the female born in *jyeṣṭhā nakṣatra* may prove to be adverse for her *Jyeṣṭha* brother-in-law.

Case – 7.9 (Horoscope No. 25-*vide* p.189)

The native is born in Libra ascendant. 7th lord Mars aspects 7th house. Significator of husband Jupiter is in the 6th house. Moon falls in *Jyeṣṭhā nakṣatra* in 4th quarter in 2nd house. After some time of her birth, her mother expired due to which her father married again. She didn't get the complete love and affection which was her due. She had to bear the pain of death of her brother as well. This was not all, her married life was also not very happy. She suffered the curse of widowhood on January 23rd, 1969 when she was young. After bearing all these grieves, she herself expired on May 30th, 2001. The aspect of 7th lord on the 7th house could not save her spoiled married life. All this happened due to her birth in *jyeṣṭhā nakṣatra*.

Case – 7.10 (Horoscope No. 54)

This horoscope belongs to a multimillionaire who achieved this great height at very early age due to

Case : 7.10 *Horoscope No. : 54*

Date	: 28.01.1965	Time	: 14:32:00
Place	: Mumbai	Lat 18°:58′	Long 72°:50′
Ayanāmśa	: 23:21:53	Sidereal Time	: 22:23:01

Pln	**Degree**	**Rāśi**	**Nakṣatra**	**Pad**
Asc	21:53:15	Tau	Rohiṇī	4
Sun	14:52:37	Cap	Śrāvaṇa	2
Mon	28:07:54	Sco	Jyeṣṭhā	4
Mar	04:40:46	Vir	U Phālgunī	3
Mer	27:29:24	Sag	Uttarāṣāḍha	1
Jup	23:17:19	Ari	Bharanī	3
Ven	26:41:47	Sag	Uttarāṣāḍha	1
Sat	10:45:48	Aqu	Satabhiṣā	2
Rah	28:45:52	Tau	Mṛgśirā	2
Ket	28:45:52	Sco	Jyeṣṭhā	4

Lagna Chart **Navāmśa Chart**

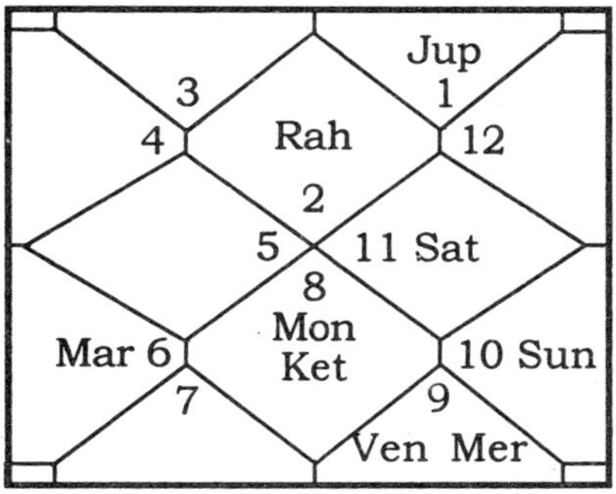

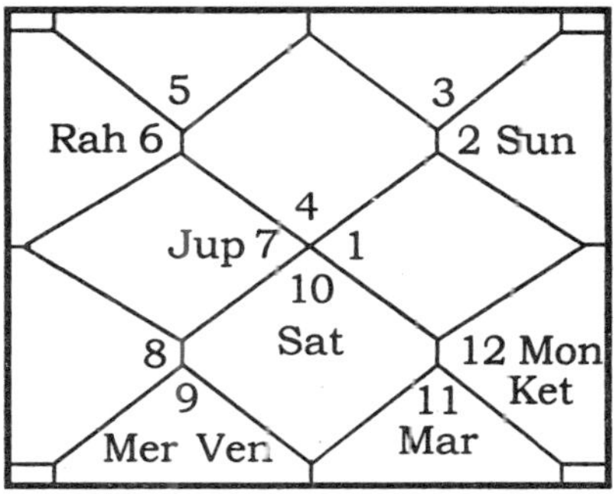

Balance of Vimśottarī Daśā of **Mercury 2Y 4M 17D**

Name of Event	Date of Event	Major Period	Sub Period
Very late Marriage	11.02.2003	Moon	Rahu

his talent, laborious nature, knowledge and excellence in his work. His 7th lord Mars is placed in the 5th house aspected by *Rāhu*. *Rāhu* aspects 7th house and debilitated Moon is placed in the 7th house. On his birth, Mercury's *daśā* of 2 years 4 months and 13 days was to be operated. 12th house is aspected by Mars and Saturn which indicates extra marital relation. He had physical relations with a lady before marriage, they decided to marry after 4 years on February 11th, 2003 during Moon-*Rāhu daśā bhukti*. This horoscope is clear example of unbalanced marriage, due to his birth in *jyeṣṭhā nakṣatra*, i.e., the native was married but it was not accepted by the society. Due to his birth in *jyeṣṭhā nakṣatra*, he had to face separation, enormous grief and this extremely talented man had lost all his comforts, glory and respect just because of a single lady.

Case – 7.11 (Horoscope No. 55)

This horoscope is of the youngest world heavyweight boxing world champion Mike Tyson, who has always been in controversy not only because of his boxing but for other things also. He was born in Libra ascendant. 7th lord Mars is in the 8th house in conjunction with *Rāhu* and Venus, which spoiled his marital happiness. Saturn in the 6th and Mars in the 8th are under *pāpakartari yoga*. Mike had to first face divorce from his first wife, later on in 1992, he was jailed for raping a beautiful lady named Disery Washington. He was also in the papers for his brutal behaviour towards his opponent. He had bitten his ear. The birth in *jyeṣṭhā nakṣatra* has aggravated the intensity of Mars.

Case – 7.12 (Horoscope No. 56)

This horoscope is of a business tycoon of India who has not only achieved great heights in the business

Case : 7.11 *Horoscope No. : 55*

Date	: 30.06.1966	Time :	15:30:00
Place	: Bronx	Lat 40°:51′	Long 73°:54′
Ayanāmśa	: 23:23:07	Sidereal Time :	10:03:49

Pln	**Degree**	**Rāśi**	**Nakṣatra**	**Pad**
Asc	24:31:56	Lib	Viśākhā	2
Sun	15:11:33	Gem	Ārdrā	3
Mon	21:52:01	Sco	Jyeṣṭhā	2
Mar(C)	29:36:59	Tau	Mṛgśirā	2
Mer	10:54:31	Can	Puṣya	3
Jup(C)	18:38:13	Gem	Ārdrā	4
Ven	11:45:52	Tau	Rohiṇī	1
Sat	06:12:23	Pis	U Bhādrapadā	1
Rah(R)	01:17:58	Tau	Kṛtikā	2
Ket(R)	01:17:58	Sco	Viśākhā	4

Lagna Chart

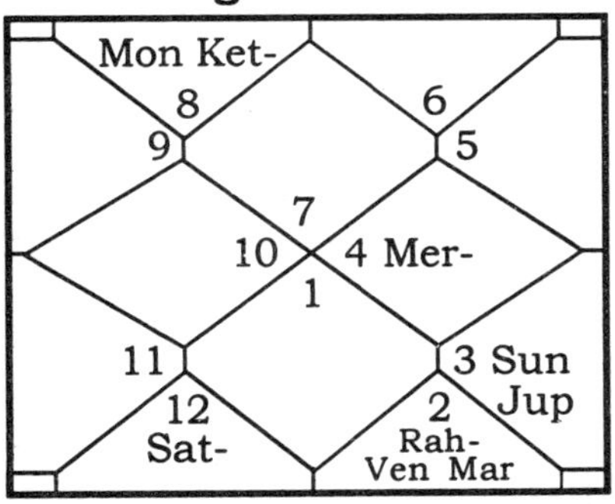

Navāmśa Chart

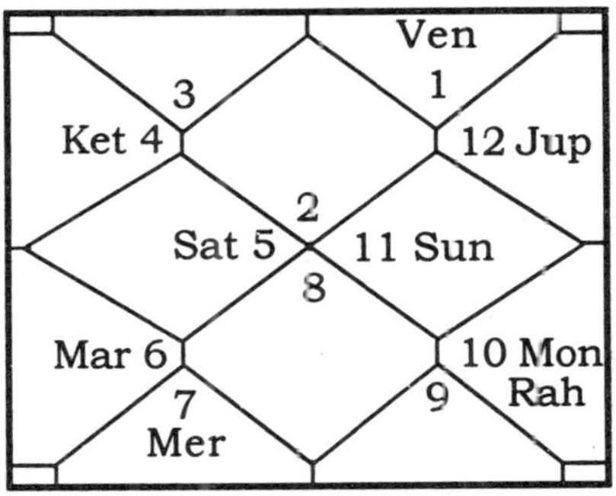

Balance of Vimśottarī Daśā of **Mercury 10Y 4M 13D**

Name of Event	Date of Event	Major Period	Sub Period
Marriage	—	—	—
Divorce from first wife	1992	Venus	Rahu

Case : 7.12 *Horoscope No. : 56*

Date	: 08.07.1949	Time	: 02:15:00
Place	: Mysore	Lat 12^0:18′	Long 76^0:37′
Ayanāmśa	: 23:09:01	Sidereal Time	: 20:53:24

Pln	**Degree**	**Rāśi**	**Nakṣatra**	**Pad**
Asc	26:38:07	Ari	Bharanī	4
Sun	22:12:55	Gem	Punarvasu	1
Mon	21:16:35	Sco	Jyeṣṭhā	2
Mar	26:22:04	Tau	Mṛgśirā	1
Mer	03:09:58	Gem	Mṛgśirā	3
Jup(R)	05:41:31	Cap	Uttarāṣāḍha	3
Ven	14:00:52	Can	Puṣya	4
Sat	09:48:28	Leo	Maghā	3
Rah(R)	28:51:41	Pis	Revatī	4
Ket(R)	28:51:41	Vir	Citrā	2

Lagna Chart

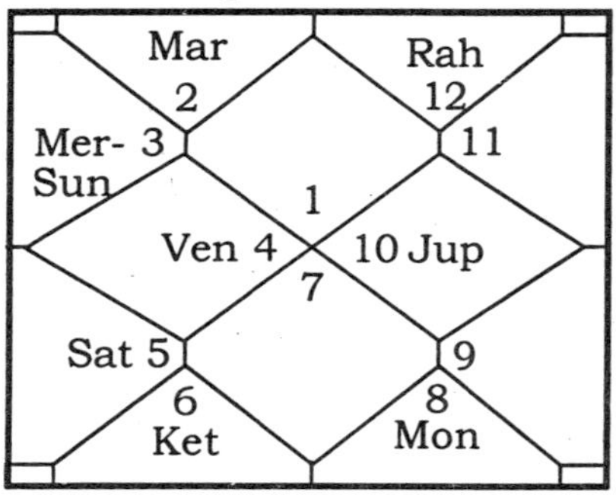

Navāmśa Chart

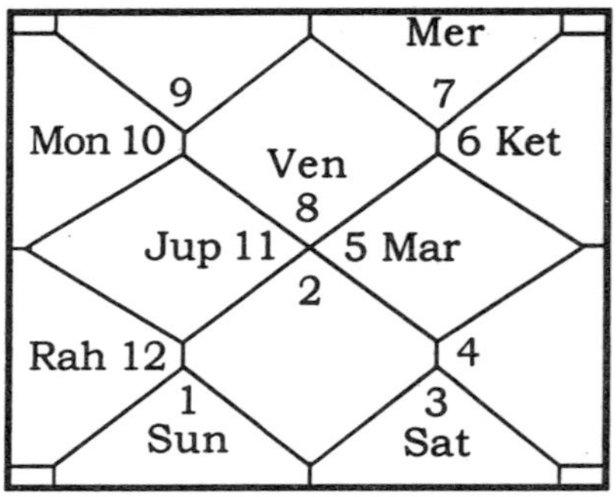

Balance of Vimśottarī Daśā of **Mercury 11Y 1M 14D**

Name of Event	Date of Event	Major Period	Sub Period
Marriage	15.05.1974	Venus	Mars

but also in the field of love. The native is born in Aries ascendant with 7th lord Venus in the 4th house in inimical sign, 7th house is also aspected by Saturn. Moon falls in *jyeṣṭhā nakṣatra* in 8th house. Since Mars is in 2nd house, the native is also *maṅgalī*. He is the father of 3 children and enjoying all comforts of life. He has gained success in all walks of life except in love. He had an affair with a lady junior to him. He had spent lot of money on her with open hands. Lady left her husband for him but she could not become her wife. The native had spent more than a crore to attract her but he was not successful. The lady has left him and she is now living with another man. All this resulted into mental imbalance of the native.

This is because of his birth in *jyeṣṭhā nakṣatra*, which resulted into the havoc in his married life and mental imbalance.

Birth in *jyeṣṭhā nakṣatra* in the first quarter is adverse for elder brother, in second quarter for younger brother, in third quarter for the mother and in the fourth quarter for the native's father. The remedy for prevention of the adversity caused to the native due to the birth in *jyeṣṭhā nakṣatra* must be done by a learned, experienced and meritorious *caryā* who is well-versed with such kinds of remedies, recitation of mantras and stotras etc. Following mantra of *jyeṣṭhā nakṣatra* should be recited 28000 times, at the rate of one thousand times every day from the day of birth of child to the day of *mūlā śānti pūja* (because *mūlā śānti pūjana* is done on 28th day after the birth of a child). Before commencing the *mūlā śānti pūjana, daśāṁśa, havana, tarpaṇa, mārjana* etc. should be done by the same mantra of *jyeṣṭhā nakṣatra*. If *śānti pūjana* work will be undertaken with proper procedure, faith and confidence, all adversities will be minimized to an appreciable extent. The mantras are as under:-

1. ॐ मातेव पुत्रं पृथ्वीं पुरीष्यमग्निं स्वेयोनावभारूयतां विश्वैर्देवैर्ऋतुभिः संविदानः प्रजापतिर्विश्वकर्मा विमुञ्चतु ।
2. ॐ आधय विद्महें परमेश्वराय धीमहि तन्नो कालि प्रचोदयात्
3. ॐ त्रातारमिन्द्रमवितारमिंद्रं हवे हवे सुखं शूरमिन्द्रम् हवयामि शुक्रं पुरूहूतमिन्द्रं स्वस्ति नो मधवा धात्विन्द्रः ॐ शुक्राय नमः।

The root of *circita* tree should be purified by the concerning mantra in a proper way and should be worned around the right arm by males and left arm by females.

If *jyeṣṭhā nakṣatra* falls on Thursday or Friday and any kind of sickness starts on that day, the native will recover only after 10 days. If *jyeṣṭhā nakṣatra* falls on any other day, the native will recover only after 15 days.

The native born in *jyeṣṭhā nakṣatra* must not do any transactions with the native born in *pūrvaṣāḍhā, śrāvaṇa, śatabhiṣā, ārdrā, punarvasu and uttara phālgunī.*

With these remedies mentioned above, one can nullify the adversity of *jyeṣṭhā nakṣatra.*

Jyeṣṭhā Nakṣatra and Marriage of *Jyeṣṭhā* Boy with *Jyeṣṭhā* Girl in *Jyeṣṭhā Māsa*

Jyeṣṭhā nakṣatra is 18th as reckoned from *aśvinī. jyeṣṭha* means eldest. *Jyeṣṭha* is the third Hindi month as counted from caitra. So, there is a possibility of four *jyeṣṭhās* coming together. Eldest son, eldest daughter, birth in *jyeṣṭhā nakṣatra* and marriage in *Jyeṣṭhā māsa.* If three *jyeṣṭhās* are combined in any marriage, the tragedy and mishappenings in their married life are bound to come. Mishappening covers a vast meaning, e.g., unhappy conjugal life, mental or physical separation, divorce, loss of either spouse etc. Here, I have discussed various cases of the natives who were born in *jyeṣṭhā nakṣatra* and all of them suffered in one or the other way. Here I will discuss the case of my most affectionate, loving, exceptionally charming and most attractive daughterly girl.

She is extremely close and very dear to me. She learnt astrology under my guidance with full dedication, faith, concentration and confidence and thus, I am very much concerned with her conjugal happiness which is eclipsed heavily due to negative role of three *Jyeṣṭhās*. Since she is my most loving and innocent child, I will explain both the phases of her life.

Sometime ago, there lived a noble king of Awadh. He was an extremely pious monarch, renowned for his supreme judgement, esteemed, and adored by his people. He lived in a magnificent palace resplendent with luxurious grandeur.

After some time, the king was blessed with a pretty female child. Even in her infancy, the young cherub was amiable, charming and incredibly enchanting in beauty. She was deeply adored and cared for her delicacy, with immense affection. She had numerous exquisite dolls to play with and a separate room for her toys and garments. Even at school, she soon became the most popular child. She always secured first position and later acquired high academic qualifications.

Now we are discussing about gorgeous beauty and youth of the princess, which created historical sensation everywhere. That is a long story, though here that is out of context.

This is the study of the birth chart of this captivating baby who was adored by all. With her childlike appearance and innocence, she easily procured the admiration of all who came in her contact. With the passage of time, she blossomed into an ethereal nymph like beauty with a blooming, graceful and elegant figure. Her grace, charm and dignified appearance remained unexcelled.

The passing years greatly enhanced the delicacy of her features. Her well-built supple figure was with oval face looked flushed and radiant like the freshness of the morning dew surrounded by the golden brown hair like crown. Her radiant smile revealed pearl like well set teeth and her laughter was like the twinkle of bells. Her large, lustrous and dazzling eyes were capable of attracting anyone's heart. Her courteous demeanor, soberness and etiquette had enhanced the graceness and grandeur of her appearance. Her perfectly poised and enameled figure, like an orchid under glasses, was exquisite without any blemish. Her rising beauty aroused a range of emotions and left a wealth of desires within a man's heart.

The sharpness and extreme intelligence of the princess was shining and radiating over her innocent face and impressive personality. However, she never lacked with self-respect and self-confidence, which always made her most important and adorable.

This exceptionally beautiful, charming and most captivating princess who was innocent, pious and absolutely free from the feelings or liking for anyone, got married with a good looking, smart, energetic and dynamic boy whose father was the friend of king of Awadh. The birth of her husband took place in *jyeṣṭhā nakṣatra.* The princess and her life partner both were eldest in their families. The marriage was settled and engaged in *jyeṣṭhā māsa* (month). Now four *jyeṣṭhās* were together in the marriage of the princess. *Kālidāsa* writes in *Purva Kalāmṛta:-*

ज्येष्ठे मासि करग्रहो न शुभकृत् ज्येष्ठांगना पुत्रयो
ज्यैष्ठे मास्यपि जातयोश्च यदि वा ज्येष्ठोडुसम्भूतयोः ।
दम्पत्योर्यदि येन केन विधिना ज्येष्ठत्रयं चास्ति चेत्
त्रिज्येष्ठाह्वय दोषदो हि सततं नाप्यांघ गर्भद्वये ।।

i.e., the eldest child's marriage whether a boy or girl is prohibited in *jyeṣṭhā māsa. Trijyeṣṭhā* means that three *jyeṣṭhās* should never be united, i.e., eldest son and eldest daughter which are termed as *jyeṣṭhā putra* and *jyeṣṭhā putrī* must not be married in *Jyeṣṭhā māsa.* If the boy or girl is born in *jyeṣṭhā nakṣatra,* marriage must not be ceremonised in *Jyeṣṭhā māsa,* to avoid any kind of disaster and damage to their married life.

There was a matching point of 24.50 points out of 36, there was no *nāḍī doṣa* and *graha maitrī* of a high order was also present as the birth sign of the boy was Scorpio and that of Princess was Leo. The *gaṇa doṣa* was present as the *gaṇa* of the boy was *rākṣasa* and the princess was born in *manuṣya gaṇa.*

The princess had lot of sweet dreams and high expectations from her husband. Soon after marriage, the princess and her parents realised that they were terribly mistaken by granting this match. It was too late then. The princess got every thing there except harmony, true feeling of belonging and love acceptance of her ambitions, desires and dreams. After sometime of her marriage, she was immensely criticised. However, she remained quite. Moreover, there was no one with who she could feel comfortable in sharing her feelings. The princess was introvert in nature. Therefore, she never complained to anyone.

Meantime, one of her uncle who loved the princess as his own, could realise that she is unhappy. He took her in confidence and asked about her problems. She started crying like a small child and told him whatever she was facing. She felt protected, supported and secured under the shelter of her uncle. The husband of the princess also regarded that uncle like his father. The problems and tensions of their married life started reducing after the advice of the uncle. Later the princess started getting inclined towards her uncle. So much so, that at times she even started ignoring few desires of her husband. Gradually her husband started misunderstanding the uncle and her relation with him became a strong point of conflict, confrontation and confusion between them. Their relationship got bitter. The uncle realised that the marital maladies of the princess has increased due to his intervention.

On 6th April 2002, when *jyeṣṭhā nakṣatra* was rising, the princess left her husband's house forever without even consulting the uncle. Thus, the role of *jyeṣṭhā nakṣatra* once more created panic in their lives. She was seeking divorce. The negative role of birth in *jyeṣṭhā nakṣatra* of her husband created unaccomodable miseries, problems, griefs, tension, frustrations and depression in their married life. It was a critical juncture when the husband of princess realised and learnt about her exaggerated and explosive attitude. Afterwards he began to improve his indecent behaviour. He sacrificed and tried to adjust with his wife. Initially the princess was not ready to adjust with him anymore. However, his continued decency and softness gradually made a place in her mind and a feeling of respect and attachment also crept in her heart for her husband. She immediately took the decision to leave the palace, and patch up with her husband.

We can see that she and her husband suffered a lot owing to birth in *Jyeṣṭhā nakṣatra* both being *jyeṣṭhā* in their families and settlement and engagement in *jyeṣṭhā māsa*. We advise all against such marriages and follow the suggestions of *Kālidāsa* as mentioned earlier about *jyeṣṭhā nakṣatra*. May God now bless the Princess conjugal bliss of a high degree and full of love.

Many more illustrations may be given here to show the adversity caused by *jyeṣṭhā nakṣatra* in respect of marital happiness but it will go beyond the scope of this book. In one case, I found that the native was an Engineer and within one year of marriage after the delivery of a child, his wife ran away with her boyfriend. All the persons of the family went to jail and had to stay there for many months and the Engineer is still living without wife. In fact the husband was charged that wife committed suicide due to his misconduct. He was born in *jyeṣṭhā nakṣatra*.

Thus it has been observed by me that the birth in *jyeṣṭhā nakṣatra* makes the married life quite critical, miserable and problem. At Many times it creates havoc, sometime one may suffer loss of his or her life partner and at times, he or she may be got married with a frigid girl or impotent person. At times, the birth in *jyeṣṭhā nakṣatra* causes separation due to misunderstandings or due to extra marital relationship. Thus the birth in *jyeṣṭhā nakṣatra* is very adverse especially for the purpose of conjugal bliss. If any girl is born in *jyeṣṭhā nakṣatra*, she should not be married with the boy born in *jyeṣṭhā nakṣatra*.

Due to limited space, I am not giving the examples of those couples where both the partners were born in *jyeṣṭhā nakṣatra* and the tragedy or death of one of them took place soon after marriage. This is a point of observation for the scholars of astrology and they may kindly give their humble opinion about it. Lot of work is required for the births which take place in *mūlā nakṣatras*. Scholars of astrology should come forward for finding out the views of those who are born in these *asterism* of *mūlās* as it is most important for all of us.

विद्या विवादाय धनं मदाय शक्तिः परेषां परिपीडनाय।
खलस्य साधोर्विपरीतमेतद् ज्ञानाय दानाय च रक्षणाय।।

Crook's knowledge is for dispute, his money is for ego and his power is for giving pains to others. Contrary to this, a gentleman's knowledge is for cognition, his wealth is for charity and his power is for defending others.

Chapter-8

DETERMINANTS FOR DEATH OF WIFE

Early loss of husband is the biggest curse for any woman, therefore, sages have enumerated number of planetary combinations for widowhood in their classical works but they have not given as much space for the combinations leading to the loss of wife. Second marriage in case of early death of wife is fairly common which is not a common practice in case of a widow. It is seen that remarriage in males is not uncommon even after attaining the age of 50 or more. However, women are unfortunate in this respect because marriage of a widow is still not commonly acceptable. Here in this chapter, we will look into the combinations responsible for early death of wife among male natives.

If malefics and evil lords, i.e., lords of evil houses influence 7th house, 7th lord and Venus by conjunction or aspect, wife dies earlier than the husband. The strength of affliction decides early or late loss of wife. If 7th house and its lord are afflicted by many malefics and by close degree of affliction, loss of wife is likely to come early. Death of wife may be in a later age when such afflictions are checked by benefic conjunction or aspect or when the degree of affliction is milder.

Mars is the worst killer. When Mars joins *lagna*, 2nd, 4th, 7th, 8th or 12th, he is capable of killing the wife, particularly when he is in enemy's sign. When such a Mars is afflicted or 7th house is afflicted and no benefic joins or aspects such a Mars, death of wife is certain, soon after marriage. When such a Mars is close to the *bhāva-madhya* of any of the above-mentioned *bhāva*, the death of the wife will be witnessed very early. When Mars is situated in any of the above houses from *lagna*, Moon, Sun or Venus, but he is *yogakāraka* or lord of *trikoṇa* from the central point, he alone may not be the killer of wife. When Mars is *svagrāhī* in friendly house in *mūla trikoṇa* or in exaltation or is with benefic association, then too he alone may not be the cause of death of the wife.

When Mars is conjoined with Jupiter or with waning Moon, his evil qualities are checked unless influenced by any other malefic. When Mars is in 7th house, 7th lord is in the 5th house and Mars is in the *navāṁśa* of Venus, the wife of the native dies. When Mars conjoins with Venus in the 5th, 7th, 9th house, he causes the death of the wife of the native, if not aspected or conjoined by any other benefic provided 7th house and its lord are weak, afflicted, debilitated and 7th lord obtains malefic *navāṁśa* or *navāṁśa* of the 8th or 2nd lord.

Before proceeding further, we quote hereunder few classical verdicts in regard to the death of wife for the benefit of readers. These aphorisms should not be applied verbatim but the horoscopes should be examined in the light of the combinations mentioned in these *ślokas*. Conclusions should be drawn only after intelligent analysis of each and every aspect, signs, house, planets and their *navāṁśa* etc. Few of these aphorisms are as below:-

पापो बुधोऽनंगगतो हि पुंसां निहन्ति नारीं विदधाति दुर्भगाम् ।
शुभर्क्षगः सौम्ययुतो विधत्ते नानाविधं स्त्रीं स्फुटरश्मिजालः।।

Jātakadīpikā

If Mercury falls in the 7th house, then it kills the wife of the native but if Mercury is in benefic sign or with benefics, then the adversities are nullified but provides the native association with number of females.

राहुः सप्तभवने दत्ते रिष्टं निहन्ति नारीञ्च ।
चाण्डालिनीं गतचित्तां कुरुते पापग्रहैर्दृष्टः ।।

Jātakadīpikā

If *Rāhu* is placed in the 7th house and is aspected by malefics, then it kills the wife of the native or it makes the wife of the native rude as a devil.

शन्यारफणिसंयुक्ते कलत्रेशो यदा भवेत् ।
क्रूरषष्ट्यंशके वापि कलत्रमरणं वदेत् ।।

Sarvārthacintāmaṇi

Early death of wife should be predicted if the lord of the 7th house is with Saturn, Mars and *Rāhu* and is located in a malefic *ṣaṣṭyaṁśa.*

सुतेशे दारभं याते तदीशे पापसंयुते ।
शुक्रो बलविहीनश्चेद्गर्भेण स्त्रीमृतिर्भवेत् ।।

Sarvārthacintāmaṇi

If the lord of the 5th house is located in the 7th and the lord of the 7th house is with a malefic and Venus is weak, the wife or the native dies as a result of pregnancy.

कलत्रे वा कुटुम्बे वा पापदृग्योगसम्भवे ।
तदीशो बलहीने तु कलत्रांतरभाग्भवेत् ।।

Sarvārthacintāmaṇi

If there are malefic planets in the 7th and 2nd house and their lords are weak, the native loses his first wife and has to marry another lady.

सप्तमे चाष्टमे पापे व्यये भूसुतसंयुते ।
अदृश्ये यदि नाथेन कलत्रांतरभाग्भवेत् ।।

Sarvārthacintāmaṇi

If malefics occupy the 7th and 8th house and Mars is located in the 12th house and if the 7th house is not aspected by its own lord, the native loses his first wife and has to marry a second time.

पापमध्यगते शुक्रे जामित्रेशोऽथवा पुनः ।
जामित्रे पापमध्ये जायारिष्टं वदेद्बुधः ।।

Scholars predict early death of spouse in case Venus is hemmed between malefic heavenly bodies while in addition, the 7th house or its lord is also similarly placed, i.e., between malefics.

The horoscope discussed below can be referred in this context.

Case No. 8.1 – (Horoscope No. 57)

The native is a famous *Paṇḍā* of *Vindhyavāsinī* temple. He got married on April 30th, 1996 during Jupiter-Jupiter *daśā bhukti.* He was blessed with a son on August 17th, 1997 during Jupiter-Saturn period. The family life of the native had been miserable. On April 21st, 2000 when the native was through the sub-period of Mercury in the major period of Jupiter, his wife committed suicide by poisoning herself. The native and his father were charged and imprisoned.

Case : 8.1 *Horoscope No. : 57*

Date	: 12.10.1978	Time :	20:05:00
Place	: Mirzapur	Lat 27°:41′	Long 79°:33′
Ayanāmśa	: 23:33:35	Sidereal Time :	21:16:27

Pln	**Degree**	**Rāśi**	**Nakṣatra**	**Pad**
Asc	09:02:38	Tau	Kṛtikā	4
Sun	25:21:16	Vir	Citrā	1
Mon	07:50:06	Aqu	Satabhiṣā	1
Mar	21:59:05	Lib	Viśākhā	1
Mer(C)	03:49:55	Lib	Citrā	4
Jup	12:30:16	Can	Puṣya	3
Ven	28:39:27	Lib	Viśākhā	3
Sat	15:57:25	Leo	P Phālgunī	1
Rah	03:10:56	Vir	U Phālgunī	2
Ket	03:10:56	Pis	P Bhādrapadā	4

Lagna Chart

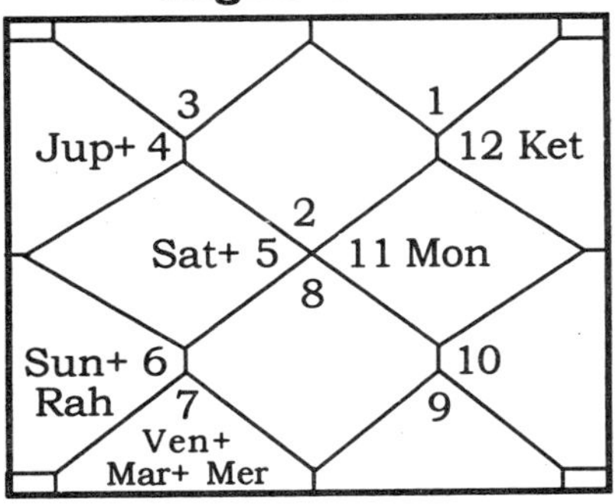

Navāmśa Chart

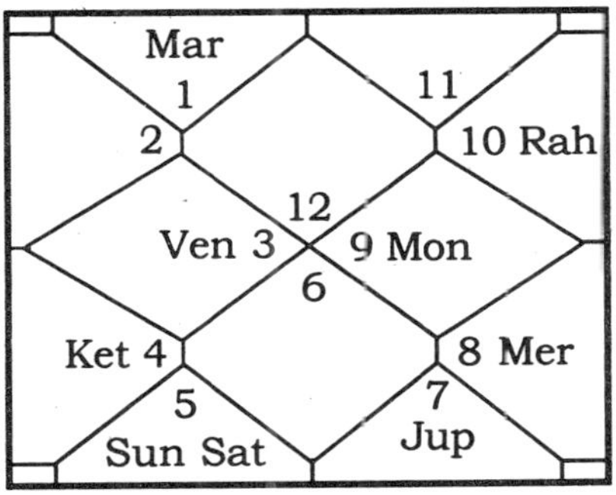

Balance of Vimśottarī Daśā of **Rahu 16Y 5M 2D**

Name of Event	Date of Event	Major Period	Sub Period
Marriage	30.04.1996	Jupiter	Jupiter
Death of wife	21.04.2000	Jupiter	Mercury

In this horoscope, 7th lord Mars occupies the 6th house in association with 6th lord Venus and 2nd and 5th lord Mercury and this combination is aspected by Saturn. The 7th lord Mars is under the adverse influence and is heavily afflicted and indicates death of wife at an early age. The Sun occupies the 5th house over the axis of *Rāhu* and *Ketu*, hence *pāpakartari yoga* is formed because the Sun is hemmed between Mars and Saturn. Mercury is combust and is conjoined with inimical 7th lord Mars and is aspected by Saturn. Therefore, the married life of the native was full of maladies. It may be noted that even the aspect of an exalted Jupiter over the 7th and 9th house could not prevent the disaster of loss of wife.

In *Jyotiṣārṇava Navinatama* the author mentions in the *śloka* No. 204 of *chapter* 2 as under:-

षष्ठाष्टमव्ययस्थे च मदेशो दुर्बलेऽपि च ।
नीचराशिगते शुक्रे दारनाशं विनिर्दिशत् ।।

That the subject will lose his spouse early if the 7th lord, bereft of strength, is in the 6th, 8th or 12th house while Venus is in debility.

In the case discussed above, the 7th lord is the 6th alongwith afflicted Venus, which resulted into the death of his wife.

Case No. 8.2 – (Horoscope No. 58)

1st Marriage – February 20th, 1975 during *Rāhu*–Venus *daśā bhukti*.

1st Wife death – April 17th, 1982 during Jupiter–Jupiter *daśā bhukti*.

2nd Marriage – July 13th, 1982 during Jupiter – Saturn *daśā bhukti*.

The native was married on February 20th, 1975 with a charming female. She was a loving, dedi-

Case : 8.2 *Horoscope No. : 58*

Date	: 30.06.1953	Time :	03:17:00
Place	: Dehradun	Lat 30°:19′	Long 78°:03′
Ayanāmśa	: 23:12:41	Sidereal Time :	21:29:53

Pln	**Degree**	**Rāśi**	**Nakṣatra**	**Pad**
Asc	14:25:44	Tau	Rohiṇī	2
Sun	14:36:21	Gem	Ārdrā	3
Mon	21:00:55	Cap	Śrāvaṇa	4
Mar(D)	17:15:15	Gem	Ārdrā	4
Mer	09:59:28	Can	Puṣya	2
Jup	18:39:08	Tau	Rohiṇī	3
Ven	29:06:13	Ari	Kṛtikā	1
Sat	27:22:19	Vir	Citrā	2
Rah	10:07:31	Cap	Śrāvaṇa	1
Ket	10:07:31	Can	Puṣya	3

Lagna Chart

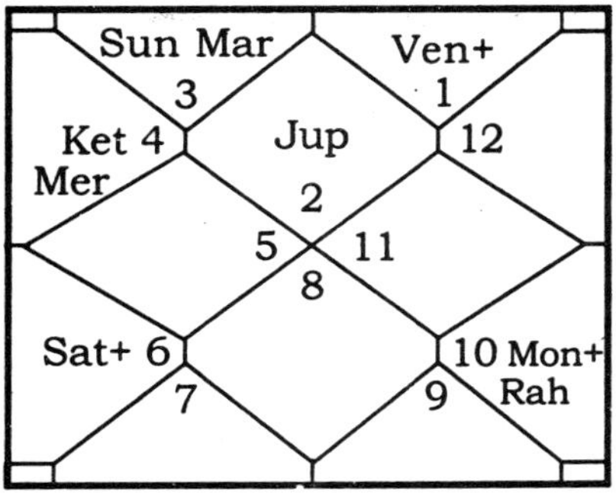

Navāmśa Chart

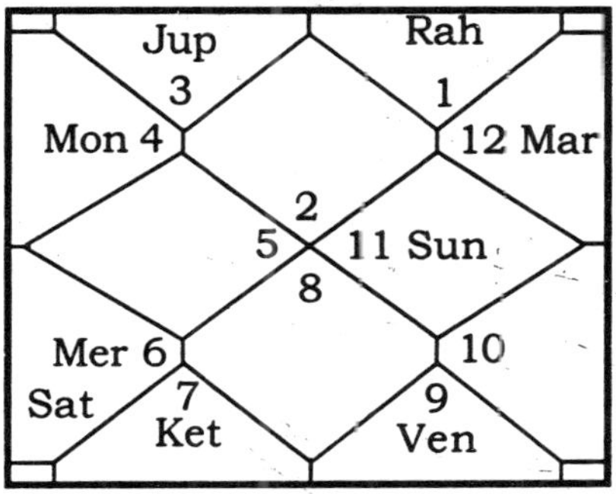

Balance of Vimśottarī Daśā of **Moon 1Y 8M 26D**

Name of Event	Date of Event	Major Period	Sub Period
1st Marriage	20.2.1975	Rahu	Venus
Death of 1st wife	17.4.1982	Jupiter	Jupiter
2nd Marriage	13.7.1982	Jupiter	Saturn

cated and loyal wife. This was the time of great struggle for the native when he was living with his wife and children in a small room. One day, the wife was cooking when she was caught by fire badly and as a result of which she died on April 17th, 1982 during the sub and major period of Jupiter. The native who claimed to love his wife very much, remarried in less than 3 months period on July 13th, 1982 during Jupiter-Saturn *daśā bhukti*. What kind of love it was that he remarried within a period of three months after the death of wife! He should have waited for at least a year. This is an irony of women that they are not supposed to remarry after the death of their husband or even if they are remarried, they have to face lot of criticism and have to undergo immense struggle. I have rarely seen that any woman remarried within less than a year after the death of her husband and the remarriage in female is rare whereas among men, it is common. How do they forget their loving wife and adorable wife within a few days and start dreaming about their second marriage !

However, the negative role of Jupiter in respect of early loss of wife can also be seen in this horoscope. The wife of the native died during the major and sub-period of Jupiter. 8th and 11th lord Jupiter occupies the ascendant. The 2nd house, which denotes the death of spouse, is occupied by malefic Sun and Mars and is aspected by Saturn. There is mutual aspect between Mars and Saturn. Saturn aspects both 7th house and 7th lord. Thus the 7th house is under the influence of Mars, Saturn and Jupiter. In this horoscope, Jupiter, Mercury, Venus and Mars obtain the *navāṁśa* of dual sign, i.e., that of Mercury and Jupiter, which indicates two marriages. The *lagna* lord Venus falls in a fiery sign Aries and obtains fiery *navāṁśa* Sagittarius. 7th lord Mars and *lagna* lord Venus both obtain *navāṁśa* of Jupiter and in *navāṁśa* chart, both aspect Jupiter as well. Mars is killer of wife who is 7th lord and aspects 8th house and obtains Jupiter's *navāṁśa.* Therefore the wife of the native died during sub and major period of Jupiter. The second marriage of the native took place on July 13th, 1982 during the sub-period of Saturn in the major period of Jupiter with the younger sister of the first wife of the native. Saturn is *yogakāraka* planet and is aspected by Jupiter and Mars, Saturn is the 9th lord which indicates the sister of wife and second marriage as well. In *bhāva* chart, Saturn is shifted in the 6th, Venus in the ascendant and Moon in the 10th. Thus Moon and Saturn who are aspected by Jupiter are devoid of the same in *bhāva* chart. The native is a high level contractor of civil works. All the concerning planets Jupiter, Mercury, Saturn, Mars and Venus obtain *navāṁśa* of dual sign which resulted into more than one marriage and early death of first wife.

Case No. 8.3 – (Horoscope No. 59)

1st Marriage – January 1936 during Mercury – Saturn *daśā bhukti.*

Death of 1st wife – December 1939 during *Ketu*-Moon *daśā bhukti.*

2nd Marriage – December 1941 during *Ketu – Rāhu daśā bhukti.*

Native died – October 22nd, 1969

2nd wife died – October 19th, 1986

The native was a very famous, successful and prosperous person. Various honours were conferred on him and he was the founder of association of engineers. He had a magnetic and very influential

Case : 8.3 *Horoscope No. : 59*

Date : 17.06.1913 Time : 06:13:00

Place : Bareilly Lat 28°:20′ Long 79°:24′

Ayanāmśa : 22:38:54 Sidereal Time : 23:39:17

Pln	Degree	Rāśi	Nakṣatra	Pad
Asc	14:53:16	Gem	Ārdrā	3
Sun	02:33:50	Gem	Mṛgśirā	3
Mon	11:23:50	Sco	Anurādhā	3
Mar	07:21:14	Ari	Aśvinī	3
Mer	19:17:14	Gem	Ārdrā	4
Jup(R)	22:35:10	Sag	Pūrvāṣāḍha	3
Ven	18:12:08	Ari	Bharanī	2
Sat(C)	17:15:58	Tau	Rohiṇī	3
Rah(R)	06:33:53	Pis	U Bhādrapadā	1
Ket(R)	06:33:53	Vir	U Phālgunī	3

Lagna Chart

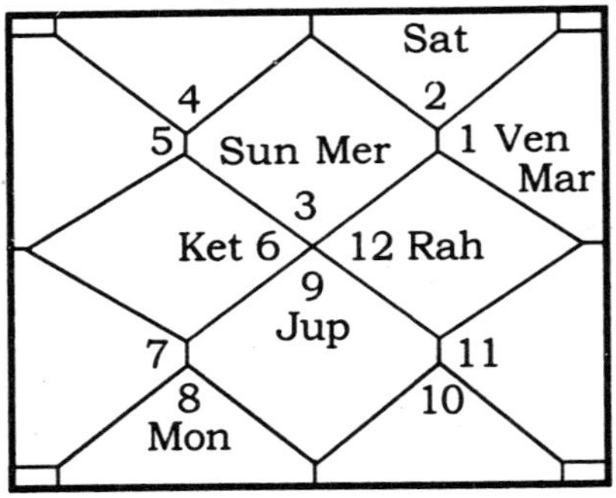

Navāmśa Chart

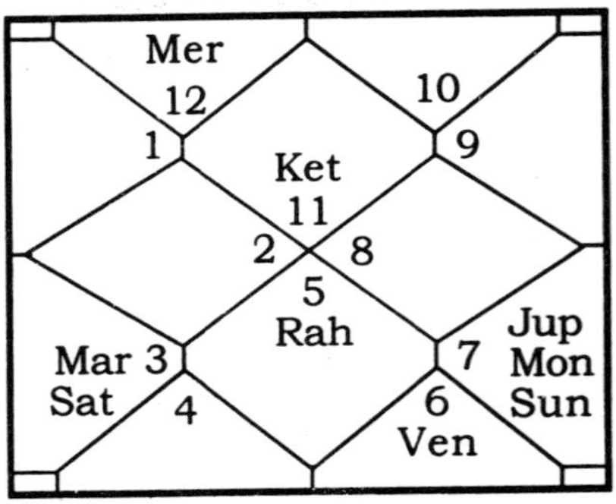

Balance of Vimśottarī Daśā of **Saturn 7Y 6M 3D**

Name of Event	Date of Event	Major Period	Sub Period
1st Marriage	January, 1936	Mercury	Saturn
Death of 1st wife	December, 1939	Ketu	Moon
2nd Marriage	December 1941	Ketu	Rahu
Native Death	22.10.1969		
Death of 2nd wife	19.10.1986		

personality. He got married in January 1936 but the wife of the native expired during 1939 due to liver cirrhosis. The native was blessed with two sons from his first wife, who also died during infancy due to liver ailment. The negative role of Jupiter may again be seen as Jupiter occupies its own sign Sagittarius in 7th house under retrograde motion. The *lagna* lord Mercury and 7th lord Jupiter fall in own and dual sign. This is a clear indication of two marriages. Venus is also hemmed between first-rate malefics Saturn and *Rāhu*, which also indicates the possibility of two marriages.

पाप मध्ये मृषे द्विभार्याम् संभवः

It has also been mentioned that if Venus is hemmed between malefics, i.e., *pāpakartri yoga* is around Venus, there is a possibility of two marriages. Thus, in this horoscope, two marriages are indicated.

The first marriage took place in January 1936 during Mercury-Saturn *daśā bhukti*. Saturn is the 9th lord and aspects the 2nd, 6th and 9th house. Mercury is the lord of *lagna* and 4th house and has given rise to *Bhadrikā Mahāpuruṣa Rājayoga*. The first wife died after 3 years in December 1939 during *Ketu* Moon *daśā bhukti*. Moon is the lord of 2nd house and joins the 6th house in the sign of debility under the aspect of 8th lord and 9th lord Saturn and 11th and 6th lord Mars. Thus Moon is heavily afflicted and caused death of first wife. It is not out of place to mention that death of wife is indicated by 2nd house as it is 8th from 7th. The 2nd and its lord are heavily afflicted due to joint aspect of Mars and Saturn. The death of wife, therefore, occurred during the bhukti of 2nd lord Moon in the major *daśā* of *Ketu*. The 2nd marriage took place in December 1941 during sub-period of *Rāhu* in the major period of *Ketu*. *Rāhu* is the dispositor of Jupiter who occupies the 7th house, therefore, second marriage took place during sub-period of *Rāhu* in the major period of *Ketu* with 10 year younger female. The native suddenly lost his life on October 22nd, 1969 in a sudden illness and his wife died on October 19th, 1986.

Case No. 8.4 – (Horoscope No. 60)

1st Marriage – May 1924 during *Ketu* – Jupiter *daśā bhukti*

Death of 1st wife – December 1929 during Venus–Venus *daśā bhukti*.

2nd Marriage – 1933 during Venus – Mars *daśā bhukti*

Death – January 5th, 1995 during Jupiter – Mercury *daśā bhukti*.

The native was a Principal. He was born in last *pāda* of *aśleṣā nakṣatra*, which belongs to *mūla*. Saturn, Mars and Moon are placed in their own signs. All planets are hemmed between *Ketu* and *Rāhu*. Native got married in 1924 during *Ketu*-Jupiter *daśā bhukti*. Jupiter is the lord of 9th house and joins 2nd house in Taurus and is 5th from *daśā* lord *Ketu*. First wife expired in December 1929. Venus is the lord of 2nd and 7th house and became *mārakeśa* for wife. Venus is combust and is conjoined with Sun and Saturn and is hemmed between malefics. Native is strong *maṅgalī* as the Mars occupies the Aries ascendant and aspects the 7th, 8th, 4th, Moon and *Rāhu*. Here Venus, Jupiter, Moon and Mercury obtain dual *navāṁśa* indicating two marriages. The second marriage took place during Venus-Mars *daśā bhukti* as Mars aspects the 7th house and obtains *vargottama navāṁśa* and

Case : 8.4 *Horoscope No. : 60*

Date	: 08.03.1906	Time :	09:23:00
Place	: Bareilly	Lat 28°:20′	Long 79°:24′
Ayanāmśa	: 22:32:38	Sidereal Time :	20:10:24

Pln	**Degree**	**Rāśi**	**Nakṣatra**	**Pad**
Asc	21:26:14	Ari	Bharanī	3
Sun	24:08:04	Aqu	P Bhādrapadā	2
Mon	19:22:59	Can	Aśleṣā	1
Mar	00:38:38	Ari	Aśvinī	1
Mer(C)	07:35:11	Pis	U Bhādrapadā	2
Jup	07:12:57	Tau	Kṛtikā	4
Ven(C)	29:28:12	Aqu	P Bhādrapadā	3
Sat(C)	14:14:59	Aqu	Satabhiṣā	3
Rah	28:12:53	Can	Aśleṣā	4
Ket	28:12:53	Cap	Dhaniṣṭhā	2

Lagna Chart

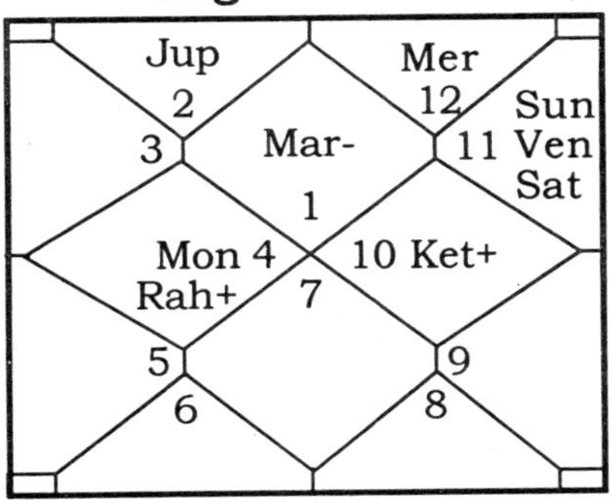

Navāmśa Chart

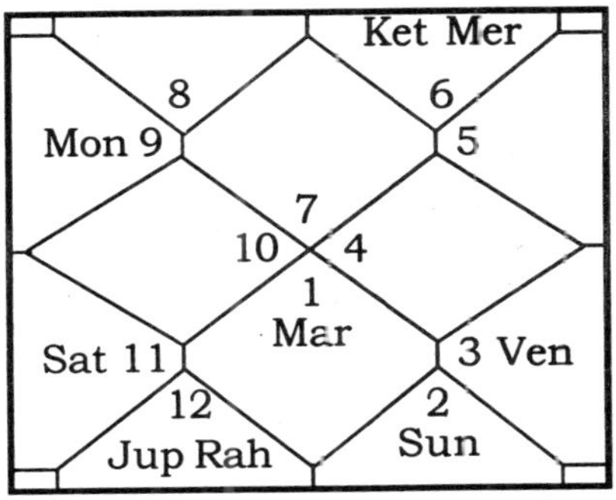

Balance of Vimśottarī Daśā of **Mercury 13Y 6M 13D**

Name of Event	Date of Event	Major Period	Sub Period
1st Marriage	May, 1924	Ketu	Jupiter
Death of 1st wife	December, 1929	Venus	Venus
2nd Marriage	1933	Venus	Mars
Death of native	5.11.1995	Jupiter	Mercury

is 7th from *navāṁśa lagna*. In this horoscope, Mars, Saturn and Jupiter obtain their own *navāṁśa*. The native was blessed with three daughters including one from first wife. The native lived nearly for 90 years and expired on January 5th, 1995 in the sub-period of Mercury in the major period of Jupiter. Mercury is combust, 3rd lord, debilitated and placed under *pāpakartari yoga* by Mars and Saturn. The second wife of the native was about 10 years younger to him and died in April 1996.

Case No. 8.5 – (Horoscope No. 61)

Marriage – February 7th, 1979 during Jupiter – *Rāhu daśā bhukti.*

Death of wife – September 2nd, 2003 during Mercury–Venus *daśā bhukti.*

The marriage took place on February 7th, 1979 during Jupiter *Rāhu* period. Jupiter occupies the 10th house and Saturn falls in 2nd in the sign of exaltation under retrograde motion. 7th lord Jupiter falls over the axis of *Rāhu* and *Ketu* and is aspected by 8th lord Mars. Jupiter also suffers *kendrādhipati doṣa* and is *bādhakādhipati* as well. Venus is hemmed between *Ketu* and Sun and falls in own sign Taurus, 2nd and 7th houses indicate death of wife. Here the 2nd house is occupied by 5th and 6th lord retrograde Saturn. 7th lord Jupiter is aspected by Mars and falls over the axis of nodes which indicates premature death of wife. Since Saturn occupies the 2nd house and is aspected by 7th lord Jupiter and *lagna* lord Mercury, the native led a married life of about 24 years. The wife died due to massive cardiac arrest during Mercury-Venus period. Mercury is placed in 8th house and Venus is 2nd lord who is placed in the 2nd house from Mercury. Therefore,

Case : 8.5 *Horoscope No. : 61*

Date	: 28.04.1954	Time	:	16:45:00
Place	: Karnal	Lat 29°:41′		Long 76°:59′
Ayanāmśa	: 23:13:33	Sidereal Time	:	06:46:29

Pln	**Degree**	**Rāśi**	**Nakṣatra**	**Pad**
Asc	16:55:34	Vir	Hastā	3
Sun	14:24:05	Ari	Bharanī	1
Mon	13:10:10	Aqu	Satabhiṣā	2
Mar	11:48:52	Sag	Mūlā	4
Mer(C)	02:48:49	Ari	Aśvinī	1
Jup	01:33:19	Gem	Mṛgśirā	3
Ven	06:13:34	Tau	Kṛtikā	3
Sat(R)	12:41:32	Lib	Svāti	2
Rah(R)	24:31:29	Sag	Pūrvāṣāḍha	4
Ket(R)	24:31:29	Gem	Punarvasu	2

Lagna Chart

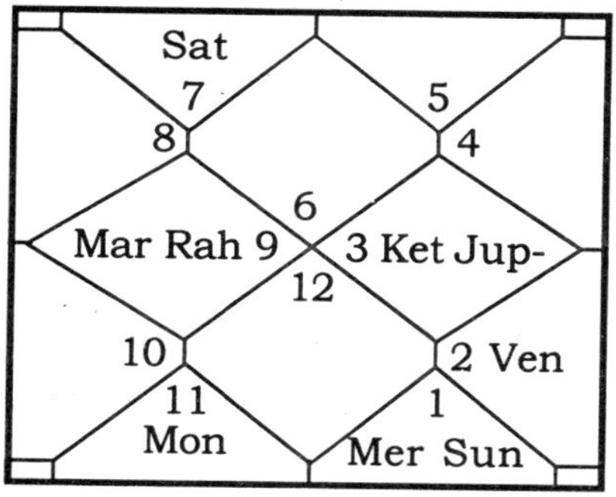

Navāmśa Chart

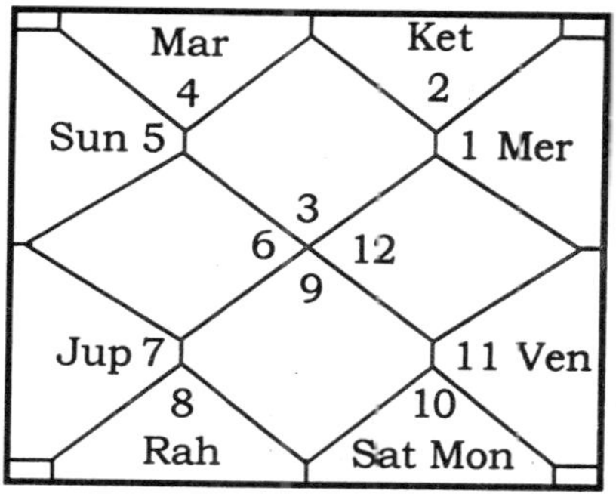

Balance of Vimśottarī Daśā of **Rahu 9Y 2M 19D**

Name of Event	Date of Event	Major Period	Sub Period
Marriage	07.02.1979	Jupiter	Rahu
Death of wife	02.09.2003	Mercury	Venus

Mercury-Venus period resulted into the death of wife of the native.

Case No. 8.6 – (Horoscope No. 62)

1st Marriage – 1951 during *Rāhu* – Mercury *daśā bhukti*

Death of wife – July, 1958 during *Rāhu* – Mars *daśā bhukti.*

2nd marriage – April 24th, 1959 during Jupiter – Jupiter *daśā bhukti.*

The native is a renowned scholar of *mantra śāstra.* He is an author of around more than two dozen books on *mantra, tantra* and *yantra śāstra.* He has written more than 300 articles and has edited various journals. He is a *sāttvika* and simple *Brahmin* and has completely dedicated his life for the noble mission of promotion and propagation of peace and happiness in the live of fellow human beings.

He was born when Cancer ascendant was rising. The wife of the native died during the sub-period of Mars in the major period of *Rāhu* in July 1958. *Rāhu* occupies the 7th house in association with Saturn and Venus. Jupiter aspects the 7th house and occupants of the 7th. Here two marriages are indicated because Venus is hemmed between *Rāhu* and Saturn. Mars is placed in the 8th house from *lagna* lord Moon, *Rāhu* falls in *dhaniṣṭhā nakṣatra* which is ruled by Mars.

In *navāṁśa* chart, *Rāhu* and Mars are associated in Virgo. In *bhāva* chart, *Rāhu* is shifted in the 8th house and *Ketu* in 2nd. Affliction of the 2nd and 7th house and placement of *Ketu* in 2nd indicates death of first wife and placement of Venus between *Rāhu* and Saturn also shows two marriages. The death of first wife, therefore, took place during the sub-period of Mars in the major period of *Rāhu* as both are placed in 6th and 8th respectively. *Lagna*

Case : 8.6 *Horoscope No. : 62*

Date	: 02.12.1933	Time	:	21:30:00
Place	: Jaipur	Lat 26°:53′		Long 75°:50′
Ayanāmśa	: 22:56:11	Sidereal Time	:	01:47:30

Pln	**Degree**	**Rāśi**	**Nakṣatra**	**Pad**
Asc	11:42:37	Can	Puṣya	3
Sun	17:06:29	Sco	Jyeṣṭhā	1
Mon	23:43:25	Tau	Mṛgśirā	1
Mar	17:15:26	Sag	Pūrvāṣāḍha	2
Mer	27:12:00	Lib	Viśākhā	3
Jup	24:03:42	Vir	Citrā	1
Ven	04:08:29	Cap	Uttarāṣāḍha	3
Sat	18:44:12	Cap	Śrāvaṇa	3
Rah(R)	29:12:49	Cap	Dhaniṣṭhā	2
Ket(R)	29:12:49	Can	Aśleṣā	4

Lagna Chart

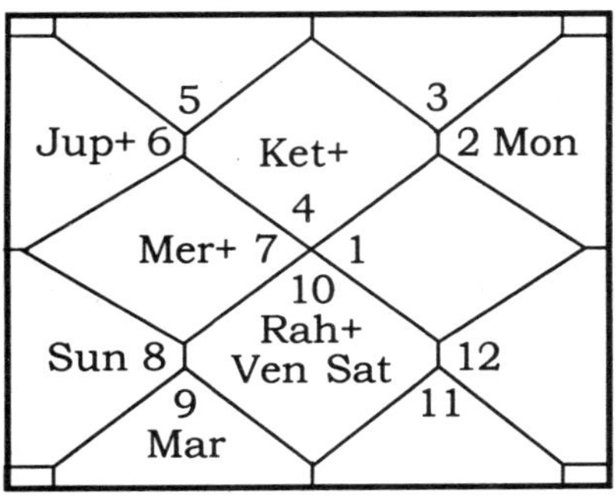

Navāmśa Chart

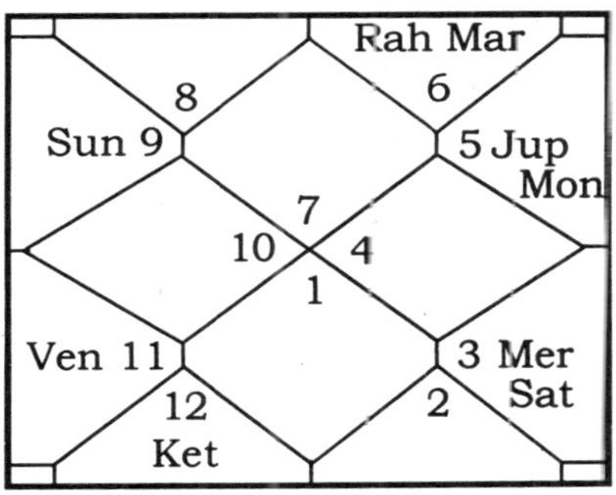

Balance of Vimśottarī Daśā of **Mars 6Y 9M 16D**

Name of Event	Date of Event	Major Period	Sub Period
1st Marriage	Jan., 1951	Rahu	Mercury
Death of 1st wife	July, 1958	Rahu	Mars
2nd Marriage	20.04.1959	Jupiter	Jupiter

lord Moon falls in *nakṣatra* of Mars, i.e., *mṛgaśirā* and Mars is 8th from Moon. 2nd lord Sun falls 7th from Moon in the sign of Mars, Scorpio and the Sun also falls in *jyeṣṭhā nakṣatra*. Sun and Moon are *saṁsaptaka* and both are under the influence of Mars and Mars is placed under *pāpakartari yoga*. Therefore, sub-period of Mars became *māraka* for the wife of *ācārya*.

The *ācārya* got remarried on April 24th, 1959 during Jupiter *daśā bhukti*. Jupiter is the 9th lord and aspects the 7th lord Saturn, 4th and 11th lord Venus, *Rāhu*, the 12th house, *lagna* lord Moon and the 9th house. Therefore, the marriage took place in major period and sub-period of Jupiter. The native has crossed 70 years of age and is living happily with his second wife and obedient and prosperous children.

Case No. 8.7 – (Horoscope No. 63)

The native is the topper of Roorkee University in Electrical Engineering. He had high aspirations for his sweet home, made of his wife and children. By the grace of God, he was decently employed in government organization and got married in early 1993 with a beautiful girl named, Chhaya, during Mercury-Venus *daśā bhukti*. Venus happens to be *yogakāraka* for Aquarius ascendant and obtains own *navāṁśa*. Mercury is placed in own sign in triangle and is shifted in the 4th house with Venus in *bhāva* chart. Therefore, the native was blessed with a charming but egoistic and arrogant wife during Mercury-Venus *daśā bhukti*. Position of Mars in the 7th house in Leo is mainly responsible for unhappy married life resulting into suicide by the wife. She delivered a daughter during December 1993. Just after one month of the delivery, she put

Case : 8.7 *Horoscope No. : 63*

Date	: 02.07.1963	Time :	23:01:00
Place	: Roorkee	Lat 29°:52′	Long 77°:53′
Ayanāmśa	: 23:20:33	Sidereal Time :	17:22:41

Pln	Degree	Rāśi	Nakṣatra	Pad
Asc	23:11:15	Aqu	P Bhādrapadā	1
Sun	16:46:05	Gem	Ārdrā	4
Mon	29:19:06	Lib	Viśākhā	3
Mar	22:22:45	Leo	P Phālgunī	3
Mer(C)	03:52:05	Gem	Mṛgśirā	4
Jup	23:53:19	Pis	Revatī	3
Ven	00:52:14	Gem	Mṛgśirā	3
Sat(R)	29:05:27	Cap	Dhaniṣṭhā	2
Rah(R/C)	27:04:26	Gem	Punarvasu	3
Ket(R)	27:04:26	Sag	Uttarāṣāḍha	1

Lagna Chart

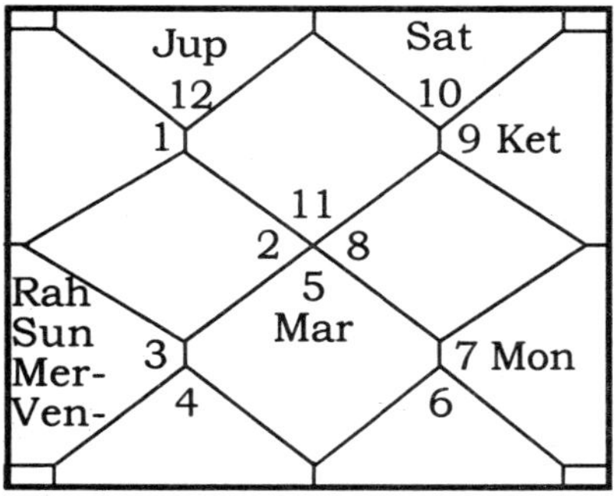

Navāmśa Chart

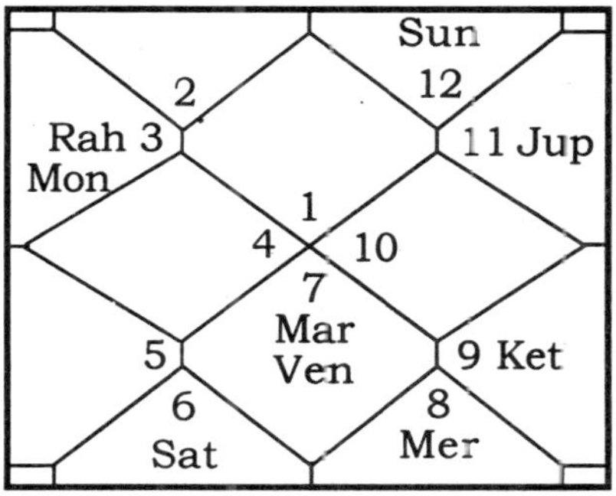

Balance of Vimśottarī Daśā of **Jupiter 4Y 9M 24D**

Name of Event	Date of Event	Major Period	Sub Period
Marriage	1993	Mercury	Venus
Death of wife	1994	Mercury	Sun

off all her ornaments and valuables on her bed between 1.00 – 2.00 am and went out of her home leaving behind her husband and daughter. She jumped in a big canal and committed suicide. Native and all other members including his parents who were nearly 70 years old, were sent to jail. The native had to live behind the bars for many months. The wife died during the sub-period of Sun in the major period of Mercury. Mercury is combust and the Sun is the lord of 7th house and falls in *ārdrā nakṣatra* of *Rāhu*. The 7th lord Sun is eclipsed due to association with *Rāhu*. The Sun is associated with *Rāhu*, Mercury and Venus, therefore, the Sun is heavily afflicted. Moreover, the 2nd house and its lord Jupiter are also heavily afflicted due to joint aspect of Saturn and Mars. This indicates death of wife since 2nd house is 8th from 7th and rules death of spouse. Jupiter falls in *revatī nakṣatra* which is ruled by Mercury and Mercury and Venus fall in *nakṣatra* of Mars whereas Mercury obtains *navāṁśa* of Mars and the Sun obtains *navāṁśa* of Jupiter, i.e., 2nd lord. Therefore, the wife committed suicide when the native was passing through the sub-period of Sun in the major period of Mercury, the 7th and 8th lords, respectively.

Here, I would like to draw the attention of readers towards the placement of Mars in the 7th house of leo. It has been quoted at various places that the placement of Mars in Leo or Aquarius anywhere does not cause *kuja doṣa* as given below. We humbly opine that this view about *kuja doṣa* does not hold good. In the present case, Mars occupies the 7th house identical to Leo sign but he faced lot of marital maladies, troubles, frustrations and even imprisonment. The native was compelled to give five lakh rupees to the parents of the wife for compromise and withdrawal of the case. Even after 10 years of this unforgettable tragedy, the native has not remarried as yet. He has decided never to marry. The native lost his service after prosecution and could not get any suitable job so far. All his education, intelligence, merits and influential personality have been heavily eclipsed.

Case No. 8.8 – (Horoscope No. 64)

Marriage – June 11th, 1973 during Venus – Mercury *daśā bhukti.*

Death of wife – June 7th, 1995 during – Mars Mercury *daśā bhukti.*

The native is a politician. He is very smart and handsome and used to be called a lady killer. Apart from his passion to make love with absolutely new females and switching over from one to another, he is rolling in money. He had a love marriage on June 11th, 1973 during Venus- Mercury *daśā bhukti.* His wife used to be highly depressed and upset due to harsh behaviour and passionate activities of her husband. She jumped from the high roof and committed suicide on June 7th, 1995. The native was charged for her murder and had to undergo imprisonment which was critically painful like death, according to his own statement. The wife committed suicide during Mars-Mercury *daśā bhukti.* Mars is 8th lord and joins the 7th house, it means that he will suffer death like pain and trouble due to any woman. Mercury, the lord of 3rd and 6th house falls over the axis of nodes. Mercury obtains *navāṁśa* of its debilitation. The 2nd house which indicates death of spouse as it is 8th from 7th house, is aspected by Mars and Saturn, both of them indicate death of wife before the native. 7th and 2nd lord Venus is heavily afflicted due to conjunction

Case : 8.8 *Horoscope No. : 64*

Date	: 10.09.1950	Time	:	20:41:00
Place	: Sagar	Lat 23°:50′	Long 78°:43′	
Ayanāmśa	: 23:10:06	Sidereal Time	:	19:42:12

Pln	**Degree**	**Rāśi**	**Nakṣatra**	**Pad**
Asc	10:19:01	Ari	Aśvinī	4
Sun	24:09:52	Leo	P Phālgunī	4
Mon	04:42:24	Leo	Maghā	2
Mar	26:29:17	Lib	Viśākhā	2
Mer(R)	06:57:06	Vir	U Phālgunī	4
Jup(R)	07:21:14	Aqu	Satabhiṣā	1
Ven	07:31:42	Leo	Maghā	3
Sat(C)	28:49:41	Leo	U Phālgunī	1
Rah(R)	05:15:20	Pis	U Bhādrapadā	1
Ket(R/C)	05:15:20	Vir	U Phālgunī	3

Lagna Chart

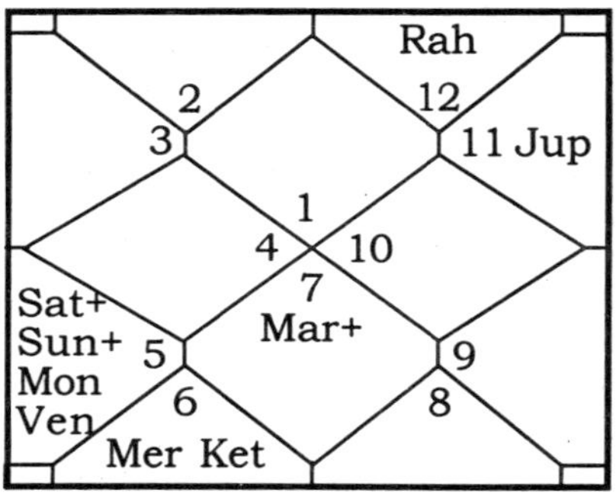

Navāmśa Chart

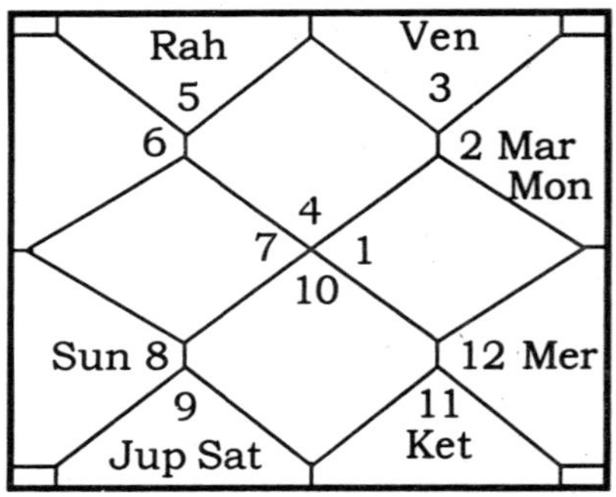

Balance of Vimśottarī Daśā of **Ketu 4Y 6M 10D**

Name of Event	Date of Event	Major Period	Sub Period
Marriage	11.06.1973	Venus	Mercury
Death of wife	07.06.1995	Mars	Mercury

with inimical Sun and Moon in inimical sign Leo. Venus obtains *navāṁśa* of Mercury. Mars obtains *navāṁśa* and sign of Venus. Mercury is placed under *pāpakartari yoga* over the axis of *Rāhu* and *Ketu*. Mercury is hemmed between Mars and Saturn and is 12th from 8th and *lagna* lord Mars. Therefore, the wife committed suicide when the native was passing through the sub-period of Mercury in the major period of Mars.

Case No. 8.9 – (Horoscope No. 65)

1st Marriage – January 24th, 1950 during Mercury– Jupiter *daśā bhukti*.

Death of wife – January 20th, 1952 during Mercury–Saturn *daśā bhukti*.

2nd marriage – May 5th, 1952 during Mercury–Saturn *daśā bhukti*.

The native was a police officer. He was married on January 24th, 1950 during Mercury-Jupiter *daśā bhukti*. Jupiter is the 7th lord whereas Mercury falls in 2nd house in Libra. The first wife died soon after marriage during Mercury-Saturn period. 5th and 6th lord Saturn occupies 3rd house which is 8th from 7th lord Jupiter and 2nd from major period lord Mercury. 4th house indicates a sweet home which is also afflicted as its lord Jupiter is placed in 8th house in Aries in *aśvinī nakṣatra*. This is a clear indication of death of first wife. However, the 2nd lord Venus is also afflicted due to association of Saturn and *Ketu*. Affliction of Venus and its placement between malefics is clear indication of two marriages. Saturn and Venus both fall in *jyeṣṭhā nakṣatra*. It has been found invariably that *kalatra kāraka* Venus, Moon or 7th lord if are placed in *jyeṣṭhā nakṣatra*, adversities like loss of wife, separation or other marital maladies are bound to

Case : 8.9 *Horoscope No. : 65*

Date	: 04.11.1928	Time :	04:29:00
Place	: Bareilly	Lat 28^0:20′	Long 79^0:24′
Ayanāmśa	: 22:51:31	Sidereal Time :	07:08:24

Pln	**Degree**	**Rāśi**	**Nakṣatra**	**Pad**
Asc	22:13:15	Vir	Hastā	4
Sun	18:25:34	Lib	Svāti	4
Mon	10:26:37	Can	Puṣya	3
Mar	15:57:59	Gem	Ārdrā	3
Mer	01:11:35	Lib	Citrā	3
Jup(R)	11:41:34	Ari	Aśvinī	4
Ven	20:54:22	Sco	Jyeṣṭhā	2
Sat	24:11:41	Sco	Jyeṣṭhā	3
Rah	07:46:41	Tau	Kṛtikā	4
Ket	07:46:41	Sco	Anurādhā	2

Lagna Chart

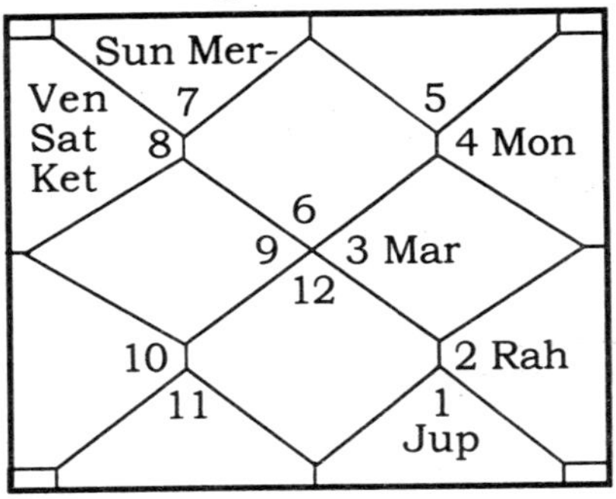

Navāmśa Chart

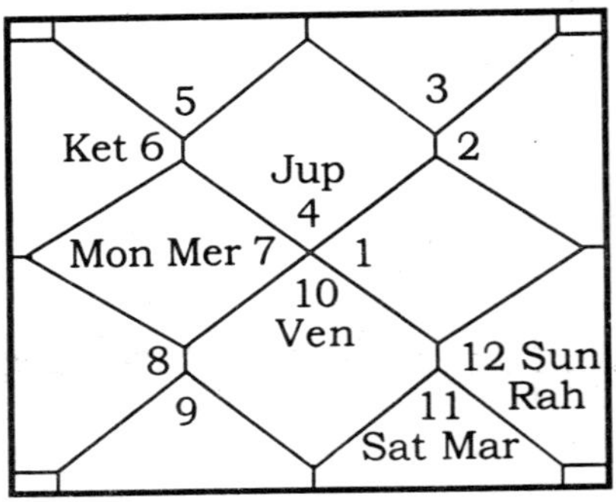

Balance of Vimśottarī Daśā of **Saturn 8Y 10M 12D**

Name of Event	Date of Event	Major Period	Sub Period
1st Marriage	24.01.1950	Mercury	Jupiter
Death of wife	20.01.1952	Mercury	Saturn
2nd Marriage	05.05.1952	Mercury	Saturn

happen. In this horoscope, the indication of death of first wife is quite evident during Mercury-Jupiter *daśā bhukti* as both own *lagna* and 7th house and occupy 2nd and 8th house respectively. This is in addition to the affliction of Venus by *Ketu* and Saturn. Within six months of the death of first wife, he remarried and has been blessed with five daughters and one son.

Case No. 8.10 – (Horoscope No. 66)

Marriage – October 10th 1981 during Moon-Jupiter *daśā bhukti*.

Death of wife – August 31st, 1997 during Jupiter–Jupiter *daśā bhukti*.

1st son – June 21st, 1984 during *Rāhu* – Mercury *daśā bhukti*.

2nd son – September 15th, 1984 during *Rāhu* – Mercury *daśā bhukti*.

The horoscope belongs to the Prince of England, Charles. He lost his wife, Diana, one of the most charming beauty of her time, during a tragic car accident on August 31st, 1997 during *Rāhu*-Jupiter *daśā bhukti*. Charles got married in 1981 during Moon-Jupiter *daśā bhukti*. Here Saturn is the 2nd lord and joins 7th under the benefic aspect of Jupiter. Affliction of the 2nd house or its lord must be examined to know about the death of wife prior to her husband. The 7th lord Saturn occupies the 2nd house in Leo in inimical sign. Mars and Saturn both aspect 8th house; both fall in *nakṣatra* of *mūla jyeṣṭhā* and *Maghā*. Debilitated Venus is under *pāpa kartari yoga*. Thus, the 2nd house is heavily afflicted. Lord of 2nd house, Sun is debilitated and falls over the axis of nodes. Therefore, his wife met with a terrible accident resulting into death. The death of the wife took place during the major period of *Rāhu*

Case : 8.10 *Horoscope No. : 66*

Date	: 14.11.1948	Time :	22:15:00
Place	: London	Lat 51°:30′	Long 00°:05′
Ayanāmśa	: 23:08:23	Sidereal Time :	01:50:40

Pln	**Degree**	**Rāśi**	**Nakṣatra**	**Pad**
Asc	23:08:33	Can	Aśleṣā	2
Sun	29:19:30	Lib	Viśākhā	3
Mon	07:48:43	Ari	Aśvinī	3
Mar	27:50:25	Sco	Jyeṣṭhā	4
Mer	13:52:52	Lib	Svāti	3
Jup	06:45:16	Sag	Mūlā	3
Ven	23:17:43	Vir	Hastā	4
Sat	12:07:49	Leo	Maghā	4
Rah(R)	11:52:07	Ari	Aśvinī	4
Ket(R)	11:52:07	Lib	Svāti	2

Lagna Chart

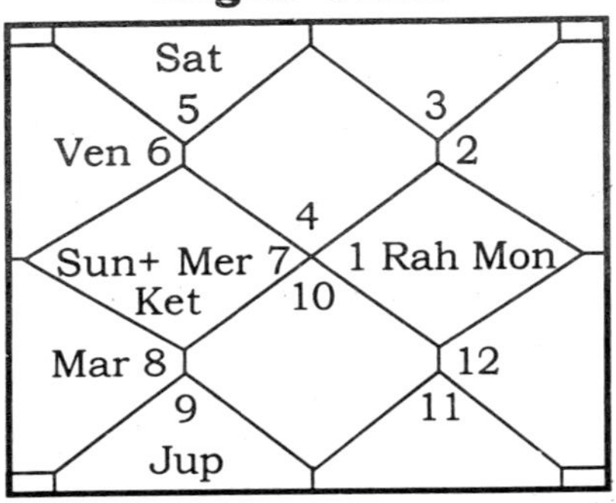

Navāmśa Chart

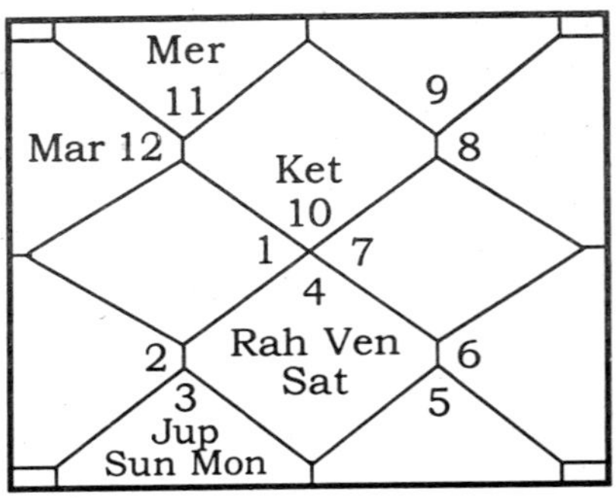

Balance of Vimśottarī Daśā of **Ketu 2Y 10M 23D**

Name of Event	Date of Event	Major Period	Sub Period
Marriage	10.10.1981	Moon	Jupiter
Death of wife	31.08.1997	Rahu	Jupiter

and sub-period of Jupiter. Jupiter falls in *mūlā nakṣatra*. To find out the period of the death of wife is a tough task. Try to judge which planet is strong enough to kill the wife. The death of wife may take place during the *daśā bhukti* of that planet or during the *daśā bhukti* of the *navāṁśa* lord of that planet. Here Mars is 8th from *lagna* lord Moon who falls in Scorpio in *jyeṣṭhā nakṣatra* and Mars obtains *navāṁśa* of Jupiter. Thus, the tragedy occurred when the native was under the vibrations of sub-period of Jupiter.

Case No. 8.11 – (Horoscope No. 67)

Marriage – June 4th, 1969 during Jupiter-Jupiter *daśā bhukti*.

Death of wife – January 22nd, 2003 during Saturn-Jupiter *daśā bhukti*.

The native is a great astrologer of worldwide fame. He has various instances of accurate prediction to his credit. He is the proprietor, editor and publisher of two reputed astrological journals. He has written number of research oriented books in astrology.

The native got married on June 4th, 1969 during Jupiter-Jupiter *daśā bhukti*. Jupiter occupies the 2nd house under retrograde motion in Martian sign Scorpio and in the *nakṣatra* of *yogakāraka* Saturn. Placement of retrograde Saturn in the 10th house under the aspect of retrograde Jupiter, *lagna* lord Venus and 10th lord Moon. There is *vinimaya parivartana rājayoga* between Saturn and Moon. These combinations have made the native great, successful, famous and renowned personality. Here we are concerned with the death of wife only which took place on January 22nd, 2003 when the native was passing through the sub-period of Jupiter in the major period of Saturn. Here Mars is a *mārakeśa*

Case : 8.11 *Horoscope No. : 67*

Date	: 19.03.1947	Time	:	21:00:00
Place	: Cuttack	Lat 20°:26′		Long 85°:56′
Ayanāmśa	: 23:06:55	Sidereal Time	:	08:59:05

Pln	**Degree**	**Rāśi**	**Nakṣatra**	**Pad**
Asc	18:15:35	Lib	Svāti	4
Sun	05:04:26	Pis	U Bhādrapadā	1
Mon	28:46:56	Cap	Dhaniṣṭhā	2
Mar(C)	18:38:49	Aqu	Satabhiṣā	4
Mer(R)	16:26:54	Aqu	Satabhiṣā	3
Jup(R)	04:24:20	Sco	Anurādhā	1
Ven	23:36:59	Cap	Dhaniṣṭhā	1
Sat(R)	09:02:35	Can	Puṣya	2
Rah(R)	12:01:10	Tau	Rohiṇī	1
Ket(R)	12:01:10	Sco	Anurādhā	3

Lagna Chart

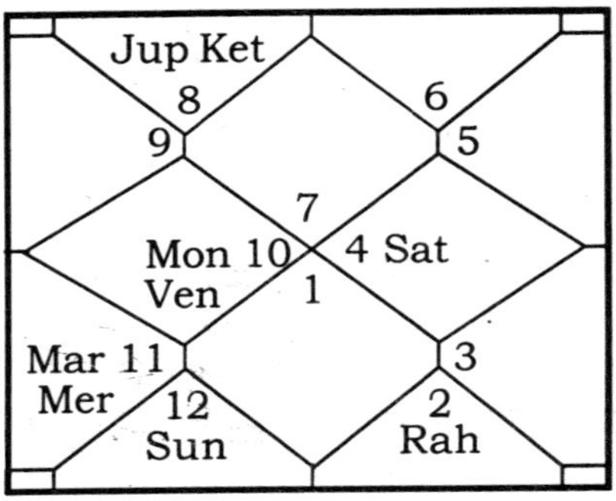

Navāmśa Chart

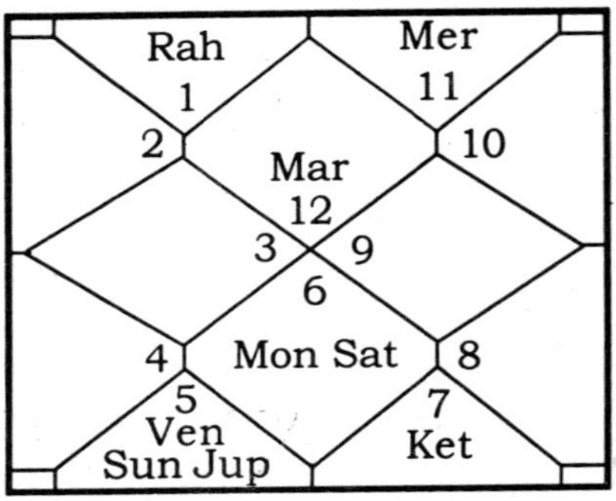

Balance of Vimśottarī Daśā of **Mars 4Y 1M 20D**

Name of Event	Date of Event	Major Period	Sub Period
Marriage	04.06.1969	Jupiter	Jupiter
Death of wife	22.01.2003	Saturn	Jupiter

and Jupiter occupies the sign of Mars. Mars and Jupiter both aspect the 8th house. Mars obtains *navāṁśa* of Jupiter and sign of Saturn. Therefore, major period of Saturn and sub-period of Jupiter resulted in sudden death of the wife of the native.

Case No. 8.12 – (Horoscope No. 68)

The native was a Chartered Accountant who later became very successful and famous industrialist in PVC business. His marriage took place on December 2nd, 1968 during Jupiter-Venus Period. *Lagna* and 2nd lord Saturn is debilitated in 4th house under retrograde motion. 7th lord Moon occupies the 10th house and 10th lord Venus occupies the 7th house. 4th and 11th lord Mars joins ascendant under retrograde motion. Saturn and *Ketu* are under close conjunction and both fall in *aśvinī nakṣatra*. Mars and Saturn aspect each other. This is as per *rāśi* chart. Many planets are shifted in *bhāva* chart. Except Jupiter, Venus and Mercury, all six planets are shifted backwards. Affliction of 2nd lord Saturn due to mutual aspect with Mars killed his first wife on October 22nd, 1981 during Saturn-Venus period. The mutual exchange between 10th and 7th lord and the aspect of Jupiter over the 7th house, 9th lord Mercury, 5th lord Venus, 7th and 9th house resulted into second marriage on January 23rd, 1984 during Saturn-Sun *daśā bhukti* with a very beautiful girl who is 22 years younger to him and who was working as his Secretary before marriage. She got deeply impressed by the influential personality of the native. In this horoscope, 2nd and 7th lord Saturn and Moon are 7th from each other with *Ketu* and *Rāhu* respectively. *Kārmic control* planets Venus and Mars are opposite to each other. In *bhāva* Chart, placement of the 8th lord Sun in the 7th house

Case : 8.12 *Horoscope No. : 68*

Date	: 19.08.1939	Time	: 17:30:00
Place	: Mahuda	Lat 23°:45′	Long 86°:15′
Ayanāmśa	: 23:01:00	Sidereal Time	: 15:32:45

Pln	**Degree**	**Rāśi**	**Nakṣatra**	**Pad**
Asc	20:00:56	Cap	Śrāvaṇa	4
Sun	02:35:14	Leo	Maghā	1
Mon	02:43:36	Lib	Citrā	3
Mar(R)	01:02:33	Cap	Uttarāṣāḍha	2
Mer(R)	19:13:06	Can	Aśleṣā	1
Jup(R)	15:04:54	Pis	U Bhādrapadā	4
Ven(C)	27:50:06	Can	Aśleṣā	4
Sat(R)	08:13:40	Ari	Aśvinī	3
Rah(R)	08:24:30	Lib	Svāti	1
Ket(R)	08:24:30	Ari	Aśvinī	3

Lagna Chart

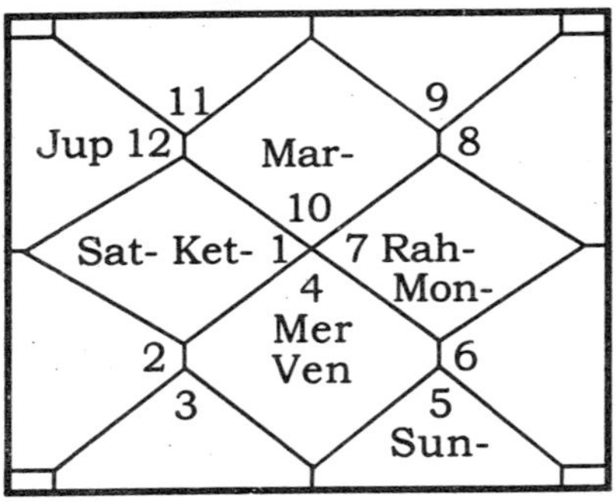

Navāmśa Chart

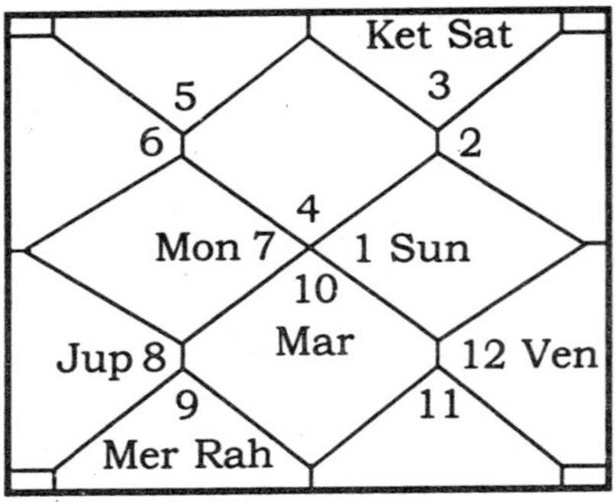

Balance of Vimśottarī Daśā of **Mars 2Y 0M 24D**

Name of Event	Date of Event	Major Period	Sub Period
1st Marriage	02.12.1968	Jupiter	Venus
Death of wife	22.10.1981	Saturn	Venus
2nd Marriage	23.01.1984	Saturn	Sun

indicates death of wife prior to him especially due to aspect of Jupiter on the 7th house and its occupants.

Case No. 8.13 – (Horoscope No. 69)

Marriage – December 4th, 1973 during Saturn – Mars *daśā bhukti.*

Death of wife – May 17th, 2002 during *Ketu*–Saturn *daśā bhukti.*

The native is an executive engineer who was married on December 4th, 1973 during Saturn-Mars *daśā bhukti.* Both the planets are conjoined in the 9th house. Saturn is the 4th lord and Mars is the lord of the ascendant. Jupiter is lord of 2nd house and is placed over the axis or nodes in the ascendant. 7th lord Venus joins the 12th house with Mercury and inimical Moon under the aspect of Mars. The 7th lord Venus is hemmed between malefic planets and is aspected by Mars. Thus, the 7th lord is heavily afflicted and the lord of the 2nd house has also been placed under affliction. Therefore, the combination of death of wife prior to her husband is present in this horoscope. Whenever, the 2nd and 7th house or their lords are afflicted, unless *lagna* is strong, the death of wife takes place before the native. The wife died on May 17th, 2002 when the native was passing through the sub-period of Saturn and the major period of *Ketu. Ketu* falls in the ascendant and Saturn falls in the 9th house in *aśleṣā nakṣatra.* Saturn is the 4th lord and joins the 9th house with debilitated Mars and under the aspect of benefic Jupiter. The combination occurred in the house of fortune, therefore, the wife of the native is fortunate enough to obtain *akhaṇḍa saubhāgya yoga* after leading a long married life with the native. In fact, she suffered from cancer

Case : 8.13 *Horoscope No. : 69*

Date	: 16.10.1947	Time	:	09:12:28
Place	: Kanpur	Lat 26°:27′		Long 80°:19′
Ayanāmśa	: 23:07:24	Sidereal Time	:	10:39:02

Pln	**Degree**	**Rāśi**	**Nakṣatra**	**Pad**
Asc	08:05:51	Sco	Anurādhā	2
Sun	28:48:36	Vir	Citrā	2
Mon	22:18:20	Lib	Viśākhā	1
Mar	15:21:08	Can	Puṣya	4
Mer	23:32:45	Lib	Viśākhā	2
Jup	05:15:22	Sco	Anurādhā	1
Ven	10:05:35	Lib	Svāti	2
Sat	27:24:08	Can	Aśleṣā	4
Rah(R)	00:31:51	Tau	Kṛtikā	2
Ket(R)	00:31:51	Sco	Viśākhā	4

Lagna Chart

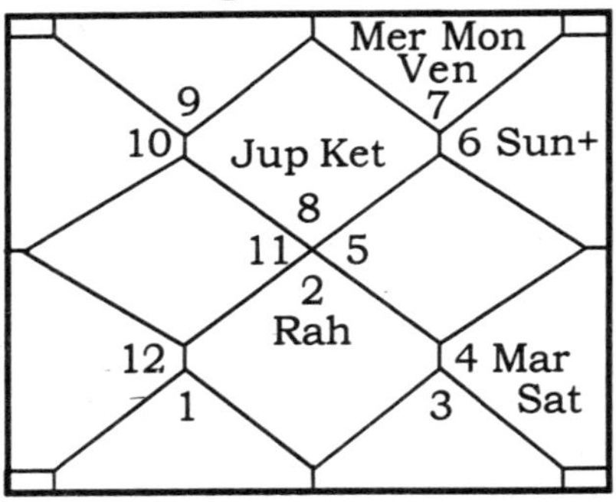

Navāmśa Chart

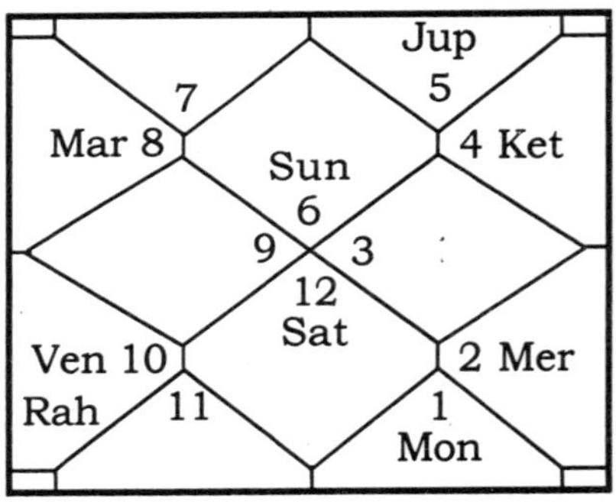

Balance of Vimśottarī Daśā of **Jupiter 13Y 2M 24D**

Name of Event	Date of Event	Major Period	Sub Period
Marriage	04.12.1973	Saturn	Mars
Death of wife	17.05.2002	Ketu	Saturn

of ovaries for 4 years. It was a troublesome and painful death of the wife of the native though she was blessed with *māṅgalya*. I had foreseen the death of this lady 8 or 9 years before the actual happening while preparing the life reading of the native and his wife. I had written that she will be suffering from any dreaded and incurable disease after August 1998 or so and she would be suffering till the middle of 2002 when she would depart for the final abode. However, cancer was diagnosed in October 1998 and in spite of the best endeavours and treatment, she could not be cured. Thus, the affliction of the 2nd and 7th lord resulted into the death of the wife of the native earlier to him.

Case No. 8.14 – (Horoscope No. 70)

Date of marriage – 1947 during sub-period of Saturn, in the major period of Mercury.

Death of wife – 1950 during *Ketu* Mars *daśā bhukti*.

The native was born in Leo ascendant with *yogakāraka* Mars. The 7th lord Saturn occupies the 6th house in own sign Capricorn over the axis of *Rāhu* and *Ketu*. The lord of the 2nd house Mercury is conjoined with inimical Jupiter, friendly Venus and the Sun but the 2nd house is hemmed between malefics. Moon falls in *aśleṣā nakṣatra* in own sign in the 12th house over the axis of *Rāhu* and *Ketu*. *Rāhu* obtains *navāṁśa* of Mars and Mars aspects the 7th house. 8th house is aspected by Mars and Saturn both, therefore, the death of wife took place during the year 1950 when the native was passing through the sub-period of Mars in *Ketu*. It may be noted that the planets, which afflict, conjoin or aspect the 7th house adversely, may cause death of wife of the native during their *daśā bhukti*. Here

Case : 8.14 *Horoscope No. : 70*

Date : 31.10.1934 Time : 03:15:00

Place : — Lat 21°:42′ Long 70°:40′

Ayanāmśa : 22:57:01 Sidereal Time : 05:01:43

Pln	Degree	Rāśi	Nakṣatra	Pad
Asc	23:31:43	Leo	P Phālgunī	4
Sun	13:50:01	Lib	Svāti	3
Mon	19:50:52	Can	Aśleṣā	1
Mar	14:29:03	Leo	P Phālgunī	1
Mer(R/C)	21:15:00	Lib	Viśākhā	1
Jup(D)	11:19:59	Lib	Svāti	2
Ven(C)	09:02:30	Lib	Svāti	1
Sat	28:33:46	Cap	Dhaniṣṭhā	2
Rah(R)	12:37:39	Cap	Śrāvaṇa	1
Ket(R)	12:37:39	Can	Puṣya	3

Lagna Chart

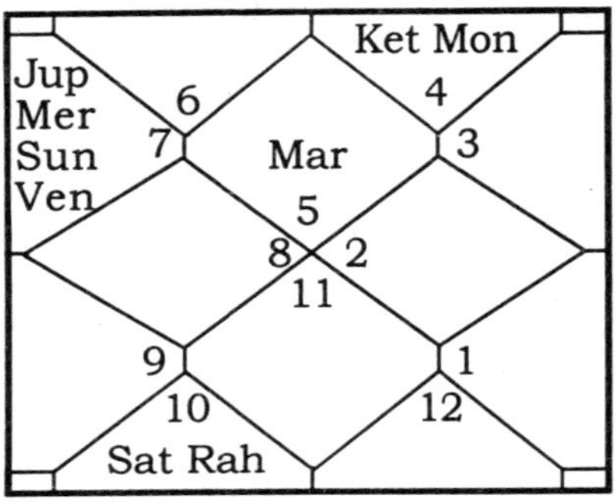

Navāmśa Chart

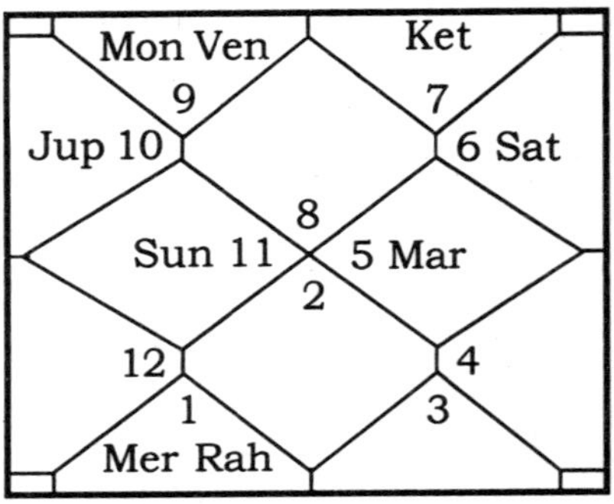

Balance of Vimśottarī Daśā of **Mercury 12Y 11M 10D**

Name of Event	Date of Event	Major Period	Sub Period
Marriage	1947	Mercury	Saturn
Death of wife	1950	Ketu	Mars

Saturn is the 7th lord which is afflicted by *Rāhu* and as *Rāhu* obtains *navāṁśa* of Mars, death took place during the sub-period of Mars. Early death of wife can also be evaluated in this horoscope because the 7th house is afflicted from *lagna* and from Moon as well.

COMBINATIONS FOR THE DEATH OF WIFE

We have following observations to make regarding to the death of wife earlier than the native. Those are fortunate women, who die when their husbands are alive, i.e., they attain *māṅgalya* or *akhaṇḍa saubhāgya*. The wife is fortunate if she attains *māṅgalya*. At the time of judgement of the horoscope of females, importance must be emphasized on the 9th house as well. If the 9th house is afflicted, weak or placed under *pāpakartari yoga* or is occupied by the lord of the *trikas* or the lord of *trikas* join the 9th house under affliction, the female may not attain *akhaṇḍa saubhāgya* in spite of well disposed 2nd, 7th and 8th house. In case the 9th house is well fortified and is occupied by benefics, lord of *Kendras* or *Trikoṇa*, she will be fortunate to die before her husband provided the 2nd house or its lord is strong or occupied by benefics. In addition to the strong and well disposed 7th house. If 8th house is occupied by benefics like Jupiter, one may be blessed with *māṅgalya yoga* provided the 9th house is also well disposed. In the exhaustive study of *māṅgalya* and *vaidhavya* we have observed that in few case, when Jupiter was placed in the 8th house in own sign or in the 7th house in own sign, they suffered loss of their husband when 9th house was weak, afflicted or ill disposed. In other cases under the similar placement of Jupiter, but with strong 9th house, the women enjoyed *māṅgalya yoga*. In the horoscope of the wife of the native of the horoscope No. 13, the wife was having Jupiter and Sagittarius in the 8th house and was blessed with *akhaṇḍa saubhāgya* because her 9th house was also strong. These considerations are very essential while examining the horoscope whether the husband will die before wife or his wife will die before her husband. In the horoscope of the native, if following combinations are present, the wife will die prior to her husband. The husband may or may not remarry, this is the other aspect of the astrology which we have not touched here.

1. If the 2nd house is afflicted, joined by malefics or the lord of 8th. 6th or 12th house are under the aspect of first-rate malefic planets, the wife will die prior to her husband provided 7th house is also weak and ill-disposed.
2. If the lord of the 2nd house occupies the 8th house with malefics, or with the lord of the Trikas or the 7th lord is under the aspect of malefics, the wife will die before her husband.
3. If malefics like Mars, Saturn, *Rāhu* or Sun occupy the 7th house, and the 2nd house is also weak or ill-disposed, the wife will meet with end of her life earlier than her husband.
4. If the 8th house and ascendant are strong, well-disposed and occupied by benefics, the husband will live longer than his wife.
5. The combination of Mars and Mercury in the 7th house is also adverse for the long life of the wife. If Mercury is the lord of the 8th house and joins the 7th house under malefic aspect or with the placement of the lord of the 7th, 12th or 8th house the wife of the native will die early.
6. If the 7th lord is either Mars or Saturn and is under the mutual aspect with Saturn and Mars or Mars and Saturn are conjoined together, the

wife may die before the native. It will be most certain if the 7th lord will fall in *jyeṣṭhā nakṣatra* and Mars will also fall in any *nakṣatra* of *mūlas*.

7. Even retrograde Jupiter in own sign, Sagittarius or Pisces may kill the wife of the native, if such a Jupiter is aspected by Mercury of own sign from ascendant. but it will happen so only if the second house is under heavy affliction of Mars, Saturn or *Rāhu* and 2nd lord is ill-disposed. The wife may die provided the ascendant is strong.
8. The aspect of strong Mars on the 7th house and Moon jointly may kill the wife at an early age provided the 7th lord is combust, afflicted or placed under *pāpakartari yoga.*
9. If Venus or 7th lord is placed under *pāpa kartari yoga,* i.e., Mars, Saturn, *Rāhu* or *Ketu* are placed around the 7th lord or Venus, the death of the first wife will take place before the native even if benefics like Jupiter occupy the 2nd house.
10. If *Rāhu* is placed in the 7th house and is aspected by malefics, then it kills the wife of the native provided the 2nd house is occupied by Saturn or Mars.
11. Combination of Venus, Saturn and Sun in the 7th house is quite adverse for long life of the wife. Similarly the combination of *Rāhu,* Venus and Saturn is adverse for wife. She dies earlier.
12. If Mars is the lord of 12th or 8th house and joins the 7th house, and the 7th lord is conjoined with Venus or Saturn, the wife will die before her husband even if the 2nd house is occupied by first rate benefic Jupiter. Probability of death of wife, gains further strength soon after marriage, if in any of the above point, 7th lord or Moon fall in *jyeṣṭhā nakṣatra.*

13. If the native is born in Aries, and Mars joins the 7th house, under the aspect of Saturn, the husband may kill his wife or may become cause of death of his wife provided the 2nd and 7th lord Venus fall in the sign of any of the luminary especially in Leo and is hemmed in between the luminaries, the Sun and the Moon.
14. If Mars is placed 8th from *lagna* lord Moon and the 7th house from *lagna* is also under the influence of Mars or Saturn, the death of wife takes place in front of her husband.
15. For Libra ascendant, Mars is lord of 2nd and 7th houses and if it is placed in the 7th house in Aries under the mutual aspect of Saturn, one becomes killer of wife and if Mars is placed under *pāpakartari yoga* with Mercury, the wife expires prior to her husband.
16. In any of the above case, if the 2nd house is occupied by malefics like Mars, Saturn, *Rāhu* and *Ketu* and lord of the 2nd house occupies any of the trikas, the death of wife will take place soon after marriage but if the 2nd house is not much afflicted, the death of wife may take place in advance age. The judgement of the age should be made on the basis of the intensity of the affliction of the 7th and 2nd house or their lords.
17. If the lord of the 5th house is located in the 7th and lord of the 7th house is with malefic, and Venus is weak, the wife of the native dies as a result of pregnancy.
18. If malefics occupy the 7th and 8th house and Mars is located in the 12th house and if the 7th house is not aspected by its own lord, the native looses his first wife and has to marry second time.

19. The strongest planet responsible for death of first wife should be examined properly. The *daśā bhukti* of the *navāṁśa* lord occupied by that planet may kill the wife during its *daśā bhukti*. The death of wife may take place during the *daśā bhukti* of 2nd lord, planet placed in the 2nd house or *navāṁśa* lord of the occupant of the 2nd house. The death of wife may also take place during the *daśā bhukti* of the lord of the 7th house or occupant of the 7th house or the *navāṁśa* lord of the occupant of the 7th house.

मौनं कालविलम्बश्च प्रयाणं भूमिदर्शनम् ।
भ्रूकुस्यत्यमुखी वार्ता नकारः षड्विधः स्मृतः ।।

When one has to deny something, there are six ways out, e.g., keeping oneself silent, prolonged consideration, leaving the place, eyeing downward, raising eyelashes, or starting conversation with another person.

Chapter-9

REMEDIES FOR MARITAL MALADIES AND WIDOWHOOD

It is not sufficient to be able to know that a woman is likely to suffer widowhood at an early age due to unnatural and violent death of her husband. It is equally important to know the measures and remedies to prevent widowhood. Mainly there are following curative measures :-

1. Matching of horoscopes of boy and girl before settlement of marriage.
2. Selection of appropriate and most suitable *muhūrta* for marriage.
3. Recitation of appropriate *mantra* and *stotra* to prevent widowhood.
4. Observation of *vrata* with full faith and dedication.
5. Donation of suitable articles and money to the desirable persons.

All these remedial measures have their own importance and benefits. The parents, who want their children to lead happy and ever lasting married life, should consult any knowledgeable, meritorious, experienced and honest astrologer who is rarely available, who is well-conversed with the significance, importance of *muhūrta*. Most appropriate *muhūrta* for marriage can prevent marital disasters provided sincere efforts are made in selection of appropriate *muhūrta* on the basis of the horoscopes of bride and bridegroom especially when indications of marital disasters, such as widowhood and divorce are present in the birth-chart. Selection of appropriate *muhūrta* for marriage is not a simple work as it is made out to be now a days. It requires wide knowledge of the subject and experience. We shall be explaining about the art of selection of *muhūrta* for the purpose of marriage in our forthcoming title *Mars : Remedies for marital Maladies and Widowhood.*

Matching of horoscopes to save all kinds of adversities, disasters and problems of marriage is most essential. This is usually taken into consideration by the parents of a boy and girl before fixing their marriage. Mostly they approach the so called astrologers and pandits who do not know much about the matching of charts for marriage. Importance is emphasized on matching points, *nāḍī doṣa* and *maṅgalī doṣa* only. We regret to say that these so-called *Pandits* do not even know the basis of matching horoscopes of *nāḍī doṣa* and *maṅgalī doṣa*, does not promise happy married life. We know couples, who are leading quite prosperous and happy married life with good understanding, though there are only three matching points present in their birth-charts out of 36. Points are matched on the basis of constellation of Moon, why other eight planets and their *nakṣatras* should not be taken into consideration? We have explained about the art of matching of horoscope in our voluminous work *Predicting Marriage* in the *chapter* "Does matching help?" We have evaluated *graha melāpaka* and *Bhāva melāpaka* in addition to *nakṣatra melāpaka* for accurate and appropriate matching of birth-charts for high degree of conjugal bliss. We are working on this most useful subject for the benefit of one and all. This work is entitled as *Match Making Mystiques*, which is written on the basis of various aspects of matching and practical study and illustrations of horoscopes of hundreds of couples.

Recitation Of Suitable Mantra And Stotra To Prevent Widowhood

Our sages were visionaries to advise the forthcoming generation of various *suktas*, *stotras* and *mantras* to prevent various kinds of miseries, mishaps and maladies of married life. We have a wide experience of the subject of curative measures and preventive art. We will be giving here various mantras and stotras which can certainly prevent the curse of widowhood, provided these remedial measures and *mantras* are followed properly with correct pronounciation, absolute faith, dedication and *sāttvika* living with honesty and loyalty towards husband.

Any *mantra* or *stotra* must be done after proper *ṣoḍaśopacāra pūjana* of the concerning deity and taking proper *saṅkalpa* for the same. *Saṅkalpa* is nothing but a pledge or promise to the concerning deity that the person will be reciting or chanting so many number of the particular *mantra* for so many days to please the deity to get the blessings for the fulfillment of one's wishes, that particular ambition and to nullify the adverse effect of malefic planets over the person etc. In *saṅkalpa*, one should pronounce his or her name along with the name of his father or her husband with *gotra* as well. The day and date, i.e., *this vār*, *samvat* and place of worship should also be pronounced. In fact before taking up any worship *anuṣṭhāna*, *mantra jāpa* and *vrata* etc. first of all we should introduce or define ourselves and the date, day and year should also be spoken alongwith the name of place. In the second half of the *saṅkalpa*, name of deity, purpose of *saṅkalpa* and number of *mantra* should be spoken. Mostly *saṅkalpa* is read in Sanskrit but it is not at all essential. The *saṅkalpa* may be read or spoken in any language in which one can easily and correctly express oneself.

Mars plays a vital role in loss of spouse and especially to curse widowhood to a woman. It is correctly believed that Mars is the significator of widowhood and Jupiter is the significator of *saubhāgya*. *Maṅgalī* girls are afraid of widowhood as placement of Mars in the ascendant, 7th or 8th house gives rise to the untimely loss of husband. We assure such *maṅgalī* natives that widowhood can be prevented provided one is sincere to take up remedial measure as advised by our sages.

Following are the most important preventive, most useful and appropriate mantras which a woman can recite regularly. It will be advantageous if *maṅgalī* girls recited or read these *mantra* and *stotra* before finalisation of marriage. If the girl is having combination of widowhood in her birth chart, she must take up remedial measure soon after she has come of age. The most important, useful and tested mantras to prevent one from the adversities and evils of Mars are given below. Most of these remedial measures are rarely known and are not found anywhere in published books on the subject. The remedial measures should be followed very sincerely with full faith and belief if one is suffering from *kuja doṣa*. The *mantras* are not for fun and frolic. Any kind of worship, *mantra*, *japa* and *vrata* etc. should not be undertaken during their menstruation periods by woman. The woman will be highly benefitted to prevent all marital disaster and mishappenings by proper, appropriate and correct use of *mantra* and *stotra*.

Remedial Measures

When Mars is adversely placed in the birth-chart and such placement of Mars indicates any kind of marital disaster, divorce, widowhood or any other mishappening such as murder, attack by criminals, accident, fight, conflict, confrontation, surgical operation or obstruction in child birth. One should recite the *mantra* of Mars in a proper way. Mantras of Mars are of various kinds but the Vedic mantras are most effective and give lasting results however everybody can not recite the Vedic mantra of Mars and therefore, there are other small and simple *mantras*. The recitation of these mantras are simple and can easily be undertaken by even those who can not read correct Sanskrit.

We are making an honest effort to write all kinds of *mantras* relating to Mars for the benefit of readers and sufferers.

Remedial Measure No. 1

Recitation of *mantra* is most useful for the prevention of *kuja doṣa*, widowhood, separation and marital maladies of all kinds, if Mars plays a negative role in birth-chart in regard to marriage. If one can not read lengthy *mantras* and *stotras* in Sanskrit, he can easily recite small *Vedic*, *Paurāṇika* or *tāntrika mantras* for at least 10,000 times. It is advised that the number of mantras should be four times in *Kaliyuga* to get best results. So the subject should recite these mantras for 40,000 in total and should perform *daśāṁśa*, *havana*, *tarpaṇa*, *mārjana* etc. either by himself or through a learned *ācārya*.

Vedic Mantra of Mars

Viniyoga -अग्निर्मूर्द्धेति मन्त्रस्य विरूपाक्ष ऋषिः गायत्री छन्दः भौमो देवता मंगलप्रीतये जपे विनियोगः ।

Mantra - ॐ क्रां क्रीं क्रौं सः ॐ भूर्भुवः स्वः ॐ अग्निर्मूर्द्धा दिवः ककुत्पतिः पृथिव्याऽअयम् अपा ग्वं रेता ग्वं सिजिवन्ति। ॐ स्वः भुवः भूः ॐ सः क्रौं क्रीं क्रॉं ॐ भोमाय नमः।

This is the most useful and important Vedic *Mantra* of Mars "ग्वं" to be pronounced as *Gvang*.

Tāntrika Maṇtra of mars No. 1.

If one can not read Vedic *Mantra* of Mars correctly, he or she should recite *tāntrika mantra* of Mars regularly.

ॐ क्रॉं क्रीं क्रौं सः भौमाय नमः।

Paurāṇika Mantra

This is *Paurāṇika Mantra* and can be easily recited.

धरणीगर्भसम्भूतं विद्युत्कान्तिसमप्रभम्।
कुमारं शक्तिहस्तं च मंगलं प्रणमाम्यहम्।।

Tāntrika Mantra of Mars No. 2.

ॐ भौम भौमाय नमः

Angāraka Mantra Of Mars

ॐ अं अंगारकाय नमः

Tāntrika Maṇtra of Mars No. 3.

ॐ ह्रीं णमो सिद्धाणं।

These all *mantras* should be recited 10,000 times to eliminate the adverse results of Mars but to get the best results, four times of this, that is 40,000 times, the *mantra* relating to Mars are required to be recited. It is a prerequisite in *Kaliyuga* that any *mantra* gives its best effects when it is recited four times, then that of the number of *mantra* advised to be done in other *yugas*, such as *satyayuga*. *Dvāpara* and *Tretāyuga*. Probably it is so because one is surrounded by enumerable evils, sins of various kinds and crimes in *Kaliyuga*. The following mantra should also be done alongwith the *Vedic*, *tāntrika* or *Paurāṇika manṭra*.

ॐ ह्रीं वासुपूज्यप्रभो नमस्तुभ्यं मम शान्तिः शान्तिः।

This *mantra* should be recited 108 times alongwith other *mantras* to get the lasting and permanent results.

Kārttikeya, son of *Śiva*, Army General of *devatās*, is the ocean of knowledge who moves on a holy, pure and chaste peacock; the above mentioned *mantra* should be recited alongwith the *mantras* of Mars to get more advantage and to produce acceleration in the results of the *mantras*. *Kārttikeya* has red complexion, like blood or *kumkum*. Worship of *Kārttikeya* should be done with red sandal, red rose flower, *roli*, red betel nut, red *kesar*, red coral and red sweets.

Following stotra belongs to *Kārttikeya* who slew *Tārakāsura*. This *stotra* may also be read for the enhancement of the beneficial results quickly.

Kārttikeya Stotra :

ॐ श्रीगणेशाय नमः
स्कन्द उवाच:
योगीश्वरो महासेनः कार्तिकेयोऽग्निनन्दनः ।
स्कन्दः कुमारः सेनानिः स्वामि शङ्करसम्भवः ।।
गंगेयस्ताम्रचूडश्च ब्रह्मचारी शिखिध्वजः ।
तारकारिरुमापुत्रः क्रौञ्चारिश्च षडाननः ।।
शब्दब्रह्मसमुद्रश्च सिद्धः सारस्वतो गुहः ।
सनत्कुमारो भगवान् भोगमोक्षफलप्रदः ।।

शरजन्मा गणाधीशः पूर्वजो मुक्तिमार्गकृत् ।
सर्वागमप्रणेता च वांछितार्थप्रदर्शनः ।।
अष्टाविंशतिनामानि मदीयानीति यः पठेत् ।
प्रत्यूषे श्रद्धया युक्ता मूको वाचस्पतिर्भवेत् ।।
महामन्त्रमयानीतं मम नामानुकीर्तनम् ।
महाप्रज्ञामवाप्नोति नात्र कार्या विचारणा ।
इति श्रीरुद्रयामले प्रज्ञाविवर्धनाख्यं श्रीमत्कार्तिकेयस्तोत्रम् ।

नामावलीः
स्कान्ध वन्दे नमोऽस्तु ते जय षण्मुखनाथ नमोऽस्तु ते।
मुरूगा गुहने नमोऽस्तु ते जय वल्ली वल्लभ नमोऽस्तु ते।
कार्तिकेय नमोऽस्तु ते जय कतिरकाम वासा नमोऽस्तु ते।
दण्डायुधपाणि नमोऽस्तु ते जय तिरूपुरनकुन्द्र नमोऽस्तु ते।
दैवयाने समेता नमोऽस्तु ते जय अनाथ रक्षक नमोऽस्तु ते।
दीनबन्धु नमोऽस्तु ते जय दीन नाथ नमोऽस्तु ते।
देव देव नमोऽस्तु ते जय देवनाथ नमोऽस्तु ते।
भक्तवत्सल नमोऽस्तु ते जय पतितपावन नमोऽस्तु ते।
गुह मुरूगा षण्मुखा उडिपि सुब्रह्मण्य।
तिरूचेन्दूर वेला कातिरकामनाथा।
देवयानी समेता पलनिमलै आण्डवा।
ॐ शरवणभव गुह मुरूगेशा।।
षण्मुखा बाल षण्मुखा बाल षण्मुखा बाल षण्मुखा।
सुब्रह्मण्य शिव सुब्रह्मण्य शिव सुब्रह्मण्य शिव सुब्रह्मण्य।
भक्तवत्सल भक्तवत्सल भक्तवत्सल भक्तवत्सल।
पतितपावन पतितपावन पतितपावन पतितपावन।।
बोल् षण्मुख बोल् षण्मुख षण्मुख षण्मुख बोल् ।
शिव शिव शिव शिव सुब्रह्मण्य शरवणभव बोल्।।

Remedial Measure No. 2

Maṅgala Caṇḍikā Mantra

The following *mantra* must be read by all *maṅgalī* females irrespective of the fact that they are strong or weak *maṅgalī*. Mars can exhibit its adversity at any stage of life whenever concerning *daśā bhukti* is operative over the native. Influence of Mars may create much turbulence in the 21st, 28th, 35th or 42nd years of age, provided one comes under the influence of adverse planetary vibrations of *daśā bhukti* as well.

Mātā Gaurī, i.e., *mātā Pārvatī* is the goddess of the *saubhāgya* of females. It is a common belief in all females that regular worship of *mātā Gaurī* will provide them *akhaṇḍa saubhāgya*. It is advisable to have a small idol of *mātā Gaurī* made of copper or brass, bronze or *aṣṭadhātu*. Get the *prāṇa pratiṣṭhā* should be done by some learned, experienced and knowledgeable *ācārya*. Worship *mātā Gaurī* by doing *ṣoḍaśopacāra pujā* every day. First of all, light a five-sided lamp (*pañcamukhī dīpaka*), thereafter complete the *ṣoḍaśopacāra* or *pañcopacāra pūjana* of *mātā Gaurī*. Thereafter, recite the following mantra for at least 28 times every day. The recital may be enhanced gradually from 28 to 56 and after a month or so to 108. It may be noted that recitation of the number of *mantras* can not be reduced after increasing it. Therefore, the number should be increased only when one has intense desire and sufficient time to increase the number of *mantras* recital in a proper way. This is to be done with full faith and concentration before goddess *Gaurī*.

रक्ष रक्ष जगन्मातर्देवि मंगलचण्डिके।
हारिके विपदां राशौ हर्षमंगलकारिके।।
हर्षमंगलदक्षे च हर्षमंगलदायिके।
शुभे मंगलदक्षे च शुभे मंगलचण्डिके।।
मंगले मंगलार्हे च सर्वमंगलमंगले।
सदा मंगलदे देवि सर्वेषां मंगलालये।।

Remedial Measure No. 3

Maṅgala Caṇḍikā Stotra

One of the most powerful prayers is *maṅgala Caṇḍikā stotra*, addressed to goddess *Candikā*, an incarnation of *Pārvatī*.

In our sacred *Purāṇas*, an account goes thus, Lord *Nārāyaṇa* speaks to *Nārada*: "Now listen to the sacred story of *maṅgala Caṇḍikā* which is agreeable to the Vedas and dearest even to those scholars who know of everything. The term *Caṇḍī* denotes *Dakṣā* (or the all skillful deity). *maṅgala* means auspicious. She is capable of causing any and every auspicious event. The term *Caṇḍī* further denotes *Durgā* while the term *maṅgala* denotes the planet Mars, the son of earth. Since the goddess is dear to Mars or *Kuja*, she also is known as *maṅgala Caṇḍikā*. She appears before her devotees as mercy personified and is the muse of women. Once upon a time, lord *Śaṅkara* also obtained her blessings before slaying the fierce demon called *Tripura*".

Narrating the above account, lord *Viṣṇu* reveals the following sacred and the most auspicious *mantra*, which should not be conveyed to hypocrites or to people who do not have any reverence for it.

Maṅgala Caṇḍikā Stotra With *Mantra* And *Dhyāna*

ॐ ह्रीम् श्रीम् क्लीम् सर्वपूज्ये देवि मंगलचण्डिके।
ऐं क्रूं फट् स्वाहेत्येवं चाप्येकविंशाक्षरो मनुः।।
पूज्यः कल्पतरुश्चैव भक्तानां सर्वकामदः।
दशलक्षजपेनैव मन्त्रसिद्धिर्भवेन्नृणाम्।
मन्त्रसिद्धिर्भवेद् यस्य स विष्णुः सर्वकामदः।
ध्यानं च श्रूयतां ब्रह्मन् वेदोक्तं सर्वसम्मतम्।।
देवीम् षोडशवर्षीयां शश्वत्सुस्थिरयौवनाम्।
सर्वरूपगुणाढ्यां च कोमलांगीं मनोहराम्।।
श्वेतचम्पकवर्णाभां चन्द्रकोटिसमप्रभाम्।

वधिशुद्धांशुकाधानां रत्नभूषणभूषिताम्।
बिभ्रतीम् कबरीभारं मल्लिकामाल्यभूषिताम्।
बिम्बोष्ठीं सुदन्तीं शुद्धां शरत्पद्मनिभाननाम्।
ईषद्धास्यप्रसन्नास्यां सुनीलोत्पललोचनाम्।
जगद्धात्रीम् च दात्रीम् च सर्वेभ्यः सर्वसम्पदाम्।
संसारसागरे घोरे पोतरूपां वरां भजे।
देव्याश्च ध्यानमित्येवं स्तवनं श्रूयतां मुने।
प्रयतः संकटग्रस्तो येन तुष्टाव शंकरः।
शंकर उवाच्
रक्ष रक्ष जगन्मातर्देवि मंगलचण्डिके।
हारिके विपदां राशे हर्षमंगलकारिके।।
हर्षमंगलदक्षे च हर्षमंगलचण्डिके।
शुभे मंगलदक्षे च शुभ मंगलचण्डिके।।
मंगलं मंगलार्हे च सर्वमंगलमंगले।
सतां मंगलदे देवि सर्वेषां मंगलालये।।
पूज्या मंगलवारे च मंगलाभीष्टदैवते।
पूज्ये मंगलभूपस्य मनुवंशस्य संततम्।
मंगलाधिष्ठातृदेवि मंगलानां च मंगले।
संसारमंगलाधारे मोक्षमंगलदायिनि।।
सारे च मंगलाधारे पारे च सर्वकर्मणाम्।
प्रतिमंगलवारे च पूज्ये च मंगलप्रदे ।
स्तोत्रेणानेन शम्भुश्च स्तुत्वा मंगलचण्डिकाम्।
प्रतिमंगलवारे च पूजां कृत्वा गतः शिवः ।।
देव्याश्च मंगलस्तोत्रं यः शृणोति समाहितः।
तन्मंगलं भवेच्छश्वन्न भवेत् तद्मंगलम्।।

Meaning: (Lord *Nārāyaṇa* proceeds) "The principal *mantra* containing 21 letters – *Om Hrīm Śrīm Klīm Sarva Pūjya Devī Maṅgala Caṇḍike, Im Krūm Phatt Svāhā* – as given by Manu (the progenitor of human beings) when recited, well is capable of fulfilling all of one's desires like the divine Boon-giving Tree.

This *mantra's siddhi* can be attained by reciting the same for ten lakh (10,00,000) times. O Brahmin (*Nārada*) listen to me with attention! This widely acceptable prayer (*dhyāna*, now being told) is honoured even by the *devatās*. Goddess *maṅgala Caṇḍikā*, who is ever youthful, and always looks like a sixteen year old damsel. Endowed with wholesome beauty and virtues, she is soft bodied and heart robbing. Her complexion is akin to that of white *campaka* flower and her charming radiance is equal to that of one crore Moons. She applies jasmine in her hair. Her lips are reddish, resembling the brilliant lotus of the spring season and adores a captivating smile. Both her eyes resemble the blossoming blue lotuses. She fulfils all the desires of everyone (who bows before her) and is a boat to cross the ocean of mundane journey and is the Excellent one. I (Lord *Viṣṇu*) always sing her glory. O sage, that was the *mantra* to please *maṅgala Caṇḍikā*. Now listen to her stotra or praises (as told by Lord *Śiva*).

Stotra: Lord *Śiva* says, "O *maṅgala Caṇḍike*! the mother of the Universe, you are the destroyer of all the dangers, and are ever ready to bestow auspiciousness. Protect me, protect me. The joyous *maṅgala Caṇḍike*, you distribute happiness and auspiciousness with open (or free) hands. You are the all auspicious *śubha maṇgala Caṇḍikā* and the auspiciousness of all other auspiciousness. O Devi! your nature is to bestow auspiciousness to virtuous people. You are the abode of auspiciousness for one and all. Devi you are the favourite deity of the planet *maṅgala* (or *Kuja*). You should be (unfailingly) worshipped on Tuesdays (as on other days). You are the honourable deity of *Maṅgala*, a king of Manu dynasty. O presiding deity of auspiciousness! you are auspicious even for the auspiciousness. All the auspiciousness of the universe takes shelter in you. You are the bestower of auspiciousness containing emancipation. O Devi! giver of auspiciousness on being worshipped on Tuesdays, you are the essence of the universe and are beyond all Karmas or deeds."

Lord *Nārāyaṇa* further says: Thus *maṅgala Caṇḍikā* has been first worshipped by Lord *Śiva* on all Tuesdays, so also by Mars. One who recites or listens to this stotra, will never receive any inauspiciousness. He will beget auspicious results."

When a man or a woman recites the above *mantra* and *stotra* regularly and with devotion, he or she will have no obstacles in his or her life, will be married early and will lead a happy life. The worship should be commenced on a Tuesday and be continued.

This is extremely favourable for those natives (whether males or females) having *kuja doṣa* of any magnitude. Such evils of Mars will completely vanish, marriage will take place and matrimonial life will be fully auspicious in every aspect. Also those without *kuja doṣa* will also stand to gain timely marriage and attend happiness.

Recitation of this *maṅgala Caṇḍikā stotra* (or the entire story) can be resorted to by those who are likely to be affected by transit of Mars. Those who are subjected to other kinds of blemishes by an afflicted Mars at birth (like disease, litigation etc.) can also undertake the recitation of this *maṅgala Caṇḍikā stotra* regularly.

Remedial Measure No. 4

Pārvatī Svayamvara mantra

This *mantra* can also be recited alongwith the above mentioned *maṅgala Caṇḍikā mantra*. *Ṣoḍaśopacāra pūjana* (16 faceted worship) is not required but five-faced lamp, i.e., the *Pañcamukhī Dīpaka* must remain lighted throughout the worship and recitation of *mantra*.

बालार्कायुतसत्प्रभां करतले लोलाम्बुमालाकुलां ।
मालां सन्दधतीं मनोहरतनुं मन्दस्मितोद्यन्मुखीम् ।
मन्दं मन्दमुपेयुषीं वरयितुं शंभुं जगन्मोहिनीं
वन्दे देवमुनीन्द्रवन्दितपदां इष्टार्थदां पार्वतीम् ।।

Remedial Measure No. 5
Maṅgala stotra No. 1

This *stotra* is very useful which should be done by male and female alike who are passing through the adverse vibrations of Mars. After *ṣoḍaśopacāra pūjana* of *Maṅgala graha*, proper *saṅkalpa* of *Maṅgala stotra* recitation be undertaken. Thereafter, take a small amount of water in the cup of your palm and offer this to ground after reading the *viniyoga*. Thereafter, read *maṅgala stotra* correctly with absolute faith and concentration in the amazing and astonishing power of *Maṅgala Deva*.

अस्यांगारकस्तोत्रस्य विरूपांगिरस ऋषि ।
गायत्री छन्दः भौमप्रीत्यर्थ जपे विनियोगः।
अंगारकः शक्तिधरो लोहितांगो धरासुतः।
कुमारो मंगलो भौमो महाकायो धनप्रदः।।
ऋणहर्ता दृष्टिकर्ता रोगकृद्रोगनाशनः।
विद्युत्प्रभो व्रणकरः कामदो धनहृत् कुजः।।
सामगानप्रियो रक्तवस्त्रो रक्तायतेक्षणः।
लोहितो रक्तवर्णश्च सर्वकर्मावबोधकः।।
रक्तमाल्यधरो हेमकुण्डली ग्रहनायकः।
नामान्येतानि भौमस्य यः पठेत्सततं नरः।।
ऋणं तस्य च दौर्भाग्यं दारिद्र्यं च विनश्यति।
धनं प्राप्नोति विपुलं स्त्रियं चैव मनोरमाम्।।
वंशोद्योतकरं पुत्रं लभते नात्र संशयः।

योऽर्चयेद्दहि भौमस्य मंगलं बहुपुष्पकैः।।
सर्वा नश्यन्ति पीडाश्च तस्य ग्रहकृता ध्रुवम्।।
इति श्रीस्कन्दपुराणे अंगारकस्तोत्रं संपूर्णम्।

Remedial Measure No. 6

Maṅgala stotra No. 2

Same results will be derived by the *sādhaka* as mentioned above. However, different *stotras* have been written by different sages and their *devatā* and *Ṛṣis* may be different. One should select the *stotra* on the basis of his or her birth-chart.

गणाधिपो भानुशशी धरासुतो बुधो गुरुर्भार्गवसूर्यनन्दनौ ।
राहुश्च केतुश्च परे नवग्रहाः कुर्वन्तु वः पूर्णमनोरथं सदा ।
उपेन्द्र इन्द्रो वरुणो हुताशनस्त्रिविक्रमो भानुसखश्चतुर्भुजः ।
गन्धर्वयक्षोरगसिद्धचारणाः कुर्वन्तु वः पूर्णमनोरथं सदा।
नलो दधीचिः सगरः पुरूरवा शाकुन्तलेयो भरतो धनंजयः ।
रामत्रयं वैन्यबलौ युधिष्ठिरः कुर्वन्तु वः पूर्णमनोरथं सदा।
मनुर्मरीचिर्भृगुदक्ष नारदाः पराशरो व्यास वशिष्ठ भार्गवाः ।
वाल्मीकि कुम्भोद्भव गर्ग गौतमाः कुर्वन्तु वः पूर्णमनोरथं सदा ।
रंभा शची सत्यवती च देवकी गौरीच लक्ष्मीश्च दितिश्चरुक्मिणी ।
कूर्मो गजेन्द्रः सचराचरा धरा कुर्वन्तु वः पूर्णमनोरथं सदा ।।
गंगा च क्षिप्रा यमुना सरस्वती गोदावरी वेत्रवती च नर्मदा ।
सा चन्द्रभागा वरुणा त्वसी नदी कुर्वन्तु वः पूर्णमनोरथं सदा ।
तुंग प्रभासे गुरुचक्रपुष्करौ गयाऽ विमुक्ता बदरी वटेश्वरः ।
केदार पंपासरसश्च नैमिषः कुर्वन्तु वः पूर्णमनोरथं सदा ।
शंखश्च दूर्वासित पत्रचामरो मणिः प्रदीपो वररत्नकांचनम् ।
सम्पूर्णकुम्भः सुहुतो हुताशनः कुर्वन्तु वः पूर्णमनोरथं सदा ।
प्रयाणकाले यदि वा सुमंगले प्रभातकाले च नृपाभिषेचने ।
धर्मार्थकामाय जयाय भाषितं व्यासेन कुर्यात्तु मनोरथं हि तत् ।।

Remedial Measure No. 7
Maṅgala stotra 3

We have written about two *maṅgala stotras* as above. *Kaśyapa ṛṣi* has written both of these *stotras*. This *stotra* has been written by Garga *ṛṣi*. This is very prominent and useful *maṅgala stotra* and works tremendously where all other *maṅgala stotra* do not fulfil the desire. This *maṅgala stotra* should be read with absolute faith and confidence.

विनियोगः अस्य श्री भौमस्तोत्रस्य गर्गऋषिः मंगलो
देवता त्रिष्टुप् छन्द ऋणापहरणे
जपे विनियोगः ।
ध्यान रक्ताम्बरो रक्तवपुः किरीटी
चतुर्मुखो मेघगदो गदाधृक् ।
धरासुतः शक्तिधरश्च शूली
सदा अमस्या वरदः प्रशांतः ।।
स्तोत्र मंगलो भूमिपुत्रश्च ऋणहर्ता धनप्रदः ।
स्थिरात्मजो महाकायः सर्वकामार्थसाधकः
लोहितो लोहितांगश्च सामगानां कृपाकरः ।
धरात्मजः कुजो भौमो भूतिदो भूमिनंदनः ।।
अंगारको यमश्चैव सर्वरोगापहारकः ।
वृष्टेःकर्ताऽपहर्ता च सर्वकाम फलप्रदः ।।
एतानि कुजनामानि नित्यं यः श्रद्धया पठेत ।
ऋणं न जायते तस्य धनं प्राप्नोत्यसंशयः ।।
अंगारकोऽतिबलवानपि यो ग्रहाणां
स्वेदोद्भवस्मिन्नस्य पिनाकपाणेः
आरक्त चन्दन सुशीतलवारिणा यो
प्यभ्यर्चिततोऽथ विपुलां प्रददाति सिद्धिम् ।
भो भो धरात्मज इति प्रथितः पृथिव्याम्
दुःखावहो दुरितशोकसमस्तहर्ता ।
नृणामृणं हरति तान्धनिनः प्रकुर्यात्
यः पूजितः सकलमंगलवासरेषु ।।

एकेन हस्तेन गदां विभर्ति
त्रिशूलमन्येन ऋजुक्रमेण ।
शक्तिं सदान्येन वरं ददाति
चतुर्भुजो मंगलमादधातु ।।
यो मंगलो मंगलमादधाति
मध्यग्रहे यच्छति वाञ्छितार्थम् ।
धर्मार्थ कामादि सुखं प्रभुत्वं
कलत्र पुत्रैनं कदा वियोगः ।।
कनकमयशरीरस्तेजसा दुर्निरीक्ष्यो
हुतवहसमकान्तिर्मालवे लब्धजन्मा ।
अवनिजतनयेषु श्रूयते यः पुराणो
दिशतु मम विभूतिः भूमिजः सप्रभावः ।।

Remedial Measure No. 8

Aṅgāraka stotra

Aṅgāraka stotra is very famous and most useful of Vedic *stotra* of Mars. This can be read in addition to *mantras* of Mars where the adversity and malefic results of Mars are pronounced very deeply. The women who are suffering from *kuja doṣa* resulting into miserable married life, destruction and disaster, they are advised to recite *aṅgāraka stotra* atleast once every day. This *stotra* may be recited 7, 14 or 21 times depending upon the adversity caused by Mars in the birth-chart of the native. However, this is harmless in all respect.

Viniyoga

अस्याऽङ्गारकस्तोत्रस्य विरूपांगिरस ऋषिः
गायत्रीच्छंदः भौमप्रीत्यर्थजपे विनियोगः ।

Stotra

अंगारकः शक्तिधरो लोहितांगो धरासुतः ।
कुमारो मंगलो भौमो महाकायो धनप्रदः ।

ऋणहर्त्ता दृष्टिकर्त्ता रोगकृद्रोगनाशनः ।
विद्युत्प्रभो व्रणकरः कामदो धनहृत् कुजः ।
सामगानप्रियो रक्तवस्त्रो रक्तायतेक्षणः ।
लोहितो रक्तवर्णश्च सर्वकर्मावरोधकः ।
रक्तमाल्यधरो हेमकुण्डली ग्रहनायकः ।
नामान्येतानि भौमस्य यः पठेत् सततं नरः ।
ऋणं तस्य हि दौर्भाग्यं दारिद्र्यं च विनश्यति ।
धनं प्राप्नोति विपुलं स्त्रियं चैव मनोरमाम् ।
वंशोद्योतकरं पुत्रं लभते नाऽत्र संशयः ।
योऽर्चयेदह्नि भौमस्य मंगलं बहुपुष्पकैः ।
सर्वा नश्यंति पीडा च तस्य ग्रहकृता ध्रुवम् ।।

Remedial Measure No. 9

Maṅgala kavaca

The function of *maṅgala kavaca* is different than *maṅgala stotra. Maṅgala kavaca* should be recited where protection and safety is required. This is very useful for those in whose birth chart, serious combination of accident and violent death is indicated.

Viniyoga

अस्य श्रीमंगलकवचस्तोत्रमंत्रस्य कश्यप ऋषिः ।
अनुष्टुप छंदः। अंगारकी देवता ।
भौमपीडापरिहारार्थं जपे विनियोगः ।
रक्तांबरो रक्तवपुः किरीटी चतुर्भुजो मेषगमो गदाभृत् ।
धरासुतः शक्तिधरश्च शूली सदा मम स्याद्वरदः प्रशांतः ।
अंगारकः शिरोरक्षेन्मुखं वै धरणीसुतः।
श्रवौ रक्तांबरः पातु नेत्रे मे रक्तलोचनः।
नासां शक्तिधरः पातु मुखं में रक्तलोचनः।
भुजौ मे रक्तमाली च हस्तौ शक्तिधरस्तथा।
वक्षः पातु वरांगश्च हृदयं पातु लोहिताः।
कटिं मे ग्रहराजश्च मुखं चैव धरासुतः।

जानुजंघे कुजः पातु पादौ भक्तप्रियः सदा ।
सर्वाण्यन्यानि चांगानि रक्षेन्मे मेषवाहनः ।
य इदं कवचं दिव्यं सर्वशत्रुनिवारणाम् ।
भूतप्रेतपिशाचानां नाशनं सर्वसिद्धिदम् ।
सर्वरोगहरं चैव सर्वसंपत्प्रदं शुभम् ।
भुक्तिमुक्तिप्रदं नृणां सर्वसौभाग्यवर्धनम् ।
रोगबंधविमोक्षं च सत्यमेनन्न संशयः ।।
इति श्रीमार्कण्डेयपुराणे मंगलकवचं संपूर्णम् ।।

Remedial Measure No. 10

Maṅgala kavaca

This *Maṅgala kavaca* is most useful for those who are suffering due to malefic effect of Mars over them. This is wonderful *kavaca*, ruins enemies or they are badly defeated in the fight. If one is suffering from evil spirits, the reading of the *kavaca* will remove all such problems. This prevents all kinds of ailments especially those which are indicated by Mars such as blood pressure, muscular trouble, injury, burns, cuts, boils and operation etc. This *kavaca* of Mars prevents rivalry, punishment, penalty and gives all kinds of happiness, wealth, prosperity and fulfilment of desires.

Viniyoga

अस्य श्रीअंगारककवचस्तोत्रमंत्रस्य कश्यप ऋषिः ।
अनुष्टुप् छंदः । अंगारको देवता ।
भौमपीत्यर्थे जपे विनियोगः।

Dhyāna

रक्ताम्बरो रक्तवपुः किरीटी चतुर्भुजो मेषगमो गदाभृत् ।
धरासुतः शक्तिधरश्च शूली सदा मम स्याद्वरदः प्रशांतः ।

Kavaca

अंगारकः शिरोरक्षेन्मुखं वै धरणीसुतः ।
श्रवौ रक्तांबरः पातु नेत्रे मे रक्तलोचनः ।
नासां शक्तिधरः पातु मुखं मे रक्तलोचनः ।
भुजौ मे रक्तमाली च हस्तौ शक्तिधरस्तथा ।
वक्षः पातु वरांगश्च हृदयं पातु रोहितः ।
कटिं मे ग्रहराजश्च मुखं चैव धरासुतः ।
जानुजंघे कुजः पातु पादौ भक्तप्रियः सदा ।
सर्वाण्यन्यानि चांगानि रक्षेन्मे मेषवाहनः ।
य इदं कवचं दिव्यं सर्वशत्रुनिवारणम् ।
भूतप्रेतपिशाचानां नाशनं सर्वसिद्धिदम् ।
सर्वरोगहरं चैव सर्वसंपत्प्रदं शुभम् ।
भुक्तिमुक्तिप्रदं नृणां सर्वसौभाग्यवर्धनम् ।
रोगबंधविमोक्षं च सत्यमेतन्न संशयः ॥

Remedial Measure No. 11
Ṛṇamocana maṅgala stotra

Ṛṇamocana maṅgala stotra is useful for getting rid of debts and loans. Many times, placement of Mars in 12th, 2nd or 8th house may give rise to debts and as a result of which the native may have to lead a painful married life and suffer poverty, misunderstandings and differences. One may even commit suicide, if one is suffering from the problems of heavy loans and he is not able to pay the same in spite of his best results. Therefore, he must read *ṛṇamocana maṅgala stotra* which will bless the subject with prosperity, property, wealth, happiness and success in various aspects of life.

मंगलो भूमिपुत्रश्च ऋणहर्त्ता धनप्रदः ।
स्थिरासनो महाकायः सर्वकर्मावरोधकः ॥
लोहितो लोहितांगश्च सामगानां कृपाकरः ।
धरात्मजः कुजो भौमो भूतिदो भूमिनंदनः ॥

अंगारको यमश्चैव सर्वरोगापहारकः ।
वृष्टेःकर्ताऽपहर्ता च सर्वकाम फलप्रदः ।।
एतानि कुजनामानि नित्यं यः श्रद्धया पठेत ।
ऋणं न जायते तस्य धनं शीघ्रमवाप्नुयात् ।।
धरणी गर्भसंभूतं विद्युत्कान्ति समप्रभम् ।
कुमारं शक्तिहस्तं च मंगल प्रणमाम्यहम् ।।
स्तोत्रमंगारकस्यैतत् पठनीयं सदा नृभिः ।
न तेषां भौमजा पीडा स्वल्पाऽपि भवति क्वचित् ।।
अंगारक ॐ महाभाग ॐ भगवन् ॐ भक्तवत्सल ।
त्वां नमामि ममाशेषमृणमाशु विनाशय ।।
ऋणरोगादि दारिद्रयं ये चाऽन्ये ह्यपमृत्यवः ।
भय क्लेश मनस्तापा नश्यन्तु मम सर्वदा ।।
अतिवक्र ॐ दुराराध्य ॐ भोगमुक्तजितात्मनः ।
तुष्टो ददासि साम्राज्यं रुष्टो हरसि तत्क्षणात् ।।
विरिञ्चि-शक्र-विष्णूनां मनुष्याणां तु का कथा ।
तेन त्वं सर्वसत्त्वेन ग्रहराजो महाबलः ।।
पुत्रान् देहि धनं देहि त्वामस्मि शरणं गतः ।
ऋणदारिद्रयदुःखेन शत्रूणां च भयात्ततः ।।
एभिर्द्वादशभिः श्लोकैर्यः स्तौति च धरासुतम् ।
महतीं श्रियमाप्नोति ह्यपरो धनदो युवा ।।

Remedial Measure No. 12

Maṅgala yantra

Maṅgala yantra should be prepared in triangular shape having 21 small triangles as given in the design of *maṅgala yantra.* This *yantra* should be inscribed either over a sheet of gold or of copper in appropriate *muhūrta.* Position of Moon and the rising *nakṣatra* should be a favourable one on the basis of birth chart. We will not discuss here about the *muhūrta* as it is a different subject. It is always advisable to prepare the *yantra* in the bright lunar half of *Vaiśākha* or *Mārgśīrṣa māsa.* Favourable *nakṣatra, tārā, yoga* synchronizing with Tuesday will be the ideal period for the preparation of *maṅgala yantra*. After preparation of *yantra* in appropriate and favourable period, regular worship of so prepared *yantra* should be done every day for at least one year. The worship should be done with the help of red *candan*, red flower, *rolī*, kesar etc. *Prāṇa pratiṣṭhā* of the *yantra* is most essential which may be got done by any learned, experienced and expert *ācārya*. This *prāṇa pratiṣṭhā yantra* should be worshipped in the following manner. This is called *ṣoḍaśopacāra pūjana* of *maṅgala yantra*.

Saṅkalpa

देशकालौ स्मृत्वा मम जन्म राशेः सकाशान्नामराशेः सकाशाज्जन्मलग्नाद्वर्षलग्नाद्वा गोचराच्चतुर्थाष्टमादित्यद्य-निष्टस्थानस्थित भौम सर्वानिष्ट फल निवृत्तिपूर्वक तृतीयैकादश शुभस्थान स्थित वद्युत्तम फलप्राप्त्यर्थं आयुरारोग्यवृद्धयर्थमृणच्छेदार्थममुकरोग विनाशार्थवा पुत्र प्राप्त्यर्थं श्री मंगल देवता प्रसन्नतार्थें भौमव्रतं करिष्ये। तदंगत्वेन न्यास ध्यान पूजार्घ्यदानादिकं च करिष्ये।

Viniyoga

ॐ अस्य मंत्रस्य विरूपाक्ष ऋषिः गायत्री छंदः धरात्मजोभौमोदेवता हां बीजम् हं सः शक्तिः सर्वेष्ट सिद्धये जपे विनियोगः ।

Ṛṣyadinyāsa

ॐ विरूपाक्ष ऋषये नमः - शिरसि।
गायत्री छन्दसे नमः - मुखे।
धरात्मज भौम देवतायै नमः - नेत्रयोः।
हां बीजाय नमः - गुह्ये
हं सः शक्तये नमः - पादयोः
विनियोगाय नमः - सर्वांगे

Karanyāsa

ॐ ॐ भौमाय - अंगुष्ठाभ्यां नमः ।
ॐ हां भौमाय - तर्जनीभ्यां नमः ।
ॐ हं भौमाय - मध्यमाभ्यां नमः ।
ॐ सः भौमाय - अनामिकाभ्यां नमः ।
ॐ खं भौमाय - कनिष्ठिकाभ्यां नमः ।
ॐ खः भौमाय - करतलकरपृष्ठाभ्यां नमः ।

Hṛdayanyāsa

ॐ ॐ भौमाय - हृदयाय नमः ।
ॐ हां भौमाय - शिरसे स्वाहा ।
ॐ हं भौमाय - शिखायै वषट् ।
ॐ सः भौमाय - कवचाय हुम् ।
ॐ खं भौमाय - नेत्रत्रयाय वौषट् ।
ॐ खः भौमाय - अस्त्राय फट् ।

Sarvāṅganyāsa

ॐ मंगलाय नमः - अंध्रयोः।
ॐ भूमिपुत्राय नमः - जानुनो।
ॐ ऋणहर्त्रे नमः - ऊर्वोः।
ॐ धनप्रदाय नमः - कट्योः।
ॐ स्थिरासनाय नमः - गुह्ये
ॐ महाकायाय नमः - उरसि।
ॐ सर्वकर्मावरोधकाय नमः - वाम बाहौ।
ॐ लोहिताय नमः - दक्षिण बाहौ।
ॐ लोहिताक्षाय नमः - कंठे ह्यगलाह
ॐ सामगानां कृपाकराय नमः - मुखे।
ॐ धरात्मजाय नमः - नासिका।
ॐ कुजाय नमः - नेत्रयोः।
ॐ भौमाय नमः - ललाटे।
ॐ भूतिदाय नमः - भ्रुवो।

ॐ भूमिनंदनाय नमः - मस्तके।
ॐ अङ्गारकाय नमः - शिखायाम्।
ॐ यमाय नमः - सर्वांगे।
ॐ सर्वरोग प्रहारिणे नमः - मूर्द्धादिहस्तांतम्।
ॐ वृष्टिकर्त्रे नमः - मूर्द्धादिपादांतम्।
ॐ वृष्टिहर्त्रे नमः - चरणादिमस्तकांतम्।
ॐ सर्वरोगापहारकाय नमः - दश दिक्षु च।
ॐ आराय नमः - नाभौ।
ॐ वक्राय नमः - वक्षसि।
ॐ भूमिनंदनाय नमः - मूर्ध्नि।

After all kinds of *nyāsa* as mentioned above, one should do *dhyāna* as given below:-

Dhyāna

जपाभं शिवं स्वेदजं हस्तपद्मैर्गदा शूलशक्ती करे धारयंतम्।
अवंती समुत्थं समेषासनस्थं धरानन्दनं रक्त वस्त्रं समीडे।।

Thereafter the worship of *tāmra pātra* (copper pitcher), i.e., *kalaśa* should be done.

Pīṭha Pūjā, worship of *savartho bhadra chakra king bhadra maṇḍala* should be done after their preparation over the *pītha* a where all other powers and deities have been called and placed.

ॐ यं मण्डूकादि परतत्त्वांत पीठ देवताभ्यो नमः।

Thereafter, worship of nine *shakti's* should be done in the following order:-

ॐ वामायै नमः।
ॐ ज्यैष्ठायै नमः।
ॐ रौद्राय नमः।
ॐ काल्यै नमः।
ॐ कल विकरण्यै नमः।

ॐ बल विकरण्यै नमः।
ॐ बल प्रमथिन्यै नमः।
ॐ सर्वभूतदमन्यै नमः।

In the middle

ॐ मनोन्मयै नमः।

Get *maṅgala yantra* inscribed over a sheet of gold or copper whose *prāṇa-pratiṣṭhā* must be got done by any *paṇdit* or *ācārya* in the proper way. Thereafter, bathe or *snāna* the yantra with pure water and by *pañcāmṛta*, and thereafter, again with pure water. Afterwords offering of flowers should be done on all 21 triangle of the *maṅgala yantra* with the help of following mantras.

ॐ नमो भगवते सकलगुणात्मशक्ति युक्ताय भूमिपुत्राय योगपीठात्मने नमः।

After offering of flowers, concentrate on *maṅgala deva yantra* and invite him humbly with pleasant mood by reciting *maṅgala gāyatrī mantra.*

ॐ अंगारकाय विद्महे शक्तिहस्ताय धीमहि तन्नो भौमः प्रचोदयात्।

Thereafter, do *ṣoḍaśopacāra pūjana*, i.e., worship with flower, tilak, incense, sweets, fruits, bettle nuts etc. by using *maṅgala gāyatrī mantra* and by offering red flowers, red *candana*, red clothes etc.

Āvaraṇa pūja

After *āvaraṇa pūja*, do *ṣaḍaṅga pūjā* by extending rice grains in all directions.

ॐ ॐ भौमाय हृदयाय नमः ।
हृदय श्रीपादुकां पूजयामि तर्पयामि नमः।

ॐ हां भौमाय शिरसे स्वाहा ।
शिरः श्रीपादुकां पूजयामि तर्पयामि नमः।
ॐ हं भौमाय शिखायै वषट् ।
शिखा श्रीपादुकां पूजयामि तर्पयामि नमः।
ॐ सः भौमाय कवचाय हुम् ।
कवच श्रीपादुकां पूजयामि तर्पयामि नमः।
ॐ खं भौमाय नेत्रत्रयाय वौषट् ।
नेत्रत्रय श्रीपादुकां पूजयामि तर्पयामि नमः।
ॐ खः भौमाय अस्त्राय फट् ।
अस्त्र श्रीपादुकां पूजयामि तर्पयामि नमः।

Puṣpāñjali

ॐ अभीष्ट सिद्धिं मे देहि शरणागतवत्सलः ।
भक्त्या समर्पये तुभ्यं प्रथमावरणार्चनम्।।

Thereafter read all 21 names of Mars and put one flower every time over *maṅgala yantra* in various triangles one after another.

ॐ मंगलाय नमः।
मंगल श्रीपादुकां पूजयामि तर्पयामि नमः।
ॐ ॐ भूमिपुत्राय नमः।
भूमिपुत्र श्रीपादुकां पूजयामि तर्पयामि नमः।
ॐ ऋणहर्त्रे नमः।
ऋणहर्तृ श्रीपादुकां पूजयामि तर्पयामि नमः।
ॐ धनप्रदाय नमः।
धनप्रद श्रीपादुकां पूजयामि तर्पयामि नमः।
ॐ स्थिरासनाय नमः।
स्थिरासन श्रीपादुकां पूजयामि तर्पयामि नमः।
ॐ महाकायाय नमः।
महाकाय श्रीपादुकां पूजयामि तर्पयामि नमः।
ॐ सर्वकर्मावरोधकाय नमः।
सर्वकर्मविरोधक श्रीपादुकां पूजयामि तर्पयामि नमः।

ॐ लोहिताय नमः।
लोहित श्रीपादुकां पूजयामि तर्पयामि नमः।
ॐ लोहिताक्षाय नमः।
लोहिताक्ष श्रीपादुकां पूजयामि तर्पयामि नमः।
ॐ सामगानां कृपाकराय नमः।
सामगानां कृपाकर श्रीपादुकां पूजयामि तर्पयामि नमः।
ॐ धरात्मजाय नमः।
धरात्मज श्रीपादुकां पूजयामि तर्पयामि नमः।
ॐ कुजाय नमः।
कुज श्रीपादुकां पूजयामि तर्पयामि नमः।
ॐ भौमाय नमः।
भौम श्रीपादुकां पूजयामि तर्पयामि नमः।
ॐ भूतिदाय नमः।
भूतिद श्रीपादुकां पूजयामि तर्पयामि नमः।
ॐ भूमिनंदनाय नमः।
भूमिनंदन श्रीपादुकां पूजयामि तर्पयामि नमः।
ॐ अंगारकाय नमः।
अंगारक श्रीपादुकां पूजयामि तर्पयामि नमः।
ॐ यमाय नमः।
यम श्रीपादुकां पूजयामि तर्पयामि नमः।
ॐ सर्वरोग प्रहारिणे नमः।
सर्वरोग प्रहरी श्रीपादुकां पूजयामि तर्पयामि नमः।
ॐ सर्ववृष्टिकर्त्रे नमः।
सर्ववृष्टिकर्तृ श्रीपादुकां पूजयामि तर्पयामि नमः।
ॐ सर्वरोगापहारकाय नमः।
सर्वरोगपहारक श्रीपादुकां पूजयामि तर्पयामि नमः।

Puṣpāñjali

Aṣṭa Mātṛka Pujana

ॐ ब्राह्म्यै नमः ।
ब्राह्मी श्रीपादुकां पूजयामि तर्पयामि नमः।
ॐ माहेश्वर्यै नमः ।
माहेश्वरी श्रीपादुकां पूजयामि तर्पयामि नमः।
ॐ कौमार्यै नमः ।
कौमारी श्रीपादुकां पूजयामि तर्पयामि नमः।
ॐ वैष्णव्यै नमः ।
वैष्णवी श्रीपादुकां पूजयामि तर्पयामि नमः।
ॐ वाराह्यै नमः ।
वाराही श्रीपादुकां पूजयामि तर्पयामि नमः।
ॐ इन्द्राण्यै नमः ।
इन्द्राणी श्रीपादुकां पूजयामि तर्पयामि नमः।
ॐ चामुण्डायै नमः ।
चामुण्डा श्रीपादुकां पूजयामि
तर्पयामि नमः।
ॐ महालक्ष्म्यै नमः ।
महालक्ष्मी श्रीपादुकां पूजयामि तर्पयामि नमः।
ॐ ब्राह्म्यै नमः ।
ब्राह्मी श्रीपादुकां पूजयामि तर्पयामि नमः।

Puṣpāñjali

Daśa Digpāla Pūjana

ॐ लं इन्द्राय नमः । ॐ रं अग्नेय नमः ।
ॐ मं यमाय नमः । ॐ क्षं नैर्ऋत्ये नमः ।
ॐ वं वरूणाय नमः । ॐ यं वायवे नमः ।
ॐ कुं कुबेराय नमः । ॐ हं ईशानाय नमः ।
ॐ आं ब्रह्मणे नमः । ॐ ह्रीं अनंताय नमः ।

Puṣpāñjali

Indrādika Pujana

ॐ वं वज्राय नमः । ॐ शं शक्तये नमः ।
ॐ दं दण्डाय नमः । ॐ खं खंगाय नमः ।
ॐ पं पाशाय नमः । ॐ अं अंकुशाय नमः ।
ॐ गं गदायै नमः । ॐ त्रि त्रिशूलाय नमः ।
ॐ पं पद्‌माय नमः । ॐ चं चंक्राय नमः ।

Puṣpāñjali

Naivedya : After *āvaraṇa pūjā* offer sweets, gur, wheat etc.

Ācamana : thereafter offer water. Thus after doing *ṣoḍaśopacāra pūjana, arghya* that is offering of water to *Maṅgala Deva* should be done.

Arghya : Take water and put *rolī*, red flower, sugar, red sandal and money therein. This water over *maṅgala yantra* with absolute faith and devotion.

ॐ भूमिपुत्र महातेजः स्वेदोद्भव पिनाकिनः।
सुतार्थिनं प्रपन्नत्वां गृहाणार्घ्यं नमोस्तुते।।
रक्तप्रवाल संकाश जपाकुसुम सन्निभः।
महीसुत महाबाहो गृहाणार्घ्यं नमोस्तुते।।

After *arghya pradakṣiṇā*, i.e., *parikramā* of *maṅgala yantra* should be done and 21 names of Mars should be pronounced.

Draw three lines on the ground with the help of a piece of kher wood, thereafter rub these lines by speaking out the following mantras:-

दुःख दौर्भाग्य नाशाय पुत्रसंतान हेतवे।
कृतरेखात्रयं वाम पादेनैतत्प्रभार्जूम्यहम्।।
ऋण दुःख विनाशाय मनोऽभीष्टार्थ सिद्धये।
मर्जियाम्यसिता रेखांस्तिस्त्रो जन्मत्रयोद्भवाः।।

Puṣpāñjali

ॐ धरणीगर्भ संभूतं विद्युत्तेज समप्रभम्।
कुमारं शक्ति हस्तं च मंगलं प्रणमाम्यहम्।।
ऋणहर्त्रे नमस्तुभ्यं दुःखदारिद्र्य नाशिने।
नमामिद्योतमानाय सर्वकल्याण कारिणे।।
देवदानवगन्धर्वयक्ष राक्षस पन्नगाः।
सुखं यान्ति यतस्तस्मै नमो धरणि सूनवे।।
योवक्रमतिमापन्नो नृणां विघ्नं प्रयच्छति।
पूजितः सुखं सौभाग्यं तस्मैक्ष्मासूनवे नमः।।
प्रसादं कुरु मे नाथ मंगलप्रद मंगलः।
मेष वाहन रूद्रात्मन्पुत्रान्देहि धनं यशः।।

Thereafter *Brāhmaṇa bhojana* and appropriate *dakṣiṇā* to them is essential without which *anuṣṭhāna* will remain incomplete. If the whole process is done without the help of any *Paṇdit*, even then *dakṣiṇā*, i.e., some money should be given to a *Paṇdit*.

Puraścaraṇa

Worship of *maṅgala deva yantra* should be done likewise. Recite the Vedic mantra of Mars for 40,000 times. At many places where the adversity is so threatening that even the death may take place, the recitation of 6 lakh *mantra* of Mars has been advocated by few *ācārya* for a complete *puraṣcaraṇa*.

Remedial Measure No. 13

Name of Mars – By reading various names of Mars as listed below, adversities created by Mars gets nullified. If one is unable to read various *stotras*, *kavaca* and *mantras* of Mars, he or she can easily read various names of Mars to eliminate the adversities, problems, tensions, disaster, accidents, operation, death and widowhood etc. These names of Mars should be read correctly.

ॐ महीसुताय नमः	ॐ महाभागाय नमः
ॐ मंगलाय नमः	ॐ मंगलप्रदाय नमः
ॐ महावीराय नमः	ॐ महाशूराय नमः
ॐ महाबलपराक्रमाय नमः	ॐ महारौद्राय नमः
ॐ महाभद्राय नमः	ॐ माननीयाय नमः
ॐ दयाकराय नमः	ॐ मानदाय नमः
ॐ अपर्वणाय नमः	ॐ क्रूराय नमः
ॐ तापत्रयविवर्जिताय नमः	ॐ सुप्रतीपाय नमः
ॐ सुताम्रक्षाय नमः	ॐ सुब्रह्मण्याय नमः
ॐ सुखप्रदाय नमः	ॐ वक्रस्तंभादिगमनाय नमः
ॐ वरेण्याय नमः	ॐ वरदाय नमः
ॐ सुखिने नमः	ॐ वीरभद्राय नमः
ॐ विरूपाक्षाय नमः	ॐ विदूरस्थाय नमः
ॐ विभावसवे नमः	ॐ नक्षत्रचक्रसंचारिणे नमः
ॐ क्षत्रपाय नमः	ॐ क्षात्रवर्जिताय नमः
ॐ क्षयवृद्धिविनिर्मुक्ताय नमः	ॐ क्षमायुक्ताय नमः
ॐ विचक्षणाय नमः	ॐ अक्षीणफलदाय नमः
ॐ चतुर्वर्गफलप्रदाय नमः	ॐ वीतरागाय नमः
ॐ विज्वराय नमः	ॐ विश्वकारणाय नमः
ॐ नक्षत्रराशिसञ्चाराय नमः	ॐ नानाभयनिकृन्तनाय नमः
ॐ वन्दारुजनमान्दाराय नमः	ॐ वक्राकुञ्चितमूर्द्धजाय नमः
ॐ कामनीयाय नमः	ॐ दयासाराय नमः
ॐ कनत्कनकभूषणाय नमः	
ॐ भव्यफलदाय नमः	ॐ भक्ताभयवरप्रदाय नमः
ॐ शत्रुहन्त्रे नमः	ॐ शमोपेताय नमः
ॐ शरणागतपोषणाय नमः	ॐ साहसिने नमः
ॐ सद्गुणाध्यक्षाय नमः	ॐ साधवे नमः
ॐ समरदुर्जयाय नमः	ॐ दुष्टदूराय नमः
ॐ शिष्टपूज्याय नमः	ॐ सर्वकष्टनिवारकाय नमः
ॐ दुश्चेष्टावारकाय नमः	ॐ दुःखभञ्जनाय नमः

ॐ दुर्धराय नमः ॐ हरये नमः
ॐ दुःस्वप्नहंत्रे नमः ॐ दुर्धर्षाय नमः
ॐ दुष्टगर्वविमोचनाय नमः ॐ भरद्वाजकुलोद्भताय नमः
ॐ भूसुताय नमः ॐ भव्यभूषणाय नमः
ॐ रक्तांबराय नमः ॐ रक्तवपुषे नमः
ॐ भक्तपालनतत्पराय नमः ॐ चतुर्भुजाय नमः
ॐ गदाधारिणे नमः ॐ मेषवाहाय नमः
ॐ मिताशनाय नमः ॐ शक्तिशूलधराय नमः
ॐ शक्ताय नमः ॐ शस्त्रविद्याविशारदाय नमः
ॐ तार्किकाय नमः ॐ तामसाधाराय नमः
ॐ तपस्विने नमः ॐ ताम्रलोचनाय नमः
ॐ तप्तकाञ्चनसंकाशाय नमः ॐ रक्तकिञ्जल्कसन्निभाय नमः
ॐ गोत्राऽधिदेवाय नमः ॐ गोमध्यचराय नमः
ॐ गुणविभूषणाय नमः ॐ असृजे नमः
ॐ अंगारकाय नमः ॐ अवन्तीदेशाधीशाय नमः
ॐ जनार्दनाय नमः ॐ सूर्ययाम्यप्रदेशस्थाय नमः
ॐ थूने नमः ॐ याम्यहरिन्मुखाय नमः
ॐ त्रिकोणमण्डलगताय नमः ॐ त्रिदशाधिपसन्नुताय नमः

Remedial Measure No. 14

Candra Maṅgala Stotra– For prevention of *candra maṅgalī doṣa* this *candra maṅgala stotra* may be recited by the women who are *maṅgalī* as reckoned from Moon. This would eliminate the possibility of matrimonial disharmony and problems regarding children, prosperity, wealth etc.

चन्द्रः कर्कटकप्रभुः सितनिभश्चात्रेय गोत्रोद्भव
श्चाग्नेयश्चतुरस्र वारुणमुखश्चापोऽप्युमाधीश्चरः ।
षट् सप्तानि दशैक शोभनफल शौरिः प्रियोऽर्को गुरुः
स्वामी यामुनदेशजो हिमकरः कुर्यात् सदा मंगलम्।।

Remedial Measure No. 15

Bhauma maṅgala stotra: This *Bhauma stotra* should be recited by the women who are suffering from various problems of married life, ill health, lack of happiness and prosperity. Though various *maṅgala stotras* have been given which are very useful and tested by us and various *ācārya* of astrology. This is small *maṅgala stotra* of four lines which may be read or recited by those who can not read long *maṅgala stotra* in Sanskrit. This *stotra* is also very useful for the prevention of all problems caused by Mars due to its adverse placement in the birth chart in one or the other way.

भौममंगलस्तोत्रम्
भौमो दक्षिणादिक् त्रिकोण यमदिग् विघ्नेश्चरो रक्तभः
स्वामी वृश्चिक मेषयोः सुरगुरुश्चाऽर्कः शशी सौहृदः।
ज्ञोऽरिः षट्त्रिफलप्रदश्च वसुधा स्कन्दौ कमाद् देवते
भारद्वाजकुलोद्भवः क्षितिसुतः कुर्यात् सदा मंगलम्।।

Remedial Measure No. 16

Mantras – Prevention of Widowhood – This is very useful and effective mantra to prevent the loss of husband, even if the combinations of widowhood are present in the birth chart. We have given various *stotra* of Mars, *Kārttikeya, saubhāgyastotra śatanāma stotra, maṅgala kavaca, dhūmāvatī mahāvidyā, mātaṅgī mahāvidyā mantra,* and *yantra* etc., in this context. It is quite possible that all women may not be well conversant with the correct recital and accurate pronounciation of Sanskrit. They should recite 1, 3 or 5 *mālās* of following *mantra* every day.

1. ॐ ॐ ह्रीं ॐ क्रीं ह्रीं ॐ स्वाहा

2. *Ṛṣi-Bhṛgu*

Deity (Devatā) - Agni

इमां नारीरविधवाः सुपत्नीराञ्जनेन सर्पिषा संस्पृशन्ताम्
अनश्रवो अनमीवाः सुरत्ना आरोहन्तु जनयो योनिमग्रे ।
व्याकरोमि हविषाहमेतौ ब्रह्मणा व्यहं कल्पयामि।
स्वधां पितृभ्यो अजराँ कृणोमि दीर्घेणायुषा समिमान्त्सृजामि।।

Remedial Measure No. 17

Saubhāgyastotra śatānāma stotra – For *saubhāgya* of the women and for absolute prevention of widowhood. This is a well-known and popular *saubhāgyastotra śatanāma stotra.* A woman who recites it at least once every day can never suffer loss of her husband even if she has adverse combination in her chart as regards the life of her partner. This *stotra* has been tested number of times by innumerable women who were blessed with *akhaṇḍa saubhāgya.* We advise all women in whose horoscope 7th or 8th house is afflicted by the placement of malefics or by the relationship of these houses with trikas, Mars, Saturn or *Rāhu*, the reading of this *stotra* will certainly promote the quality and quantity of conjugal bliss.

निशम्यैतज्जामदग्न्यो माहात्म्यं सर्वतोऽधिकम् ।
स्तोत्रस्य भूयः पप्रच्छ दत्तात्रेयं गुरूत्तमम् ।।
भगवन्स्त्वन्मुखाम्भोजनिर्गतवाक्सुधारसम् ।
पिबतः श्रोत्रमुखतो वर्धतेऽनुक्षणं तृषा ।।
अष्टोत्तरशतं नाम्नां श्रीदेव्यो यत्प्रसादतः ।
काम सम्प्राप्तवांल्लोके सौभाग्यं सर्वमोहनम् ।।
सौभाग्यविद्यावर्णानामुद्धारो यत्र सः स्थितः ।
तत्समाचक्ष्व भगवन् कृपया मयि सेवके ।।
निशम्यैवं भार्गवोक्तिं दत्तात्रेयो दयानिधिः ।
प्रोवाच भार्गवं रामं मधुराक्षरतपूर्वकम् ।।

श्रृणु भार्गव यत्पृष्टं नाम्नामष्टोत्तरं शतम् ।
श्रीविद्यावर्ण रत्नानां निधानमिव संस्थितम् ।।
श्रीदेव्या बहुधा सन्ति नामानि श्रृणु भार्गव ।
सहस्त्रशतसख्यानि पुराणेष्वागमेषु च ।।
तेषु सारतरं ह्येतत् सौभाग्याष्टोत्तरात्मकम् ।
यदुवाच शिवः पूर्वे भवान्यै बहुधार्थिवः ।।
सौभाग्याष्टोत्तरशतनामस्तोत्रस्य भार्गव ।
ऋषिरुक्तः शिवश्छन्दोऽनुष्टुप् श्रीललिताम्बिका ।।
देवता विन्यसत् कूटत्रयेणावत्यं सर्वतः ।
ध्यात्वा सम्पूज्य मनसा स्तोत्रमेतदुदीरयेत् ।।

अथ नाममन्त्रः

ॐ कामेश्वरी कामशक्तिः कामसौभाग्यदायिनी ।
कामरूपा कामकला कामिनी कमलासना ।।
कमला कल्पनाहीना कमनीयकलावती ।
कमलाभारतीसेव्या कल्पिताशेषसंसृतिः ।।
अनुत्तरानघानन्ताद्भुतरूपानलोद्भवा ।
अतिलोकचरित्रातिसुन्दर्यातिशुभप्रदा ।।
अघहन्त्रयतिविस्तारार्चनतुष्ठामित्तप्रभा ।
एकरूपैकवीरैकनमचैकान्तार्चनप्रिया ।।
एकैकभावतृष्ठैकरसैकान्तजनप्रिया ।
एधमानप्रभावैतद्भक्तपातकनाशिनी ।।
एलामोदमुखैनोऽद्रिशक्रायुधसमस्थितिः ।
ईहाशून्येप्सितेशादिसेव्येशानवरानांगना ।।
ईश्वराज्ञापिकेकारभाव्येप्सितफलप्रदा ।
ईशानेतिहरेक्षेषदरूणाक्षीश्वरेश्वरी ।।
ललिता ललनारूपा लयहोना लसत्तनुः ।
लयसर्वा लयक्षोणिलयकर्त्री लयात्मिका ।।
लघिमा लघु मध्याढ्या ललमानालघुद्रुता ।
हयारूढाहतामित्रा हरकान्ता हरिस्तुता ।।

हयग्रीवेष्टदा हालाप्रिया हर्षसमुद्धता ।
हर्षणा हल्लकाभांगी हस्त्यन्तैश्वर्य—दायिनी ।।
हलहस्ताचिंतपदा हविर्दानप्रसादिनी ।
रामा रामार्चिता राज्ञी रम्या रमयी रतिः ।।
रक्षणी रमणी राका रमणीमण्डलप्रिया ।
रक्षिता खिललोकेशी रक्षोगणनिषूदिनी ।।
अन्तान्तकारिण्यम्भोजक्रियान्तकभयंकरी ।
अम्बरूपाम्बुजकराम्बुजजातवरप्रदा ।।
अन्तः पूजाक्रियान्तदः अन्तर्ध्यानवचोमयी ।
अन्तकारातिवामांकस्थितान्तस्सुखरूपिणी ।।
सर्वज्ञा सर्वगा सारा समा समसुखा सती ।
संतति सतता सोमा सर्वा सांख्या सनातनी ॐ ।।
एतत् ते कथित राम नाम्नामष्टोत्तर शतम् ।
अति गोप्यमिदं नाम्नां सर्वतः सारमुद्धतम् ।।
एतस्य सदृशं स्तोत्रं त्रिषु लोकेषु दुर्लभम् ।
अप्रकाश्यमभक्तानां पुरतो देवताद्विषाम् ।।
एतत् सदाशिवो नित्यं पठन्त्येन्ये हरादयः ।
एतत्प्रभावात् कदर्पस्त्रैलोक्यं जयति क्षणात् ।।
सौभाग्याष्टोत्तरशतनामस्तोत्रं मनोहरम् ।
यस्त्रिसंध्यं पठेन्नित्यं न तस्य भुवि दुर्लभम् ।।
श्री विद्योपासनवत्तामेतदावश्यकं मतम् ।
सकृदेतत् प्रपठतां नान्यत् कर्म विलुप्यते ।।
अपठित्वा स्तोत्रमिदं नित्यं नैमित्तिकै कृतम् ।
व्यर्थीभवति नग्नेन कृतं कर्म यथा तथा ।।
सहस्रनामपाठादौभक्तस्त्वेतदुदीरयेत् ।
सहस्रनामपाठस्य फलं शतगुणं भवेत् ।।
सहस्रधा पठित्वा तु वीक्षणान्नाशयेद्रिपून् ।
करवीररक्तपुष्पैर्हुत्वा लोकान् वशं नयेत् ।।
स्तम्भयेत् पीतकुसुमैर्नीलैरुच्चाटयेद् रिपून् ।
मरिचैर्विद्वेषणाय लवंगैर्व्याधिनाशने ।।

सुवासिनीर्ब्राह्मणान् वा भोजयेद्द यस्तु नामभिः ।
यश्च पुष्पैः फलैर्वापि पूजयेत् प्रतिनामभिः ।।
चक्रराजेऽथवान्यत्र स वसेच्छ्रीपुरे चिरम् ।
यः सदाऽऽवर्तयन्नास्ते नामाष्टशतमुत्तमम् ।।
तस्य श्री ललिता राज्ञी प्रसन्ना वाञ्छितप्रदा ।
एतत्ते कथितं राम श्रणु त्वं प्रकृतंब्रुवे ।।

Meaning :

Paraśurāma showed great interest and curiosity to know more and more about 108 names of *Śrī Devī*. He prayed *Ṛṣi Dattātreya* again and again to give more knowledge about *Saubhāgyastotra śatanāma*. Ultimately *ṛṣi* got pleased, accepted the requests of *Bhārgava Vaṁśīya Paraśurāma*, and replied very softly:

O *Paraśurāma*, The 108 names, about which you want to know are the precious gems and are saved secretly as a treasure. Although there are one lac names of the Goddess *Śrī Vidyā* expressed in different holy books like *Purāṇas* and *Āgamas* but 108 names are main. They were told by Lord *Śiva* to goddess *Pārvatī* on her repeated requests. *Śiva* is the *ṛṣī* and *Śrī Lalitāmbikā* is the God of this powerful *stotra anuṣtup* metre. It should be recited by the devotee in meditative state by heart and with total concentration towards Tripura *Sundarī Śrī Lalitā Devī*. Names are:-

Kāmeśvarī, Kāmaśakti, Kāmasaubhāgyadāyinī, Kāmarūpā, Kāmakalā, Kāminī, Kamalāsanā, Kamalā, Kalanāhinā, Kamanīyā, Kalāvatī, Padmajā, Bhāratī, Sevyā, Anuttarā, Anaghā, Anantā, Adbhutrūpā, Analodbhavā, Atilokacaritrā, Atisundarī, Atiśubh-apradā, Aghahantrī, Ativistarā, Arcanatuṣṭā, Amitaprabhā, Ekarūpā, Ekavīrā, Ekanathā, Ekāntā, Arcanapriyā, Ekaikabhāvatuṣṭā, Ekārasā, Ekāntajana-priyā, Aidhmanprabhā, Vaidhatabhaktapātakanāśhinī,

Elāmodmukhā, Enodrī, Śakāyudh-samasthiti, Ihāśuntā, Ipsitaiśādi-sevyā, Iśānvārāṅgaṇā, Iśvarā, āyāpika, Ikārbhāvyā, Ipsitfalpā, Iśhana, Hareśhaisāa, Aruṇākṣī, Iśwarā, Iśwarī, Lalitā, Lalanārūpā, Layahīnā, Lasattanu, Layasarvā, Layakṣorī, Layakartrī, Layātmikā, Laghimā, Laghumadhyā ādyā, Lalamānā, Layadrutā, Hayāruḍhā, Hatamitrā, Harkāntā, Haristutā, Hayagrāva, aṣhtada, Hālāpriyā, Harṣasamudbhavā, Harṣṇā, Hallakā-bhāngī, Hastantaiwaryadāyinī, Halhastarchitpadā, Havirdānaprasādinī, Rāmā, Rāmārcitā, Rajanī, Ramyā, Rati, Rakṣiṇī, Ramaṇī, Rākādityādiāmaṇdalapriyā, Rakṣitā, Akhilālokeśī, Rakṣogaṇaniśudinī, Antānta-kāriṇī, Ambhojakiyāntakabhayankarī, Ambarūpā, Ambujakarā, Ambujatvarpradā, Antaḥpujyā-Kiyāntantadā, Antardhyāna-vimocinī, Antkarātivāmankasthitā, Antahṣukhrupinī, Sarvamyā, Sarvagā, Sārā, Sama, Samasukhā, Satī, Santati, Santatā, Somā, Sarvā, Saṅkhyā, Sanātanī.

O *Paraśurāma* ! These are *aṣṭotatra śatanāma*. These are the gist of the secret names of *Devī*. Such a stotra is rarely found in *triloka*. It should not be expressed in front of those who don't have faith in Goddess. It is very powerful and effective *stotra*. *Kāmdeva* conquers *triloka* with the help of this *stotra*. The person who recites it in all three *sandhyās* regularly and with total concentration, nothing is impossible for him on this earth. All *Nitya* and *naimittika karmas* are ineffective without this *stotra*. If a devotee recites it one thousand times, he can destroy his enemies even by his vision. One can control a person by using red *karavīra* (*kanera*) flower in *yajña* alongwith recitation of this *stotra*, by using yellow ones can terrify his enemies, by using blue ones, can defeat his enemies, by using black pepper or red chillies, can kill his enemies and by using clove, can cure the diseases. If the recitation is done in form of *japa*, Goddess fulfils all his desires and nothing is impossible for him.

It has been experienced number of times that the female, who reads this *stotra* regularly, never suffers loss of husband during her life span. There is no possibility of her widowhood, even if so indicated in her birth chart.

Following *mantra* should also be recited by all women to eliminate the possibility of widowhood, especially by those who are not able to recite above stotra due to lack of Sanskrit knowledge.

ॐ ॐ ह्रीं ॐ क्रीं ह्रीं ॐ स्वाहा ।।

Remedial Measure No. 18

Brahma kṛta sarva maṅgala stotra – For prevention of *kuja doṣa* and happy and auspicious married life.

On completion of the above narration, by Lord *Nārāyaṇa*, sage *Nārada* asks him: "O Lord, you have narrated to me the method of performing the *vrata* with its effects and the wonderful *stotra* of *Durgā* (as recited by Lord *Brahmā* and known as *sarva maṅgala stotra*). Now I desire to listen the story of this auspicious *Gaurī Vrata* – who is the first noble soul to spread it to the mortal soul?"

ब्रह्माकृतं जयदुर्गास्तोत्रम् । ॐ नमो जयदुर्गायै ।
ब्रह्मोवाच दुर्गे शिवेऽभये माये नारायणि सनातनि ।
जये मे मंगल देहि नमस्ते सर्वमंगले ।।
दैत्यनाशार्थवचनो दकारः परिकीर्तितः ।
उकारो विघ्ननाशार्थवाचको वेदसम्मतः ।।
रेफो रोगघ्नवचनो गश्च पापघ्नवाचकः ।
भयशत्रुघ्नवचनश्चाकारः परिकीर्तितः ।।
स्मृत्युक्तिस्मरणाद् यस्य एते नश्यन्ति निश्चितम् ।
अतो दुर्गा हरेः शक्तिर्हरिणा परिकीर्तिता ।।

विपत्तिवाचको दुर्गश्चाकारो नाशवाचकः ।
दुर्गं नश्यति या नित्यं सा दुर्गा परिकीर्तिता ।।
दुर्गो दैत्येन्द्रवचनोऽप्याकारो नाशवाचकः ।
तं ननाश पुरा तेन बुधैर्दुर्गा प्रकीर्तिता ।।
शश्च कल्याणवचन इकारोत्कृष्टवाचकः ।
समूहवाचकश्चैव वाकारो दातृवाचकः ।।
श्रेयःसंघोत्कृष्टदात्री शिवा तेन प्रकीर्तिता ।
शिवराशिर्मूर्तिमती शिवा तेन प्रकीर्तिता ।।
शिवो हि मोक्षवचनश्चकारो दातृवाचकः ।
स्वयं निर्वाणदात्री या सा शिवा परिकीर्तिता ।।
अभयो भयनाशोक्तश्चाकारो दातृवाचकः ।
प्रददात्यभयं सद्यः साभया परिकीर्तिता ।।
राजश्रीवचनो माश्च याश्च प्रापणवाचकः ।
तां प्रापयति या सद्यः सा माया परिकीर्तिता ।।
माश्च मोक्षार्थवचनो याश्च प्रापणवाचकः ।
तं प्रापयति या नित्यं सा माया परिकीर्तिता ।।
नारायणार्धांगभूता तेन तुल्या च तेजसा ।
तदा तस्य शरीरस्था तेन नारायणी स्मृता ।।
निर्गुणस्य च नित्यस्य वाचकश्च सनातनः ।
सदा नित्या निर्गुणा या कीर्तिता सा सनातनी ।।
जयः कल्याणवचनो ह्याकारो दातृवाचकः ।
जयं ददाति या नित्यं सा जया परिकीर्तिता ।।
सर्वमंगलशब्दश्च सम्पूर्णैश्वर्यवाचकः ।
आकारो दातृवचनस्तद्दत्री सर्वमंगला ।।
नामाष्टकमिदं सारं नामार्थसहसंयुतम् ।
नारायणेन यद् दत्तं ब्रह्मणे नाभिपंकजे ।।
तस्मै दत्त्वा निद्रितश्च बभूव जगतां पतिः ।
मधुकैटभौ दुर्गान्तौ ब्रह्माणं हन्तुमुद्यतौ ।।
स्तोत्रेणानेन स ब्रह्मा स्तुतिं नत्वा चकार ह ।

Meaning : O mother *Durgā*, *Śivā* (the spouse of Lord *Śiva*), the fearless, the illusion, *Nārāyaṇī* (a part of *Nārāyaṇa*), *Sanātanī* (the Eternal, one who is beyond *Guṇas*), the success giver, grant me auspiciousness, the all auspicious mother, my obeisance to you. In *Durgā* – "Da" stands as an appellation for destroyer of demons; *U* stands as a synonym of destroyer of obstacles. The destroyer of diseases is implied by *Ra* while *Ga* denotes destroyer of sins. A·stands for destroyer of fear and foes (Thus she is the "destroyer" of all these evils). By mere recitation of name *Durgā*, demons are destroyed. She is said to be the energy of Lord *Viṣṇu*, as stated by Śrī Hari himself. The term "*Durgā*" – without a long vowel at the end denotes "danger" while *Ā* denotes destroyer (दुर्ग + आ = दुर्गा). Since she destroys dangers, she is known as *Durgā*. *Durgamāsura*, the kind of demons is also denoted by the term *Durgā* while Ā means destroyer. Hence she is known as *Durgā*, the destroyer of *Durgamāsura*. In the term *Śivā*, the character *śa* denotes auspiciousness, *i* denotes the best and *va* is for a giver. Thus *Durgā* is a heap of auspiciousness and a giver of the best of the articles. And that is why, she is known as *Śīvā*. The meaning of *abhayā* is destroying fear (i.e., fearlessness) and *Ā* means giver. Hence she is known as *Abhayā*. In the term *Māyā*, *Mā* denotes the kingdom and *Yā*, the obtainer of a kingdom. Again in *Māyā*, *Mā* denotes emancipation and *Yā* the obtainer. Thus *Māyā* means one who will obtain emancipation by worship of the mother. This goddess dwells in the body of Lord *Nārāyaṇa* and is akin to him in radiance, hence she is revered as *Nārāyaṇī*. *Sanātana* denotes one who is everlasting and beyond guṇas. *Jaya* means success. A denotes the giver. So she is known a *Jayā*, the success giver. *Sarva Maṅgalā* denotes wholesome wealth giver. So she is the giver of wholesome wealth or auspiciousness. These eight names of the Mother are full of quintessence and this *stotra* contains the meanings of such names. Lord *Nārāyaṇa* taught these to Lord *Brahmā* seated on a Lotus emanating from the navel of Lord *Viṣṇu*. After the discourse, Lord *Nārāyaṇa* went into sleep taking shelter in *yoganidrā* (Lord *Viṣṇu's* sleep at the end of a *yuga* ; Meditational sleep. Lord *Viṣṇu's* sleep personified and said to be a form of Goddess *Durgā*) when the two demons, *Madhu* and *Kaiṭabha*, struck the scene to extinguish Lord *Brahmā*. Then *Brahmā* praised Mother *Durgā* with these names.

Remedial Measure No. 19
For Happy and Early Marriage

Jānakī kṛta Pārvatī stotra – Many times, marriage of girls gets appreciably delayed or denied due to adverse placement of planets including Mars. Those girls would be married decently, happily and would enjoy high degree of conjugal bliss if they would read *Jānakī kṛta Pārvatī stotra*. This stotra has been written by *Mātā Jānakī* as a prayer of *Mātā Pārvatī*. They will be blessed with *akhaṇḍa saubhāgya* who will read it regularly. It is best to read the *stotra* during the *vrata* of *Mātā Gaurī* after performing proper *ṣoḍaśopacāra pūjana* of Gaurī.

शक्तिस्वरूपे सर्वेषां सर्वाधारे गुणाश्रये ।
सदा शंकरयुक्ते च पतिं देहि नमोऽस्तु ते ॥
सृष्टिस्थित्यन्तरूपेण सृष्टिस्थित्यन्तरूपिणि ।
सृष्टिस्थित्यन्तबीजानां बीजरूपे नमोऽस्तु ते ॥
हे गौरि पतिमर्मज्ञे पतिव्रतपरायणे ।
पतिव्रते पतिरते पतिं देहि नमोऽस्तु ते ॥

सर्वमंगलमांगल्ये सर्वमंगलसंयुक्ते ।
सर्वमंगलबीजे च नमस्ते सर्वमंगले ।।
सर्वप्रिये सर्वबीजे सर्वाशुभविनाशिनि ।
सर्वेशे सर्वजनके नमस्ते शंकरप्रिये ।।
परमात्मस्वरूपे च नित्यरूपे सनातनि ।
साकारे च निराकारे सर्वरूपे नमोऽस्तु ते ।।
क्षुतृष्णेच्छा दया श्रद्धा निद्रा तन्द्रा स्मृतिः क्षमा ।
एतास्तव कलाः सर्वा नारायणि नमोऽस्तु ते ।।
लज्जामेधातुष्टिपुष्टिशान्तिसम्पत्तिवृद्धयः ।
एतास्तव कलाः सर्वा सर्वरूपे नमोऽस्तु ते ।।
दृष्टादृष्टस्वरूपे च तयोर्बीजफलप्रदे ।
सर्वानिर्वचनीये च महामाये नमोऽस्तु ते ।।
शिवे शंकरसौभाग्ययुक्ते सौभाग्यदायिनि ।
हरिम् कान्तं च सौभाग्यं देहि देवि नमोऽस्तु ते ।।
स्तोत्रेणानेन याः स्तुत्वा समाप्तिदिवसे शिवाम् ।
नमन्ति परया भक्त्या ता लभन्ति हरिं पतिम् ।।
इह कान्तसुखं भुक्त्वा पतिं प्राप्य परात्परम् ।
दिव्यं स्यन्दनमारूह्य यान्त्यन्ते कृष्णसंनिधिम् ।।

Meaning: *Jānakī* said (addressing *Pārvatī*): "You are the form of *śakti*. You are the substratum of the entire Universe. You are the ocean of all virtues and are the enjoyer of happiness of perpetual association with Lord *Śiva*. Obeisance unto thee. Give me the best of the husbands. Creation, stability and destruction are your forms. You are the form of the seeds of creation, stability and destruction. Obeisance unto thee. You are the knower of the secrets of (the need of) a husband. O *Gaurī*, a devotee of husband, the affectionate to husband, give me husband. Obeisance to you ! You are the auspicious form of all auspiciousness. You are endowed with the wealth of all kinds of auspiciousness. You are dear to all, the form of seeds of all, the destroyer of all inauspiciousness, the ruler of all and the mother of all. O beloved of *Śaṅkara*, obeisance to you. O form of *Paramātmā*, the everlasting, *Sanātanī* (the Eternal, or beyond *Guṇas*) you are endowed with form and are also formless, the form of all, obeisance unto thee. Hunger, thirst, desire, kindness, sleep, indolence, memory and forgiving disposition – these are all your rays. O *Nārāyaṇī*, bashfulness, intelligence, happiness, energy, peace, wealth and increase – all these are also your rays. O the form of all, obeisance unto thee. Both Visible and Invisible are your forms. You are the giver of the seed and fruit to those visible and invisible. None can describe you. O great illusion, obeisance unto thee. O spouse of *Śiva* (or O giver of auspiciousness) you are endowed with the wealth of fortunes emanating from Lord *Śiva*. O *Devī*, only *Śrī* Hari is my most beloved, and only He is my fortune. Please give him unto me. Obeisance unto thee."

Those women who after performing *Gaurī vrata*, read this *stotra* of *Pārvatī* (as told by *Jānakī*) and bow before the Mother, will obtain one like Lord Hari as their husband. They will enjoy happiness with their husband in this world and after quitting this world, aboard the divine air-borne vehicle (*Puṣpaka Vimāna*) and reach the abode of Lord *Śrī Kṛṣṇa*.

This is the end of *Gaurī Vrata* as told by Lord *Nārāyaṇa*. The recitation of the praises showered by *Sītā* on *Pārvatī* as a concluding part of the Vow is thus essential. Every aspirant will recite it without fail in order that results in full are obtained without delay.

Remedial Measure No. 20

For Happy and Intact Marriage – *Rādhikā Śri kṛṣṇa stotra* – This is highly useful *stotra* for all aspects of married life. A girl who is unmarried even after following various rectificational measures, will definitely be blessed with decent husband and happy married life, should she read *Rādhikā Śrī Kṛṣṇa stotra* thrice every day. Divorce and miseries of married life can also be ruled out by regular use of this *stotra*. The importance of this stotra has been explained hereunder.

Sarasvatī, Lakṣmī, Gaṅgā, Durgā, Veda *Mātā Sāvitrī* (*Śruti prasūḥ* = the progenitor of the Vedas) have all attained admiration by offering prayers at your feet. Such feet, I adore my lord again and again. I bow down before that Lord even by mere touch of whose servants, i.e., devotees and penance the (already) sacred shrines become purified (or become more sacred)".

Whoever reads this *stotra* three times a day during three junctions, he becomes the servant of Lord Hari and attains the same good luck as *Rādhā* did.

If one who is in danger recites this story with full devotion, then one will immediately attain wealth (of happiness and lucre). One will recover even such articles that have been lost or stolen long ago. His kinsfolk will progress and he will obtain mental happiness.

If a worried person recites this (regularly), he will be relieved.

Differences with husband, progeny and friends will be resolved by reciting this *stotra* for a month and the Lord will appear before the devotee.

If an unmarried girl listens to this account (or she herself reads this account) for one full year, she will get a husband who is as charming and as virtuous as *Lord Kṛṣṇa*.

So concludes Lord *Nārāyaṇa* in his discourse to *Brahmarṣi Nārada.*

The aspirant, whether a female or a male, reading this part of *vrata*, as narrated by Lord *Nārāyaṇa* will have all these desires fulfilled including getting an auspicious marriage. There are other benefits of reciting this *stotra* addressed to Lord *Kṛṣṇa* as reflected in the above translation. This being one of the most important ancient vows, I have fully explained all the details not bothering for space.

गोलोकनाथगोपीश मदीशः प्राणवल्लभः ।
हे दीनबन्धो दीनेशो सर्वेश्वर नमोऽस्तु ते ।।
गोपेश गोसमूहेश यशोदानन्दवर्धनः ।
नन्दात्मज सदानन्द नित्यानन्द नमोऽस्तु ते ।।
शतमन्योर्मन्युभग्न ब्रह्मदर्पविनाशक ।
कालीयदमन प्राणनाथ कृष्ण नमोऽस्तु ते ।।
शिवानन्तेश ब्रह्मेश ब्राह्मणेश परात्परः ।
ब्रह्मस्वरूपाय ब्रह्मज्ञ ब्रह्मबीज नमोऽस्तु ते ।।
चराचरतरोबीजं गुणातीत गुणात्मक ।
गुणबीज गुणाधार गुणेश्वर नमोऽस्तु ते ।।
अणिमादिकसिद्धीश सिद्धेः सिद्धस्वरूपक ।
तपस्तपस्विस्तपासां बीजरूप नमोऽस्तु ते ।।
यदनिर्वचनीयं च वस्तु निर्वचनीयकं ।
तत्स्वरूपं तयोर्बीजं सर्वबीजं नमोऽस्तु ते ।।
अहं सरस्वती लक्ष्मीदुर्गा गंगा श्रुतिप्रसूः ।
यस्यपादार्चयान्नित्यं पूज्या तस्मै नमो नमः ।।
स्पर्शेन यस्य भृत्यानां ध्यानेन च दिवानिशम् ।
पवित्राणि च तीर्थाणि तस्मै भगवते नमः ।।
इत्येवमुक्त्वा सा देवीजले संन्यस्य विग्रहम् ।
मनः प्राणंश्च श्रीकृष्णे तस्थौ स्थाणुसमा सती ।।
राधाकृतं हरेः स्तोत्रं त्रिसंध्यं यः पठेन्नरः ।

हरिभक्तिं च दास्यं च लभेद्राधागतिं ध्रुवं ॥
विपत्तौ यः पठेद्भक्तस्य सद्यः सम्पत्तिमाप्नुयात् ।
चिरकालगतंद्रव्यं हृतं नष्टं च लभ्यते ॥
बन्धुवृद्धिर्भवेत्तस्य प्रसन्नं मानसं परम् ।
चिन्ताग्रस्तः पठेद्भक्त्या परां निवृत्तिमाप्नुयात् ॥
पतिभेधे पुत्रभेधे मित्रभेधे च संकटे ।
मासं भक्त्या यदि पठेद्सद्यः संदर्शनं लभते् ॥
भक्त्याकुमारी स्तोत्रं च श्रुणुयाद् यदि ।
श्रीकृष्णासदृशं कान्तं गुणवन्तं लभेद् ध्रुवम् ॥

Meaning : "O Lord of heavens, the lord of *Gopikā kanyās*, My lord, the Beloved of my life force, the kinsfolk of the poor, the lord of the poor, the lord of the cowherds, the lord of the herds of cows, the improver of *Yaśodā's* happiness, the progeny of Nanda, one who delights in the Good, one who is ever happy, my obeisance to you."

"O Govinda, the destroyer of the ire of Lord Indra, you have destroyed even the pride of lord *Brahmā*. O Slayer of *Kāliya* (the fierce seven hooded Cobra in *Yamunā*), the lord of my life, *Śrīkṛṣṇa*, my obeisance to you."

"You are the lord of *Śiva* and Ananta (the endless *Viṣṇu*) and also the lord of *Brahmā* and *Brāhmaṇas*. You are *Parātpara* – beyond even the age of *Brahmā* (which is said to be one thousand crores of human years), (or you are beyond the foreseeable future), you are *Brahmā*, the knower of *Brahmā* and the *bīja* of *Brahmā*. My obeisance unto thee."

"You are the seed of the movable and immovable universe. You are beyond *guṇas* (*sattva* etc.), you are synonym of *guṇas*, you are the seed of *guṇas*, you are the substratum of *guṇas*, and you are the lord of *guṇas*. My obeisance unto thee."

"My lord, you are the possessor of *aṇimā* and such other *siddhis* or attainments (which are eight in number, viz., *mahimā, garimā* etc.) and you are the attainment of even those (eight) attainments. O Sage ! you are yourself Penance. You are the seed of Penance. Whatever definable and indefinable articles exist, all this is your form. You are the seed of the said two, i.e., definable and indefinable. My lord having the form of the seed of all, obeisance unto thee."

Remedial Measure No. 21
Ekadanta śaraṇāgati stotra

For all kinds of conjugal happiness for proper and easy solution of matrimonial disharmony, and for other problems of life.

सदात्मरूपं सकलादिभूतसमायिनं सोऽहमचिन्त्यबोधम् ।
अनादिमध्यान्तविहीनमेकं तमेकदन्तं शरणं व्रजामः ।।
अनन्तचिद्रूपमयं गणेशमभेदभेदादिविहीनमाद्यम् ।
हृदि प्रकाशस्य धरं स्वधीस्थं तमेकदन्तं शरणंव्रजामः।।
समाधिसंस्थं हृदि योगिनां यं प्रकाशरूपेण विभातमेतम्।
सदा निरालम्बसमाधिगम्यं तमेकदन्तं शरणं व्रजामः।।
स्वबिम्बभावेन विलासयुक्तां प्रत्यक्षमायां विविधस्वरूपाम्।
स्ववीर्यकं तत्र ददाति यो वै तमेकदन्तं शरणं व्रजामः।।
त्वदीयवीर्येण समर्थभूतस्वमायया संरचितं च विश्वम् ।
तरीयकं ह्यात्मप्रतीतिसंज्ञं तमेकदन्तं शरणं व्रजामः ।।
त्वदीयसत्ताधरमेकदन्तं गुणेश्वरं यं गुणबोधितारम् ।
भजन्तमत्यन्तमजं त्रिसंस्थं तमेकदन्तं शरणं व्रजामः ।।
ततस्त्वया प्रेरितनादकेन सुषुप्तिसंज्ञं रचितं जगद् वै।
समानरूपं ह्युभयत्रसंस्थं तमेकदन्तं शरणं व्रजामः ।।
तदेव विश्वं कृपया प्रभूतं द्विभावमादौ तमसा विभान्तम्।
अनेकरूपं च तथैकभूतं तमेकदन्तं शरणं व्रजामः ।।
ततस्त्वया प्रेरितकेन सृष्टं बभूव सूक्ष्मं जगदेकसंस्थम्।

सुप्तात्विकं स्वप्नमनन्तमाद्यं तमेकदन्तं शरणं व्रजामः ।।
तदेव स्वप्नं तपसा गणेश सुसिद्धरूपं विविधम् बभूव।
सदैकरूपं कृपया च तेऽद्य तमेकदन्तं शरणं व्रजामः ।।
त्वदाज्ञया तेन त्वया हृदिस्थं तथा सुसृष्टं जगदंशरूपम्।
विभिन्नजाग्रन्मयमप्रमेयं तमेकदन्तं शरणं व्रजामः ।।
तदेव जाग्रद्रजसा विभातं विलोकितं त्वत्कृपया स्मृतेन।
बभूव भिन्नं च सदैकरूपं तमेकदन्तं शरणं व्रजामः ।।
सदैव सृष्टाप्रकृतिस्वभावात्तदन्तरे त्वं च विभासि नित्यम्।
धियः प्रदाता गणनाथ एकस्तमेकदन्तं शरणं व्रजामः ।।
त्वदाज्ञया भान्ति ग्रहश्च सर्वे प्रकाशरूपाणि—विभान्ति खे वै।
भ्रमन्ति नित्यंस्वविहारकार्यास्तमेकदन्तं शरणं व्रजामः ।।
त्वदाज्ञया सृष्टिकरो विधाता त्वदाज्ञया पालक एकविष्णु।
त्वदाज्ञया संहरको हरोऽपि तमेकदन्तं शरणं व्रजामः ।।
यदाज्ञया भूमिजलेऽत्र संस्थे यदाज्ञयापः प्रवहन्ति नद्यः।
स्वतीर्थसंस्थश्च कृतः समुद्रस्तमेकदन्तं शरणं व्रजामः ।।
यदाज्ञया देवगणा दिविस्थाददन्ति वै कर्मफलानि नित्यम्।
यदाज्ञया शैलगणाः स्थिरा वै तमेकदन्तं शरणं व्रजामः ।।
यदाज्ञया शेषधराधरो वै यदाज्ञया मोहप्रदश्च कामः ।
यदाज्ञया कालधरोऽर्यमा च तमेकदन्तं शरणं व्रजामः ।।
यदाज्ञया वाति विभाति वायुर्यदाज्ञयाग्निर्जठरादिसंस्थः ।
यदाज्ञया सचराचरं च तमेकदन्तं शरणं व्रजामः ।।
यदन्तरे संस्थितमेकदन्तस्तदाज्ञया सर्वमिदं विभाति ।
अनन्तरूपं हृदि बोधकं यस्तमेकदन्तं शरणं व्रजामः ।।
सुयोगिनो योगबलेन साध्यं प्रकुर्वते कः स्तवनेन स्तौति।
अतः प्रणामेन सुसिद्धिदोऽस्तु तमेकदन्तं शरणं व्रजामः ।।
।। इति श्री मुद्गलपुराणे एकदन्तशरणागति स्तोत्रम् संपूर्णम् ।।

Translation : The sages addressing Lord *Gaṇeśa* (the Single Tusked Deity) praise him thus:

"We seek shelter in Lord *Gaṇeśa* who possesses a virtuous nature, who is the source of beginning of everything, who is bereft of illusion, who is indicative of the inconceivable thought of, I am that Supreme Being, who is bereft of beginning, middle and end, and who is the symbol of Oneness."

"We seek shelter in Lord *Gaṇeśa* who is the endless Soul, who is the lord of *gaṇas* (groups of gods' armies), who is bereft of "non-difference" and difference, who is the beginning, one whose heart is endowed with the brilliance of wisdom and who is surrounded by intellect (posited in his intelligence).

"We seek shelter in Lord *Gaṇeśa* who is in *samādhi* (Yogic meditation), who shines in the hearts of *yogis*, one who can be experienced through meditation."

"We seek shelter in Lord *Gaṇeśa* who is sportive with the reflections of his own form, whose illusion can be directly seen, who has many forms and who gives his own strength (to the seekers)."

"This entire Universe is created through the power of your illusion. You are beyond the three stages of awakening, dreaming and sleeping. You are the reflection of *Paramātmā*. We seek shelter in you, O Lord *Gaṇeśa*."

"You are the ruler, O single tusked God, you are the lord of *guṇas* (qualities), you are the preceptor of these *guṇas*, and you endlessly sing the praise of that unborn *Paramātamā*, you are in all the three (viz., three worlds, three qualities and three stages). We seek shelter in you, O Lord *Gaṇeśa*."

"The world known as *Suṣupti* (complete unconsciousness) is created by your own initiation (lit. sounding call). In both the (other) stages, you are endowed with an equal form. We seek shelter in you. Lord *Gaṇeśa*."

"That world of unconsciousness was in the remote past enveloped in darkness. With your mercy, it unfolded in two forms. With all its many forms, it is one. We seek shelter in you Lord *Gaṇeśa.*"

"Only with your initiative, this minute world is created which has taken shelter in you. We seek shelter in you, Lord *Gaṇeśa,* who is virtuous, full of dreams and bereft of end or beginning."

"That minute world is dream which because of your penance turned all perfect and numerous. Because of your mercy, the world is endowed with one form. We seek shelter in you lord *Gaṇeśa.*"

"Upon your orders, that dream which was radiant in your heart has been turned into the excellent creation of this minute world which is marked by numerous awakenings. We seek shelter in you Lord *Gaṇeśa,* who has unbounded energy."

"That awakening world has become evident with the quality of passion (or desire) and is seen by your mercy. Though you have one form, you appear in several forms. O Lord *Gaṇeśa,* we seek shelter in you."

"With an innate nature (for creation), you have created this world and radiantly occupy it. Only Lord *Gaṇeśa* is the giver of intelligence. We seek shelter in you Lord *Gaṇeśa.*"

"Only with your orders, all the planets and brilliant stars shine in the firmaments. Only upon your orders these planets and stars carry out their duties of moving in the skies. We seek shelter in you Lord *Gaṇeśa.*"

"Only upon your orders, Lord *Brahmā* has created this Universe. Only upon your orders, *Viṣṇu* who is second to none administers the Universe and upon your orders, Lord *Śiva* destroys it. We seek shelter in you, O Lord *Gaṇeśa.*"

"We seek shelter in such lord *Gaṇeśa* with whose orders only, earth and water came to exist, on whose orders the rivers flow with water and on whose orders the oceans exist with the boundaries of water."

"We seek shelter in such Lord *Gaṇeśa* upon whose command Gods bestow effects of *Karma* (on the earthly beings), and on whose orders mountains remain still."

"We seek shelter in such Lord *Gaṇeśa* upon whose orders the *Śeṣanāga* (the divine Cobra) carries the earth on its hood, upon whose orders Manmatha (the God of love) instills passion and upon whose orders the Sun God adores the wheel of Time (which is said to be *kālapuruṣa* leading every phase of earthly developments)."

"We seek shelter in such Lord *Gaṇeśa* upon whose orders, the Wind God blows wind, upon whose orders the fire God dwells in abdomens (creating hunger which keeps the world active) and upon whose orders, this entire movable and immovable universe keeps on moving."

"Lord *Gaṇeśa* dwells in the hearts of one and all. Only with his orders, this entire Universe bristles with brilliance. His form is endless. Remaining in everyone's hearts, he creates awareness. We seek shelter in such Lord *Gaṇeśa*."

"Excellent of the saints attain him with the power of their meditation. Who can (sufficiently) sing his praise? Yet, merely by our offering obeisance, he grants us excellent achievements. We seek shelter in such Lord *Gaṇeśa*."

Thus ends the *stotra* of shelter in Lord *Gaṇeśa* in the *Mudgala Purāṇa*.

Remedial Measure No. 22

Bhagavatī Mātaṅgī

Mātaṅgī is the name of the daughter of *Mātaṅga Muni*. *Mātaṅgī stotra* and worship of *Mātaṅgī Devī* is most useful for the blessings of *Mātā Sarasvatī* and to be well versed in music. *Mātaṅgī stotra* is very powerful and most effective in giving all kinds of conjugal bliss, marital happiness, *akhaṇḍa saubhāgya*, desired husband, early marriage and prevention of all kinds of problems, adversities, obstacles and negative effect of various planetary configuration. Women who want to lead happy, prosperous and everlasting conjugal life, must read *Mātaṅgī stotra* regularly. *Mantra* and *stotra* of *Mātaṅgī Devī* enhances the countenance and physical appearance and beauty of females.

Mātaṅgī Dhyāna

श्यामांगीं शशिशेखरान्त्रिनयनां रत्नसिंहासनस्थिताम् ।
वेदैर्ब्बाहुदण्डैरसि खेटकं पाशांकुशधराम ।।

Mātaṅgī Yantra

Prepare the *Mātaṅgī yantra* as given below. The *yantra* should be worshipped properly in 16 phases with the help of fresh flowers and other things which are used in *ṣoḍaśopacāra pūjana*. Thereafter, recite *Mātaṅgī mantra* as given below for 108 times.

Mātaṅgī Mantra

ॐ ह्रीं क्लीं हूं मातंग्यै फट स्वाहा ।।

Procedure (*Viniyoga*)

अस्य श्रीमातंगीमन्त्रस्य दक्षिणामूर्तिऋषिः विराट् छन्दः श्रीमातंगोदेवता ह्रीं बीजं हूं
शक्तिः क्लीं कीलकं मम सर्ववांछितार्थसिद्धये जपे विनियोगः ।

Ṛṣyādinyās

दक्षिणामूर्तिऋषये नमः ह्यशिरसिह विराट्छन्दसे नमः ह्यमुखेह श्रीमातंगी देवतायै नमः ह्यहृदयेह ह्रीं बीजाय नमः ह्यगुह्येह हूं शक्तये नमः ह्यपादयोःह क्लीं कीलकाय नमः ह्यनाभौह विनियोगाय नमः ह्यसर्वांगेह ।

Karahṛdayādinyāsa

ह्रीं क्लीं हूं ह्रीं क्लीं हूं ।

श्यामां शुभ्रांशुभालां त्रिकमलनयनां रत्नसिंहासनस्थां
भक्ताभीष्टप्रदात्रीं सुरनिकरकरासेव्यकञ्जाङ्घ्रियुग्माम् ।
नीलाम्भोजांशुकान्ति निशिचरनिकरारण्यदावाग्निरूपां पाशं
खड्गं चतुर्भिर्वरकमलकरैः खेटकञ्चांकुशञ्च ।।
मातंगीमावहन्तीमभिमत भयदां मोदिनीं चिन्तयामि ।।

There is also another, meditational verse

श्यामांगीं शशिशेखरां त्रिनयनां सद्रत्नसिंहासने संस्थां
रत्नविचित्रभूषणयुतां संक्षीणमध्यस्थलाम् ।
आपीनस्तनमण्डलां स्मितमुखीं वन्दे दधानां क्रमाद्
वेदैर्बाहुभिरङ्कुशासिलतिके पाशं तथा खेटकम् ।।

Mānasopacāra Pūjana

ॐ ह्रीं क्लीं हूं मातंग्यै फट् स्वाहा ।

Mātaṅgī Stotra

आराध्य मातश्चरणाम्बुजे ते ब्रह्मादयो विस्तृत कीर्तिमापुः।
अन्ये परं वा विभवं मुनीन्द्राः परां श्रियं भक्तिपरेण चान्ये।1।
नमामि देवीं नवचन्द्रमौलेर्मातंगिनीं चन्द्रकलावतंसाम् ।
आम्नायप्राप्तिप्रतिपादितार्थंप्रबोधयन्तीं प्रियमादरेण ।2।
विनम्रदेवस्थिरमौलिरत्नैर्विराजितं ते चरणारविन्दम् ।
अकृत्रिमाणां वचसां विशुक्लं पदात्पदं शिक्षितनूपुराभ्याम्।3।
कृतार्थयन्तीं पदवीं पदाभ्यामास्फालयन्तीं कलवल्लकीं ताम् ।
मातांगिनी सद्हृदयां धिनोमि लीलांशुकां शुद्धनितम्बबिम्बाम् ।4।
लीलादलेनार्पितकर्णभूषां माध्वीमदोद्घूर्णितनेत्रपद्माम ।

घनस्तनीं शम्भुवधूं नमामि तडिल्लताकान्तिमनर्घभूषाम्।5।
चिरेण लक्ष्यां नवलोमराज्यां स्मरामि भक्त्या जगतामधीशे।
वलित्रयाढ्यं तव मध्यबिम्बं नीलोत्पलांशुश्रियमावहन्तीम्।6।
कान्त्या कटाक्षैः कमलाकराणां कदम्बमालाञ्चितकेशपाशाम्।
मातंगकन्यां हृदि भावयामि ध्यायेयमारक्तकपोलबिम्बम्।7।
बिम्बाधरन्यस्तललामवश्यमालोललीलालकमायताक्षम् ।
मन्दस्मितं ते वदनं महेशि स्तुत्याऽनया शंकरधर्मपत्नीम् ।8।
मातंगिनी वागधिदेवतां तां स्तुवन्ति ये भक्तियुता मनुष्याः ।
परां श्रियं नित्यमुपाश्रयन्ति परत्र कैलासतले वसन्ति।9।

Remedial Measure No. 23

Dhūmāvatī Mantra, Dhyāna, Yantra, Sādhana

There are ten *mahāvidyā* on the name of ten most important deities to be worshiped for the accomplishment of various ambitions of life. Every deity of *mahāvidyā* has a vast field of its influence over the mankind. One should select the most appropriate and suitable deity for the particular purpose. These *mahāvidyās* are:-

1. *Kālī*
2. *Tārā*
3. *Bāla tripura sundarī*
4. *Bhūmeśvarī*
5. *Tripura bhairavī*
6. *Chinnmastā*
7. *Dhūmāvatī*
8. *Baglāmukhī*
9. *Mātaṅgī*
10. *Kamalā*

All auspicious and inauspicious works, activities and ambitions are covered by these 10 deities. Each deity has a specific role in and action over a few particular aspects. *Dhūmāvatī* is empowered to defeat or eliminate enemies, for prosperity and begetting children, *Bhagavatī Dhūmāvatī* prevents widowhood, that is the loss of husband most effectively.

Once *Pārvatījī* was very hungry. In spite of her repeated requests provide some edibles. *Bhagavān Śaṅkara* asked her to wait for a while. *Pārvatījī* could not bear the hunger any longer and losing all her patience engulfed *Bhagavān Śaṅkara*. Thus, she lost her husband and suffered the curse of widowhood. However, *Bhagavān Śaṅkara*, with the help of *yogamāyā* became alive again. But lot of smoke was coming out of the body of *Pārvatījī*. She prayed *Bhagavān Śaṅkara* to pardon her for this stupid act. *Bhagavān Śaṅkara* relented and said that she will be worshipped in this world as *Dhūmāvatī*. Those who will worship her with dedication and faith, will be blessed with victory over enemies, good children, wealth, prosperity and *saubhāgya*. This is the worship of *Mātā Pārvatī* personified as widow. Those who are likely to suffer such curse of widowhood in their lives, must worship *Dhūmāvatī Devī* so that they may never suffer loss of husband. This should be done in the following manner.

Dhūmāvatī Dhyāna

विवर्ण्णा चञ्चला दुष्टा दीर्ग्घा च मलिनाम्बरा ।
विमुक्तकुन्तला रूक्षा विधवा विरलद्विजा।।
काकध्वजरथारूढ़ा विलम्बितपयोधरा ।
शूप्प–हस्तातिरूक्षाक्षा धूपहस्ता वरान्विता ।।
प्रवृद्धघोणा तु भृशङ्कुटिला कुटिलेक्षणा ।
क्षुत्पिपासार्द्दिता नित्यम्भयदा कलहास्पदा ।।

Following *mantra* should be recited 108 times for *mantroddhāra.*

Dhūmāvatī's Mantra

धूं धूं धू मा व ती ठः ठः ।

Dhūmāvatī Yantra : *Dhūmāvatī yantra* should be prepared as given below with the help of sandal stick or pen by *aṣṭagana* over *bhojapatra* copper or gold plate. This *yantra* should be properly worshipped by *ṣoḍaśopacāra pūjana* and the concerning *mantra* should be recited as explained below.

Results of *Mantra* for *Dhūmāvatī*

धनहृष्टा धनपुष्टा दानाध्ययनकारिणी ।
धनरक्षा धनप्राणा धनानन्दकरी सदा ।।
शत्रुग्रीवाच्छिदाछाया शत्रुपद्धतिखण्डिनी ।
शत्रुप्राणहराहार्या शत्रून्मूलनकारिणी ।।
मदिरामोदयुक्तो वै देवीध्यानपरायणः ।
तस्य शत्रु क्षयं याति यदि शक्रसमोऽपि वै ।।

Viniyoga – अस्य श्रीधूमावती मन्त्रस्य स्कन्दऋषिः पङ्क्तिश्छन्दः श्रीधूमावतीदेवता धूं बीजं स्वाहा शक्तिः प्रणवः कीलकं मम शत्रुक्षयार्थे विनियोगः।
Ṛṣyādinyāsa – स्कन्दर्षये नमः शिरसि । पङ्क्तिच्छन्दसे नमः मुखे ।श्रीधूमावतीदेवतायै नमः हृदये। धूं बीजाय नमः गुह्ये। स्वाहा शक्तये नमः पादयोः। प्रणवकीलकाय नमः नाभौ । विनियोगः नमः सर्वांगे । कर हृदयादि न्यास

Dhyāna

श्यामांगीं रक्तनयनां श्यामवस्त्रोत्तरीयकम् ।
वामहस्ते शोधनं च दक्षहस्ते तु शूर्पकम् ।।
धृत्वा विकीर्णकेशां च धूलिधूसरविग्रहाम् ।

लम्बोष्ठीं शुभ्रदशनां लम्बमानां यशोधराम् ॥
संलग्नभ्रूयुगयुतां कटुदंष्टोष्ठवल्लभाम् ।
कृसरंतु कुलुत्थोत्थं भग्नभाण्डतले स्थितम् ॥
तिलपिष्टसमायुक्तं मुहुर्मुहुश्च भक्तितम् ।
महिषीश्रृंगताटंकी लम्बकर्णातिभीषणाम् ॥
भजे धूमावती देवीं शत्रुसंहारकारिणीम् ।
सर्वसिद्धिप्रदात्रीं च मातरं शोकहारिणीम् ॥

Dhūmāvatī Mālā Mantra

ॐ धूं धूमावति चतुर्दशभुवननिवासिनि सकलग्रहोच्चाटनि सकलशत्रुरक्तमांसभक्षिणि मम शरीररक्षिणि भूतप्रेत पिशाचब्रह्मराक्षसादि सकलग्रहसंहारिणि मम शरीर परमन्त्र परयन्त्र परतन्त्रनिवारिणि आत्ममन्त्रयन्त्रतन्त्र प्रकाशिनि मम शरीरे परकट्टु परवाटु परवेट्टु परजप परहोम परशून्य परवृष्टि परकौतुक परौषधादिच्छेदिनि चिट्टेरि काहेरि कन्नेरि पाट्टेरि शुनककाट्टेरि प्ररिटिकाट्टेरि दर्भकाट्टेरि पातालकाट्टेरि सकलजतिकाट्टेरि ग्रहच्छेदिनि मम नाभि कमलस्थान संचारग्रहसंहारिणि धूम्रलोचनि उग्ररूपिणि सकलविषच्छेदिनि सकलविषसंचयान् नाशय नाशय मारय मारय विषमज्वर तापज्वर शीतज्वर वातज्वर लूतज्वर पयत्यज्वर श्लेष्मज्वर मोहज्वर सान्निपातज्वर पातालकाट्टेरिज्वर प्रेतज्वर पिशाचज्वर कृत्रिमज्वर नानादोषज्वर सकलरोगनिवारिणि सकलग्रहच्छेदिनि शिरःशूलाक्षिशूल कुक्षिशूल कर्णशूल नाभिशूल कटिशूल पार्श्वशूल गण्डशूल गुल्मशूलांगशूल सकलशूलान् निर्धूमय सकालग्रहान् निवारय निवारय रां रां रां रां रां क्षां क्षां क्षां क्षां क्षां खैं खैं खैं खैं खैं धूं धूं धूं धूं धूं फ्रें फ्रें फ्रें फ्रें फ्रें धूं धूं धूं धूं धूं धूमावति मां रक्ष रक्ष शीघ्रं शीघ्रमागच्छागच्छ क्षिप्रमेवारोग्यं कुरू कुरू फट् धूं धूं धूमावति स्वाहा।

This *mantra* of *Dhūmāvatī* will give best results if it is done on lunar or solar eclipse, *akṣaya tritīyā* holy night. After recitation of *mantra* for 108 times on these auspicious *muhūrta* many adversities, evil spirits, ill, luck, ailments etc. can be removed.

वन्दे कालाभ्रनीलां विकलितवदनां काकनासां विकर्णां
सम्मार्जिन्युल्कशूर्पैर्युत मुसलकरां वक्रदन्तां विषास्याम्।
ज्येष्ठां निर्वाणवेषां भृकुटितनयनां मुक्तकेशामुदारां
पीनोत्तुङ्गाद्रितुङ्गस्तनभरनमितां निष्कृपां शत्रुहन्त्रीम् ।।

Remedial Measure No. 24

Pavamāna Sūkta : Remedy for marital disharmony, separation and other adversities of conjugal disorder.

There is difference between *stotra* and *sūkta*. *Stotra* is a prayer while *sūkta* is a verdict which gives more lasting and quick results. *Pavamāna sūkta* have been taken from *Atharva Veda* under *Paippalāda Saṁhitā*. These 21 *ślokas* are mentioned there as *pavamāna sūkta*, for elimination of all adversities of married life. The women who read it with firm faith get rid of all problems connected with their family and conjugal life. We had given *pavamāna sūkta* in our first book *Vaivāhika Vilamba ke Vividha Āyāma Evam Mantra* for the benefit of readers. I received hundreds of letters from women who followed this remedy for happiness of their family life and to overcome the differences with their husband owing to one or the other reason. These women obtained astonishing results after reciting *pavamāna sūkta* which is given below. Those women who are suffering or are likely to suffer from vagaries of married life, are advised to read this *stotra* atleast once every day in regular *pūjā*. However, we have never advised *pavamāna sūkta* to the women who are likely to suffer loss of their husband due to affliction of concerning planets and houses in their concerning birth charts. *Pavamāna sūkta* is best for preventing misunderstandings, difference of opinion, conjugal disharmony, mental or physical separation and divorce.

In order to stop/control the severe clashes and conjugal disputes in married life, *pavamāna sūkta* proves to be immensely powerful, energetic and effective. It has remarkable potence to show positive results. If the situations in marital relationships are uncontrollable and all efforts fail to show results, usage of ordinary mantras prove ineffective, this *sūkta* must be used. Positive results are bound to come.

This *sūkta* is written in *Paippalāda Saṁhitā* of the *Atharvaveda*. It contains twenty one *ślokas* in which Lord *Pavamāna* is worshipped because the whole universe, air, earth, water, heaven, days, night, all directions, Sun, Moon, planets, fire, altar, altarages, mountains, rivers, seas, oceans, clouds, past, future and even God *Prajāpati* are purified by him, hence devotee prays for his/her purification also.

Timing events are operated by *daśā bhukti* of planets. Any particular planet for a particular subject may be *māraka* if it is adversely placed in the birth chart. Therefore, propitiation of that planet is also essential which is out of the scope of this work. However, we are giving hereunder the *Vedic*, *paurāṇika* and *tāntrika maṇtra* of all nine planets, which should be recited by the native himself or by any learned and experienced *ācārya* or pandits. The *mantra* of all planets should be recited for specific number of times such as the Vedic *mantra* of Saturn and Mars are to be recited 23,000 and 10,000 times respectively. In *Kaliyuga* the number of recitals should be four times as ordained for best results.

सहस्राक्षं शतधारमृषिभिः पावनं कृतम् ।
तेन सहस्रधारेण पावमानः पुनातु माम् ।। 1
येन पूतमन्तरिक्षं यस्मिन्वायुरधिश्रितः ।
तेन सहस्रधारेण पवमानः पुनातु माम् ।। 2
येन पूते द्यावापृथिवी आपः पूत अथो स्वः ।
तेन सहस्रधारेण पवमानः पुनातु माम् ।। 3
येन पूते अहोरात्रे दिशः पूता उत येन प्रदिशः
तेन सहस्रधारेण पवमानः पुनातु माम् ।। 4
येन पूतौ सूर्याचन्द्रमासे नक्षत्राणि भूतकृतः सह येन पूताः
तेन सहस्रधारेण पवमानः पुनातु माम् ।। 5
येन पूता वेदिरग्नयः परिधयः सह येन पूताः ।
तेन सहस्रधारेण पवमानः पुनातु माम् ।। 6
येन पूतं बर्हिराज्यमथो हविर्येन पूतो ।
यज्ञो वषट्कारी हुताहुतिः ।
तेन सहस्रधारेण पवमानः पुनातु माम् ।। 7
येन पूतौ व्रीहियवौ याभ्यां यज्ञो अधिनिर्मितः ।
तेन सहस्रधारेण पवमानः पुनातु माम् ।। 8
येन पूता अस्वा गावो अथोपूता अजावयः ।
तेन सहस्रधारेण पवमानः पुनातु माम् ।। 9
येन पूता ऋचः सामानि यजुर्ब्राह्मणं सह येन पूतम्
तेन सहस्रधारेण पवमानः पुनातु माम् ।। 10
येन पूता अथर्वाङ्गिरसो देवताः सह येन पूताः ।
तेन सहस्रधारेण पवमानः पुनातु माम् ।। 11
येन पूता ऋतवो येनार्तवा येंयः संवत्सरो अधिनिमि तः ।
तेन सहस्रधारेण पवमानः पुनातु माम् ।। 12
येन पूता वनस्पतयो वानस्पत्या ओषधयो वीरुधः सह येन पूताः।
तेन सहस्रधारेण पवमानः पुनातु माम् ।। 13
येन पूता गन्धर्वाप्सरसः सर्पपुण्यजनाः सह येन पूताः।
तेन सहस्रधारेण पवमानः पुनातु माम् ।। 14
येन पूताः पर्वताः हिमवन्तो वैश्वानराः परिभुवः सह येन पूताः।

तेन सहस्रधारेण पवमानः पुनातु माम् ।। 15
येन पूता नद्यः सिन्धवः समुद्राः सह येन पूताः ।
तेन सहस्रधारेण पवमानः पुनातु माम् ।। 16
येन पूता विश्वेदेवाः परमेष्ठी प्रजापतिः ।
तेन सहस्रधारेण पवमानः पुनातु माम् ।। 17
येन पूतः प्रजापतिर्लोकं विश्वं भूतं स्वराजभार ।
तेन सहस्रधारेण पवमानः पुनातु माम् ।। 18
येन पूतः स्तनयित्नुरपामुत्सः प्रजापतिः ।
तेन सहस्रधारेण पवमानः पुनातु माम् ।। 19
येन पूतमृतं सत्यं तपो दीक्षां पूतयते ।
तेन सहस्रधारेण पवमानः पुनातु माम् ।। 20
येन पूतमिदं सर्वं यद्भूतं यच्च भाव्यम् ।
तेन सहस्रधारेण पवमानः पुनातु माम् ।। 21

Remedial Measure No. 25

Mantra of *Rāmāyaṇa :* The mentioned *śloka* is taken from a Hindu epic *Rāmacaritamānasa* written by *Tulasīdāsa.* This *śloka* is for those females who either can not or have some problem in reading the texts of Sanskrit or they can not determine themselves to follow all the instructions to do the *mantras* or *stotras.*

चन्द्रहास हर मम परितापं
रघुपति विरह अनल संजातं ।।
शीतल निशित बहसि बर धारा
कह सीता हर मम दुख भारा ।।

On any Sunday when *Puṣya nakṣatra* is ascendant, a gold sword of an inch long is made and *ṣoḍaśopacāra pūjana* of *Sītājī* is required to be done. The *mantra* should be recited 1000 times everyday, i.e., 10 *Mālās.* One has to blow from mouth over the sword of gold while reading or reciting the above *mantra.* This should be continued for 41 days and after completing it, woman should bath most comprehensively. Thereafter, she should wear new and beautiful clothes and she should decorate herself by *sindūr*, *bindī*, gold ornaments and other materials. She should adorn this sword around her neck by reciting the above *mantra* for 108 times. All women will be highly benefited with *akhaṇḍa saubhāgya* and all her desires will be fulfilled.

Remedial Measure No. 26

(Vedic *Puraṇa* and *Tāntrika Mantras* of all nine planets)

Mantra of Sun

1. ॐ घृणिः सूर्य आदित्योम् ।

Viniyoga – अस्य श्री सौरमन्त्रस्य देवभागऋषिः गायत्री छन्दः सूर्यो देवता तत्प्रसादसिद्धयर्थे जपे विनियोगः।

Ṛṣyādinyāsa – देवभाग ऋष्ये नमः शिरसि। गायत्री छन्दसे नमो मुखे। सूर्यदेवतायै नमो हृदये । विनियोगाय नमः सर्वांगे ।

Dhyāna - ध्यान धृतपद्मद्वयं भानुं तेजोमण्डलमध्यगाम्। सर्वाधिव्याधिशमनं छायाश्लिष्टतनुं भजे ।।

2. ॐ ह्रॉं ह्रीं ह्रौं सः सूर्याय नमः ।

7000 *mantras* should be done and *arghya* to Sun must be given with the help of red flowers, red sandal etc. everyday.

3. Vedic *Mantra* of Sun

Viniyoga – आकृष्णेनेत्यस्य हिरण्यस्तूपांगिरस ऋषिः त्रिष्टुपछन्दः सूयो–देवता सूर्यप्रीतये जपे विनियोगः ।

Maṇtra –ॐ ह्रॉं ह्रीं ह्रौं सः ॐ भूर्भुवः स्वः ॐ आकृष्णेन रजसा वर्तमानो निवेशयान्तमृतं मर्त्यञ्चा ।
हिरण्ययेन सविता रथेना देवो याति भुवनानि पश्यन् ।
ॐ स्वः भुवः भूः ॐ सः ह्रौं ह्रीं ह्रॉं ॐ सूर्याय नमः ।।

4. *Paurāṇika Mantra*

जपाकुसुमसंकाशं काश्यपेयं महाद्युतिम् ।
तमोऽरिं सर्वपापघ्नं प्रणतोऽस्मि दिवाकरम् ।।

Mantras of Moon

ॐ श्रॉं श्रीं श्रौं सः चन्द्रमसे नमः ।

11,000 *mantras* must be recited and *arghya* must be given with white sandal and white flower.

Viniyoga – इममित्यस्य देववात ऋषिः अत्यष्टिश्छन्दः चन्द्रो देवता चन्द्रप्रीतये जपे विनियोगः।

Mantra – ॐ श्रॉं श्रीं श्रौं सः भूर्भवः स्वः ॐ इमन्देवा असपत्न सुवध्वम्महते क्षत्राय महते ज्यैष्ठयाय महते जान्राज्यायेन्द्रस्येन्द्रियायाय । इममुष्य पुत्रममुष्यै पुत्रमस्यै विशऽएष वोमी राजा सोमोऽस्माकं ब्राह्मणानां राजा । ॐ स्वः भुवः भूः ॐ सः श्रौं श्रीं श्रॉं ॐ चन्द्रमसे नमः ।

Paurāṇika Mantra

दधिशङ्खतुषाराभं क्षीरोदार्णवसन्निभम् ।
नमामि शशिनं सोमं शम्भोर्मुकुटभूषणम् ।।

Maṇgala Mantra

ॐ क्रॉं क्रीं क्रौं सः भौमाय नमः ।

Mantra must be done 11,000 times and *pūjana* is to be done with red sandal and red flower.

Vedic *Mantra*

Viniyoga अग्निर्मूर्द्धेति मन्त्रस्य विरूपाक्ष ऋषिः गायत्री छन्दः भौमो देवता मंगलप्रीतये जपे विनियोगः ।

Mantra – ॐ क्रॉं क्रीं क्रौं सः ॐ भूर्भूवः स्वः ॐ अग्निर्मू

र्द्धा दिवः ककुत्पतिः पृथिव्याऽअयम् अपा रेता शिजिन्वति।
ॐ स्वः भुवः भूः ॐ सः क्रौं क्रीं क्रॉं ॐ भौमाय नमः।

Paurāṇika Mantra

धरणीगर्भसम्भूतं विद्युत्कान्तिसमप्रभम् ।
कुमारं शक्तिहस्तं च मंगलं प्रणमाम्यहम् ।।

Mantra of Mercury

ॐ ब्रॉं ब्रीं ब्रौं सः बुधाय नमः ।

Mantra must be recited 9000 times and *pūjana* is to be done with multi-coloured flowers.

Vedic *Mantra*

Viniyoga – उदबुध्यस्येति मन्त्रस्य परमेष्ठी ऋषिः त्रिष्टुप छन्दः बुधो देवता बुध प्रीत्यर्थे जपे विनियोगः।
Mantra – ॐ ब्रॉं ब्रीं ब्रौं सः भूर्भवः स्वः ॐ उदबुद्धयस्वाग्ने प्रतिजागृहि त्वमिष्टापूर्ते सह गवं सृजेथा मयञ्च ।
अस्मिन्त्सधस्थेऽअद्धयुत्तरस्मिन् विश्वेदेवा यजमानश्च सीदत
ॐ स्वः भुवः भूः ॐ सः ब्रौं ब्रीं ब्रॉं ॐ बुधाय नमः।

Paurāṇika Mantra

प्रियङ्गुलिकाश्यामं रूपेणाप्रतिमं बुधम् ।
सौम्यं सौम्यगुणोपेतं तं बुधं प्रणमाम्यहम् ।।

Mantra of Jupiter

ॐ ज्रॉं ज्रीं ज्रौं सः गुरवे नमः ।

This *mantra* is done 19,000 times alongwith the *pūjana* with *keśar*, sandal and yellow flower.

Vedic *Mantra*

Viniyoga – बृहस्पति इति मन्त्रस्य गृत्समद ऋषिः त्रिष्टुप छन्दः बृहस्पतिर्देवता बृहस्पतिप्रीतये जपे विनियोगः ।
Mantra – ॐ ज्रॉं ज्रीं ज्रौं सः ॐ भूर्भुवः स्वः ॐ

बृहस्पतेऽअतियदर्योऽअर्हाद्युमद्विभाति ऋतुमज्जनेषु।
यद्दीदयच्छवसऽऋतप्रजाततदस्मासु द्रविणं देहि चित्रम्।
ॐ स्वः भुवः भूः ॐ सः ज्रौं ज्रीं ज्रॉं ॐ बृहस्पतये नमः।

Paurāṇika Mantra

देवानाञ्च ऋषीणाञ्च गुरुं काञ्चनसन्निभम् ।
बुद्धिभूतं त्रिलोकेशं तं नमामि बृहस्पतिम् ।।

Mantra of Venus

ॐ द्रॉं द्रीं द्रौं सः शुक्राय नमः ।

Mantra must be recited 16000 times and *pūjana* must be done with white flower and white sandal.

Vedic *Mantra*

Viniyoga – अन्नात् परिस्रुत इति मन्त्रस्य अग्निसरस्वतीन्द्रा ऋषयोऽति जगती छन्दः शुक्रो देवता शुक्रप्रीतये जपे विनियोगः ।

Mantra – ॐ द्रॉं द्रीं द्रौं सः ॐ भूर्भुवः स्वः ॐ अन्नात् परिस्रुतो रसं ब्रह्मणा व्यपिवत् क्षत्रम्पयः सोमं प्रजापतिः। ऋतेन सत्यमिन्द्रियंविपान शुक्रमन्धसऽ इन्द्रस्येन्द्रियमिदम्पयोमृतम्मधु । ॐ स्वः भुवः भूः ॐ सः द्रौं द्रीं द्रॉं ॐ शुक्राय नमः ।

Paurāṇika Mantra

हिमकुन्दमृणालाभं दैत्यानां परमं गुरुम् ।
सर्वशास्त्रप्रवक्तारं भार्गवं प्रणामाम्यहम् ।।

Mantra of Saturn

1. ॐ प्रॉं प्रीं प्रौं सः शनये नमः ।
2. ॐ खॉं खीं खौं सः शनये नमः ।

Any one of the above *mantras* may be done 23,000 times alongwith the *pūjana* of Saturn with blue flowers and sandal but during *pūjana*, these must continuously be lighted with *dīpaka* filled with mustard oil.

Viniyoga – शन्नोदेवीरिति मन्त्रस्य दध्यङ्ङाथर्वण ऋषिः गायत्री छन्दः आपो देवता शनैश्चरप्रीतये जपे विनियोग।
Mantra – ॐ खाँ खीं खौं सः ॐ भूर्भुवः स्वः ॐ शन्नो देवीरभिष्टयऽ आपो भवन्तु पीतये । शं योरभिस्रवन्तु नः। ॐ स्वः भुवः भूः ॐ सः खौं खीं खाँ ॐ शनैश्चराय नमः।

Paurāṇika Mantra

ॐ नीलाञ्जनसमाभासं रविपुत्रं यमाग्रजम् ।
छायामार्तण्डसम्भूतं तं नमामि शनैश्चरम् ।।

Mantra of *Rāhu*

ॐ भ्राँ भ्रीं भ्रौं सः राहवे नमः ।

This *mantra* must be recited 18,000 times and in night *pūjana* of *Rāhu* dev must be done alongwith the blue coloured flower and sandal.

Vedic *Mantra*

Viniyoga – कयानश्चित्र इति मन्त्रस्य वामदेव ऋषिः गायत्री छन्दः राहुर्देवता राहुप्रीतये जपे विनियोगः ।
Mantra – ॐ भ्राँ भ्रीं भ्रौं सः ॐ भूर्भुवः स्वः ॐ कया नश्चित्र आभूवदूती सदावृधः सखा । कयाशचिष्ठयावृता। ॐ स्वः भुवः भूः ॐ सः भ्रौं भ्रीं भ्राँ ॐ राहवे नमः ।

Paurāṇika Mantra

ॐ अर्धकायं महावीर्य चन्द्रादित्यविमर्दनम् ।
सिंहिकागर्भसम्भूतं तं राहुं प्रणमाम्यहम् ।।

Mantra of *Ketu*

ॐ प्रॉं प्रीं प्रौं स्रः केतवे नमः ।

Mantra must be recited 17000 times and *pūjana* must be done with ash-coloured flower and sandal.

Vedic *Mantra*

Viniyoga – केतुं कृण्वन्निति मन्त्रस्य मधुच्छन्दा ऋषिः गायत्री छन्दः केतवो देवताः केतुप्रीतये जपे विनियोगः। *Maṇtra* – ॐ प्रॉं प्रीं प्रौं स्रः भूर्भुवः स्वः ॐ केतुं कृण्वन्नकेतवे पेशोमर्याऽअपेशसे । समुषद्भिरजायथाः। ॐ स्वः भुवः भूः ॐ स्रः प्रौं प्रीं प्रॉं ॐ केतवे नमः।

Paurāṇika Mantra

ॐ पलाशपुष्पसंकाशं तारकाग्रहमस्तकम् ।
रौद्रं रौद्रात्मकं घोरं तं केतुं प्रणमाम्यहम् ।।

PREVENTION FROM UNTIMELY AND UNNATURAL DEATH

The above remedial measures are concerned with prevention of widowhood, elimination of *kuja doṣa*, promotion of conjugal harmony and removal of the possibilities of separation, setbacks, suicide, suppression, accidents, death and for the neutralization of the negative planetary vibrations causing ailments like cancer, heart trouble, mental disorder, hemorrhage and nervous breakdown. Apart from these remedial measures, our sages have given us most powerful *mṛtyunjaya, mahā mṛtyunjaya, sanjīvanī mṛtyunjaya, laghu mṛtyunjaya* etc. for the cure, relief and prevention of such ailments and untimely deaths. That is a separate subject, which will be dealt some time in a separate cover. We are giving here *mantras* of *mahā mṛtyunjaya, pāśupatāstra* and *Indrākṣī stotra* here which have strength to cure the native and to protect him from unnatural, untimely and unexpected demise.

Remedial Measure No. 27

Mantra of *Mahā mṛtyunjaya : Mahā mṛtyunjaya, mṛtyunjaya sanjīvanī maṇtra, laghu mṛtyunjaya mantra, anuṣṭubha tryambaka mantra prayoga, Gāyatrī mantra garbhita tryambaka mantra, kṣatabhsara mṛtyunjaya mantra, mṛtyunjaya kavaca* and various types of *mṛtyunjaya mantra* for essential to be recited by *paṇdit* or *ācārya* or self as and when required. These are to be used alongwith the specific *mantra, stotra, sūkta* etc. for preventing widowhood which we have detailed in the beginning of the text. The book named *Mahāmṛtyunjaya* by Dr. Rudra Deva Tripathi is most authentic and authoritative in this regard.

Remedial Measure No. 28

Viṣṇu Sahasranāma : This is a very effective and quite useful *stotra* in which thousand different names of lord *Viṣṇu* are there. *Viṣṇu* is *pālanahāra*, i.e., the protector. Those who are suffering from incurable and complicated ailments, they should read *Viṣṇu sahasranāma.* Books of *Viṣṇu sahasranāma* are available everywhere for further details.

Remedial Measure No. 29

Pāśupatastra : Prevention from untimely death to be written.

Essential No. of Readings of *Pāśupatastra*

Mantra

ॐ अस्य पाशुपतास्त्रशान्तिस्तोत्रस्य भगवान् वेदव्यास ऋषिः अनुष्टुप् छन्दः श्रीसदाशिवपरमात्मा देवता सर्व विघ्नविनाशार्थे पाठे विनियोगः।

Viniyoga – ॐ नमो भगवते महापाशुपताय अतुलवीर्य पराक्रमाय त्रिपञ्चनयनाय नानारूपाय नानाप्रहरणोद्यताय सर्वांगरक्ताय भिन्नांजनचयप्रख्याय श्मशानवेतालप्रियाय सर्वविघ्ननिकृन्तनरताय सर्वसिद्धिप्रदाय भक्तानुकंपिनेऽसंख्यवक्त्रभुजपादाय तस्मिन् सिद्धाय वेतालवित्रासिने शाकिनीक्षोभजनकाय व्याधिनिग्रहकारिणे पापभंजनाय सूर्यसोमाग्निनेत्राय विष्णुकवचाय खड्गवज्रहस्ताय यमदंडवरुणपाशाय रुद्रशूलाय ज्वलज्जिह्वाय सर्वरोगविद्रावणाय ग्रहनिग्रहकारिणे दुष्टनाशक्षयकारिणे।

ॐ कृष्णपिंगलाय फट् । हुंकारास्त्राय फट् । वज्रहस्ताय फट्। शक्तये फट् । दंडाय फट् । यमाय फट्। खड्गाय फट्। नैर्ऋताय फट् । वरुणाय फट् । वज्राय फट् । पाशाय फट्। ध्वजाय फट् । अंकुशाय फट् । गदायै फट् । कुबेराय फट्। त्रिशूलाय फट्। मुद्गराय फट् । चक्राय फट् । पद्माय फट्। नागास्त्राय फट् । ईशानाय फट् । खेटकास्त्राय फट् । मुंडाय फट्। मुंडास्त्राय फट् । कंकालाख्याय फट् । पिच्छिकास्त्राय फट्। क्षुरिकास्त्राय फट् । ब्रह्मास्त्राय फट् । शक्त्यस्त्राय फट्। गणास्त्राय फट् । सिद्धास्त्राय फट्। पिलिपिच्छास्त्राय फट्। गन्धर्वास्त्राय फट् । पूर्वास्त्राय फट् । दक्षिणास्त्राय फट्। वामास्त्राय फट् । पश्चिमास्त्राय फट् । मंत्रास्त्राय फट् । शाकिन्यस्त्राय फट् । योगिन्यस्त्राय फट् । दंडास्त्राय फट्। महादंडास्त्राय फट् । नमोऽस्त्राय फट् । शिवास्त्राय फट्। ईशानास्त्राय फट् । पुरुषास्त्राय फट्। अघोरास्त्राय फट् । सद्योजातास्त्राय फट् । हृदयास्त्राय फट् । महास्त्राय फट् ।

गरुडास्त्राय फट् । राक्षसास्त्राय फट् ।
दानवास्त्राय फट्। नरसिंहास्त्राय फट्।
त्वष्ट्रस्त्राय फट् । सर्वासास्त्राय फट्।
नः फट् । वः फट् । पः फट् । फः फट् ।
भः फट्। श्रीः फट् । पैः फट् । भूः फट् ।
भुवः फट्। स्वः फट्। महः फट् । जनः फट् ।
तपः फट् । सत्यं फट् । सर्वलोक फट्।
सर्वपाताल फट् । सर्वतत्व फट् । सर्वप्राण फट्।
सर्वनाड़ी फट् । सर्वकारण फट्। सर्वदेव फट् ।
ह्रीं फट् । श्रीं फट्। हूं फट् ।
स्त्रुं फट् । स्वां फट्। लां फट् ।
वैराग्याय फट् । मायास्त्राय फट् ।
कामास्त्राय फट्। क्षेत्रपालास्त्राय फट्।
शॅंकारास्त्राय फट् । भास्करास्त्राय फट् ।
चन्द्रास्त्राय फट्। विघ्नेश्वरास्त्राय फट् ।
गोः गां फट् । स्त्रौं स्त्रौं फट् ।
ह्रीं ह्रौं फट् । भ्रामय भ्रामय फट् ।
सन्तापय सन्तापय फट् । छादय छादय फट् ।
उन्मूलय उन्मूलय फट्। त्रासय त्रासय फट् ।
संजीवय संजीवय फट् । विद्रावय विद्रावय फट्।
सर्वदुरितं नाशय नाशय फट् ।।

After reading these *mantras*, *daśāṁśa*, *havana*, *tarpaṇa*, *mārjana* should be done by following *mantras*:-

ॐ नमो भगवते महापाशुपताय नमः स्वाहा
ॐ कृष्णपिंगलाय फट् स्वाहा ।

Pāśupatāstra should be read 1100 times in very serious cases of ailments like cancer, AIDS, Hepatitis-B, brain tumor, Leukemia etc. However, *Pāśupatāstra* is quite effective even it is done 125 times. In the case of ordinary ailments like Tuberculosis, neurological problems, stomach trouble, arthritis and cervical spondylitis etc. *daśāṁśa, havana, tarpaṇa,* and *mārjana* are also essential for the best results. It is always advisable to recite the *mantra* of *Mahākālī* to enhance the results of *Pāśupatāstra.*

Remedial Measure No. 30

Mantra of *Mahākālī* : We are giving here under the *mantra* of *Mahākālī,* which has been strengthened to cure and prevent death like serious troubles and incurable ailments.

Mantra – क्रीं क्रीं क्रीं ॐ हूं हूं ह्रीं ह्रीं महाकाली क्रीं क्रीं क्रीं हूं हूं ह्रीं ह्रीं स्वाहा ।।

Remedial Measure No. 31

Indrākṣi ṣtotra (Prevents untimely widowhood and death) : This is a wonderful *stotra,* which is most effective and as good as *mahā mṛtyunjaya, sanjivanī mṛtyunjaya,* and *Pāśupatāstra* or even more potent than that. The *ṣoḍaśopacāra pūjana* is done of *Indrākṣi Devī* before reciting the *Indrākṣī stotra,* which is given below. This is rarely known *stotra* and not commonly used by the astrologers, *paṇdits,* and *ācāryas.* We have experienced the wonderful results of *Indrākṣī stotra* where other measures failed or were not much effective. It is always advisable to recite *Indrākṣī stotra* if the 5th house is under the influence of Venus either by occupation, ownership or by strong aspect. *Daśāṁsa, havana, tarpaṇa, mārjana* should essentially be done for best benefic results and for absolute recovery of the patient.

Indrākṣī Stotra comprises the sacred names of Goddess *Indrākṣī.* Lord Indra worshipped the goddess by these divine names. Whoever recites this *stotra* hundred times becomes free from diseases, and if he thousand times, all his wishes are fulfilled. Undoubtedly this is a powerful *stotra* expressed by Lord Indra.

इन्द्राक्षीं द्विभुजां देवीं पीतवस्त्र समन्विताम्।
वामहस्ते वज्रधरां दक्षिणे च वरप्रदाम्।।

इन्द्राक्षीं नाम सज्योतिनानारत्नविभूषिताम्।
प्रसन्न वदनाम्भोजामप्सरोगण सेविताम्।।

इन्द्र उवाच
इन्द्राक्षी नाम सा देवी देवतैः समुदाहृता।
गौरी शाकंभरी देवी दुर्गा नाम्नाति विश्रुता।।

कात्यायनी महादेवी चन्द्रघण्टा महातपा।
गायत्री सा च सावित्री ब्रह्माणी ब्रह्मवादिनी।।

नारायणी भद्रकाली रुद्राणी कृष्णपिंगला।
अग्निज्वाला रौद्रमुखी कालरात्रिस्तपस्विनी।।

मेघश्यामा सहस्राक्षी विष्णुमाया जलोदरी।
महोदरी मुक्तकेशी घोररूपा महाबला।।

अच्युता भद्रदा नन्दा रोगहन्त्री शिवप्रिया।
शिवदूती कराली च प्रत्यक्ष परमेश्वरी।।

महिषासुर हन्त्री च चामुण्डा सप्तमातरः।
इन्द्राणी चेन्द्ररूपा च रुद्रशक्तिः परायणा।।

शिवा च शिव रूपा च शिवशक्ति परायणा।
सदा सम्मोहिनी देवी सुन्दरी भुवनेश्वरी।।

आर्या दाक्षायणी चैव गिरिजा मेनकात्मजा।
वाराही नारसिंही च भीमा भैरवनादिनी।।

श्रुति स्मृतिर्धृतिर्मेधा विद्या लक्ष्मीः सरस्वती।
अनन्ता विजया पूर्णा मानस्तोकापराजिता।।

भवानी पार्वती दुर्गा हैमवत्यम्बिका शिवा।
शिवा भवानी रुद्राणी शंकरार्धशरीरिणी।।

मृत्युंजया महामाया सर्वरोग प्रणाशिनी।
ऐरावत गजारूढा भूषिता कंकणप्रभा।।

एतैर्नामपदैर्दिव्यैः स्तुता शक्रेण धीमता।
शतमावर्तते यस्तु मुच्यते व्याधि बन्धनात्।।

आवर्तयेत्सहस्रं यो लभते वांछितं फलम्।
इन्द्रेण कथितं स्तोत्रं सत्यमेव न संशयः।।

We have given several preventive and remedial measures regarding the rectification of marital disorders, unhappy married life, conjugal disasters, separation, suppression, suspicion, setbacks, widowhood, loss of wife, and sufferings of spouses by serious and incurable ailments. We would like to invite the attention of our readers towards effectiveness of these *mantras, stotras, sūktas* etc. We are research scholar of astrology and have come across the birth charts of more than a lakh of natives seriously and sincerely and have seriously and sincerely advised these measures as and when required. Most positive results have been experienced both by us and the devotees. Many families who were ruined due to marital mishaps, they have astonishingly regained their happiness, love and their sweet home by following suitable measures applicable to them. To select a suitable measure for a particular native also requires lot of knowledge and experience. It is beyond the scope of this book to discuss the selection of appropriate and suitable deity, concerning *mantra, stotra* etc. We are planning to discuss it quite exhaustively in a separate cover captioned as *Remedies for Marital Maladies.*

Remedial Measure No. 32

Vrata (Strong Remedial Measure) : *Vrata* is one of the most important, easier and common ways of rectification of various kinds of maladies. If a planet is adversely placed in a birth chart, the gems of the planet will enhance the adversity of that planet for example if Mars is placed in any of the sensitive houses giving rise to *kuja doṣa,* wearing of coral or moonga must not be advised as that will enhance the intensity of *kuja doṣa.* In such case, *vrata,* donation and prayer are the only ways to eliminate or curtail the adverse effects of the concerning planet.

Generally in our country, innumerable persons both male and female observe vrat but they don't know many important factors to be adopted during the observance of *vrata.* Here I will explain the method of observance of a *vrata* immaculately, so that one can get the best results of the *vrata* in form of accomplishment of ambitions.

The first and most important basis of *vrata* is faith. A *vrata* will be fruitless without faith and belief in its efficiency. The ordained *vrata* should be undertaken with full faith and belief that the God or Goddess so evoked would be pleased by ones reverence. *Vrata* is to dedicate your particular day to the deity. The day has to be passed with full sanctity and piousness and devotion to Almighty

God and Goddess along with sincerity, honesty and simplicity with faith, confidence and holiness in addition to absolute involvement in spiritual and religious thinking and devotion. Generally any kind of meal is avoided during *vrata*. In present era our sages allow us to partake of little and special food without any kind of salt, only once during the day so that the routine activities may not be disturbed and one may not experience physical weakness. The scanty food, i.e., *alpāhāra* is taken only to provide essential strength and energy to the body and not for taste. In almost all the *vrata* use of salt in the food has been prohibited because its usage determines the taste of food.

The norms of *vrata* should be followed prior to and during the *vrata*. It is essential that no extra meal be taken to hide over the difficult times during the *vrata*. Normal meals should be taken the previous evening and in case of married ladies as well as gentlemen, there should be a complete abstinence from sexual acts on the days preceding and following the vrat period. Otherwise the *vrata* will be blemished. The person observing the *vrata* should not even sit or lie on the bed during the *vrata*. Even the touch of others' clothes should be avoided.

One should purify oneself with a good cleansing bath and wear clean inner garments and apparels on the proposed day. The subject should face either north or east direction and undertake the oath of *vrata* or *saṅkalpa* according to following steps: -

1st Step: *Saṅkalpa* (Pledge):

Face North or East direction while holding water, rice, whole betel nut, money and flowers in hand.

2nd Step:

Identification of the person, place and time. The person should speak his own name followed by father or husband's name. Specify the date, day, *pakṣa*, month and *nakṣatra*. The person should also state the *gotra* and name of place.

3rd Step:

State the name of the *vrata* and the name of deity connected with the *vrata*. This should be followed by stating the special wish or objective.

It is important that the process of pledging is performed while undertaking any kind of *vrata*. This is called *saṅkalpa* in which one promises or pledges to observe *vrata* on any particular day.

During the *Vrata* following precautions are prescribed:

> क्रोधात् प्रमाद्दाल्लोभाद्द् वा व्रतभंगो भवेद्द् यदि ।
> दिनत्रयं न भुञ्जीत ......।।

In *Garuḍa Purāṇa*, it is stated that those who observe vrats, should always keep in mind that about the loss of temper, laziness, greediness and temptation etc., otherwise the *vrata* will be broken. In that case, one should not have meal for three consecutive days and start the *vrata* afresh.

The person should remain silent as much as possible, should not converse especially with an atheist, disbeliever, a critic of the *vrata*, a contemptuous person or with women who are menstruating. The person should avoid common gossip, anger, jealousy, hatred, etc. He should not lie at all during the *vrata*, prayers etc. otherwise the *vrata* will automatically be violated.

After *saṅkalpa* and other *pūjā* activities, one

should always touch the place on the ground, where one sat, with both hands and then with the forehead otherwise the major part of the effect of the worship and *vrata* will go to Indradeva.

If by any mischance, any of these rules is broken, the *vrata* can be started again by making due correction etc., by donating money, cloths, fruits, flowers, grains etc. (The original rule of correction has been prescribed as donation of a cow and gold).

अस्कृज्जलपानाच्च सकृत्ताम्बूल भक्षणात् ।
उपवासः प्रणश्येत दिवास्वापच्च मैथुनात् ।।

In *Viṣṇu Purāṇa*, it has been mentioned that one should not drink water again and again or sleep during day time or eat tobacco or betel during *vrata*. One should not also indulge in any kind of sexual act during *vrata*, otherwise the *vrata* will be broken.

Meals may not be taken altogether or may be taken once a day during *vrata* but only in company of one's same generation, or after setting apart meals for Brahmin. Sleeping is normally prohibited during *vrata*, eating of betel, nuts, chocolates, mouth freshners and any kind of tasty food even if does not contain salt or cereals is strictly prohibited. It is so because little food is taken to maintain routine strength for work. And as far as possible the person should pray the God or Goddess invoked and read good and purifying literature etc. one should meditate and think about God. *Vrata* may also get broken by repeatedly drinking water or juice etc.

It is very difficult for a normal working person to undergo a 24-hour *vrata* these days, so it may be substituted by *vrata* that is only up to the evening. Whatever be the case, it is necessary that the *vrata* is undergone and completed with full adherence to the rules and regulations, if at all undertaken.

Undertaking a *vrata* means that you are pledging to the God or Goddess that you would be concentrating or praying, thoughts would be virtuous, avoiding all sorts of indulgence, including food and water. It is dedication to the God or Goddess of your faith and belief with complete devotion.

Before breaking the *vrata* in the evening, one should sit on an *āsana* (mat) and concentrate on God or Goddess invoked and repeat one's wish and the fact that one observed *vrata* on such a date and for such a purpose and that now one is breaking the *vrata*. One should plead forgiveness for any mistakes that may have been committed during the *vrata*.

Vratas are of several kinds and all of them can not be discussed here, however, the brief explanation of the concept of *vrata* should clear the understanding of *vrata*. *Vrata* are very effective if undertaken properly and definitely prove fruitful. Besides, using them to pacify planets, please Gods and Goddesses and to attain a special desire, *vratas* are also very effective when used as preventive measures against evils and impending misfortunes etc.

Vrata should be observed by those persons who are truthful, honest, kind hearted, religious, wise and sincere.

For examples, it has been rightly said :

नास्ति स्त्रीणां पृथग्यज्ञो न व्रतं नाप्युपोषणम् ।
भर्तृशुश्रूषयैवैता लोकानिष्ठान् व्रजन्ति हि ।।

It means that a woman should serve her husband only. She should neither observe any *vrata* nor she should perform any worship without the consent of her husband. A woman can get heaven etc. only by serving her husband and remain loyal towards him. No worships, religious *yajna* or *vrata* is more important for woman than serving her husband.

Vrata should neither be started nor be closed within three days of the rise or combustion of Venus and Jupiter, for getting best and early results.

व्रतारम्भे मातृपूजां नान्दीश्राद्धं च कारयेत् ।

Before commencement of any *vrata*, worship of *Gaṅapati*, *Mātrikā* and *Pañcadevatā*, must be done and thereafter *Nāndī Śrāddha* should be performed. A small statue, in gold, of the deity for whom *vrata* is being undertaken, should be got made. Thereafter *śoḍaśopacāra pūjana* of the deity should be done.

भर्ता पुत्रः पुरोधाश्च भ्रातापत्नी सखापि च ।
यात्रायां धर्मकार्येषु कर्तव्या प्रतिहस्तकाः ।।

If one can not observe *vrata* due to some problem or obstruction or being on journey, one should get it done through his or her representative, husband, wife, elder son, Purohita, brother or friend. If none of these is available, *vrata* can be got done by Brahmins.

Our *ṛṣis* and sages had foreseen the mental status and intellectual inclination, education, dedication, discipline, faith, concentration, pronounciation and other aspects of the natives of *Kaliyuga*. They have prescribed very easy as well as very tough *mantra* and *stotra* etc., for different categories of the knowledge of the natives based on their knowledge, merits and abilities to read, recite and to perform the same. They have given a very easy and simple remedy, which can be obtained by sincere adherence *vrata*. But, however, *vrata* is commonly advised to them who have strong faith and will but they can not read text in Sanskrit.

Vrata can be kept even by those who have language problem or by those who are highly educated but due to difference in culture, their pronounciation in Sanskrit is incorrect. *Vrata* can also be kept by those who can read and recite *mantra* and *stotra* and they further want to get quick results and can also afford to keep *vrata* in addition to adhering to remedies arising from *mantras* and *stotra*. Selection of appropriate and suitable *vrata* is not a tough job. Mostly the *vrata* of Tuesdays is required by all *maṅgalī* women and men. In this *vrata* intake of salt is absolutely prohibited. Before proceeding further towards the details of specific *vratas*, we are giving few important and essential points which should be remembered and followed by all during keeping of *vrata* :-

1. There must be a feeling of true and absolute dedication towards the concerning deity, that is Almighty. The day of *vrata* is not just to keep fast or to eat nothing but is a day of living with pious minds and deeds. A day is dedicated to the deity. One surrenders himself and goes in the shelter of concerning power for his or her blessings for the accomplishment of ambitions. One should eat little so that routine may not be disturbed but the food should be pious, i.e., *sāttvika* and *sākṣma*.
2. Women are advised not to observe *vrata* during menstrual periods. Most important *vrata* of *Karavā Cautha* should also not be observed during the period of impurity. Sages have very strictly stressed this point. One should otherwise donate 380 cows with mounting of gold on their horns. If the *saṅkalpa* has been taken, *vrata* should be completed if menstrual periods begin

after *saṅkalpa* has been taken and the *mantra* of *prāyaścitta* should be done when the menstrual period is over.

3. If possible, cleaning of teeth with toothpaste made of chemicals is also not advisable.
4. One should not meet any woman who is having menstrual periods provided it is known.
5. One should not make a contact with any correct male or female if known.
6. One should utilize his time by reading books or magazines on auspicious subjects or by listening or doing bhajana etc. One should not read any murder or mystry novels, books, stories and one should also avoid such type of serial on television so that the purity of mind may not be disturbed even for a short period.
7. Evening meal as prescribed in various vratas should be taken with the person of equal status such as husband, wife, brother, sister, sister-in-law etc. but not with mother, father, son, daughter or parent-in-laws. complete meals like *parāṭhā, sabjī,* should be prepared. However, in the evening meals of *vratas* other than Tuesdays, only one cereal should be taken as food but there may be several vegetables.
8. In the *vrata* on Tuesday, one should take sweet food, fruits, milk etc. during 12 noon to 3 PM. *Cūrmā* is the best intake for the Tuesday.
9. The commencement and ending any *vrata* is the toughest task. No *vrata* should be started verbatim and it should not be closed without proper procedure. Otherwise, the subject will have to suffer by the curse of concerning deity. Any *vrata* should be commenced only after firm faith, appropriate advise of any competent and meritorious astrologer. The selection of suitable

vrata be done only by a good astrologer. Essentials as mentioned above should be followed during *vrata*. Generally, the *vrata* should be stopped only after the fulfilment of desires. However, the *vrata* can be closed due to any other reason, if it becomes essential. But *vrata* should never be stopped without proper procedure, which is called *udyāpana*. *Udyāpana* is to pray and thank at the feet of concerning deity for the fulfilment of ambitions and to beg excuse for shortcomings, errors, and faulty worship. This is done after comprehensive *ṣoḍaśopacāra pūjana* of the deity for which any standard book of *vrata* can be referred.

Udyāpana of *Vrata*

Udyāpana means to make prayers for accomplishment of ambitions and to be excuse for the mistakes, errors and shortcomings, defects which might have occurred during *vratas*, at the time of completion or the total duration of *vrata* as said in *Saṅkalpa*. *Udyāpana* is done when any particular *vrata* is to be closed, i.e., to be discontinued. Starting and closing of the *vrata* should be done after repeated thinking and after making a strong determination. If a *vrata* is started and that gets discontinued due to one or the other reason, that becomes fruitless until unless *udyāpana* is done. *Udyāpana* is a particular and specific process of worship of the concerning deity at the moment of completion of *vrata* as suggested by sages and saints in various tales such as *vratarka*.

Vrata is observed for fulfilment of any desire or will. *Udyāpana* is mostly done when the period of *saṅkalpa* is over. It is a process of worship in which we offer thanks to the deity for the blessing we receive and desire gets fulfiled as an outcome. One has to express his gratitude and obligation to the concerned deity. After *ṣoḍaśopacāra pūjana*, i.e., sixteen–fold worship one must beg excuse for any known or unknown shortcoming and faults, which might have occurred during the duration of *vrata*.

These are a few important 10 points to be seriously observed during *vrata*. We have discussed a lot about procedure about *vrata* in our forthcoming book *Mars : Marital Maladies and Remedies*.

Remedial Measure No. 33

Maṅgala Gaurī Vrata : This *vrata* is observed on all Tuesdays of *srāvaṇa māsa*. But strong *maṅgalī* girls should observe this *vrata* throughout their lives. *Vrata* of *maṅgala Gaurī* eliminates all kinds of possibilities of widowhood if there is any. A separate book of *maṅgala Gaurī vrata* should be consulted and followed as instructed.

Remedial Measure No. 34

Vaṭa Sāvitrī Pujā : This *vrata* is observed by almost all women of our country of India on *amāvāsyā*, i.e. on new Moon day of *jyeṣṭha māsa* every year. For details of this *vrata*, a separate book of this *vrata* should be consulted.

Remedial Measure No. 35

Sacred *Gaurī Vrata* : There is a very detailed account in our *Purāṇas* on this rare and most efficacious *vrata* or vow for *Gaurī Pārvatī*. One who reads or recites this story every day, for one year, will get worthy spouse. (By implication, this is meant for unmarried men also to be blessed with a timely marriage).

We are now giving in this *chapter* this story and the manner of undertaking this *vrata* (vow), in full containing *mantra, dhyāna* and *stotra* (the three essential limbs of a worship), as given above for *maṅgala Caṇḍikā stotra*, ignoring space restraints, in order that a wider section of deserving readers stands to benefit (even by merely reading it every day). Since a vow is not complete without an example, we are giving *Sītā's stotra* of *Durgā* as part of *Gaurī Vrata*, whereby *Sītā* acquired lord *Rāma* (*Viṣṇu*) as her beloved husband which is also a part of *Gaurī vrata* narrated by the *Purāṇas*. Thus, what is being given below is a complete account of the *Gaurī Vrata*.

Once sage *Nārada* asked lord *Nārāyaṇa* about the method of performing *Gaurī vrata* (the vow to propitiate *Devī Gaurī*), the articles to be given away in charity, the secrets revealed at the end and such other details.

Lord *Nārāyaṇa* narrates to *Nārada* as under:-

"The vow called *Gaurī vrata* is now being explained. Initially, women (of ancient times) had performed this *vrata* in the month of *Mārgaśīrṣa*. Men also will attain the four ends (viz. *dharma, artha, kāma* and *mokṣa*) apart from devotion to lord *Śrīkṛṣṇa* by performing this *vrata*. This is famous in various lands. It is deemed that this *vrata* has been in place since remote past by tradition. By this *vrata*, a woman obtains a highly affectionate husband. A girl, i.e., the aspirant should fast on the previous day, i.e., before commencement of the month concerned), wash off the clothes (to be used the next day) and lead a restrained life. On the next day, i.e., on the day the month of *Mārgaśīrṣa* commences, i.e., *śukla pakṣa*, padyami, or the first lunar day of the bright half of *Mārgaśīrṣa* month, with the Sun transiting in Scorpio), she should take bath in near by river and wear the previously washed robes. In a sacred pot, the six prescribed deities, viz., *Gaṇeśa*, *Sūrya*, Agni (fire), *Viṣṇu*, *Śiva* and *Durgā* should be invoked. These deities should be worshipped with various articles offering the five kinds of *upacāras* (oblations like clothes and ornaments). Before the *kalaśa* (sacred pot), a square *vedī*, i.e., square area of ground to serve for sacrificial altar, having receptacles for the sacrificial fire) should be prepared. Sandal, incense, *kasturī* (musk) and *kumkuma* (saffron) should be applied on the *vedī*. An idol of *Durgā* with ten arms should be got made of sand. A mark of saffron should be applied on the forehead of the idol, and an offer of camphor and sandal should also be made on the other parts of the body of the idol. (In genuinely difficult cases, as in these days, a normal picture of *Pārvatī* will be sufficient as an aid for unflinching concentration). The goddess should be invoked with prayers. Then the following *mantra* should be recited.

1. *Mantra*

हे गौरि शंकरार्धांगी यथा त्वं शंकरप्रिया, तथा मां कुरु कल्याणि कान्तकान्तां सुदुर्लभां ।

Meaning : "O goddess Gaurī, the half of lord *Śaṅkara*, just as you are the beloved of *Śaṅkara*, you the giver of auspiciousness, make me the beloved wife – such a wife that will not be so easily available for a charming man"

The idol of *Durgā* should be worshipped with the above cited *mantra*, after taking a *saṅkalpa* (or vow to complete the worship) alongwith the following *mūla mantra*, stipulated in *Sāma Veda*.

ॐ श्रीदुर्गायै सर्वविघ्नविनाशिन्यै नमः ।

Meaning : Om, obeisance to *Śrī Durgā*, the destroyer of all obstacles).

Reciting these *mantras*, the goddess should be prayed with the most secretive prayers enjoined in the *Sāmaveda* (being described below) which is not available even to the most excellent of sages. Men of attainment pray to *Durgā*, the destroyer of evil manifestations, on these lines.

2. *Dhyāna*

Goddess *Durgā*, *Śivā* (the auspicious one), *Śiva Priyā* (the beloved of lord *Śiva*), *Śaivī* (one who has the closest alliance with lord *Śiva*) and the adorer of the chest region (abode of love) of lord *Śiva*. On her glittering face, smiles are wide spread. She has a great fame. Her eyes are charming. She is rich with fresh and everlasting (undecaying) youth. She wears ornaments studded by jewels. Her arms are decorated with bejewelled bracelets and bangles. Her feet adore jewel studded anklets. Her ear ornaments increase the beauty of her cheeks. On her forehead, marks of musk and saffron appear. Her robes are purified with flames of fire. She adores on her head a jewel rich diadem. Garlands made of the most excellent gems of parijata flowers hang on her body, from neck to feet. Her hips is very hard and heavy. She is somewhat leaning forward with her heavy chest and freshening youth. *Brahmā* and other gods ever praise her. Her physical splendour puts the radiance of even one crore Suns to shame. Her lips are reddish like a red gourd. The brightness of her body is akin to *campaka* flower. Her teeth humiliating even a garland of pearls increase the charm of her face. She is the giver of emancipation and desired boons. The beauty of the moon faced goddess defies even the full moon of the autumnal season. I worship that deity.

3. *Stotra*

The deity should be worshipped with the stotra as sung by lord *Brahmā*. This is known as *Brahmākṛta* sarva *maṅgala Stotra* (or the all-auspicious praise sung by lord *Brahmā*, addressed to *Durgā*). This *stotra* has been given in the same *chapter* earlier.

Remedial Measure No. 36

Maṅgala Yantra : To make the *yantra* one should get up early in the morning (*Brāhma Muhūrta*) on any Tuesday. After one has finished one's routine works, one should make the *yantra* with pomegranate pen and with *aṣṭagandhā* on *bhojpatra* as given below.

गजाग्नि दिश्याथ नवाद्रि बाणा पातालं रुद्रा रस सविलिख्य।
भौमस्य यन्त्र क्रमासे विधार्य मनिष्टनाशं प्रवदन्ति गगा ॥
ॐ नमः

Nine squares are made, then in the first row, 8, 3, 10 are written respectively. In the second row, 9, 7, 5 and in the third row, 4, 11, 6 are written respectively. On adding any of three digits in a row, column or diagonal, the total comes to 21.

Remedial Measure No. 37

Āyurvedic Remedy For Mars : Leaves of Bilva tree and of *maulśrī*, small red flower, hing, all must be immersed in water in night and one should bathe from this mixture in the morning usage copper vessel. This also nullifies the maṅgal doṣa to a great extent.

Remedial Measure No. 38

Ghaṭa Vivāha or *Viṣṇu Pratimā Vivāha* :

सावित्र्याश्च व्रतं कृत्वा वैधव्यविनिवृत्तये
अश्वत्थादिभिरूढ्वा दद्यात्तां चिरजीविने ।

Muhūrtgaṇpati Mahilaye Jyotiṣa, P. 70

If the combination of widowhood or *viṣhangana* is present in the horoscope of a woman, then she must observe *Vaṭa Sāvitrī vrata.* This falls on new Moon day of *jyeṣṭha māsa* every year. Her marriage should be ceremonised with the *Pīpal* tree, *Viṣṇu Pratimā, Śaligrāma* or Kumbha to nullify the evil results and adverse happenings after marriage.

If the girl is suffering from *maṅgalī doṣa, kumbha vivāha* or *ghāṭa vivāha* or *Viṣṇu pratimā vivāha* is done so as to nullify the adversity caused by Mars. *Viṣṇu pratimā vivāha* should be done with full rituals just like the actual marriage. It is believed that Lord *Viṣṇu,* becomes the first husband of the girl, all adversities caused by Mars to the female resulting into marital disasters, mishaps or widowhood will go to lord *Viṣṇu* since lord *Viṣṇu* is the supreme power, i.e., the God, so these adversities will automatically be nullified and he will not be harmed. Kumbha *vivāha* is usually but wrongly done after the settlement of the marriage of the girl with someone. In fact, *kumbha* or *ghaṭa vivāha* should be done before the settlement of any kind of engagement of the girl. However, in this marriage *kanyādāna* is prohibited. This is a *gandharva vivāha* with lord *Viṣṇu,* which she does herself secretly. *Kanyādāna* of one girl can not be done twice by the parents otherwise they will have to face the results of this sin for giving their daughter to different husbands one after another. So the girl takes up the *saṅkalpa* of marriage with lord *Viṣṇu*. After the completion of performance of marriage rituals, the girl takes out her bangles, *sārī* and other garments which she was wearing at the time of *Viṣṇu pratimā vivāha*. She should hand over her clothes to the *Ācārya* who got the marriage done. The bangles should be broken thereafter and the *kalaśa* or *kumbha* should be immersed in a river.

Thereafter, she will pray to lord *Viṣṇu* to permit her for the second marriage with so and so. It is believed that lord *Viṣṇu* has granted the permission to the girl for the second marriage. The girl should always keep the idol of lord *Viṣṇu* with her. On all auspicious occasions and celebrations, she should pay her regards to that idol of lord *Viṣṇu* or if the idol is not there or the same has not been used in *Viṣṇu pratimā vivāha*, she should imagine lord *Viṣṇu* as her first husband to pay her regards and prayers to him. At the time of Viṣṇu *pratimā vivāha*, brief *ṣoḍaśopacāra pūjana* and *prāṇa pratiṣṭhā* of the idol of gold, copper or brass should be done before the commencement of the ritual. We have suggested in a number of strong *maṅgalī* females to perform *Viṣṇu pratimā vivāha* before the settlement of their marriage. Out of hundreds of such cases, so far only one girl whose horoscope has been explained in earlier *chapter*, lost her husband in an accident after about ten years of marriage in spite of *Viṣṇu pratimā vivāha*. We believe that she lead a high class and happy married life in spite of strong combinations of widowhood in her horoscope due to *Viṣṇu pratimā vivāha*. However, except for this case, many strong *maṅgalī* women in whose horoscope even widowhood is indicated are leading happy married lives with their husband. This kind of *ghaṭa vivāha* protects widowhood in early age of the female.

Remedial Measure No. 39

Donation For Mars : We believe that donation is the most powerful rectificational measure to nullify all adversities caused by various planets. There is nothing parallel to it provided that it is done according to one's capacity. Donation should be quite a lot in quantity and amount. In fact, we have forgotten completely about donation. In earlier age, people used to donate villages, unaccountable gold, wealth, eatables, silver, gems etc. Donation should be so much that the donor should be extremely satisfied by giving a part of property or wealth. The *saṅkalpa* should be done in any language by the donor that he is donating such articles to the person mentioned by name followed by mentioning the name of his father, gotra, date, purpose and the place where *saṅkalpa* is being taken. The person who is accepting the donation, should utter loudly that he accepts the donation from the donor mentioned by name etc. Any donation is incomplete without money without which one does not get the benefit of donation. Donation should be given to the deserving person and one has to make efforts in finding out the suitable recipient for donation.

The donation for Mars can be given to Brahmins and *Kṣatriya* natives. One should donate liberally with faith and dedication in the power of the *Maṅgala* Deva. Following *śloka* should be quoted in connection of the donation to please Mars and to get the best advantage and results for the attainment of *saubhāgya*, high degree of conjugal bliss, wealth, children, prosperity, popularity, sound health, elimination of enemies, conquer of rivals, criminals, opponents, and to get rid of ailments and untimely death etc. Once again, we strongly emphasize on the remedies of Mars and all other planets etc. by way of donation frequently and liberally. This will certainly make the life happy, prosperous, loving, caring, adjusting and healthy.

Śloka

प्रवालगोधूममसूरिकाश्च रक्तं वृषं चापि गुडं सुवर्णम्
आरक्त वस्त्रं करवीरपुष्पम् ताम्रं हि भौमाय वदन्ति दानम्।

1. Gura, Gram, red *masūra*, red cloth, copper, *keśar*, *kastūrī*, gold, coral, weapons, red sandal, red flower, money, wheat, red bull may be donated on Tuesday to please *Maṅgala devatā*.
2. 1.25 Kg. of revaḍi may be dropped in the river or any water stream flowing south hard, to please *Maṅgala devatā*. The money can always be donated in lieu of these articles as all such articles can be purchased by means of money. Donation is the strongest measure to solve all problems, tensions, failures, dissatisfaction, disharmony and diseases but one must know the art of donation and for that, one must have full faith and intense desire and inner conscience to help the deserving person by donating money and articles to them.

We have given here 38 strong remedial measures to get rid of most of the problems of life caused by Mars and for prevention of widowhood in particular. Before taking up any remedial measures, one should consult any worthy astrologer or *ācārya* or the measure should be undertaken after his guidance or supervision to avoid mistakes and faults. Pronounciation must be absolutely correct and proper procedure must be followed for obtaining best results and quick effects of these preventive measures.

A sincere and honest approach has been made to explain various tested remedies for marital maladies so as to prevent discord and miseries of conjugal life and most of all to nullify every probability for the loss of life partner and attaining *Akhaṇḍa Saubhāgya* by all means. I believe honourable readers will be highly benefitted by learning rare combinations and aphorisms on this most important branch of marriage which had been continuously ignored and not taken seriously and religiously so far.

We strongly trust that our readers will be largely and widely benefitted and that will be a true reward to the work on specialised branch of the subject.

****

नन्द गोप गृहे जावा यशोदा गर्भ संभवा
ततस्तौ नाशयिष्यामि विन्ध्याचल निवासिनी।।